ARTHUR BALFOUR'S GHOSTS

An Edwardian Elite and the
Riddle of the Cross-Correspondence
Automatic Writings

Trevor Hamilton

imprint-academic.com

Copyright © Trevor Hamilton, 2017

The moral rights of the authors have been asserted.
No part of this publication may be reproduced in any form
without permission, except for the quotation of brief passages
in criticism and discussion.

Published in the UK by
Imprint Academic, PO Box 200, Exeter EX5 5YX, UK

Distributed in the USA by
Ingram Book Company,
One Ingram Blvd., La Vergne, TN 37086, USA

ISBN 9781845409135

A CIP catalogue record for this book is available from the
British Library and US Library of Congress

*For Anne,
Dan and Ralph*

Contents

List of Illustrations	viii
Preface and Acknowledgements	ix
Important Note on the Selection, Presentation and Assessment of Material	xi
Introduction	1

Part 1. The Development of the Cross-Correspondences from 1901–1936

1. **Margaret Verrall and Diana Raikes:** The Beginnings — 11

2. **The Return of Myers?** The Syringa Flower; the Sealed Envelope and the Valley at Hallsteads; the Unexpurgated Autobiography — 23

3. **Paranormal Cognition in Margaret Verrall's Early Scripts** — 32

4. **The Life and Automatic Writing of Trix Fleming:** Her Researcher, Alica Johnson, and the Theory of the Cross-Correspondences — 36

5. **Paranormal Cognition in Trix Fleming's Scripts:** Myers, Gurney, Oliver Lodge, Roden Noel, Richard Hodgson, Winifred Coombe-Tennant, Everard Feilding, the Verralls, and Miscellaneous and Untraced References — 48

6. **The Trance Automatic Writing Medium Leonora Piper in the US and the UK** — 63

7. **The Life and Automatic Writings of Winifred Coombe-Tennant to 1919:** The Death of Daphne Coombe-Tennant; Early Paranormal Phenomena; Affair with Gerald Balfour; the Story of the Palm Maiden (May Lyttelton) and the Knight (Arthur Balfour); the Wizard of Melrose (Francis Maitland Balfour); the Peacock Lady (Laura Lyttelton); and the Messianic Child (Henry Coombe-Tennant) — 83

8. The Later Scripts and Last Years of Margaret Verrall: Post-Mortem Communication from A.W. Verrall; and Interpretive Disagreements with Gerald Balfour & John George Piddington   114

9. The Life and Automatic Writing of Helen Verrall/Salter   127

10. Winifred Coombe-Tennant: The End of the Affair with Gerald Balfour; Her Later Scripts and the Last Years of Arthur Balfour; the Education and Career of Henry Coombe-Tennant   133

11. The Minor Automatists: The Mackinnon Family from Aberdeen; Dame Edith Lyttelton; Kenneth and Zoë Richmond; and Mrs Wilson   147

Part 2. Assessing the Cross-Correspondence Automatic Writings

12. Were the Cross-Correspondences Unambiguous, Consistent and Meaningful?   159

13. Did the Scripts Demonstrate Paranormal Cognition?   184

14. Could One Be Sure that the Cryptic Nature of the Cross-Correspondences was not the Product of a Psychological Artefact?   196

15. Was the Process of Communication Interactive and was it Clear that the Communicators Both Initiated and Signalled Cross-Correspondences and Understood and Accurately Responded to Messages and Requests from the Investigators?   212

16. Did the Cross-Correspondences Occur within a Reasonable Time Frame and Above Chance Expectation and Were They Widely Distributed Amongst the Automatists?   221

17. Were All Normal Avenues for Acquiring the Information Ruled Out?   228

18. Were the Correspondences (Including the Overall Story and the Plan) Tweaked by Wishful Thinking, Over-Subtle Interpretation, or Deliberate Selection?	236
19. Were the Aims, Intentions, and Long-Term Predictions of the Communicators Fulfilled?	260
Afterword	278

Appendices

Appendix 1: The Flow of Scripts 1901–1936	280
Appendix 2: Ave Roma Immortalis Complete Scripts	282
Appendix 3: The Hope Star Browning Complete Scripts	287
Appendix 4: List of Types of Symbols in the Scripts	291
Archives	294
Select Bibliography and References	295
Index	328

List of Illustrations

The Balfours: From top left clockwise; Arthur; Francis Maitland; Eleanor (who married Henry Sidgwick); and Gerald.

The Verralls: From top left clockwise; Helen Verrall (who married W.H. Salter); her mother Margaret Verrall; and Margaret's husband, Arthur Verrall.

The Friends: From top left clockwise; Oliver Lodge; Edmund Gurney; Richard Hodgson; and Henry Sidgwick.

The Myers: From top left clockwise; the mature Myers; the young Myers around the time of his trip to Greece; Myers' wife, Eveleen; and Leckhampton House, their Cambridge home.

The Mediums (also see Helen and Margaret Verrall above): From top left clockwise; Leonora Piper; Rosalie Thompson; Winifred Coombe-Tennant; and Trix Fleming.

The Script Interpreters (see also Margaret Verrall and Winifred Coombe-Tennant above): Top left J.G. Piddington; mid-left Alice Johnson; right side group photograph of five SPR presidents—from left clockwise: Hans Driesch; Gerald Balfour; J.G. Piddington; Lawrence Jones; and Eleanor Sidgwick.

The Messianic Child, Henry Coombe-Tennant, and the Palm Maiden, May Lyttelton.

Burne-Jones' Peacock Memorial for Laura Lyttelton.

Preface and Acknowledgements

I would like to thank the following institutions for access to their records and the ability to make use of them: the Society for Psychical Research archive at Cambridge University Library, the Society for Psychical Research online library of their *Proceedings*, *Journal*, and online Encylopaedia,Trinity College, Cambridge (the Wren Library), and the Houghton Library Harvard, and the American Society for Psychical Research, New York. The online records of the Balfour family archive in Edinburgh were searched but no material has been taken from them.

Short quotations and extracts from other sources are within the accepted guidelines for the purpose of criticism and discussion and are fully attributed. Any errors in accuracy or non or incorrect attribution are apologised for and will be corrected in any future edition. Illustrations and images are largely from the SPR's own records, or out of copyright, or untraceable, though every effort has been made to do so. Any omissions will be corrected as stated above. Thanks to the National Portrait Gallery, the Keep/Special Collections Sussex University, Mary Evans Picture Library, the Victoria and Albert Museum, and Colin Salter (Tall Tales from the Trees website) for their permissions. I would particularly like to thank Tricia Robertson for advice, permission, and help with some of the illustrations, and for her sturdy encouragement in this most difficult of fields. I also owe a debt of gratitude to her close friend, the late Archie Roy, author of *The Eager Dead*, for his courageous and enthusiastic pioneering work in this field. I would also like to thank Adrian Parker for his general interest in and support for this work.

I wish to acknowledge, with gratitude, financial assistance for the research on which this book is based, from the Perrott-Warrick trust.

I owe a profound and specific obligation to Alan Gauld for his support and advice and for allowing me to take away and scan thirty-one volumes of printed scripts and the commentaries on them, in order to photocopy each individual page and then scan them (over many long months) into a manageable and searchable format. The book would not have been possible without this act of generous trust.

A special note of thanks must also go to Carlos Alvarado for his invaluable work in disseminating, in useful and perceptive articles, the historical resources of the Parapsychology Foundation, and for his efforts to encourage a less Anglo Saxon perspective in this field.

My brother David gave, to a complete neophyte, invaluable advice on the technology of scanning.

I would also like to thank Ralph Crane for access to the letters between Trix Fleming and Maud Diver; Barbara Fisher for extracts from her intended biography of Trix Fleming; Mark Coombe-Tennant for permission to access the Houghton archive and for his interest and encouragement; Peter Lord for his excellent edition of Winifred Coombe-Tennant's diaries and for general information. Robin Darwall-Smith, the archivist at Magdalen College, Oxford, was very helpful on the academic background of John George Smith (as Piddington was called then). Lis Warwood and Marc Demarest were hugely resourceful in tracking down his business and personal records and those of Rosalie Thompson.

Finally, I have to thank my wife Anne, and my son Daniel, for their unfailing love and encouragement, despite my involvement in a project which must at times have seemed to them both puzzling and something of a pain in the neck.

The subject matter of this book is so complex in range, variety, and volume that there are bound to be many errors, despite my best efforts, still undetected in the text. Such mistakes will be fully acknowledged and corrected in any future edition.

Important Note on the Selection, Presentation and Assessment of Material

Quotations around words like 'discarnate' and terms like 'ostensibly', 'allegedly', and so forth, are, as far as possible, not deployed in the text. This is to reduce the density of an inevitably highly complicated document. There is no attempt by this to either endorse or reject the paranormal elements in the narrative. For reasons of space and expense only a sample of parts of significant cases and scripts can be presented in some detail but it is hoped that there is enough depth in the documentation provided to enable the reader to get a more than superficial sense of the issues involved in making a judgement on this highly intricate and daunting body of material. There is no substitute, in the final analysis, for an examination of the individual scripts themselves, or at the least, a study of the detailed extracts printed in the *Proceedings* of the Society for Psychical Research. Selections from scripts are generally indented to make them stand out in the text. Those parts of the scripts which were originally in Greek and Latin have been translated. The translations are those of the first investigators. Words enclosed in square brackets are summaries of script material, bridging statements, or descriptions of drawings. Words enclosed in conventional brackets are explanatory and contextual comments. The script extracts are not consistent in layout, spelling, and punctuation and have been condensed because of limited space. But they remain faithful to the overall meaning. For the same reason, only essential references are provided in the text. For more detail on this consult the online Society for Psychical Research abstracts catalogue.

It should be noted that, though careless phrasing might accidently imply this, the Society for Psychical Research, past or present, holds no collective view on the cross-correspondences or any other phenomena that it may study.

Introduction

Why Arthur Balfour's ghosts and why link his name with the cross-correspondence automatic writings? He is known in the twenty-first century, if at all, as an aristocratic politician of a century ago, and some people may well link him with the Balfour Declaration of 1917 which promised a home for the Jewish people in Palestine. Yet, during his long political career, the intimate involvement of his family in the interpretation and construction of the cross-correspondences has not yet been fully explored from the full range of original sources, and has profound implications for the proper assessment of the huge body of data generated by automatists and investigators alike. The bizarre messages that emerged from the scripts focused largely on him, his lost love, May Lyttelton, and his brother Gerald's child by Winifred Coombe-Tennant, one of the participating mediums. It is important to analyse and weigh these personal elements since many reputable scholars (who were not aware of this personal equation) have stated that the cross-correspondence automatic writings provided some of the best, if not the best, evidence for the post-mortem survival of individual consciousness and personality.

The evidence began to build up shortly after the death of Frederic William Henry Myers on 17 January 1901 in Rome at the Hotel Primavera (Skrupskelis 1994: 156). He had a reputation in his earlier years as a classical scholar, poet, and man of letters, but in later life he was known for his energetic and wide-ranging work on behalf of the Society for Psychical Research. His conclusions and much though not all of the evidence to support them were published in his posthumous masterpiece *Human Personality and Its Survival of Bodily Death*. He had come to believe that the survival of bodily death did in fact take place. Therefore, it was hardly surprising that his former colleagues in the SPR should have looked eagerly for any indications of his continuing existence and that one, Margaret Verrall, offered him the opportunity to make contact through automatic writing. She could not have realised at the time that this would lead to the generation of well over three thousand scripts from a number of automatists between 1901 and 1936 which told an incredible tale that went far beyond the post-mortem survival of one individual. This narrative, which was constructed by the first investigators, all of whom had been

Myers' personal friends and collaborators, strongly requires an up to date and, within the obvious human limitations, an independent appraisal.

There are several reasons for this. First, the claims made for the scripts. Alan Gauld (1983: 77) has written that they are 'undoubtedly the most extensive, the most complex and the most puzzling of all ostensible attempts by deceased persons to manifest purpose, and in so doing to fulfil their overriding purpose of proving their survival'. They have, in addition, the advantage of being a permanent paranormal object: that is, the original spontaneous event by its very nature was creating a record that could be examined again and again. Second, the complete body of material has rarely been studied in detail by later researchers because of its inaccessibility and convoluted nature. Therefore, there is always the suspicion that the original interpreters selected those items from the scripts that confirmed their prior belief in survival and, conversely, that critics of the cross-correspondences may never have engaged in sufficient detail with the material in order to come to an informed opinion. The final reason is the staggering and bizarre claim made about the future destiny of Henry Coombe-Tennant: *prima facie*, an extraordinary conclusion for investigators of such calibre to come to.

Two different but related types of phenomena impressed the early researchers and a number of later scholars. There appeared to be highly specific verbal similarities between the scripts of different automatists which could not be explained by chance coincidence or normal contact between the individuals concerned. Alice Johnson (1907–09: 369) defined them as 'independent references to the same topic found in the scripts of two or more writers'. These connections were labelled cross-correspondences, a term which was first employed by J.G. Piddington (1903–04: 294) in his study of the medium Rosalie Thompson. In addition, examples of what one might call paranormal cognition were scattered throughout the scripts. These included predictions, descriptions of environments, facts about individuals, communications highly characteristic of the deceased individuals' personalities and beliefs, and the demonstration of skills, all of which transcended the mental capacities and physical and temporal location of the automatist involved.

A cross-correspondence was often simple—a phrase or topic clearly repeated in the writing of two or more automatists. It could be cryptic or complex—'where the idea is suggested by allusions, or conveyed in a disguised form' (Saltmarsh 1938: 35, 41–2). It could also be symbolic and part of a much larger hermeneutical structure, though this dimension took a number of years for the interpreters to identify. These, and other types of cross-correspondence, are discussed in detail in the text.

The content of the cross-correspondence, whether simple or complex, was heavily literary, classical, historical, biblical, artistic, and cultural. It was communicated in English, Greek, and Latin with a smattering of French, German, and Italian. A number of abstract and representational drawings also appeared in the scripts. The elements of the more convoluted cross-correspondences tended to be dispersed across the automatists over a period of time, and the key to their reassembly could be a specific historical event like the rise of Rome, the rule of a Rennaisance prince, a poem, a passage in a novel, a play, or sources even more esoteric. Sometimes aspects of the lives of the communicators formed the cross-correspondence and so the two central characteristics of the phenomenon—verbal connections across scripts and paranormal cognition—merged into one. In some cases, the fragmentary elements just formed, over a variable period of time, an interesting progressive puzzle in the scripts of a single automatist.

Any reader new to this subject might immediately, and with a certain irritation, ask why was there any need for this complex, allusive, highly verbal and literary method of communication? Why not just concentrate on providing first-rate evidence of survival through the methods of high quality mental mediumship? Alice Johnson (see below) argued that evidence from traditional mediumship was highly susceptible to alternative explanations, namely that the material could have been generated by telepathy or clairvoyance, and that there was clear evidence in the scripts that the communicators were aware of this objection and devised the cross-correspondence method to circumvent it. Gerald Balfour (1927: iii–xxvi) concluded that this cryptic method had the additional advantage of preventing the ultimate purposes of the communicators being revealed before the appropriate time.

The main automatists were (writing pseudonym in brackets): Margaret Verrall, classics lecturer at Newnham College, Cambridge, and the wife of A.W. Verrall, classics fellow and tutor of Trinity College, Cambridge; their daughter Helen, also a classicist and later an SPR researcher and official; Alice 'Trix' Fleming (Mrs Holland), sister of Rudyard Kipling, and herself a gifted writer; Winifred Coombe-Tennant (Mrs Willett), sister-in-law of F.W.H. Myers, a magistrate, Liberal political activist, and an individual strongly committed to supporting Welsh life and culture; Leonora Piper, the only professional medium; Diana Raikes (Mrs Forbes), the wife of Justice Raikes KC; the Mackinnon family (Macs) from Aberdeen; Mrs Wilson, wife of a high-ranking Army officer; Dame Edith Lyttelton (Mrs King), a social reformer, public servant, playwright, and the second wife of the politician Alfred Lyttelton (their child, Antony, who died of meningitis before his second birthday, figured in the cross-correspondences); and Kenneth Richmond (a psychoanalyst and SPR official) and his wife Zoë.

The communicators were: F.W.H. Myers; Edmund Gurney; Henry Sidgwick (all three fellows of Trinity College, Cambridge, and co-founders of the Society for Psychical Research and all dead by 1901 — see Hamilton 2009: 111-17; Gauld 1968: 137-49); Laura Lyttelton (née Tennant) who died after childbirth on Easter Eve in 1886 and whose son Christopher died at the age of two. She was the first wife of Alfred Lyttelton and was the daughter of Charles Tennant, a Scottish industrialist. Her sister, Margot Tennant, later married Asquith, the Liberal Prime Minister; Mary (May) Catherine Lyttelton, who died of typhus fever on Palm Sunday 1875 (she was called the Palm Maiden in the scripts). May was Alfred Lyttelton's sister and the daughter of Lord Lyttelton. Arthur Balfour, Prime Minister 1902-05, was part of their social circle, and her death devastated him; Francis Maitland Balfour, a distinguished embryologist who died in a climbing accident in 1882. He was Gerald, Arthur, and Eleanor's brother; and Annie Marshall, the wife of Myers' unstable cousin Walter. She committed suicide in 1876 and was the love of Myers' life (Hamilton: 39-47; Beer 1998: 116-88).

The first assessors of the scripts were: Alice Johnson, first-class in natural sciences from Newnham College and SPR researcher and official; J.G. Piddington, business man and Oxford classics graduate and SPR official; Sir Oliver Lodge, radio pioneer, SPR president, and celebrated physicist; Margaret Verrall; Eleanor Sidgwick (née Balfour), mathematician, co-founder and principal of Newnham College, Cambridge, and the widow of Henry Sidgwick; and Gerald Balfour, classicist, philosopher, fellow of Trinity College, and politician.

Two things stand out from this catalogue. Apart from Leonora Piper, the individuals involved were of very high intellectual calibre and social status, which boded well for the quality of the assessment of the scripts. But potentially working against this was the highly intimate nature of their relationships and networks. Most were members of the SPR, a number were Cambridge graduates (Oxford in Piddington's case) with the intellectual energy largely coming from Trinity and Newnham Colleges, and, finally, some members of the Balfour and the Lyttelton families were part of the celebrated aristocratic circle called the 'Souls' that met regularly at country houses and shared similar aesthetic and intellectual interests (Ellenberger 1982, 2015).

Given the close, interlocking nature of these groups, it is crucial to examine the methods of investigation and interpretation deployed on the scripts and any criticisms of them made at the time and later. This becomes even more important when one considers the narrative themes of the scripts, dubbed the Story and the Plan by the investigators. The former was an account of the efforts by the discarnate May Lyttelton to convince Arthur Balfour that her love for him continued beyond the grave and that she would wait, on the borders of the next world, to be reunited with him. In addition, according to Piddington, there were veiled symbolic references to the central and positive role Arthur Balfour would play for the British Empire in the last long period of his political career. The latter (the Plan) referred to the efforts of the discarnate communicators to work collectively for world peace by influencing the birth of children of remarkable qualities who had the requisite intellectual, moral, and leadership qualities to do so. Explicit, highly moving, and dramatic narratives on these two subjects occurred in the scripts of Winifred Coombe-Tennant and more allusively and faintly in others. She became the lover of Gerald Balfour in 1911 and had his child, Henry, in 1913. The scripts appeared to assign him the major role in implementing the Plan.

There has been trenchant criticism of the methodology adopted by the early investigators who stated that a statistical approach was not appropriate for the assessment of such a highly literary and subtle body of material. It has, however, been counter-argued, at least before the sheer number of scripts spiralled almost out of control, that there could have been an effort to quantify numbers of successes against numbers of failures with regard to cross-correspondences attempted and achieved, and to relate this to cross-correspondences occurring by chance in comparable material (West 1962: 107-9; Thouless 1972: 160-1; Burt 1975: 121-57; Moreman 2003: 225-42). But it is easy with hindsight to make this criticism. The scripts did not suddenly materialise in complete published form with dates, commentaries, and indices. They came haphazardly in spurts and starts over many years and often with no apparent links between them. The task of co-ordinating, interpreting, and printing the material was almost overwhelming, particularly as the investigators had other professional responsibilities both within and beyond the SPR. A robust critic of aspects of the cross-correspondences, Braude (2003: 95-100), has argued that the literary methodology, attributed to the communicators and accepted by the investigators, has compounded rather than clarified problems connected with the survival issue. Researchers adopting a more traditional and conventional perspective towards the survival issue (Doyle 2001 and, to some extent, Hyslop 1919) would have agreed.

These critical comments were based on the selective examples from the scripts quoted in the *Proceedings* of the SPR. The issue of complexity is greatly intensified when one goes back to the full original scripts. There are only a few printed sets of the complete (or almost complete) automatic writings in existence so, first, getting a set is difficult and, second, cross-referring between sets in order to evaluate any paranormal dimension is a time-consuming and tedious task. The present writer has scanned into PDF format and transferred to the computer all the scripts of the automatists that have been printed in volumes—the Verralls, Trix Fleming, Winifred Coombe-Tennant, the Mackinnons, and Mrs Wilson—and the associated commentaries by Balfour and Piddington. This speeds up the task of cross-referencing but by no means eliminates the time, effort, and energy required to make assessment judgements, or the need to refer to a substantial body of background and contextual documentation. It was not possible to do this with Leonora Piper's scripts since they were never printed in volume form. That the investigators (unconsciously) selected material to prove a pre-conceived thesis will always be a central question in her case.

A comprehensive and authoratitive evaluation of all these documents is well beyond the capacities of one individual. The intention of this book is more modest. It aims to provide an outline of the main themes in the scripts and to examine some of the more salient examples of cross-correspondences and paranormal cognition put forward by the original researchers; to establish some objective criteria for evaluating these; and to indicate the location of the key primary and secondary sources. The fundamental purpose is to act as an initial orienteering guide for other students of the cross-correspondences. One warning. It is easy to come to a superficial conclusion about them either way and it should be emphasised that an adequate appreciation of the full complexity of them, as mentioned in the earlier note on the selection, assessment, and presentation of material, requires sustained and in-depth reading. This, naturally, makes them far less appealing than some of the more graphic and sensational evidence from other sources put forward as evidence for the survival hypothesis.

A brief comment on automatic writing may be useful. It is a term which has almost completely faded from general discourse but at the end of the nineteenth century it was quite familiar in educated circles. Myers did a great deal of work on it and it helped to inform his concept of the subliminal self (Myers 1885a,c, 1887a, 1889a) but it is an under-researched area in much post-Edwardian psychology (Wegner 2002: 99–144; Moreira-Almeida 2012: 191–213; Palmer 2001: 205–17; Muhl 1930) and there are many misconceptions about the level, quality, and value of the content produced. It was called automatic writing because it was not under the conscious control of the individual and it could be induced by a variety of methods. For some people simply sitting quietly with a pencil in hand over a blank piece of paper while they read or relaxed was enough to initiate activity. Others never achieved anything or at most just managed a few heavy unco-ordinated thumps (Payne 1992: 134–42).

Others found using a planchette to be effective. This was a heart-shaped piece of wood on rollers with a pencil fixed to it. A hand lightly resting on the wood quite frequently sent the pencil skittering around the paper spelling out messages which were often gibberish but which occasionally made surprising sense. The Ouija (yes/no) was slightly different in that the operators(s) would use a pointing device which was free standing on a board with yes and no and the letters of the alphabet pre-marked on it. Sometimes the device was replaced by a wine glass. The main method used in the cross-correspondences, however, was basic automatic writing but these other techniques were occasionally employed and sometimes the medium would go into a trance or semi-trance state and produce automatic speech. The nature and proportion of these various methods varied, given the individual preferences and abilities of the automatists involved.

The actual writing was quite diverse in size, shape, execution, presentation, and legibility and on occasions it seemed to bear a fair resemblance to the handwriting of the communicator in life. One could argue, in the case of the cross-correspondences, that the printed versions in the *Proceedings* and the private published scripts are sanitised and presentable versions of the originals (only a relatively small proportion of these survive). It is, therefore, difficult for the researcher to identify if there has been any 'tweaking' of meaning in the transfer from original handwritten script to printed page. On the other hand the original investigators appear to have been scrupulous in identifying where such misinterpretation might have occurred.

In any attempt to make a systematic evaluation of this material one has to address what Cunningham (2012) has called the content source problem in modern mediumship research. How can one use the content of mediumistic communications to determine the origins of those communications? This was very much the question Myers attempted to answer when he made his own enquiry into automatic writing. He identified several potential origins for the material: content from the automatist's own mind, from other living minds, from the unembodied intelligence of unknown consciousnesses, and from the surviving personality that purported to communicate (Myers 1904a vol 1: 118–19). These sources might well blend and interact with each other, making the clarity of the communication and its origin particularly difficult to estimate and verify. And the establishment of different potential origins is only a small step along the road to actually identifying the 'correct' source.

Braude (2003: 196) has put the issue succinctly: is anything paranormal going on and can the material be linked causally to the post-mortem communicators? One can address these points by posing a number of more detailed subsets of these questions as assessment criteria: were the cross-correspondences, of whatever type, unambiguous, consistent, and meaningful? Did they demonstrate paranormal cognition? Might not the cryptic nature of the cross-correspondences have been merely a psychological artefact (the dreamy, ruminative activity characteristic of much normal subliminal mentation)? Was the process interactive and was it clear that the communicators both initiated and signalled cross-correspondences and understood and accurately responded to messages and requests from the investigators? Did the cross-correspondences occur within a reasonable time frame and above chance expectation and were they distributed sufficiently widely amongst the automatists? Were all normal avenues for acquiring the information ruled out? Had the cross-correspondence been tweaked by wishful thinking or over-subtle interpretation or deliberate selection? And were the aims, intentions, and long-term predictions of the communicators fulfilled? It should be stressed, for a variety of obvious reasons, that conscious collaborative fraud is ruled out in this context and that in order to make sound and reliable assessment judgements all the appropriate criteria need to be covered.

The book is organised as follows. The first part outlines a narrative of the phenomena as they developed from 1901 to 1936 and brings together a body of historical material which has not been found in one place before and some of which has only recently become available. The second part applies the above criteria to a number of significant examples of the cross-correspondences and of paranormal cognition. The appendices provide, amongst other things, some background quantitative information on the scripts themselves, two examples of the complete body of material from which two famous cross-correspondences were drawn, comments on the structure of the symbolism in the scripts, and there is a bibliography locating the primary and secondary resources on which this book is based. Finally, a curious aside, to which the reader no doubt will respond according to their prior beliefs, preferences, and experiences. It appears that there was opposition on the part of some of those on the other side as to whether the whole process of the cross-correspondences should take place at all.

Trix Fleming 27/4/1910:

> Many purposes are clearer to us than to you—but not all—indeed not all—and to those who still need such crutches the pleasanter conditions of earth life appear still to persist—the meals—the hours of rest—but these are childish things and should be set aside—Perhaps it is easier for those simpler personalities to appear—but I must not theorize with insufficient data—Very many of them here are out of sympathy with any attempt to communicate—we should wait the Good Time they say—but for some of us that time is now.

Part 1.

The Development of the Cross-Correspondences from 1901–1936

1

Margaret Verrall and Diana Raikes
The Beginnings

The Balfours of Whittingehame (their grand house in the Scottish border country of the Lothians) were a remarkable family. They were clever, insular and self-sufficient. They disliked socialising with the local gentry and they went to great lengths to avoid casual callers. There was a mile long drive, through a deep narrow glen, leading to the house, and so visitors could be spotted in sufficient time for evasive action to take place. If indoors the Balfours would hide in the large, cold, gloomy house, white blinds down excluding the sun; if outside, at tennis or croquet, they would quickly and silently cluster under the concealing limbs and foliage of a large tree, till the 'bounders' had gone (Harris, P. 1989; Balfour, F.1930).

They were the children of James Maitland Balfour and his wife Lady Blanche, a sister of Lord Salisbury (Prime Minister 1885, 1886, 1897), the head of the powerful and influential Cecil family. There were eight of them: Arthur Balfour (Prime Minister 1902–1905); his sister Eleanor, mathematician, psychical researcher, and co-founder of Newnham College, Cambridge; Frank Balfour, an outstanding embryologist who died in a climbing accident in 1882; Gerald Balfour, classicist, politician, and psychical researcher; Eustace, a colonel in the territorials and an architect; Alice, Arthur's housekeeper, a gifted amateur naturalist who made a twelve hundred mile journey by wagon through Southern Africa; Evelyn, the wife of and collaborator with Lord Rayleigh, a Noble Prize winner for Physics; and Cecil, the black sheep of the family (one has a certain residual sympathy for poor Cecil) who died in Australia. It is ironic that at least four members of this gifted and private family should figure in the cross-correspondence automatic writings which, within the admittedly narrow world of psychical research, became the most publicised and celebrated of paranormal cases.

This, however, was for the future. In 1901 the main focus appeared to be firmly on any indication that Myers' consciousness and individuality had survived death. Two mediums, Mrs Thompson and Miss Wingfield, provided some evidence of his activity post-mortem but much of this early material was fragmentary, confused, contradictory, or not capable of being verified (Lodge 1909b: 284-307). One statement by Miss Wingfield, nevertheless, is of interest, to any student of the cross-correspondences, in terms of early suggestions of planning and design: 'I implore you not to lose the least scrap of evidence. It is only by putting down all the scraps you make a mosaic.' And, early in May 1901, cross-references began to appear at roughly the same time in a sitting Sir Oliver Lodge (1909b: 300-1) had with Mrs Thompson in Birmingham and in the automatic writing of Margaret Verrall at Cambridge.

Rosalie Thompson, Margaret Verrall 8/5/1901 (Thompson first, then Verrall):

1. I cannot   1. Non Possum (I cannot)
2. Some one is calling me now   2. Doing something else tonight
3. Let me be at rest   3. Desine (leave off)
4. False things may creep in   4. Falsehood is never far away

The timing, the precision, and the separation of location made them all significant—though of what? There was certainly no rush to judgement on the issue by Lodge and his colleagues. Many of the other very early communications from Mrs Thompson and Miss Wingfield, though with hints and touches of Myers' personality, had no value as evidence whatever since he had known them well and investigated them both in his lifetime. Moreover, these mediums eventually became unavailable for consultation. Miss Wingfield, who appears to have been a highly gifted sensitive, increasingly withdrew from traditional mediumship to concentrate on the production of books containing spiritual advice from her guides (Wingfield 1948); and Mrs Thompson, whose mediumship had hugely impressed Myers in life, gradually stopped giving sittings, partly because of the hostility of Mrs Myers to her, but also because of her own husband's untimely death (Hamilton 2009: 283-92).[1]

Gradually, the most sustained and detailed evidence of Myers' survival (though of a type difficult to decode and assess) began to come from Margaret Verrall, whom nobody could accuse of being credulous or a convert to the Spiritualistic hypothesis. Margaret de Gaudrion Verrall was a woman of acute mind and no nonsense rationality. She was married to a popular Cambridge and Trinity College tutor and fellow in classics, Arthur Verrall, and she herself had been a classics lecturer at Newnham College, where she continued to work part-time in later years. Both the Verralls were liberal and open-minded individuals who were prepared (she

---

[1] Mrs Thompson's later career provides food for thought. She became a detective, married again, went to South Africa, and died there. See Demarest (2014), Warwood (2014).

particularly) to swim a little against the prevailing Cambridge tide of scientific naturalism.

Margaret Verrall had joined the SPR in 1889. Her parents had been interested in psychic phenomena (see below) and she herself seemed to have a certain sensitivity, experimenting in crystal-gazing and experiencing premonitions of potential disasters (Kingsford 1920: 168-70). However, she took none of this in a superstitious or credulous sense. She sat with the two major mediums of the time, Leonora Piper and Rosalie Thompson, having a substantial twenty-two sessions with the latter and writing them up with her characteristic critical thoroughness. She classified 238 of the statements made by Mrs Thompson as true (59%), not verified (27%), and false (14%). She argued that there were a number of facts displayed not known to the medium and a number unknown to the sitter which would count against the telepathy hypothesis (Lodge et al. 1901-02: 61-244).

W.H. Salter, who married her daughter Helen, has painted this portrait of her: 'I knew her of course (for the Verralls were extremely hospitable) as a charming and sympathetic hostess, in whose house (5 Selwyn Gardens) one met all sorts of interesting people, young and old, and heard brilliant talk on all sorts of subjects. She was one of the most perceptive people I have ever known, seeming to know what one was going to say before one began to say it. In all her activities, inside and outside the home, she was eminently practical & responsible, the exact opposite of the popular idea of "psychics" and "sensitives"...' (Salter 1955a).

She admired Myers greatly and on hearing of his death wrote in her diary (Salter A/3/1): 'I must do what I can: the extraordinary range of his gifts can never be replaced, nor the intense stimulus he has given by his passionate desire to make his friends share his belief, but so far as it lies with me, it shall not be said that his work perishes with him.' One of her most endearing qualities was loyalty—loyalty to her husband increasingly crippled with arthritis, to her friend Jane Harrison whom she consoled (Sidgwick 1916; Harrison 1917) when she gained the Newnham lectureship which they had both been competing for, and which Jane had wanted so badly. She, therefore, decided to try automatic writing herself. She had previously done so with little or no success and had no real hope or belief that anything would happen, but she reasoned, quite understandably, that if Myers continued to exist, and was able to communicate at all, he might wish to do so through someone whose mind, culture, and ethos chimed with his own.

Another quality she had was calm and balance, a certain grace under pressure. And she needed this because of the general hostility towards 'Spiritualistic' practices like automatic writing. She was also unperturbed by the inexplicable noises and raps that accompanied her first attempts at automatic script and these she carefully recorded in her diary. They started almost immediately after Myers' death, as she noted on 22/1/1901 (Salter A/3/1): 'Alone in the drawing room reading Demosthenes when at 5.15 a series of light taps began apparently on the greenhouse window behind me... I went into the greenhouse & cut off some of the bits of vegetation which might have touched, but on my return the taps continued... Then I asked for them to be louder, which they were. Then I turned out the light, sat on the floor with my hands on the three legged stool, & presently there came three raps on the brass table.' Searching through her papers later, she found a letter from Myers from 1898 in which he promised he would 'rap' after death if he could. It is a nice touch and entirely consistent with her intellectual and literary habits that Margaret Verrall was reading Demosthenes at the time rather than, say, Bram Stoker's *Dracula*. Equally typical was her determination to rule out all normal explanations and to engage actively with the phenomenon rather than flee from it.

She was a secure and admired member of a particular section of the Cambridge intellectual community. She belonged to the Ladies Dining Club, whose membership was formidable and impressive. There was, in addition to Margaret Verrall: Mrs Marshall, Mrs Creighton, Mrs Arthur Lyttelton, Mrs Sidgwick, Mrs James Ward, Mrs Francis Darwin, Baroness von Hügel, Lady Horace Darwin, Mrs Prothero, and Lady Jebb. These women had married very distinguished men but had also a developed sense of their own individual and collective worth: '...one black ball was enough to exclude a proposed new member' (Shils 1996: 73–92). Margaret Verrall was part of that remarkable generation of women at Newnham and Girton Colleges who achieved intellectual distinction in a masculine Cambridge environment at a time when the attitude to the higher education of women was very mixed—part puzzled, part sympathetic, part hostile. She gained her 'qualifications', as did her daughter, Helen, under a rather grudging compromise (Beard 2000; Sutherland 2006). Women could sit the tripos examinations and were informally told how they had performed. From 1882 these results were published but it was not till 1948 that women could officially receive a degree.

Margaret Verrall had an interesting pedigree. Her father, Frederic Merrifield, was a well-known Brighton solicitor and later became clerk to the East and West Sussex county councils and a respected amateur entomologist. He had, in his earlier years, a keen and sceptical interest in Spiritualism, and published in May 1903 in the *Journal* of the SPR his account of his 1855 (written up a few weeks afterwards) experience at a séance with the celebrated medium Daniel Dunglas Home. Merrifield had attended with his fiancée, later Margaret Verrall's mother, Maria Angélique de Gaudrion. Maria's mother came from a military family, extending back to George III, called Fawcett.

This name—Fawcett—was ingeniously played on in scripts forming a cross-correspondence between Margaret Verrall and Trix Fleming's writing. It was built up through the Fawcett name on Mrs Verrall's maternal line; and on Mr and Mrs Henry Fawcett, the blind politician and postmaster and his wife, the suffragist leader, who were good friends of the Merrifields and strongly supported Margaret's plans to get a higher education; through the Latin pun on the name Fawcett (faux cecinit/the voice/fox sings/speaks) in script of 7/4/1901; and note the instruction, in the last script quoted, to look back. (The name Fawcett can mean fox on a hillside.)

Fawcett

Margaret Verrall 7/4/1901:

Faux cecinit (the voice/fox speaks/sings)

Margaret Verrall 20/4/1901:

A fox (alopex) and a vulture

Margaret Verrall 20/3/1906:

[allusions to Henry Fawcett's family] Open the last morning's paper and look for the lost word (the name Fawcett was the first name in the Births/Deaths/Marriages column)

Trix Fleming 28/2/1906:

Henry F. [and drawing of dark glasses] It was first started when we were all sitting under the cedars at Broadlands. While the sunset flared crimson on that noble window.

Trix Fleming 4/4/1906:

[Fawcett and drawing of dark glasses and riding crop, some correct details re Margaret Verrall's relatives with name Fawcett...] F. a blue jewel—set in a ring—or else in a brooch. (Miss Flora Merrifield, Margaret's sister, had a blue jewel in a brooch which came to her from a Fawcett.)

Trix Fleming 7/11/906:

Nov 6th 1884 was my date my death date—Do you remember H.F. I am not the blind one now [drawing of spectacles]. (Trix Fleming did not know of Henry Fawcett, she said, nor had she read the memoir of Henry Sidgwick (1906) which gave the date of his death.)

Margaret Verrall 11/10/1907:

You will find the foxes heads have been given to you before this—Alopex long ago.

Not only was there a double pun here: Faux = Fox = Alopex (Greek for fox or wolf). But Piddington traced a reference back to one of Margaret Verrall's sittings with Rosalie Thompson in which one of the communicators mentioned her knitting slippers with fox's heads on them. (On all this see Piddington 1943a: 443–9; 544–48).

Note: Margaret Verrall wrote her scripts in Cambridge or Yorkshire. Trix Fleming wrote hers elsewhere in the UK except for the last one written in Calcutta. She never saw the Verrall scripts.

***

Both parents strongly supported higher education for women and Margaret went to the Sidgwick's foundation Newnham Hall (later College) in 1877 to study political economy and moral sciences. She switched to classics and despite little grounding in them managed to achieve high second class honours. She became classics lecturer at Newnham, in the same year, 1880, married A.W. Verrall in 1882, and had her daughter Helen in 1883. But she continued in her classics work at Newnham (see Wyles, R. and Hall, E. 2016) and later became involved in the developing field of psychical research. She remained intellectually active and well balanced till the end, as this extract from a memorial tribute to her by her friend Jane Harrison (1917) demonstrated: 'On her mother's side she came of French stock, and of her two-fold ancestry she was most justly proud. Throughout her life her attitude towards superstition, ancient and modern, was not of protest and intolerance but of almost physical shrinking and disgust. I often tried to interest her in savage superstitions and rites—she used to shudder and say, "how can you work at such things—ugh."' That may well reflect an attitude to anthropological study not shared today, but it certainly did not reveal naivety or credulity with regard to magic and the paranormal.

Margaret Verrall's husband, Arthur, as a fellow and a tutor at Trinity College, was a significant figure in the Cambridge of the time; lanky, dark-bearded, humorous, and with a slightly perverse tendency to challenge the accepted orthodoxy of the classical literature establishment. His highly dramatic and imaginative approach to life and to the classics complemented Margaret's temperament, which was sensible, practical, and impatient of the too fanciful. From 1897 onwards arthritis increasingly began to take a hold of him and Margaret, who had helped him considerably in his pastoral work and social entertaining of students, had this problem to cope with at the very moment her automatic writing was beginning to grow in volume and complexity. She looked after him on visits to spas at home and abroad, including Algeria, Germany, and Switzerland. Verrall eventually had to relinquish his pastoral role. He had been a very popular tutor, even winning praise from Aleister Crowley, a demanding tutee if ever there was one. His arthritis, despite remissions, became so advanced that in his last years he had to be carried, like a helpless baby, to the stage from where, cross-legged, he would lecture to great dramatic effect (see Tillyard 1958 for a moving description of this).

Margaret Verrall's (1906) own account of the inception of her automatic writing, in the *Proceedings*, was lucid and sober, a far cry from the exaggerated and fanciful descriptions provided by a number of writers on the topic. She noted that it was not till she altered her grip on the pencil 'to hold it between the thumb and first finger' that after some nonsense she began to write rapidly mainly in Latin. She wrote without light purely by the flickering of the fire.

Margaret Verrall 5/3/1901:

> Evie Myers ... counsel gear nen o save trouble cant keep (Here I changed the pencil and held it between my thumb and first linger in the usual way, not in my way, **i.e.** between first and second finger.) evie vely ten yet come Name and I with many and all Let not the last sad offices to the dead be performed nor I myself to-morrow morning-star work rosy angelic I live ever little by little...thrice(?) to the world what everywhere...and I and I-do not strive after airy...following behind the tracks of the gods of many kinds is your expense for me and smiling to have moved the the other image of thy cross(?) do not avoid what I say to you, both always and everywhere, do not even once break my intent stay at home on Sunday(?) you may see whom I send to you goodbye

If one reads this sympathetically one can sense in the communicator a determined effort to break through in spite of the initial difficulty in mastering the process. On 31/3/1901 came the first intelligent use of English and, from April onwards, an increasing amount of Greek. She was only aware of the individual word as she wrote it and 'retained no recollection of what I had just written and no general notion as to the meaning of the whole'. She also commented perceptively on the lack of French which 'I know well and read as easily as English; I speak it also, and indeed constantly dream in it...' Because of this she argued that 'the subliminal strata tapped, so to speak, in the automatic writings are not those reached by the usual ways of dreaming or semi-conscious thought...'(Verrall 1906: 32; Kingsford 1920: 113–18). She further pointed out other characteristics of the scripts (which in the early days were fairly short, usually between 70 and 90 words), that they contained puns which she did not make or find interesting; that they wrote verse in Latin, Greek, and increasingly English while she was by no means a poet and found it difficult to produce even a very brief poem in English. And, finally, the scripts began to give dramatic indications of personality other than hers.

Rosalind Heywood (1959: 69), herself a gifted sensitive, stressed Margaret Verrall's courage given the prevailing attitude of the time. However, Margaret Verrall was part of what has been dubbed the intellectual aristocracy, the Oxbridge professional middle, upper-middle classes, and upper classes who furnished Oxford and Cambridge with so many academics from the mid nineteenth century onwards, and if any group had the intellectual sturdiness and self-confidence to override established prejudices, they did (Annan 1955).

Her home at 5 Selwyn Gardens was one of a number of very substantial late-Victorian properties clustered round the edges of the grounds of Corpus Christi College, probably built for the expanding academic population of Cambridge, particularly fellows newly allowed to marry and occupied then and no doubt now by distinguished and talented individuals. Next door lived James Ward, a leading Cambridge psychologist. Short walks away were Myers' home, Leckhampton House, the new College, Selwyn, which would figure in the cross-correspondences, and Newnham College itself. Some of the bricks for Verrall's and Ward's new homes were supposed to have come from George (brother of the more famous Charles) Darwin's family home (Keynes, M.E. 1976). Also, within walking range was the home of Alice Johnson, whose family was well established in the city.

Not only did Margaret Verrall receive material that began to make sense, her writing displayed links and resonances with the scripts of other mediums and automatists. Initially, the most remarkable and well documented of these early connections was with Diana Raikes (the wife of Justice Raikes KC—yet another graduate of Trinity College). Margaret Verrall received a letter from her on 23/6/1900 with regard to an impressive sitting she had recently had with Mrs Thompson. Diana Raikes sat a number of times with Mrs Thompson in 1900 (Piddington 1903a: 150) and, on one occasion, in spite of an attempt to deceive Mrs Thompson as to who her sitter was, Howard (her deceased son) correctly identified the sitter as his mother and communicated with her. Her pseudonym in these reports in the *Proceedings* of the SPR was Mrs Scott and Howard's was Geoffrey Scott. In discussing this episode Piddington quoted from a letter of Diana Raikes which revealed her exemplary upper-class background and interests: 'On the day I received the message I went out hunting, starting early, probably about 9 a.m., and returning about 3.45. I changed my habit and came down rather tired to the drawing-room, where I sat down by the fire with a book to wait for tea.' Piddington's comment was quietly amusing: 'I venture to direct the attention of a certain Continental school of psycho-physiologists to the fact that we produce here in England a fox-hunting type of automatic writer. Fox-hunting must in future, I suppose, be added to their lengthy list of "notes" of degeneracy.'

Diana Raikes had started to practise automatic writing in the hope of contacting her son, Lieutenant Francis Howard Raikes of The Rifle Brigade, who had been killed in a Boer attack at Wagon Hill, Ladysmith, on 6/1/1900. He was buried in South Africa but there is a memorial stained glass window to him in the Raikes' local church in Yorkshire, St Peter's, Norton, Malton. The Raikes lived at The Leat House, Malton. A number of cross-references concerning Howard developed in the scripts of Diana Raikes and Margaret Verrall which Margaret meticulously documented (1906: 219). She stated that 'Every note that I have on the subject is dated… the dates of Mrs Forbes' script are attested by the postmarks on the envelope in which they were sent to me; and since November, 1902, the dates of my script are attested by the postmarks and Sir Oliver Lodge's corroboration.' Three communicators emerged: Howard, Edmund Gurney, and Myers. But at this stage Margaret Verrall was certainly not prepared to identify these names with the surviving post-mortem personalities of the individuals indicated. She also stressed in the *Proceedings* that she did not just select positive connections with Mrs Raikes' scripts but 'that I give all the cases in which my script seemed to refer to Mrs. Forbes, not only those which appear to have "evidential" value.' The full account of the links (Verrall 1906: 205-75) repays detailed study but one particularly stands out because of its precision.

Margaret Verrall 28/8/1901:

> The fir-tree that has already been planted in the garden gives its own portent [plus the drawing of a sword, a suspended bugle, and possibly a crown].

All three of the drawings were part of Howard Raikes' regimental badge, particularly the bugle crucial for the direction of the infantry in battle. With regard to the fir-tree, Diana Raikes had grown some from seed sent to her by her son from abroad and she called it Howard's tree. Looking through her scripts to date and considering the question of chance coincidence, Margaret Verrall concluded: 'As bearing on the question whether such a combination is likely to have been accidental, I may say that on no other occasion has a bugle appeared in the script, nor has there been any other reference to a planted fir-tree.' Nor did this combination appear in the scripts of any of the other automatists through the long extended period of the cross-correspondences, though sword, as will be seen, frequently did, in a symbolic rather than literal sense. Finally, there was a hint of planning to communicate across mediums in that, on the same day of the Verrall script above, there occurred in Diana Raikes' script the statement that her son was looking for a sensitive through whom he could provide her with corroborative evidence. However, as one will find again and again through this study, statements in automatic writing about the writer's own concerns need to be treated with great caution.

One of the most remarkable early connections concerned a script sent by Diana Raikes to Margaret Verrall emphasising the one word — Birthday. On 14/12/1900 at a sitting with Mrs Thompson, Margaret Verrall had been given a message from the Bright Lady (as Annie Marshall, Myers' beloved, was described by the medium):

Tell Fred that [I] shan't fail to keep [my] promise about his birthday.

Margaret Verrall later discovered that this was a prediction, through Mrs Thompson, that Myers would die within a couple of years on his birthday and be with Annie (Piddington 1943a: 394; Johnson 1916b vol 2: 320-3). The prediction was not fulfilled (he died a year earlier than anticipated), but one interpretation, perhaps laboured, had 'birthday' meaning birth into the post-mortem world. In her last letter to Myers on 7/1/1901, to which she never received an answer, Margaret Verrall added as a postscript: 'When is your birthday? Is it soon?' On 23/3/1902 Diana Raikes sent Margaret Verrall a letter asking if the word 'birthday' had any meaning for her since her script had the statement: 'one word will be enough, Birthday', with instructions to send the message to Margaret Verrall. As Margaret Verrall wrote to Piddington: 'No single word that I can think of would have been so suggestive as this...' In her report in the *Proceedings* (Verrall 1906: 230) the incident had to be so disguised, because of Mrs Myers' hostility, that its evidential impact was greatly minimised. But it was quite safe to publicise the more general material in which the communicators expressed knowledge of what Margaret Verrall or Diana Raikes were doing even when Margaret Verrall was writing at the Simplon Pass in Switzerland or Diana Raikes was at Malton in Yorkshire.

It is surprising that references in Margaret Verrall's scripts to the trance automatic writings of the great American medium Leonora Piper were sparse at this stage. Only two items stood out. The first was the puzzling mixed Latin/Greek phrases 'all-seeing sphere' (panoptican sphaerae) and 'flying iron' (volatile ferrum) which occurred in a couple of early Margaret Verrall scripts. Richard Hodgson, the SPR-funded investigator of Leonora Piper in the United States, at a sitting with her in Boston had suggested that Rector get Helen Verrall to see a sphere. Hodgson knew that she was experimenting with crystal ball gazing at this time. The ambiguity occurred because Rector (one of the spirits who acted as a kind of manager or gatekeeper in the Piper trance sittings) was not sure whether Hodgson meant spear or sphere. One could argue that both aspects were communicated even if the recipient was Margaret rather than Helen Verrall since both meanings — sphere and spear — were conveyed (Verrall 1906: 216-17). Later (see Part 2) Piddington with his characteristic ingenuity discovered considerable symbolic meaning in these fragments. The second item was an attempt by Hodgson to transmit from Leonora Piper to Margaret Verrall the staggeringly boring password, stabdelta (Verrall 1906: 252). It was hardly surprising that the experiment was a resounding failure.

More successful, though not a cross-correspondence between mediums, was the effort by Arthur Verrall to test the hypothesis that telepathy, rather than discarnate spirits, was the source of his wife's automatic writing. He took three words from Electra's lament in Euripedes' *Orestes*, 'monopolon es Ao' — alone towards the dawn — or towards the one-horse of dawn (Eur. *Or.* 1004). The phrase had occurred in his degree examination in 1873 and he had stood on the steps of the examination hall afterwards discussing its meaning with two of his friends. These were probably — their rank order in the tripos in brackets — Arthur Myers (Twelfth Classic) and S.H. Butcher (Senior Classic). Verrall himself was Second Classic. Incidentally, all three of them made appearances, of varying dramatic intensity, in the automatic scripts after their deaths. One of them coined the phrase a one-horse dawn for it (as in the popular phrase a one-horse town) and this has become shorthand for his experiment.

There certainly appeared to be indirect references to the phrase in a number of Margaret Verrall's scripts between 10/4/1901 and 31/5/ 1902 (Verrall 1906: 156-67). There was a particular cluster of these in August 1901, where there were several other words in mono, allusions to dawn, and to reversals of nature, which was the context of the phrase in the play — Zeus's horror at the violent cruelty of the feuding Greek family, the House of Atreus, which caused him to reverse the course of the sun through the heavens. At the time this was seen as possibly suggesting a telepathic influence from husband to wife, albeit a far less impressive example than some of the cases that Myers himself had personally examined (see the case of Reverend P.H. Newnham and his wife: Myers 1885c: 1-63).

One-Horse Dawn (Monopolon es Ao)

A.W. Verrall 10/4/1901 transmitted:

'monopolon es Ao'/alone towards the dawn

Margaret Verrall 4/7/1901:

Yellow is the colour of the dawn

Margaret Verrall 13/8/1901:

A crested Cock that crows is the emblem

Margaret Verrall 20/8/1901:

> The long room with the many windows is near this hot room—he was outside—how plain it seems to me! But you don't know. Arthur can tell you.

Margaret Verrall 2/9/1901:

> Towards the

Margaret Verrall 4/9/1901:

> Alone with God

Margaret Verrall 9/9/1901:

> Moleskin—that is more like, the look not the meaning...Find the herb moly that will help...

Margaret Verrall 18/9/1901

> One-horsed

***

These extracts can be interpreted in a variety of ways. An effort from some source to transmit something that seems to approximate to Arthur Verrall's original message is about as far as one can go purely on the surface content presented. Margaret Verrall's verdict was (once she had been told what her husband had tried to communicate to her): '...it will be seen that the script attempts to reproduce both the word and the sense; it tries for the notions of "dawn" and of "one-horse" or "solitary"; it also attempts to reproduce the sound and the appearance both of the individual words and of the whole sentence of three words' (Verrall 1906: 159). But what was initially a partially successful experiment in telepathy expanded, under the dogged scrutiny of Piddington, into one of the most important themes in the scripts, the bringing into incarnation of a race of remarkable children through a process of spiritual eugenics (see Part 2 for details).

2

The Return of Myers?
The Syringa Flower; the Sealed Envelope and the Valley at Hallsteads; the Unexpurgated Autobiography

Margaret Verrall first publicly announced details of her automatic writing at a private meeting of members and associates of the SPR on 17/10/1902 in the large hall at 20 Hanover Square, London, where the Society had its headquarters. Sir Oliver Lodge, the president, in welcoming her, stressed the point that, regardless of its general value, the fact that this automatic writing had been developed by one of their own rather than strangers made it of even greater value (Anon 1902: 291–5). One can now see that this was a double-edged sword. To them, then, the evidence was all the more trustworthy as it came from one of their own class, and a particularly balanced, co-operative, and intelligent one at that. On the other hand, retaining objectivity and avoiding the leakage of crucial information was bound to be extremely difficult in such a situation.

Lodge then raised the crucial question on everyone's mind. Was this automatic writing the return of Myers? He probably felt easier in speculating about this since, according to Mrs Myers' diary (her husband's daily diary which she loyally tried to continue after his death: Myers 14/2), she was safely away visiting a friend in Yorkshire. Lodge was cautious in what he said. He noticed, he stated, the emphasis on predictions in Margaret Verrall's scripts since Myers himself had thought that successful predictions might provide some of the best evidence for post-mortem survival and he, Lodge, also felt there was a quality or atmosphere about the scripts which suggested some extremely intelligent influence at work. But beyond this he would not go.

Margaret Verrall's scripts did, however, show a certain persistence in describing items that later were found to have links with important events in Myers' life. On 19/4/1901 (Verrall 1906: 198 onwards) her script referred to something under the sofa in a blue cover. On 27/4/1901 the writing stated that a book was there and to tell Mrs Sidgwick about it: it was under something blue, loose, low, it was wrapped up, and they should stoop to see it. On 1/5/1901 there was mention of a jar, sweet-scented and full with an arm-chair nearby. On 3/5/1901 something blue, many books, and a portrait, perhaps, in a frame, were referred to. And finally, on 8/5/1901, 'Wooden cases Florentine pattern. She will know'. After discussion with Alice Johnson, Margaret Verrall realised that the details could match Mrs Sidgwick's room in Newnham College. There was a window-seat covered in blue cushions and nearby there was a table on which was a jar of sweet-smelling wallflowers, and by that table an armchair. There were bookcases full of books and on the wall a portrait of Henry Sidgwick. Nearby there was a Florentine chest of drawers which had been given to Mrs Sidgwick by members of her family (Verrall 1906: 195-7).

Mrs Sidgwick told Margaret Verrall on 18/5/1901 that she did in fact keep important papers under the window-seat but nothing that seemed directly to match the description in the automatic writing. It was about this time that Eveleen Myers asked Mrs Sidgwick for the return of the copy of Myers' unexpurgated autobiography which he had given to his closest friends, of whom Henry Sidgwick was one. Mrs Sidgwick told Eveleen that she had no idea where it was and it was not till the end of 1903 that she realised that in 1893 she had put the envelope containing it with the other papers under the window-seat. So it later became clear that the scripts were referring, fairly accurately, to something that later was proved to have been there at the time of the original scripts — and a document of considerable emotional and scientific importance to all concerned.

Mrs Sidgwick and Margaret Verrall had to tread a careful line with Mrs Myers who, although a very possessive woman, had some legitimate concerns re privacy. Annie Eliza Hill (Myers' great love) — the subject of the most private and moving parts of the unexpurgated autobiography — was born on 6/2/1845 and in 1865 married Walter James Marshall, the third son of William Marshall of Patterdale Hall, Cumberland. Annie died by her own hand on 29/8/1876, drowning in Ullswater below the family properties by the water's edge, Hallsteads and Old Church (Hamilton 2009). She had three sons and two daughters, and one of the sons, the Reverend Godfrey Marshall, MA Trinity College Cambridge, was still, as late as the 1930s, the rector of the church in Annie's home village, Thornton le Dale in Yorkshire (Piddington 1943a: 595-615). Moreover, Annie had a sister who survived till 1922. There were, therefore, people who could be affected by the revelation of the relationship even though it had been platonic and not to anyone's discredit.

Margaret Verrall'scripts also started to refer to the sealed envelope that Myers had left to be opened after his death. Margaret Verrall knew that Myers had done this. William James, Henry Sidgwick, and Richard Hodgson had also made this experiment at different times: the idea being that a correct message through a medium from the deceased Myers, or whomever, as to what was actually in the envelope would be formidable evidence in favour of personal survival. These references occurred fairly early on in her scripts. For example 31/5/1901: 'Diotima gives the clue.' Margaret Verrall had heard of the name but knew nothing of its meaning till she looked in Plato's *Symposium* on 1/6/1902. There she found that Diotima was the prophetess of Mantinea who had instructed Socrates on the nature of love and the importance of moving beyond physical to spiritual love. This was also an important and recurring theme in Myers' own prose and poetry.

The matter went quiet for some time till 18/12/1902 when Diana Raikes produced a number of dio references.

Diana Raikes 18/12/1902:

> with the-Dionysus *Dion-*...word of the test will be Dy...will you be so kind as to send this today...it is one of the most Hymeneal Songs — Love's oldest melody.

The script stated that it was the joint product of Edmund Gurney and Howard Raikes and that the word 'will be found in Myers own...' There was a gap but the word 'book' or 'writings' obviously completed the sense. In January 1903 the emphasis on receiving the key word from Mrs Raikes or finding it in a book of Myers' continued with the statement on 25/1/1903 that 'Love is the Bond'. Margaret Verrall became convinced that all this was more than just wishful thinking when on 10/2/1903 she read for the first time, in Myers' just published *Human Personality*, his own summary of the spiritual and cosmical elements of love as expressed by Socrates in the *Symposium* (Myers 1904a vol 1: 113-15). Finally came an explicit statement.

Margaret Verrall 13/7/1904:

> I have long told you of the contents of the envelope. You have not understood. It has in it the words from the Symposium — about Love bridging the chasm.

There were also, alongside the insistence on the message in the sealed envelope, references to the importance of a particular picture.

Margaret Verrall 31/7/1903:

> ask Mrs. Raikes whether she knows the likeness in the picture — she may know. Go to the gallery at Venice — the lady with the pearls. This both of us desire HS and I more through Helen later.

Helen Verrall 23/8/1903 (who knew nothing of this):

> Why did Mrs. Verrall not understand about those pearls. We said it plainly. It is a clue...

This matter had to be handled delicately for Mrs Sidgwick later informed Margaret Verrall that she and her husband had been told by Myers that when visiting Venice he had seen a picture of a girl with a string of pearls round her neck who bore a remarkable likeness to Annie. They do not appear to have attempted to track the picture down at the time, though a few years later Winifred Coombe-Tennant tried to do so. In addition, on 20/10/1903, Margaret Verrall learnt from Hodgson in the United States (Piddington 1921: 125) that the Greek sign for the letter S, Σ, that had begun to appear in her scripts had been used by Myers as a symbol for those parts of his sittings with Mrs Thompson at which Annie Marshall had communicated. However, the wider significance of the letter sigma was not picked up for a number of years (see below).

Given this range of evidence, all apparently linked intimately with Myers, Sir Oliver Lodge as President of the SPR had a difficult call to make. Was there really enough evidence to justify opening the sealed envelope? If he lent his authority to its opening, no one would oppose him. But if the event proved to be a failure, the cause of psychical research would suffer a devastating blow. From humble origins (Johnson G.M. 2015: 60-85), Lodge had built up a substantial scientific and public profile and shown great courage in promoting the cause of psychical research and openly expressing his belief in survival (this had come from sittings with Leonora Piper in 1889 and not from sittings with Mrs Leonard in World War I as has often been stated). In 1900 Lodge had been offered the Principalship of the new University of Birmingham. And in 1902 he was, along with his fellow seeker after truth, Arthur Conan Doyle, knighted by Edward VII. So, both as a public figure and as the man who had steered the SPR through the difficult period after the deaths of Sidgwick and then Myers, his words carried weight.

Therefore, when he examined Margaret Verrall's scripts and consequently wrote to the members of the Council of the SPR and a few other chosen individuals to come to the Society's rooms on 13/12/1904 for the opening of Myers' sealed envelope, there was real expectation that something remarkable might occur. Many of them must have speculated that if anyone could run the blockade of death, it was the passionate and determined personality of Myers. Margaret Verrall read out the message from her script and Lodge then revealed the contents of the envelope which he had taken from the bank vault where it had rested for thirteen years: 'If I can revisit any earthly scene, I should choose the *Valley* in the grounds of Hallsteads, Cumberland.' All were bitterly disappointed. None more so than Margaret Verrall and it was announced in the *Journal* for January 1905 that the experiment had been a complete failure (Anon 1905-6: 11-13).

Mrs Sidgwick, who finally discovered Myers' autobiography under her window-seat in December 1903, after, as has been seen, considerable prompting from Margaret Verrall's scripts, thought that it might be possible to reconcile these differing statements. She re-read her husband's copy of the unexpurgated autobiography, realised that the valley was obviously the setting of the scene of Myers' meetings with Phyllis (the name by which Annie was disguised in his autobiography), and that the Socratic view of love seemed to imbue the booklet, particularly certain descriptive passages of prose and some of the poetry. She showed Margaret Verrall the relevant sections in the autobiography and this persuaded them both that Myers associated Hallsteads and its valley with his love for Annie Marshall, very much a love of the spiritually transforming kind, described in Plato's *Symposium* (Mrs and Miss Verrall 1914: 354–5. See also Salter 1958a).

This was further confirmed by Margaret Verrall contacting a member of the Marshall family, W.C. Marshall (who was the architect who had designed Myers' home, Leckhampton House, now a graduate centre in the grounds of Corpus Christi College), to see if the term 'the Valley' had any meaning for them. In his reply he wrote that they all used that phrase, at Hallsteads, to describe an area that ran down past the flower garden to a sheltered area and to a small house, Old Church, which looked out across Ullswater. It had been occupied for some time by Walter Marshall whose first wife was a very great friend of Myers. It now became even clearer to Margaret Verrall that Myers associated this place and walks therein with Annie and with the highest form of love and that either the script references were 'a series of accidents, – or the work of an existing intelligence outside me – outside this world' (Salter A/3/3).

The relevant paragraph in the unexpurgated autobiography was: 'Some of the serenest hours of those mourning years [after the death of Annie] were spent in that valley in the grounds of Hallsteads, on Ullswater, which has been the setting of much of my inward life. Outside it lie the wilder beauties of Cumberland; within are a grandeur and solitude which foster without overwhelming the heart. There are tower and spire, of cedar and cypress, high walls of flowering laurel, and rhododendrums massed amid the shade. There for many a twilight hour I have paced alone, and shaken from the thick syringas their load of scent and rain. The childhood of Phyllis also had been spent in a scene resembling this: she had been nurtured amid antique simplicity, and in an ancestral moorland home.' It is quite obvious from this passage that Myers associated syringas and their scent with his love of Annie, and references to syringa crop up in a number of the scripts of the automatists.

All this had to be discussed discretely since Mrs Myers was determined not to have the full autobiography in print and hounded those with copies to give them back. Nor would she grant permission for relevant extracts to be published to substantiate the claim that Margaret Verrall's scripts were closer in essence to the message in the sealed envelope than had initially been realised. Indeed, she wrote intense and almost insulting letters to Margaret Verrall and to Mrs Sidgwick once she learnt that a report on the Verrall scripts was to appear in the *Proceedings* of the SPR (Hamilton 2009: 283-92). Gossip, slander, and innuendo would be heaped on her family, she fulminated, and the press would get hold of it. She was completely dismissive of any attempt to link the *Symposium* to the statement in the sealed envelope. As Margaret Verrall (Salter A/3/3) wearily wrote in her diary on Jan 13 1905: 'I hear that Eveleen, hurt at not being present when the envelope was opened, says that she attachs no value to my script, & that (e.g.) the Diotima business is all in the Rossetti essay!' (Myers had written an essay on Rossetti).

Assuming his survival, Myers must have been immensely frustrated at his widow twice 'blocking' his efforts to provide good survival evidence. This occurred first with regard to *Human Personality*. As Salter (1955a,b) stated: 'When *Human Personality* came to be published in 1903, even the most friendly critics were struck by the weakness of the argument at the crucial moment, where well-documented and authenticated communications from the dead were to be found and by the absence of the communications through Mrs Piper and especially Mrs Thompson to which it was known he attached great importance.' It is heartbreaking to examine Myers' diary for the years 1898 onwards and to look at the regular entry denoting a Mrs Thompson sitting. Enclosed within the sigma sign which indicated a sitting there was often an 'a' which meant that Annie Marshall had communicated. Yet no physical record whatsoever exists of these. The second block on his attempt to provide good survival evidence, as will be seen, was the public statement by Mrs Myers in 1908 that she had not yet received any evidence worth taking seriously and her refusal to allow access to the full unexpurgated autobiography which would have made the Sealed Envelope Test appear a partial success rather than an inglorious failure.

The attitude of Mrs Myers caused Margaret Verrall difficulties on a number of levels. It probably damaged her reputation with some elements of Cambridge society. It prevented the investigators from verifying personal details in the automatic writing scripts with Mrs Myers, and it vitiated for many years the quality and the presentation of the survival evidence that was accumulating. One can, however, have a certain sympathy for Mrs Myers given the number of members of the Marshall family still alive. To some extent, therefore, she was right, if somewhat oversensitive, to fear the early publication of the full autobiography. She managed to get back most of the copies that Myers had given out but fortunately for the history of psychical research three copies, as far as can be ascertained, were not returned: Hodgson's, Lodge's (technically, he returned his but kept a copy), and Sidgwick's.

Myers had, in fact, left his wife in a rather difficult position. On the one hand those interested in psychical research were keen to receive any post-mortem evidence from the most celebrated psychical researcher in the UK at the time. On the other hand, though he did want the autobiography to be more widely published and printed at some stage without any cuts, he had also written that part of it might remain unpublished for some years after his death. That put a certain amount of pressure on his wife to make the correct judgement, as his own preface clearly showed (Myers 1961):

'I desire that the following sketch should someday be published in its entirety; but it may probably be well to reserve at least part of it until some years after my death. To avert accidents, therefore, I now propose to get these pages privately printed, and to send a sealed copy to each of the following intimate friends: Professor Henry Sidgwick, Cambridge; Professor Oliver Lodge, Liverpool; Professor William James, Harvard; Dr. R. Hodgson, Boston; Sir R.H. Collins, K.C.B., Claremont; Mr. R.W. Raper, Oxford. I shall desire these friends to open the packet after my death, and I shall be grateful if any of them, in the order in which their names are mentioned, will act as my literary executors, using their discretion as to the publication of this in its entirety; but it may probably be well to reserve at least part of it until some years after my death.' One notes the phrase 'to avert accidents'. Myers obviously knew his wife well and in fact, after his death, the records of his sittings with Mrs Thompson, through whom Annie, 'the Bright Lady', communicated so convincingly, vanished without trace.

The relevant portions of the unexpurgated autobiography were only made available in 1958 to researchers through the 'courtesy of Mrs Goold-Adams and Mrs Nicholson', grand-daughters of Myers, and the complete autobiography was not published till 1961 (Salter 1958a). This secrecy and delay in publication fuelled rumours in the Spiritualist press that the SPR was concealing valuable survival evidence provided by the discarnate Myers. At a later period, reticence over the precise evidential nature of parts of Trix Fleming's and Winifred Coombe-Tennant's scripts had similar consequences.

Nevertheless, despite the failure to reveal the exact contents of the sealed envelope, the scripts continued to address the topic.

Margaret Verrall 21/12/1904:

> Orotava and the scented eve — Hodgson could tell you more —
> It is confused but I have said what it is right [sic] — you may
> not understand, but it is there, all there if you only knew.
> Wait now and write regularly — I will send a message about
> this through Mrs. Raikes — do not ask for it — it may take time.
> In January it may be clear — you are less wrong than you
> think, but there has been a mistake somewhere...

Your friend once and always—you have rightly understood, rightly felt, although you have not proved

Diana Raikes wrote to Margaret Verrall on 10/1/1905, with script of that date. She had heard from Margaret Verrall that the envelope had been opened, and that it was a failure, but Margaret Verrall had not given her any hint as to the nature of the contents of the letter, and this script contained the following:

Mrs. Verrall ... we see your effort ... you will be given [scrawls] ... look more carefully, more sensible of FWHM's meaning in a sentence all made by sympathy.

Margaret Verrall came to realise that the phrase 'Orotava and the scented eve' was an allusion to a poem by Myers entitled *Teneriffe* which was famous for its syringas, and that there were possibly scattered references to Annie and to syringa in the early scripts of her daughter Helen Verrall. Not till 20/10 1903 did Margaret Verrall learn from Richard Hodgson that Myers in his autobiography had referred to Annie as Phyllis (the name of a girl loved by a shepherd in one of Virgil's *Eclogues* (7: 59-63); Phyllis loves the hazels), and yet the name Phyllis had appeared in Helen Verrall's script on 2/8/1903 and by January 1905 Margaret Verrall suspected that Dove and White Bird in scripts also stood for Annie, since thirteen poems in the unexpurgated autobiography had Phyllis as their subject. The first one, *Love and Death*—'My bird, so wounded, soaring so, At once so tender and so brave,/He knows not through how stormy skies/My dove maintains her waveless way...'—was particularly moving given the situation in Annie's life at the time of her death.

The first investigators gradually gained some sense of this and her fraught relationship with her husband Walter (Beer 1998; Hamilton 2009), but not the full detail which made those lines so poignant. Walter had contracted syphilis, was manic depressive, and financially profligate. Myers had observed Annie's efforts, at home and abroad, to cope with that and with her five young children. This, possibly even more than her intelligence and personal attractiveness, had turned his admiration into a deep and spiritual love. Alice Johnson collected, at the end of the second volume of Fleming automatic writings, these extensive references to Annie that built up over the first decade of the scripts, but her published papers on Fleming script in the *Proceedings* were much more muted in this respect because of the continued hostility of Mrs Myers (Johnson 1916b vol 2).

There was one other interesting development that was not known of or appreciated at the time. On the same day, 13/7/1904, that Margaret Verrall received her message about the contents of the sealed envelope, Piddington drafted his own posthumous message, sealed it, and gave it to Alice Johnson to be kept locked at the SPR office in Hanover Square. It stated: 'If ever I am a spirit, and if I can communicate, I shall endeavour to transmit in some form or other the number SEVEN.' This number was chosen 'because seven has been a kind of tic with me ever since my early boyhood'. He reasoned that communication might be extremely difficult post-mortem and that such a deep rooted psychological quirk, expressed in a simple phrase like 'We are seven' or another common phrase involving seven, might have a chance of getting through (Salter 1961: 175-81). It should be stressed in the light of what followed that Margaret Verrall and the other automatists had no idea that Piddington had written and deposited a sealed envelope with Alice Johnson (she did not know the contents). On the same day, as if a signal from the communicators, Margaret Verrall in Cambridge wrote '…it is something contemporary that you are to record — note the hour — in London half the message has come…'

Over the next few years, particularly during 1907–1908, references to the number seven were distributed across the scripts of Helen Verrall, Mrs Frith, Trix Fleming, and Leonora Piper, concluding with a statement by Margaret Verrall on 27/1/1909:

> And ask what has been the success of Piddington's last experiment? Has he found the bits of his famous sentence scattered among you all? And does he think that is an accident, or started by one of you? But even if the source is human, who carries the thoughts to the receivers? Ask him that. F.W.H.M.

As in the one-horse dawn episode, it appeared that the discarnates had also intervened in this case for their own purposes (see Part 2).

3
Paranormal Cognition in Margaret Verrall's Early Scripts

The sealed envelope episode may have, in strict logic, been a failure, but Margaret Verrall was rather successful at another form of paranormal cognition, namely prevision and prediction. She was particularly scrupulous in regard to this complex area and, unlike some individuals who have experienced them, she recorded all failures as well as successes (Verrall 1906: 319–39). One remarkable prediction was that Mrs Myers would visit Boston, with her son Leo, to sit with Leonora Piper. She limited the details in her report and disguised references to Myers by using the initial H, as she did on a number of other occasions. But the original script and her comments on it in her diary make a much more vivid and powerful impact.

Margaret Verrall 29/8/1901:

> October will help. The 19th. Remember. Φ (probably but not absolutely clear in the original)

Margaret Verrall 28/9/1901:

> ...every day is nearer... The old world & the new... note the date—and the sequence—and count the days—ten more and other nine then two. Father and son... Signed Tuus.

Margaret Verrall recorded in her diary (Salter A/3/2) that on 15/10/1901 she met Leo Myers in the Great Court of Trinity who told her that he and his mother were going to America on 19/10/1901, and she encountered Eveleen Myers shortly before she left, who mentioned she had only decided to go to the States that very day. Margaret Verrall concluded, given the dates of her original scripts, that telepathy was not the source of the prediction. In late 1903 (see above) she was able to interpret the symbol Φ, Phi for Phyllis, as referring to Annie Marshall.

Another prediction, or rather prevision, concerned Eddie Marsh, the civil servant, belle lettrist, and art collecter. He was a former student of A.W. Verrall's and had often enjoyed the Verralls' hospitality. On 11/12/1901 Margaret Verrall wrote of someone reading Marmontel (an eighteenth-century French historian) on a cold night by candlelight. There was an attempt at Sidgwick's signature beneath the script. The following March, Eddie Marsh told her he had recently read Marmontel by candlelight on a cold night, and two names (mentioned in a later automatic script by Margaret Verrall), Passy and Fleury, also occurred in the passages he was looking at (Lodge 1909b: 155–9). Marsh in his autobiography confirmed this in broad outline though with minor differences in detail (Marsh 1939).

A more sinister prevision took place on 11/5/1901. Margaret Verrall's script had 'Chalk sticking to the feet has got over the difficulty'. Then there followed the drawing of a bird with a large head and an evil grin which the Verralls later referred to as the 'cockyoly bird'. They could make no sense of it till Margaret Verrall read on 16/5/1901 in the *Westminster Gazette* an abridged account of an incident earlier reported in the *Daily Mail*. It transpired that two friends investigating haunted rooms 'in one of the Inns within a stone's throw of the Law Courts' had put down powdered chalk and had captured the prints of (estimated from the print size) a large bird in the empty room. The key point was that Margaret Verrall's script and drawing took place around 11.10pm on the 11th but the incident with the chalk did not take place till around 2.30am on the 12th (Verrall 1906: 328–30).

The context of this particular piece of automatic writing is also worth commenting on. Margaret Verrall had had a small party of ladies to dinner that evening and if they were the members of her regular dining club they would have been very high-powered indeed. It was, therefore, not probably an environment conducive to ghostly thoughts. Moreover, Margaret Verrall wrote that 'after the departure of the guests I had gone upstairs, when I felt a sudden strong desire to write automatically, and came down again to find materials'. This sense of external impulse or motivation happened quite frequently with Margaret Verrall, Trix Fleming, and Winifred Coombe-Tennant, an externality that did not appear to stem from immediate psychological causes or the environmental context.

The following was another interesting prevision.

Margaret Verrall 2/4/1903:

> Now draw on five stone steps a cross [a drawing of this] and on the cross hangs a wreath, a fresh green wreath. They have come to see it there—out in the open on the hill side in the sound of the sea... Grey sky and sea and the grey gulls cry in the wind.

On 24/2/1905 and 17/3/1906 the topic was referred to again: 'Can you not find the cross on its five steps and the green wreath?' On 4/4/1906 Margaret Verrall visited a Miss Curtois, who had a photograph on her wall which reminded her of those scripts. Miss Curtois confirmed that on a pedestal of five stone steps in her mother's home village a cross was erected in her memory and that a green wreath was once placed on it. Moreover, although thirty miles from the sea, the countryside was sometimes flooded, with seagulls skimming over the flood waters (Verrall 1906: 335–9).

Lodge (1909b: 161) in his book *The Survival of Man* wrote that he, Myers, and Sidgwick had often discussed the importance of consistent, veridical predictions, as providing good *prima facie* evidence for some form of survival: predictions that were not necessarily on the grand scale which might be easily inferred by the educated and informed, but trivial, precise, and intimate ones. Some of those quoted above would fit into that category. But what about grandiose ones?

Margaret Verrall 27/1/1905:

> No this is other… A dread appearance and foul prodigies. It is not over yet the worst is still to come — not in a town — on the open road they will fall But you will not hear for six whole days… and then see the news. Lying side by side not of equal size they are and a woman among them. Did they then fall? I did not see but only know them there and the horror of it can you not feel? But wait 6 whole days.

This seems to have been a clear prediction of an incident in the Russian Revolution of 1905. The revolution started on 22/1/1905 in St Petersburg and rapidly spread to the countryside, but the investigators appear to have made no effort to match the narrative above to news reports as and when they reached the West.

Margaret Verrall summarised and commented on these early scripts in a very substantial edition of the *Proceedings* of the SPR for October 1906. Her tone was rational and analytic and her text contained absolutely no sense or awareness of the complex patterning and symbolism that, much later, Gerald Balfour and J.G. Piddington claimed could be found in them. Nor did she see them as certain evidence for the post-mortem survival of Myers and other individuals who were mentioned in the writings. Only two chapters (X and XI) discussed the early cross-correspondences; there was some collation of references to past and future events; to telepathy; to the form and style of the scripts and other general characteristics; and the great question of the survival of bodily death was at this stage subsumed under the title of 'Varieties of Dramatic Form Assumed'. Myers, Gurney, and Sidgwick had to prove that they were not merely imaginative dramatisations of Margaret Verrall's subconscious mind.

With the arrival of Trix Fleming as an automatic writer, Margaret Verrall's role and workload in the SPR expanded considerably. After the publication of her own report, her efforts shifted (in conjunction with Alice Johnson) to examining the relationship between her steadily continued automatic writing output and that of Trix Fleming, Leonora Piper, and her own daughter Helen. She therefore moved from being not only an investigator of her own scripts but also an investigator of the others' — a dual role she managed with great conscientiousness till the end of her life.

4

The Life and Automatic Writing of Trix Fleming
Her Researcher, Alice Johnson, and the Theory of the Cross-Correspondences

Trix Fleming, Rudyard Kipling's sister, who wrote to the SPR from India in 1903 for advice concerning her automatic writing, has not achieved her full recognition as a gifted automatist and as a writer generally (see Lee 2004). With regard to the latter she has only in recent years emerged from under the shadow of her brother's reputation and, with regard to the former, rumours of her mental instability and the negative effect that automatic writing had on her life and personality abounded for years. For these reasons a substantial amount of text is here devoted to providing more detailed biographical information about her as a prelude to the narrative and analysis of her automatic writing. Barbara Fisher (2014a: 44–57) has graphically outlined the commonly perceived view of Trix. 'She is largely absent from Rudyard's biographies, making rare appearances, mostly as a source of inconvenience and embarrassment.' She was seen as fey, fragile, and her literary efforts underplayed or ignored. She was written out of history reappearing towards the end of her life, as Fisher puts it, as 'a batty old lady at the Edinburgh zoo, talking to the elephants in Hindustani'.

The family attitude to Trix's interest in psychic matters (she was nicknamed Trix as a child by her father because of her tricksiness) was a little conflicted. Certainly, on her mother's side of the family, the Macdonald sisters (Flanders 2002; Taylor 1987) seem to have feared the Scottish 'second sight', but there were no objections to Trix, herself, doing palmistry etc. at fetes and on other social occasions. In fact, her father made her a black wooden box with gold relief to contain the playing cards she used for fortune-telling. Her short comic play *The Art and Craft of Palmistry* showed her fully aware of the kind of sharp observations, patter, and fishing techniques that the bogus and fraudulent often employed, and it also demonstrated an amused detachment about the practice (Lee 2004: 267-74). She clearly saw the comic, unpleasant, or deceitful side of such activities but was also aware that there was something remarkable about her own psychic abilities as they developed. Her relatives, Helen and Betty Macdonald, testified to the genuineness of her experiences—speaking to the Chinese Ambassador in his own language (which she did not know), travelling out of her body at night, and retrocognitive clairvoyance in York Minster (Lee 2004: 116–17).

She and Rudyard had a vivid and colourful early childhood with their parents Lockwood and Alice Kipling in Bombay, where her father had a post as architectural sculptor at the Jeejeebhoy School of Art. Then the children were sent back to England, as many were, because the climate was thought inimical to their health. This was harsh but explicable. What was difficult to understand was that they were placed with a Mrs Holloway in Southsea, a professional boarder, rather than with relatives. Mrs Kipling had remarkable and well connected sisters (one married Burne-Jones the artist and another Alfred Baldwin, the father of Stanley, the future prime minister; see Flanders 2002). They would have taken the children. But, Trix was left in Southsea at three years old and Rudyard at almost six. Rudyard wrote about their experiences in the story *House of Desolation* and Trix produced her version of events in *Punch and Judy*: 'unluckily Punch never forgot... Judy could and did forget details in the past... the mother want in her world was never supplied' (Fisher: 46). The traumatic impact on the children, though Trix seems to have been less harshly treated than Rudyard by Mrs Holloway, must have been huge. It is a tribute to her innate ability and spirit that she later showed great promise when sent to Notting Hill High School for Girls and was considered bright enough to try for Cambridge. This came to nothing because of lack of finance and, no doubt, the prevailing attitude to female higher education (Fisher: 47).

The family later moved to Lahore in the Punjab where Lockwood Kipling had been appointed Principal of the newly founded Art School, where Rudyard was a successful and pugnacious journalist, and where 'the family square', as he put it, was now intact, with both children back in India. Trix, however, was keen to stress (Fisher: 48) that there was none of the Charles and Mary Lamb or William and Dorothy Wordsworth nonsense, or over-intensity of relationship, between brother and sister. They were too witty, sharp, and robust for that. She collaborated with him on *Echoes* (a volume of parodies) and on some of the early *Plain Tales from the Hills*, and with all the family on *Quartette*, a collection of short stories.

At first the Kiplings seemed socially a little isolated and financially stretched. But after Lord Dufferin came out as Viceroy that began to change, particularly in 1885, Trix's first season in Simla. Situated about six to eight thousand feet above sea level with residences connected by winding paths through the pine trees, Simla was the English governing classes' refuge from the heat of the plains. It was a strange, slightly feverish and isolated environment since there was no train from the railhead at

Umballa till 1903, which meant an onward trek of two days by animal carriage.

The Kiplings became increasingly popular in some though not all sectors of Simla society. The wit of Trix's mother, Alice, was much appreciated by Lord Dufferin, who would take tea with her occasionally, and Trix, herself, became much admired for her 'ice maiden' kind of beauty. Dufferin's son (Clandeboye who, like Howard Raikes, would die at Wagon Hill) fell in love with her and had to be sent back (Ankers 1988: 127–8) to England. Trix had refused his proposal but the Vicereine decided to play safe anyway. Trix, was probably too perceptive and widely read with her finely honed literary sensibility (she had a prodigious memory for quotations and was a very fast and effortless reader) for most young men.

She began eventually to show some interest in Jack Fleming, a decade older than herself, who was a subaltern in the Queen's Own Borderers but who had been seconded to the Survey of India. Neither Rudyard nor her father Lockwood approved of her choice but both weakened under Trix's pining for Jack (their first engagement had been broken off) and her mother's belief that she needed someone mature and strong to look after her. Subconsciously, Trix may have felt the need to get away from her mother's controlling and dominant personality and that marriage, to a man who was clearly infatuated with her and who showered her with presents, might well be the answer. They were married on her 21st birthday, 11/6/1889, and they went to live in Mussoorie, North West Frontier (about a hundred miles or so from Simla in the foothills below Nepal).

The marriage seems to have been something of a disaster from the start. Trix was attractive, well read, and witty in company: Fleming was tall and distinguished looking but temperamentally completely the wrong person for the lively Trix. He showed no interest in literature and the arts (except in design and illustration) and indeed was contemptuous of Rudyard Kipling's scribbling and of literary 'riff raff' generally (Lee 2004; Johnson 1934a). Furthermore, he had a real hostility towards automatic writing and what he saw as dabbling in the occult. Though he and Rudyard disliked each other cordially, they united in their opposition to this practice. Trix Fleming privately thought that this was nonsense. She believed that the activity was harmless 'for a person of average common-sense', and, though she was careful to whom she said this, for she had a strong sense of duty and loyalty, she knew that the main problems in her life were caused by her marriage to a rather dour and unimaginative man. This temperamental incompatibility must have been exacerbated when in 1893 she and Jack went to live in Calcutta on 'small means' and her parents went back to England permanently.

Though, compared to the triumphs of Simla, Tisbury, in Wiltshire, may have seemed a come-down, Trix's parents had settled in an area where their arts and crafts and Pre-Raphaelite connections made them popular with the local aristocracy. John Lockwood Kipling had built up quite a reputation in India, as had Rudyard, and the family connection to Ned Burne-Jones, ore of the most important late-Victorian painters, was very useful. Such associations gained them entry to the Wyndhams of Clouds where 'Mr Kipperling' became the children's drawing master; they knew Arthur Morrison, the millionaire art collector; and they visited Wardour Castle, home of the Arundell family (Dakers 1993: 146-7; Ankers 1988: 133-5).

Trix and Jack Fleming had occasional leaves in England in 1893 and 1895 and then went back to Mussoorie in March 1896. She returned to England in December 1897. At some point she developed a friendship with Evelyn Pickering de Morgan, the painter (Oberhausen 2009). She wrote a number of poems stimulated by Evelyn's paintings. There were few people she could share her psychic and spiritual beliefs with and Evelyn was one. Trix was no 'dabbler'. As one of her cousins (Lee 2004: 121) remembered: 'From early girlhood she saw ghosts or spirits, and in her later years the gift developed considerably, so that she was able to converse with many who had passed into the spirit world. These experiences had no terror for her, but were only of intense interest, and she wondered why others couldn't see what she saw.' Moreover, Evelyn's mother-in-law, Sophie de Morgan (1863), had written a substantial book on Spiritualism based on the six years a medium lived in their family, which Trix may well have read.

It is not clear if Jack Fleming was with her on her return to England in 1897 but it was about this time that she had the severe breakdown which she later described in a letter to Alice Johnson on 16/4/1908 (Johnson 1916b vol 2). In this letter she attributed the cause to the popular medical explanation of anaemia, stating that she just avoided anaemia of the brain. This explanation seems to have had, with the medical profession, the same catch all value that hysteria had previously as a meaningless weasel word for explaining women's behaviour (Oppenheim 1991). However, other sources (Lee 2004) described a much more disturbing situation. It appears that she had long, stubborn silences punctuated by outbursts in which she revealed a bitter revulsion towards her husband. Recent students of Trix's life agree on this as the root cause (Fisher 2014a; Hamer 2012). Many of the problems were psychological rather than physical and only through the social licence of temporary 'madness' could she express the real cause of her unhappiness. Alice Johnson, who came to know her well, circulated a memo to the inner circle of the SPR on this (Johnson 1934a: 5). She emphasised the disastrous nature of the marriage, Trix's strong sense of conscience and her 'gentle and yielding nature', and that when away from Fleming she was often cheerful and in good health.

Trix Fleming remained in England and Europe from 1898 to 1902 doing some travelling with her parents, trying to improve her mental health, and while in Florence she encountered the remarkable, and remarkably named, Lady Walburga Paget, who was one of the leaders of Anglo-Florentine society at the turn of the twentieth century, and the wife of a retired diplomat. It was Lady Paget, with her considerable experience in *fin de siècle* alternative beliefs and practices, who first helped her to see that her psychic gifts might be managed and grounded. In the second volume of Lady Paget's diary (1924 vol 2: 351-2) there was a vivid, shrewd, and only lightly disguised portrait of Trix: 'After her came T.F., the daughter of a literary father and mother, the sister and niece of very celebrated men, herself a novelist and poet, very attractive, with the overpowering wish of being loved and admired by all, highly gifted in the way of talent, and also very psychic but unbalanced. She was born in India, and married there an officer, handsome, poor and of a depressed state of mind.'

She rejoined her husband in Calcutta in 1902 (where he had moved to continue work on the survey of India) with greater confidence in her sense of the importance of her gifts and the need to explore and develop them. In 1903 she read Myers' *Human Personality* and restarted her automatic writing. She wrote to Alice Johnson at the SPR, asking for advice about this practice, describing her earlier experiences, and stressing her current good health and mental cheerfulness. She emphasised that she had never been mesmerised, never attended a séance, that the idea of paid mediumship was repugnant to her, and that five years ago she had only discovered the clairvoyant faculty by accident (Johnson 1907-09: 170-6).

The support of Evelyn de Pickering, then Lady Paget, then Alice Johnson, and also that of her old Indian friend, the novelist Maud Diver, gave her the confidence to produce more than two hundred scripts in the next few years. These contributed enormously to the development of the cross-correspondence phenomena. Trix Fleming tried to write in the cool of the early morning and the scripts counselled her to make her mind a blank and not to worry about being made a fool of. She often had a headache before the writing but afterwards the headache would go and she would feel well. However, she still had to keep the activity secret both from Jack Fleming and from her family, and this explains the irregular production and terseness of her scripts compared to the enormous body of material generated by the Verralls and Winifred Coombe-Tennant, all of whom, in different ways, operated in much more propitious environments.

Trix Fleming returned to Europe in April 1904. There was no doubt a certain amount of travelling and visiting and Fleming might have been with her for some of the time. This could be the reason why from April 1904 there was almost no writing for a year. In February 1905, probably when Fleming would have returned to India from leave, she resumed correspondence with Alice Johnson and met her in the flesh on 6/10/1905 in the rooms of the SPR at Hanover Square. Hanover Square was a suitably impressive location for the Society, close to other academic societies and in a prestigious part of the capital just below Oxford Street. It was a far cry from the environment of professional mediumship Trix Fleming so disliked and the milieu must have reassured her. There, on 16/11/1905, she first met Margaret Verrall and they agreed on weekly joint writing sessions which continued till June 1906, Trix sending the scripts to Hanover Square from Edinburgh, Tisbury, or London, one assumes. Because of lack of documentation (her brother destroyed a lot of material at their parent's deaths and on Trix's subsequent collapse: see Allen 2007), her itinerary and location cannot be established more precisely, except where it is given at the top of the script.

It is known from various sources, however, that she began to make quite an impact on some of the leading figures of the SPR and their aristocratic connections in the spring and summer of 1906. From April 12-19 she was part of a large country house gathering at Clouds, the home of the Wyndham family, and two letters to Maud Diver vividly described the events and the fact that she was being taken very seriously by a section of the establishment (Fisher 2014a; 2014b). She mentioned Arthur Balfour's polite but shrewd conversational style and Oliver Lodge's niceness and kindness (letter of 17/4/1906). Gerald Balfour held a crystal ball for her so she could demonstrate crystal gazing. In the second letter (26/6/1906) she expressed her growing confidence in the nature of the work she was involved in: 'Telepathy is a real thing & some day we shall know how to control it. When we meet I shall/will tell you about the experiments with the wife of a Cambridge professor... [It is a] guilty secret [I keep] from Jack and my Father they think it bad for me but I have felt so much better since reading HP [*Human Personality*] and not suppressing it.'

She returned to live with her husband in Calcutta for two years while he worked on the Survey of India. The anguished tone in her scripts seemed to diminish (though it is difficult to be precise about this) and the scripts displayed a greater complexity, particularly when later cross-referred against those of the other automatists. She continued to write on Wednesdays in 1907 and into March 1908 (these scripts eventually reached Alice Johnson).

She remained in good health on her return to England in 1908. Alice Johnson stated (1934a) that Fleming remained in India till 1910 with short spells of leave back in the UK. Trix travelled with or without him, again it is not clear, to France, Spain, and Italy and, in the autumn of 1908, she met Alice Johnson again. She was encouraged to continue writing by Alice Johnson, who was particularly looking for links between her scripts and those of Margaret Verrall and Leonora Piper. She wrote weekly between

25/11/1908 and 19/5/1909 and produced 22 scripts, dividing her time, presumably, between 8 Napier Rd Edinburgh (the Fleming's house) and The Gables, Tisbury, her parent's.

She had regular trips to London, which she enjoyed as a relief from her dour Scottish relatives, and on 11/5/1909 she met Johnson again. Throughout this period she helped Alice Johnson trace possible non-paranormal sources for her script materials. She wrote her, for example, that shortly before her script of 30/6/09 which mentioned the psychical research of Everard Feilding, she had read two numbers of *Light* which described his investigation of the famous Italian physical materialisation medium Eusapia Palladino, and which also had an account of Miss Bates' lecture on automatic writing that, importantly, included references to the Verrall/Raikes cross-correspondences. She had, in addition, read some of the writings of Sir Oliver Lodge and some bits of the *Proceedings*, and all these possible sources of information were dutifully reported. She stressed to Johnson, however, that she was not eager to read much psychical research in case it cast doubt on the origins of her own scripts.

The situation changed dramatically in 1910. First, her mother died, and then in 1911 her father. Jack Fleming arrived to support her and, going through a number of papers, he discovered her continued automatic writing. This led to a major confrontation which, on top of the loss of both her parents, she found overwhelming. She now seemed to be completely abandoned by all and it must have revived the sense of utter isolation she felt when Rudyard and she had been placed in the *House of Desolation*. But she no longer had Rudyard to turn to. He disapproved of her psychical activity. He was paranoid about keeping family matters secret from the press and the public, and his wife thoroughly disliked Trix—in fact was jealous of her. Trix had a breakdown which lasted for a number of years, including a long period of exile on the island of Jersey with a nurse companion. Though suggestions of a hyperactive thyroid like her mother's, or a difficult menopause, may have played a part, the temperamental and possibly the physical incompatibility with Fleming and her extreme psychological isolation must have been at least equally painful. Rudyard Kipling's destruction of family papers makes it extremely difficult to reconstruct the psychodynamics of this and earlier periods. In later years Trix commented bitterly on this and on the financial settlement after the parents' deaths. She accused Rudyard of destroying their wills as part of his general eradication of confidential papers and that this was what prevented a more equitable provision for her. This is not quite fair. He, in fact, divided the estate between them both and invested her half leaving Fleming the interest, presumably for her continued medical needs. But it has been argued that he could have foregone any claim on what had been left by their parents and dedicated it all to Trix's health, given his considerable and increasing wealth at the time (Flanders 2002: 318).

Trix spent many years in treatment and in semi isolation. Pictures of her taken at this time show a sad decline and a great loss of vitality. But that was not the true or the best Trix. (See Lee 2004: 124–5, for Hilton Brown's portrait of her: 'Of her personal charm I need say nothing; it is sufficiently known to many readers of these words. Like her gaiety and her common sense it did not flag.') But it took time for the best of her to return. From 1925 to her death in 1949, she lived in Edinburgh in Jack's house at 6, West Coates, and she gradually seemed to recover her youthful exuberance. On one occasion, showing off to some young relatives, she encouraged an attempt at table tilting in the lounge of Bailey's Hotel, Gloucester Rd, where she always stayed on her visits to London. Fortunately or unfortunately 'the table refused to co-operate', but either way the other guests had some lively free entertainment (Lee 2004). This detachment and ability to see the comic elements in aspects of the psychic world, combined with the seriousness with which she approached the cross-correspondence work, make it difficult to interpret her automatic writing as the product of a seriously disturbed individual.

The novelist Colin MacInnes (1961: 114–19) wrote a sympathetic and humorous description of his Aunt Trix (technically his first cousin twice removed), highlighting her vivid literary and linguistic gifts and her endless talking in beautifully constructed phrases before the bewildered Jack Fleming, almost a kind of revenge for the early years when he would not talk to her, punishing her with silence. MacInnes related her love of caramel walnuts 'which delighted her because of their extraordinary resemblance to the bald head of William Shakespeare'. This gives some idea of the charm and wit which Jack Fleming did not really appreciate but which gained her the admiration of Kitchener, Lord Roberts, Curzon, and other demanding Indian grandees. She had great gifts and in another relationship and another time, and with sustained effort, could have been a celebrated writer.

Alice Johnson had no doubt that the marriage lay at the root of her mental problems. On the other side of the equation one must place the extraordinary testimony of Colin MacInnes, who stated she told him that after an out of body experience she was unable fully to return to complete participation in daily life and remained suspended in a psychic limbo for many years. It is, however, quite possible to reconcile these accounts. The way she framed her experiences may have been more for the benefit of a young nephew fond of tall stories of the Indian occult, rather than reflecting, as it probably did, an intense dissociative state consequent on childhood abandonment, the shock of her parents' deaths, and exacerbated by a self-centred, depressive, and unsympathetic husband.

Alice Johnson became a staunch supporter and friend of Trix Fleming. She was an early feminist and suffragist and came from a well-known Cambridge family. She, herself, worked closely with Mrs Sidgwick and shared her meticulous, balanced, and incisive approach to the subject of psychical research. She was a rather frail woman who drove herself hard in the work of the Society. She was a scholar of Newnham College and was placed in the first class of the natural sciences tripos in 1881. In 1884 she was appointed the first demonstrator in the Balfour Laboratory set up at Newnham, largely funded by Mrs Sidgwick in honour of her brother Francis Maitland Balfour (Richmond 1997). She also produced a number of scientific research papers. From the 1890s she was increasingly involved with the SPR and took a significant part in the Brighton thought transference experiments and did considerable work on the massive Census of Hallucinations which was published in 1894. She became the editor of the Society's *Proceedings* in 1899, worked—not always harmoniously—with Richard Hodgson to prepare Myers' *Human Personality* for publication, became Organising Secretary of the Society in 1903, and Research Officer in 1908 till she retired because of ill health in 1916. However, she lived until 1940 and was always available for informal consultation, remaining on good terms with the Salter, Balfour, and Coombe-Tennant families till the end. (See Salter and Newton 1940; and p. 129.)

Alice Johnson was a quietly remarkable woman. She reorganised and took firm control of office administration and records after the twin blows of losing Sidgwick and Myers in fairly quick succession. Lodge kept the Society going in the public mind because of his national profile and prestige but, in her undemonstrative way, Alice Johnson made an equally valuable contribution at the level of organisation and research. She also read widely in abnormal psychology and multiple personality and was familiar with the work of both Freud and Jung.

Her father, William Henry Farthing Johnson was headmaster of Llandaff House School, Cambridge, situated at 2 Regent St, not far from the railway station and close to a number of colleges. The family also had a property at 1 Millington Rd, where Alice Johnson spent much of the rest of her life. She had seven siblings: three sisters and four brothers. One brother, W.E. Johnson, was an eleventh wrangler and became a fellow of Kings. He was an intimate friend of Maynard Keynes' father, an expert on probability (Skidelsky 2003), and joined the SPR in 1884. Another brother, George William Johnson, went to Trinity College and became a senior civil servant in the Colonial Office. He was a strong supporter of political and social reform for women and Alice Johnson (1927) wrote a memoir recording his work in this and other fields. A third brother, Reginald Brimley Johnson, worked in publishing and was a well-known man of letters. Alice Johnson, like the Balfours, Verralls, and Salters, came from a formidably gifted family, and Trix Fleming had fortuitously made contact with a person whose education and interests had well equipped her to understand and support the nature of Trix's problems and her gifts.

A number of the most celebrated early cross-correspondences were derived from the connections spotted between Margaret Verrall's and Trix Fleming's scripts but they have not always been accurately described and, therefore, can appear more impressive than they actually were. A good example is the account provided by Michael Tymn (2008: 76), generally an accurate and knowledgeable populariser of the history of psychical research, of the Selwyn Text cross-correspondence. Tymn states that on the same day, 17/1/1904, Myers gave the biblical reference 1 Cor.16–13 to Trix Fleming. The same reference 'on the very same day, thousands of miles away in England', was received by Margaret Verrall. That is just not true and a clear example of the difficulties involved in summarising these complex and often tedious puzzles.

The actual sequence and content of the relevant scripts was as follows:

Margaret Verrall 25/12/1903:

> on the 17th of next month ask the question...use the daylight hours, for the night cometh when no man may work

Margaret Verrall 17/1/1904:

> The question is answered...The test [or text] and the answer are one and are given

Trix Fleming 17/1/1904:

> I am unable to make your hand form Greek characters and so I cannot give the text as I wish — only the reference 1 Cor. 16-13.

Note: Margaret Verrall wrote her two scripts in Algeria. Trix Fleming wrote hers in Calcutta. Trix Fleming never saw the Verrall scripts. Margaret Verrall saw the Fleming script in October 1905.

The text, 1 Cor.16–13, for which Trix Fleming gave the reference was a very significant text in Myers' life, for the text in Greek (minus the last two words) was carved over the gateway of Selwyn College close to both Margaret Verrall's and Myers' homes. It was: 'Watch ye. Stand fast in the faith. Quit ye like Men. [Be strong].' Myers often saw it as he walked by to visit her or the Sidgwicks not far away in Newnham College.

Margaret Verrall had, in fact, been trying to find the answer to a question set by Mrs Sidgwick. What was the last of the biblical texts that Henry Sidgwick had meditated on? Sidgwick through his life was in the habit of taking a text and meditating on it for the purposes of mental and physical self-discipline. This spiritual practice was not generally known till the publication of his memoir in 1906. The last text he meditated on was

John VI 12: 'Gather up the fragments that remain, that nothing be lost.' Margaret Verrall had no idea which text it was and her scripts of this period were sent to Sir Oliver Lodge who kept them unopened. Towards the end of 1903 the Verralls travelled to Algeria for the thermal baths and the mild climate which eased Arthur's arthritis, and her text of 25/12/1903 certainly explored a similar theme but it was not the text to which Trix Fleming provided the reference, nor was it the specific text that Mrs Sidgwick had set as a test question.

It was difficult to spot these links between scripts since different people had responsibilities for them in the early years. Lodge had received the first Margaret Verrall scripts; Margaret Verrall kept her daughter's early scripts; Alice Johnson looked after the early Fleming scripts; and, during the period of the English sittings with Leonora Piper, Piddington had access to them all. However, from the end of 1907 all of the scripts gradually came under Alice Johnson's central control at 20 Hanover Square.

In 1906 Alice Johnson was focusing on the links between Margaret Verrall's and Trix Fleming's scripts and she became increasingly aware of a steady and consistent emphasis on the need for cross-referencing them.

Margaret Verrall 18/2/1906:

> When you see the same in the other scripts with your own eyes, you will have belief in my words

And she was particularly intrigued by two lines in a Trix Fleming script in the Spring of 1906.

Trix Fleming 4/4/1906:

> Before the largest chestnut tree in Trinity blossoms —
> She will understand at Easter

Alice Johnson took these lines as referring to the theory of the cross-correspondences which she wrote was 'simmering in my mind, but first came to me clearly on the afternoon of April 12th, 1906, the Thursday before Easter. On coming back to London after Easter, I mentioned it to Mr. Piddington, and he accepted it as the probable solution. The whole of the script, up to and culminating in this phrase, seems to imply that we were on the verge of some definite step' (Johnson 1907-9: 362).

She knew that Myers and Hodgson had discussed attempts to get the same message through different mediums since this would be a powerful indicator of independent continuing purpose and personality. She believed that there was some evidence of this approach from the discarnate side in the early scripts of Margaret Verrall, Diana Raikes, and the mediumship of Rosalie Thompson. However, she theorised that, with the advent of Trix Fleming, a more sophisticated version of this approach was being attempted. Rather than the same topic/idea/phrase being transmitted through two or more mediums, she concluded that the discarnates were transmitting partial and unintelligible pieces of information which only made sense when put together with other communications. She called this the mosaic method of cross-correspondence where fragments of 'tiles' were dispersed amongst the automatists until the key was provided for their reassembly. She also used the term 'complementary' to suggest that each piece contributed to the whole but that the fundamental complementary nature of each of the pieces was not in the mind of any living automatist. It was, therefore, proof against telepathy between the living as a source of the correspondence (Johnson 1910a: 259–63).

It was clear, however, that the assessing of such cross-correspondences required a fine literary sensibility based on wide and deep cultural reading and intellectual resources. For this reason, Johnson opposed the mere counting of cross-correspondences and attempts to assess their occurrence above chance. She asserted that 'it is obvious that the data necessary for any exact calculation of probabilities are entirely lacking, while a rough empirical judgement of what one might expect to occur by chance can only be tentative and may be quite untrustworthy.' But, on the other hand, she argued that many cross-correspondences of this sort seem to have been signalled in some way like, 'Remember the word and the date', or by devices like the repetition of a word, or its being written in large letters or underlined or by mistranslations and misquotations.

The other leading SPR investigators thought Alice Johnson's thesis was worth exploring, and so Leonora Piper—the celebrated American trance medium who had so impressed the psychologist and philosopher William James, the physicist Oliver Lodge, Myers himself, and above all her main investigator, Richard Hodgson—was invited to England to see what might transpire. Since she had no classical learning and was cut off from English culture, mores, and information, this would make her scripts potentially of great evidential value, and the links between Fleming/Verralls/Piper/Coombe-Tennant scripts which were discovered and publicised in the next few years formed what one might call the golden age of the cross-correspondences, and will be considered in a later chapter.

Paranormal Cognition in Trix Fleming's Scripts
Myers, Gurney, Oliver Lodge, Roden Noel, Richard Hodgson, Winifred Coombe-Tennant, Everard Feilding, the Verralls, and Miscellaneous and Untraced References

As well as her contribution to the cross-correspondences, Trix Fleming also developed, through her automatic writing, a startling facility to access the environments, personalities, and appearances of people she had never known in life, was never to know, or had not yet met. Trix Fleming decribed the development of this strange skill or talent in a letter of 14/9/1903 to Alice Johnson. She wrote that she began automatic writing having read about it in W.H. Stead's *Review of Reviews*. This would have been in the early/mid 1890s and probably when she was visiting Clouds while staying with her parents in Wiltshire since there is a poem of that period which could possibly refer to Laura Lyttelton and her continued love for Alfred Lyttelton. It is a poem with a certain wistful charm and also a maggoty Gothic ghoulishness (Johnson 1907-09: 172):

> I whom he loved, am a ghost,
> Wandering weary and lost.
> I dare not dawn on his sight,
> (Windblown weary and white)
> He would shudder in hopeless fright,
> He who loved me the best.

The poem continued in this vein for several more stanzas. A later poem of 1901 written while in Italy and probably at the time of meeting Lady Walburga Paget seems to have picked up on a legend of a child buried under an orange tree in the garden at Bellasquardo (Johnson 1907-09: 173):

> Under the orange tree
> Who is it lies?
> Baby hair that is flaxen fair,
> Shines when the dew on the grass is wet,
> Under the iris and violet.

> Neath the orange tree
> Where the dead leaves be,
> Look at the dead child's eyes!

For the rigorous Alice Johnson these early writings were of little importance and Trix Fleming also kept a certain distance from them. As she wrote to Alice Johnson (1907-09: 190): 'In 1902 a friend sent me a MS.Book of copied "spirit writings" to read: flowery descriptions of the "Happy Land," signed with names like pantomime fairies, which I disliked intensely. I have never seen any other examples of automatic writing. The names I know to be real, which occur here and there, always distress me, but if I suppressed what had been written when it did not suit my own taste, I should feel very dishonest.'

References to Myers

On 16/9/1903 Myers made his first appearance in Trix Fleming's script. At the time she knew nothing more about Myers than she could have read in or possibly inferred from his book. Though she did know the date of his death, she certainly did not spot the literary device used in that script till it had been pointed out to her by Alice Johnson. It was the same technique Myers had used in his private diary (Myers 14/1) to disguise his love for Annie Marshall, quoting from a poem by William Morris: 'Love is enough/ while ye deemed he was sleeping/There were signs of his coming/and sounds of his feet', and distributing the lines across the bottom of several pages of that diary (Beer 1998: 149; Hamilton 2009: 41).

Trix Fleming 16/9/1903:

> F
> F/Friend while on earth with knowledge slight...
> 17/It may be that those who die suddenly suffer no prolonged...
> 1/The reality is infinitely more wonderful than our most daring...
> 01/But this is like the first stumbling attempts at expression in an...

Only the first line of each of Trix Fleming's verses has been given to demonstrate that the same technique, in this case fragmenting a date rather than lines of verse, was used.

Some play has been made of the apparent differences between the personality of the Verrall Myers and that of the Fleming Myers, and that the Fleming Myers was far more emotional. There does not, however, seem to be that much difference between them when one goes back to the original scripts rather than the extracts quoted in the *Proceedings*. There was plenty of emotion in the Verrall Myers. In addition, Alice Johnson made a very useful and perceptive comment when she pointed out that Trix Fleming was much more isolated than Margaret Verrall and that in that situation a more 'urgent'and supportive Myers was needed (1907-09: 239-

40). Also, she put forward the plausible argument that there would always be some difference in the way discarnate personalities were presented by different automatists because of the unique blend of the personalities involved and, one could add, in life Myers had been more tender and sensitive towards women than many of his contemporaries. This was a characteristic of his that Josephine Butler particularly commented on when they were working together on social and political rights for women (Hamilton 2009: 37–8).

Trix Fleming's scripts had cryptic references to key quotations that meant much to Myers in life and which were used as memorials to him after his death. There was a tablet to Myers put up in the Protestant Cemetery at Rome. William James, who was in Rome being treated by the same physician as Myers, loyally helped to oversee the process (Skrupskelis 2001: 425). It had on it an inscription from *Odyssey* 1,5 chosen and translated by Myers as 'striving to save my own soul and my comrades' homeward way'. On the brass memorial to him in St John's Church, Keswick, was inscribed another quotation: 'He asked life of Thee, and Thou gavest him a long life, even for ever and ever' (Psalm xxi 4). This text was also quoted at the end of his autobiography. There appeared to be indirect references to the Protestant Cemetery at Rome and to the memorial tablet to Myers in five Fleming scripts (108/127/135/148/197). However, the line from the *Odyssey* can be found on page 48 of his *Fragments of Prose and Poetry*, published in 1904, well before the five Fleming scripts were written, and the second text was a very familiar biblical one and sometimes carved on people's headstones. May Lyttelton had the same text (with a very minor alteration) on her headstone in Hagley churchyard. In both these cases one feels that Johnson and later Piddington made too much of too little.

There was, too, in one of Trix Fleming's scripts, a possible allusion to the first message in a sealed envelope that Myers had set up to be opened after his death. Myers had selected a two-line quotation from Wordsworth's *Laodamia*:

> July, 25 1890.
> The invisible world with thee hath sympathised;
> Be thy affections raised and solemnised.

Laodamia had begged for her husband, the first Greek hero to be slain in the Trojan war, to be returned to her from Hades and she made a wax statue of him to comfort her (Graves 2000 vol 2: 598).

Trix Fleming 26/5/1909:

> The long poem...F.W.H.M. liked it—it was one of his favourites...The one he means is in the Golden Treasury.

In his *Wordsworth* (Myers 1929: 114), Myers stressed that he preferred the first version of the poem, the one published by Arnold in his volume of selections in the Golden Treasury series, and not the third version 'with its sermonizing tone'. Myers particularly admired the lines 'Ah judge her gently who so deeply loved!/Her, who, in reason's spite, yet without crime,/Was in a trance of passion thus removed', rather than the moralistic version reflective of Wordsworth's increasing conservatism in his later years (Beer 1998: 114-15). It is, of course, possible that the intensely literary Trix Fleming had read Myers' biographical study of Wordsworth.

One can speculate that part of the appeal of the first version of *Laodamia* for Myers was the application of the above lines to Annie Marshall. Trix Fleming never knew anything about that story but frequent symbolic references to it occur in her scripts. As has been seen, Alice Johnson compiled a list of them and references to the story in Margaret and Helen Verrall's scripts (see Johnson 1916b: 314-24). These included: Phyllis, references to hazel, to Plato's symposium, Tennyson's high hill garden (Annie Marshall's maiden name was Hill), the valley, syringa, dove, white winged bird, Eurydice, Ophelia, rosemary, pansies. There are twenty-four or more references of this sort in Fleming's and the other automatists' scripts.There is even the phrase 'Annie Bird' (Trix Fleming 20/11/1906) which combined her Christian name and Myers' favourite endearment for the women he loved (see Hamilton 2009).

Her family name Marshall was also mentioned in another script which had a literary quotation which seemed to apply to the valley at Hallsteads where he and she had walked (Trix Fleming 16/6/1909). It should be stressed that Trix Fleming never had any access to the unexpurgated autobiography in which the love story was told.

References to Edmund Gurney

Edmund Gurney, Myers' great friend and co-worker, died in enigmatic circumstances at the elegant Regency Royal Albion Hotel in Brighton in June 1888. Trix Fleming knew virtually nothing about him but he began to appear in her scripts from the fourth one onwards:

Trix Fleming 16/9/1903:

> There were three workers once upon the earth
> Three that have passed through Death's great second birth
> Their work remains and some of lasting worth

This perhaps reflected Gurney's sense of an unfulfilled life. He had tried a range of careers till he found an absorbing and productive outlet for his high intellectual gifts in psychical research and had done strenuous, meticulous, and pioneering work in the collation and analysis of apparitions and the study and mapping of alternative states of consciousness in hypnotism (Myers 1888b; Epperson 1997). Though Gurney appeared quite extensively and at times persuasively in Trix Fleming's scripts, one must not be carried away by what might be called the quality of the impersonation. For example, later on the same morning came a passage in prose warning of the dangers of hypnotism. This seemed much more likely to have reflected Trix Fleming's subliminal fears since both Myers and Gurney in life strongly argued that the judicious use of hypnotism was a very valuable tool in the exploration of the subliminal consciousness. Nevertheless, Margaret Verrall on reading the early Coombe-Tennant scripts stated: 'When I read these scripts I notice the "dramatisation" which gave to "E.G." the somewhat peremptory tone that is assumed by that control in the writings of Mrs Raikes and of Trix Fleming' (Verrall c1910a: 14). Gurney, in life, could be abrupt and sarcastic and he complained to Myers that this manner sometimes lost him friends (Hamilton 2009).

Trix Fleming, though she was interested in Myers rather than Gurney, began to have visions of him. On 6/12/1905 she wrote to Alice Johnson: 'I saw the figure of a very tall thin man dressed in grey, standing with his back to the fire.' She did not recognise it as Gurney and when this was pointed out to her she stated that she was interested in Myers and not in Gurney. And in another letter she enquired: 'Do you remember the tall man in grey I saw here one evening in the winter? The other morning I went into a small room next to my own, thinking only of putting away an evening dress. The tall figure in grey was lying on the bed in a very flung-down, slack-jointed attitude. The face was turned from me, the right arm hanging back across the body, which lay on the left side. I started violently, and my foot seemed to strike a small empty bottle on the floor.'

These references and visions all appeared very impressive but one has to remember that Trix Fleming obtained some information about Gurney from her reading of *Human Personality* and the publication in 1904 of Myers' *Fragments of Prose and Poetry*, and Alice Johnson had, in fact, told Trix Fleming, some time earlier, of the circumstances of Gurney's death and, most critically, this had been forgotten by both of them (Johnson 1907–09: 286).

References to Sir Oliver Lodge

Sir Oliver Lodge, another intimate friend of Myers, was also portrayed quite vividly in Trix Fleming's scripts and, apparently, long before she met him.

Trix Fleming 17/1/1904 (anniversary of Myers' death):

'We few, we happy few, we band of brothers'
Dear old chap you have done so much in the past three
years—I am cognisant of a great deal of it but with

strange gaps in my knowledge—If I could only talk with
you—If I could only help you with some advice—I tried
more than once did it ever come—There's so much to be
learnt from the Diamond Island experiment—

Alice Johnson later identified these comments as referring to Sir Oliver Lodge, particularly since she discovered that, though Lodge had no knowledge of Diamond Island itself, the Lodge-Muirhead system of Wireless Telegraphy had been tested at the mouth of the Irrawaddy in Burma on a small island, Diamond Island. Lodge told her that Myers had been extremely interested in his work and that he and his brother Arthur had coined the term 'syntony' to describe the tuning process in wireless telegraphy. Trix Fleming did eventually remember a reference to Diamond Island in her normal reading but she did not know in January 1904 that Lodge had been an old and intimate friend of Myers nor of the warm tone of Myers' private letters to Lodge, something of which she captured in her script (Johnson 1910b: 293-8).

She also seemed to have clairvoyant access to the environment in which he lived and worked but by this time she had met him.

Trix Fleming 7/11/1906:

On the ledge of the squarish—no oblong window is not a safe
place for that solution—Of course you cannot consider poisons
out of place in a laboratory—but there is not enough locking up—
this one should be locked up—Towards the end of the room to
your left—an actinic green bottle.

Alice Johnson sent the script to Lodge for comment and he replied: 'This I find is remarkably correct. My two youngest boys have a laboratory adjacent to the house—not at the college at all—and there they do photography, make explosives, and many other things. The other night when we were all together I asked them whether they had a green bottle of poison in that laboratory, and the elder said, yes. It is on the bench, quite accessible, not on the ledge of the oblong window, but near it, and on the left. He says it has been there nearly all the winter, and is Mercuric Chloride which the Doctor gave him for a lotion,—not one of their own chemicals. I have told him that it must be either thrown away or locked up' (Johnson 1907-09: 216).

References to Roden Noel

Roden Noel was the son of the Earl of Gainsborough and had a position at Queen Victoria's court as Groom of the Chamber (Heath 1998). He resigned this position to go into business, at which he failed, and spent the remainder of his life as writer. He was a liberal but not a socialist despite having written a long poem, *The Red Flag* (which read carefully does not support extremism), known to this day. He was educated at Harrow and Trinity and became an Apostle (see Lubenow 1998). He had three children and the death of one, Eric, led to his volume of poems, *A Little Child's Monument*. His poetry was admired by some though not by Sidgwick or, one suspects, Myers, as it was too florid and emotionally unbalanced, in some ways rather like his essays in psychical research which Myers (Hamilton 2009: 158) mercilessly made fun of. There was a strong strain of overblown romanticism in most of his writing but he had a heart. Between them Margaret Verrall and Trix Fleming produced a fair amount of script material about him, even though they only had the most superficial knowledge of his life and poetry.

Margaret Verrall 7/3/1906:

> Tintagel and the sea that moaned in pain
> And Arthur's mount uplifted from the plain
> And crowding towers of quaint fantastic shape
> Ah! Never more to see
> The ripples dance
> Nor hear again the roar
> On smitten shore
> When the huge waves roll on
> Amid the salt and savour of the sea

Trix Fleming 11/3/1906:

> Ask him [Verrall] what the date May 26th 1894 meant to him — to me — and to F.W.H. [Myers] I do not think they will find it hard to recall but if so let them ask Nora [Sidgwick's wife Eleanor]. We no more solve the problem of Life by being born — I seek still — I am not oppressed with the desire to share our knowledge or optimism with you all before the time. You know who feels like that but I am content that you should wait —

Trix Fleming 14/3/1906:

> Eighteen fifteen four five fourteen — Fourteen, fifteen five, twelve — Not to be taken as they stand. See Rev. 13-18 — but only the central 8 words not the whole passage (the central 8 words were 'for it is the number of a man' and when the numbers above were turned into letters they spelled out Roden Noel) — It does not do to be clearer under existing circumstances…June 1st 1881 (?) Surely you will not need to ask about that

Trix Fleming 28/3/1906:

> Roden Noel…Cornwall…Patterson…do you remember the velvet jacket.

Roden Noel had composed a poem, *Tintadgel*, had visited Cornwall and written a book about it, had died on May 26th 1894, knew Myers and Verrall, and was an intimate friend of Sidgwick's. A.J. Patterson was a mutual friend. Noel did wear a slightly louche velvet jacket. Sidgwick's post-mortem caution about the nature of the afterlife and communicating it to the still incarnate was apposite. This characteristic was also in evidence later on in Winifred Coombe-Tennant'scripts.

The stock objection to all this, as put by Anna Hude, was cryptomnesia by Trix Fleming supplemented by her own highly dramatic imagination and by telepathy from Margaret Verrall: ' The date of his death is probably due to latent memory; it is mentioned in his [Noel's] *Collected Poems* published in 1902; a description of him in her script of March 28th points to this book, which contains his picture... That she connects him with Professor Sidgwick is, however, a circumstance indicative of an impression received from Mrs. Verrall... similar relations to Dr. Verrall and Frederic Myers is imagination; their acquaintance with Roden Noel was slight, and the date of his death could not mean very much to them' (Hude 1913: 151–4). Hude did not acknowledge the fact that Alice Johnson (Johnson 1907–09: 323) had already pointed some of this out: 'It is to be noted that this last passage is quoted in the Preface to *The Collected Poems of Roden Noel* (a passage stating Sidgwick's awareness of Noel's sensitivity to the beautiful and the spiritual in life),—from which book... many of the references to him in Mrs. Holland's and Mrs. Verrall's scripts are derivable, though they both believe they have never seen it.'

In fact, some of this is true and some of it is not. Noel did seem to be wearing a velvet jacket in the photograph at the beginning of the *Collected Poems*, and the date of his death was mentioned in the book, as was his friendship with Henry Sidgwick. And Myers knew Noel quite well (Heath 1998). There is no mention of Patterson in the introduction to the poems, though there are frequent references to A.J. Patterson in the life of Sidgwick. Trix Fleming disclaimed knowledge of the *Collected Poems* and, as far as one knows, she had not read the life of Sidgwick at the time of writing the scripts, only a couple of reviews, neither of which provided the information about the date of Noel's death or the name A.J. Patterson, as far as can be ascertained.

The Noel cross-correspondences appeared to have been first flagged up in February 1906.

Margaret Verrall 9/2/1906 (the script writing resembled Sidwick's):

In the life of Sidgwick you will find two clues to what I have said to you. two only—follow the thread.

Margaret Verrall immediately obtained a copy of the life on its publication and identified one of the clues as a letter from Sidgwick to Roden Noel about his poems in memory of his dead son Eric. Shortly after this she wrote on 7/3/1906 the script quoted above. The style certainly seemed reminiscent of Roden Noel's *Tintadgel* though Margaret Verrall hadn't noticed this at the time. The first letter had Sidgwick's famous statement: 'it is that on moral grounds, *hope* rather [than certainty] is fit for us in this earthly existence.' Notice how well this chimed with the sentiments expressed in Trix Fleming's script on 11/3/1906. Margaret Verrall thought the second clue was a letter by George Otto Trevelyan to Sidgwick. In it Trevelyan mentioned Sidgwick and himself, in youth, walking in the cloisters at Trinity and discussing the great questions of life (Johnson 1907-09: 314-15, 317).

Note: Margaret Verrall wrote her scripts in Cambridge and Trix Fleming elsewhere in the UK. However, Alice Johnson sent her a copy of Margaret Verrall's script of 7/3/1906 (Johnson 1907-09: 318) which may have triggered subliminal literary memories of Roden Noel.

Piddington, much later and ranging widely across the scripts (Piddington 1943b: 856-60), traced allusions to three more of Noel's poems mainly in Margaret Verrall's automatic writing. They were *Fowey*, *A Song of Nereids*, and *At Porthcurno*. He discovered, too, that Noel, who loved Cornwall, had written a book, *Essays on Poetry and Poets*, which contained a chapter called 'Rambles by Cornish Seas', some of whose phrases were echoed in the scripts. For example, 'briny wind and savour of turbulent sea' linked to two Margaret Verrall scripts: 'and what a smell and savour of the sea' and 'Amid the salt and savour of the sea'. Noel was a great swimmer, particularly fond of night swimming with a lantern strapped to his head (Heath 1998). There was also the virtual repetition of a phrase from one of Noel's poems 'under the shadow of a great tree'. Margaret Verrall had no memory of having read these poems. But one could argue that these were poetic platitudes that any reasonably literary person could generate.

References to the Verralls

There were some fairly precise references in Fleming's scripts to the Verralls and their environment. The most famous and frequently quoted example was the following:

Trix Fleming 7/11/1903:

> Get a proof – try for a proof if you feel this is a waste of time without
> Send this to Mrs. Verrall 5 selwyn Gardens Cambridge

The name Mrs Verrall was in *Human Personality* but not the address. Trix Fleming had never been to Cambridge nor knew of Selwyn Gardens. But the fact that the address was in *Who's Who* must always weaken the paranormality of this incident (Johnson 1907-09: 187).

Shortly before this, on 21/9/1903, Trix Fleming had already produced a good description (with minor inaccuracies) of Margaret Verrall's dining room, though like so many of the other interesting features in her scripts it took time to be recognised and appreciated (Johnson 1907–09: 194-5):

> A room that is rather narrow for its length with three windows and a long narrow table covered with a dull red cloth rather faded. The walls need repapering. The ceiling needs whitewashing. There is a portrait over the fire-place of a man. with a high fore head — the background of it is very dark — A bust on a pedestal stands in a very shadowed corner — The head is not clear — round the shoulders is a kind of bath towel like drapery. The pedestal is imitation greenish marble —
> There are a few good prints in the room — but it is not easy to see them —
> Shelves on one side have a few books and a great many papers and pamphlets on them — The room is not in the least interesting in itself but very interesting things have happened there and some men now dead still influence that room very strongly.

And, a little later on, a broadly accurate and fairly precise description of Margaret Verrall herself.

Trix Fleming 5/1/1904:

> She is not very tall — a slender figure often dressed in green dark hair — rather pushed from the forehead — straying a little from the centre parting — very mobile brows — pince-nez when she writes — A strong chin — mouth thin-lipped but sympathetic — a strong face but not a hard one — Mind admirably well balanced — Hands with long fingers — but the palms well developed — No foolish impulses — but no fear of sudden actions which seem the outcome of sudden impulse — Age — 32-33 — I forget — What importance has age to me now —

There were in fact references in three scripts by Trix Fleming to Margaret Verrall's appearance and character, though the script quoted above had shaved more than a decade off her age. The unambiguity of this portrait was to some extent blurred by the description of another slender woman with long fingers in her scripts which Piddington later claimed as referring to Mary Catherine Lyttelton (Piddington 1921: 404-07.) This raises fundamental questions about the confirmation of identity in scripts and will be considered in Part 2 in the section on paranormal cognition.

References to Richard Hodgson

Richard Hodgson died on 20/12/1905. Based in Boston, Mass., he was the dedicated SPR-funded researcher in the United States, who had, almost single-handedly, carried out an enormously detailed and painstaking investigation into the mediumship of Leonora Piper. Shortly after his death references to him began to appear in Trix Fleming's scripts, though she knew nothing about him except that she had read in a newspaper in January 1906 that he had died. On 9/2/1906 she produced a particularly persuasive script which seemed to be accompanied by a tendency for her to move from a lighter to a deeper state of trance. She did not like the feeling and with some advice from Alice Johnson was able to ward it off in later writing sessions.

The details in this Hodgson script were quite specific: Hodgson gave his name using a simple code, the name of Jessie his first love was mentioned, there was a reference to the K notation (the encrypted system he used for his confidential records), the manner of his death, his watch chain and cigar cutter (some inaccuracies here), and a description of the view from the windows of the club he had died in after a particularly vigorous game of handball. On 28/2/1906 her script contained a broadly accurate description of Hodgson's physique and his tendency to short temper, and also a reference to Münsterberg, a psychologist for whom and whose views Hodgson had a visceral dislike. On 16/5/1906 in her script, Hodgson, a man particularly responsive to the outdoor life and to nature, referred to the brilliant red flowers of one of the maples in spring, an unusual fact (most people associating the red of the maple with autumn) which Trix Fleming did not know.

In assessing this material, Alice Johnson was fortunate in that Piddington was in Boston in May 1906 (see below) and was able to confirm a number of evidential items in the scripts from records left in Hodgson's old rooms at 15 Charles Street. Allowing for a few errors of detail, the language and personality of Hodgson were well conveyed in these scripts despite Trix Fleming never having seen a portrait of Hodgson nor having access to the obituaries and tributes to him which had not yet appeared in the *Proceedings* (Johnson 1907-09: 303-10; Sidgwick 1907: 365-72).

References to Everard Feilding

Another leading member of the SPR, Francis Henry Everard Joseph Feilding, also featured in Trix Fleming's automatic writing. He was by all accounts a delightful and charming man (Feilding 1963, intro Dingwall: v–xx). He was the second son of the eighth Earl of Denbigh, and the family were Catholics. He read classics and law at Trinity College, Cambridge, and gradually moved away from the traditional Catholicism of his youth, particularly after the death of his beloved sister Clare in 1895. He joined the Council of the SPR in 1900 and was appointed joint Honorary Secretary with Piddington in 1904.

After 1905 he became involved in the hugely lucrative rubber industry in Malaya and he also developed an interest in Malay magical practices. This financial independence allowed him to spend time studying a wide variety of spectacular psychical phenomena. He investigated with humour, patience, and perception—notably a poltergeist case faked by a solicitor who smuggled in apports in his backside ('Did it hurt?' enquired Feilding solicitously, 'Only at first', said the solicitor: see Feilding 1963).

He needed all his humour and sense of detachment when in August 1906 his brother Basil drowned in the Rhine. This led to an intensification of his interest in the work of the SPR, and he was part of the team which went out to Naples to investigate the notorious Eusapia Palladino who had caused so much dissension and heartache in the SPR in the 1890s. A number of details in Trix Fleming's scripts referred to these activities but they were difficult to disentangle from her normal knowledge. Some throwaway lines in her automatic writing, as so often in the scripts, could tease, but they were not particularly convincing. There was a sly reference in one of her scripts to 'perhaps a signal may be tapped through to the nuthatch'. It was easy to miss the signifigance of this since very few people would be aware that a nuthatch pecking at a hazel branch was the crest of the Feilding family. A more easily verifiable statement occurred in the script below.

Trix Fleming 22/5/1906:

> It is the wiring—the electric lighting in the John St. house that is dangerous—The terms of the fire insurance too need supervising—Denbigh.

Both these statements were followed up in detail by Alice Johnson (1907-09: 354). Trix Fleming had had dinner with Feilding earlier in the year and Alice Johnson checked with both of them that they had not discussed fire insurance or mentioned the name Denbigh: the Earl of Denbigh was the head of the Feilding family. Johnson, however, was cautious and aware that there could have been, from some source, a subliminal recollection of these matters.

References to Winifred Coombe-Tennant

Trix Fleming did not know of and never knew Winifred Coombe-Tennant, but she produced in her automatic writing a largely accurate description of her country house, one confirmed by Gerald Balfour who was to know it well (see below). The details were quite specific. It would be unusual for a fantasy chocolate box image of a country house to mention coal and railroads, which was the situation at Cadoxton, close to the coal mining district and to the port at Swansea.

Trix Fleming 18/7/1906:

> A morning mist hangs thickly over the meadows, outlining the course of the little river—
> The boat house is rather neglected now—

Tell him to have it repaired and repainted. The second mine—
The head foreman knows—not the present man—The one who was retired soon after.
The house is not near a station but very near a railway line—
too many coal trains in an hour for country peace—

Cadoxton (pulled down after the Second World War) was about a mile from the station, but a railway line passed near the back of the house, cutting off what was originally part of its grounds and garden. Beyond and parallel with the railway was a canal, the old boundary of the grounds, on which was a practically unused boat-house. On the other side of the canal were marshes, then another railway, and beyond a small river. There were mines in the district and the traffic of the railway nearest to the house consisted chiefly of coal trains. The noise made by the frequent passing and shunting of these trains was often disturbing to people in the house and garden. Gerald Balfour commented (1927: 17), 'This description applies so accurately to Mrs. Willett's home that it is difficult to ascribe the coincidence to chance'.

There was also a reference to a London flat of the Coombe-Tennants.

Trix Fleming 16/5/1906:

A presentation clock—are those bronzes on either side? The
Angelo Day and Night—I like the books better than the carpet
But it is well to be free from foolish thoughts as to the beauty
of all ones surroundings—Which Madonna is that? I don't remember
it at all The room was always a little narrow

On 12/11/1910, Winifred Coombe-Tennant received a copy of Fleming scripts 49–239 inclusive and made a comment (7/1/1911) on the above script:

Vague ideas of connection between this script and me. The
presentation clock given by the tenants on my marriage is of
marble and bronze and has, I think, Michael Angelo's Lorenzo on
it, which forms the centre at each side of which are his Day and
Night. It has two bronze vases given with it and intended to
stand on a mantlepiece each side of the clock. It stands in a
room with books, the carpet of which is very inadequate, being an
odd piece left over from one remade, and it is a narrow room and
small. One could not walk about in it. I cannot verify seated
bronze statue on clock at present, as it is in the London flat,
which is let, and in which I was living at time of this script.

On 9/5/1912, Alice Johnson went to the flat with Winifred Coombe-Tennant and checked the details: 'Clock black marble; on the top is bronze figure, copy of M. Angelo's Lorenzo de Medici. Below the face of the clock is a plate on which is engraved: "Presented to [Mr. and Mrs. Coombe-Tennant] by the Tenants of the Estate on the occasion of their marriage

[Date]…" On each side of the clock are bronze tazzas… In the Library, where the clock used to stand on the writing table… I saw the carpet bluey-green in colour and too small for the room… [which] is small, and narrow in proportion to its length… In the drawing room is a Della Robbia plaque The figures are white on a bluey purple ground; the ornamented border has alternate bunches of dark purple grapes and groups of three round rather pale yellow fruits and trails of green leaves' (see Johnson 1916b vol 2: 4-7 for both the above incidents). The Madonna and Child was a symbol for Winifred Coombe-Tennant (even though she disliked many aspects of organised religion) for the sacred and eternal relationship between the mother and her children, and she had a Della Robbia 'Madonna and Brass' put up in the church in Cadoxton as a memorial to Daphne. She also had, as stated above, a Della Robbia plaque in her London flat (Lord 2011: 17).

Miscellaneous and Untraced References

Occasionally, Trix Fleming seemed to access events on a national or international scale and sometimes this was combined in a cross-correspondence, as below. It obviously referred to the Habsburg Emperor, Framz Joseph.

Trix Fleming 12/9/1906:

> Franz Joseph—Sept 13th to 25th—a rally on the 21st followed by a complete and unlooked for collapse—Hepatic complications

Margaret Verrall 20/9/1906:

> Now say this Mrs. [Fleming] had the warning more than a week ago but may not have understood what was meant—surely there was a note of the day Sept. 21-or 21st of some month was named.

(There is a clear link in terms of warning and the date—so a definite minor cross-correspondence. Alice Johnson checked, from the contemporary press, that it could be inferred that something of the sort had happened to the Emperor. On the other hand Trix Fleming had a penchant for gloomy medical predictions.)

Note: Margaret Verrall was in Cambridge and Trix Fleming was in India at the time of writing their respective scripts. She did not see Trix Fleming's script till October 1906.

There is, then, substantial evidence that Trix Fleming had a good track record in the area of paranormal cognition. Therefore, one should be careful not immediately to dismiss out of hand as subliminal inventions, as Alice Johnson did in her first report on Trix Fleming, the miscellaneous and contextless names and dates that occasionally occurred in her scripts. One should look, for example, more closely at the addresses that Trix Fleming received in 1903-04: Margaret Verrall's was correct, and Lambert (1971:

217-22) has made a plausible case for the identification of Agnes Lysaght, 17 Manchester Square, with other names linked to Henry Sidgwick's time at Trinity College. On the other hand, in her scripts and in the others, there were occasional dislocated references to names and places that were tiresome to follow up and which quite naturally could make one suspicious of the true source and value of the automatic writing.

Because of this remarkable capacity to tune into the living and the dead, Trix Fleming was very careful to examine her own motives and her own psychological state. As she put it in a letter of 25/2/1905 to Alice Johnson: 'I cannot tell you how glad I should be to know if the longing for recognition (it is such a passionate craving sometimes that I find myself crying out: "If I could help you—Oh! If I could only help you!" while I write) is a real influence from beyond or only my own imaginings. But why should my imagination take that form? I have been singularly free from bereavements thus far in my life and therefore my thoughts have been very seldom in the Valley of the Shadow...' (Johnson 1907-09: 240).

She was also alive to the possibility of cryptomnesia and always tried to trace and declare possible normal sources for her knowledge and she accepted that some of her scripts might just be make believe. Piddington (1943a: 239) wryly commented on Trix Fleming's creative imagination: 'Having finished with Mrs. Verrall, Hld.105 passes on to invent an entirely imaginary engagement for Everard [Feilding].'

Similarly, Trix Fleming, in a number of scripts, invented engagements for Helen Verrall and Leonora Piper's younger daughter, Minerva. As Piddington put it: 'Her trick of providing young women with husbands resembles her trick of prescribing medical treatment for real or imaginary invalids.'

6

The Trance Automatic Writing Medium Leonora Piper in the US and UK

Leonora Piper was born on 27/6/1859 at Nashua in New Hampshire (see Tymn 2013 for an overview). Like many mediums she showed psychic abilities in childhood but she was not a sickly child and was quite athletic in her teens. In appearance she was a slight, tall blonde. As a young adult she went to J.R. Cocke, a healing medium, and this led to a rapid development of her mediumistic gifts. Her main communicator and master of ceremonies became a rather dubious French doctor named Phinuit and, with him as control, she began to give readings at her home in the wooded suburb of Arlington Heights above Boston, where she lived with her husband William, a department store employee, and her parents. Though the gruff personality of Phinuit and the convulsive movements Leonora Piper made when coming out of trance alarmed a number of people, others were impressed by the high quality and specific nature of much of the evidence. It was stories about her circulating around Boston that first led to William James having a sitting (Tymn *op. cit.*: 1–2).

Leonora Piper was by far the most puzzling, contentious, and idiosyncratic of the automatists involved in the cross-correspondences. She was the only professional medium and was eventually kept on a retainer by the SPR (James 1986: 394-5). She was also the only consistent full trance medium and allegedly retained no knowledge of what happened in the trance and was, therefore, unable to use this knowledge to fabricate future convincing messages. She was, finally, different in that opinions about her were and are much more polarised than those of the other mediums, whose social status and education was more elevated than hers (Gauld 1968: 361-3).

After the death of Hodgson the question of the ownership and disposal of the Piper records to date became a matter of considerable dispute between the English and the American sections of the SPR (Berger 1988: 46-9).The English believed they had a legal right to the records since Hodgson was their secretary in America and they had, if irregularly, continued to provide funding and had stepped in to save psychical research when the separate ASPR had collapsed. Many American sitters argued that their private sittings were their private property and this trumped any general principle of research. Piddington went over to Boston in the spring of 1906 and, from the British point of view, achieved a settlement which met their interests. The Piper records came back to the SPR in England, under suitable guarantees of privacy and with an assurance that the records would be published at the earliest available opportunity. The records did come to England where they still remain but their assessment and publication, with one or two exceptions (Gauld 2014), has not taken place. The development of the cross-correspondences diverted the leadership of the SPR from this task. It was a broken promise which increasingly rankled with James Hyslop (who emerged as the leader of the new ASPR).

Leonora Piper followed her records across the Atlantic later in the year. She had found that crossing exhausting in 1889 on her first visit to England but was prepared to risk it again and responded positively to the invitation from Lodge to return in 1906. She may well have had financial reasons for this. Her physical and mental health fluctuated and she was always anxious about money, particularly after her husband's early death (James 1986: 398–400). And Myers and Lodge (unlike some of her other investigators) had always treated her and her family with warmth and kindness. She arrived in Liverpool and at first stayed with the Thompson family who had received good survival evidence from her in the past. She and her children were then taken to Lodge's house, Mariemont in Edgbaston, where they were well looked after by Lodge and his wife for several weeks, in a friendly and comfortable upper middle-class family environment. The Pipers found the removal to London after a few weeks difficult and Lodge was prepared to take them back but they managed to stick it out in chill, wintry London till they had completed the sittings the following May. Then for the last period they went to Scotland where it rained incessantly in June, and then they turned for home and arrived back in Boston to a July heat wave (Piper 1929: 128-34; 160-8). It should be remembered that Leonora Piper suffered frequently from colds and found the English climate difficult. In addition, she had the strain of adjusting to and settling her children into several new environments, all the while sitting for a large number of private sitters and being investigated *en passant* by the SPR researchers. It is very rarely acknowledged in the literature how demanding and testing this must have been for her.

Leonora Piper had by this time changed from a speaking trance medium to a writing medium and in this condition the hand became almost a separate intelligence responding and gesturing to the sitter as well as scrawling its writing on large sheets of paper. Phinuit was no longer the chief control. That was now Rector, with occasional inputs from the august Imperator. These formidable-sounding personalities were supposed to have moved from the famous medium Stainton Moses after his death to Leonora Piper and to have improved the quality of her health and her mediumship. There is some evidence for this but the process of communication still remained somewhat bizarre and off-putting to the sitter. Piddington (1908: 19–29) described it in detail. A number of cushions would be placed on the table in front of her and after some heavy breathing her head would descend onto a cushion, it would be turned gently to the left to aid breathing. In a short while the right hand would rise, make the sign of the cross, and start to write on a large block of numbered sheets of paper which would be torn off as they became filled up. It was a slow and cumbersome activity in terms of replenishing the paper, reading the automatic scrawls, and storing the records afterwards, but it had the advantage of being a permanent record of what took place at the sitting.

It is also worth quoting Miss Bates' account of Leonora Piper going into trance (1906: 136–43), since it makes crystal clear how different the alteration of consciousness was in her case compared to the much shallower dissociation displayed in the automatic writing of the other automatists: 'It was very much like watching someone under the influence of a strong anaesthetic; the same stertorous breathing and occasional low moans succeeded by perfect unconsciousness; when the whole body became relaxed and Dr. Hodgson, having drawn up a small table quickly in front of her, placed two soft cushions upon it, placing her left arm under her head in such a position as to support the latter... I may mention here how curiously "dead" and limp Leonora Piper's arm and hand became when unconsciousness set in; the blood had departed, leaving it as white and helpless as that of a corpse. By degrees, this dead look disappeared. The blood flowed once more through the veins, and as I noticed this change, the hand moved gropingly towards the pencil held out by Dr. Hodgson and finally grasped it. He had come armed with many pencils, for the writing is so rapid and generally so faint that a very sharp-pointed pencil is necessary to make it legible. Even so, it was difficult to read at times, but Dr. Hodgson's long practice and infinite patience, helped matters very much.'

She also commented (as did Piddington in Sidgwick *et al.* 1910: 84) on the difference between the trance writing state and the waking stage as Leonora Piper came round from the trance. The written communications appear to have been delivered first to Rector who then committed them to writing using Leonora Piper's hand, and this language 'is to a large degree coloured by Rector's own peculiar phraseology'. In the waking stage the communicating spirits themselves addressed Leonora Piper directly, bypassing the control. In the written stage there was little uncertainty about what had been written. In the waking stage there was sometimes confusion as to what had been said. In the written stage two way communication was possible, but rarely in the waking stage. The colouring and confusion in the waking stage seemed to be largely Leonora Pipers'. Katherine Bates also commented on the strangeness of the communicator (as happened quite often in Piper sittings) complaining that they did not or could not clearly hear the investigators' questions.

The investigators were keen to explore and build on the theory of cross-correspondences which Alice Johnson had formulated in the spring of 1906. Therefore, Myers was encouraged to develop these in a message in Latin that was read to him via the entranced Leonora Piper in December 1906 and January 1907 (Piddington 1908: 312–416). The full message was: 'We are aware of the scheme of cross-correspondences which you are transmitting through various mediums, and we hope that you will go on with them. Try *also* to give to A and B two different messages, between which no connection is discernible. Then as soon as possible give to C a third message which will reveal the hidden connection.' One should, whatever one's stance on all this, try, in fairness, to appreciate the problems associated with carrying out this task. Leonora Piper knew no Latin. The message was given in tiny bits, letter by letter, and halted when the private sitter(s) of the day arrived. The whole experiment (Piddington *op. cit.*: 313–14) lasted five and a half months from 17/12/1906 to 2/6/1907. And when Myers was tested on his understanding of the Latin, this was often combined with questions on Leonora Piper's scripts generally, as well as stopping for the sitter(s) of the day. All this involved frequent tedious and confusing repetition and much liaising between the medium, her controls, and the main discarnate communicators, Myers and Hodgson.

Piddington eventually became convinced that Myers had demonstrated his understanding of the message by the design of the Hope, Star, Browning cross-correspondence and the clear indication of such an attempt in the agreed drawing of a triangle within a circle (see appendix 3). But there were two robust and acute critics of this view in the early years, whose opinions have not, over time, been given a fair airing. One was the remarkable Anna Hude (1858–1934: see Wikipedia entry). She was a Danish woman of formidable intellectual energy and intelligence and a courageous and pioneering early feminist. As a young teacher she was raped by the family doctor and she shot him. He was injured but committed suicide later. The case was a sensational one. She was given a light sentence and then worked for the Danish National Archives, becoming the first Danish woman PhD in 1893. She had been a vigorous campaigner for female suffrage but her interests shifted in the 1900s towards psychical research and she wrote a very perceptive book on the early cross-correspondences (Hude 1913).

Anna Hude argued that it was impossible for Myers to understand the Latin message because of the difficulties involved in transmitting the Latin and, if this had been performed properly, he might well have done so. Second, that he and Piddington were talking at cross-purposes, Piddington believing that Myers' reply, Hope Star Browning, referred to the Latin message whereas Myers was thinking more generally of the range of questions that Piddington and others had been pressing on the communicators. She quoted Myers on 27/2/1907 stating: '…I believe that since you sent this message to me I have sufficiently replied to your various questions to convince the ordinary scientific mind that I am at least a fragment of the once incarnate individual whom you called Myers.' She argued that in singling out *Abt Vogler* he was really thinking of the lines: 'The wonderful dead who have passed through the body and gone/But were back once more to breathe in an old world worth their new.' In other words he was stressing the general message and not the specific cross-correspondence. The reasoning was difficult to follow but one could argue that she clearly highlighted problems with the ambiguity inherent in a number of the cross-correspondences and their interpretation.

The second significant critic was Frank Podmore, consistently on the sceptical wing of the SPR. He asserted that Myers had not grasped the concept of complex cross-correspondences as outlined in the Latin message and that he could only translate bits of the Latin. He further pointed out that Myers, through Leonora Piper, questioned the importance and value of cross-correspondences anyway (in other words there had been no grand plan or design to introduce them) and stated that 'if you establish telepathic messages, you will doubtless attribute all such to thoughts from those living in the mortal body' (Podmore 1975: 247–54).

Piddington's defence was that, in practice, the Hope, Star, Browning case demonstrated that Myers had understood the Latin message and that he had not necessarily been asked to translate the Latin message as proof of his understanding but to demonstrate by his answers that he had done so — which was not the same thing; and that communication through Rector and the other controls was always going to be very difficult and allowance should be made for this. One could add in Piddington's support and to counter Podmore that there was very clear evidence, consistently over a period of time, in early Margaret Verrall scripts, that the investigators were being urged to put scripts together and to compare them. This certainly suggested intention and prior design. Though whether the 'voice' was that of a discarnate intelligence or the automatic writer communicating required and still requires discrimination.

The debate about the Latin message and the Hope, Star, Browning case highlighted the difficulties arising from the highly literary methodology the investigators adopted. The tasks were too open-ended and complex and the lines of communication between the investigators were not always as they should have been; and there were far too many sittings with too much multiple tasking going on at the same time. Also, the process of automatic writing, while providing a permanent record of some aspects of the sitting, was defective in others. At one point Hude (1913) stated re Myers: '...he did not comprehend why the conversation had been turned that way, but said with some astonishment...' How could she possibly have known that? Only an even more detailed account listing all the behavioural elements, or the application of early audio technology, could have provided evidence for that. There was, too, a real problem in controlling, managing, and cross-referencing the output of scripts. The investigators were swept up in a great tide of documentation and hypotheses and were watching a process unfold across the automatic writers that seemed to grow exponentially in richness and subtlety. One could argue that they began to lose their grip on the phenomena, and absorbed in the detail did not stand back sufficiently to debate the best type of evidence, and the simplest methodology, for convincing the broader educated and scientific community.

In his introduction, Piddington (1908) stated that no sitter entered the séance-room till Leonora Piper was in complete trance and that there were 120 experiments all together. Successes and failures were not tabulated but only, one assumes from the text, 23 were put forward as having a certain amount of success or interest, whether initiated by the investigators or the trance personalities. Trix Fleming and Leonora Piper were in complete ignorance of the process and what Margaret and Helen Verrall knew of the other scripts was carefully recorded. As Leonora Piper's sittings were automatic writing sittings, as Piddington pointed out, they 'by their very nature record themselves' (Piddington 1908: 24). Comments by the sitters were noted. The sheets of automatic writing were always kept out of Leonora Piper's sight and taken away at the end of the session. A full manuscript copy was made and then typed up. There was no discussion about the contents of the sittings with Leonora Piper in her normal state except occasionally comments in general terms that they were of interest. Such conditions certainly would not meet the at least treble-blind conditions that modern mediumship researchers would insist on (Beischel 2010), but for the time and place, and balancing out the needs of Leonora Piper and the sitters, they were pragmatic and effective.

To modern eyes a number of these Piper cross-correspondences appear rather feeble: for example, St Paul.

St Paul

Leonora Piper 15/11/1906:

> Lodge. What we are anxious to get is correspondence messages between this medium and others
> Hodgson. Good I understand...give me a message
> Lodge. Suppose you say Julius Caesar Can you send that
> Hodgson. Yes—spell it—I will give it to her within five minutes
> I will go to [Trix Fleming]...St Paul—I will give it to her at once

Trix Fleming 31/12/1906:

> II Peter 1 15...This is a faithful saying

Helen Verrall 12/1/1907:

> The name is not right robbing Peter to pay—Paul?

Julius Caesar did not appear. St Paul did not appear directly. Piddington and Walter Prince crossed swords, rather fruitlessly from a contemporary perspective, on the value of this cross-correspondence and how much latitude the interpreter had in 'massaging' the material (Prince 1917). However, Arrow, Thanatos, Triangle within a Circle as part of the Hope, Star, Browning cross-correspondence (see appendix 3) and the convoluted Light in West, amongst others, all have good claims to be taking seriously.

Arrow

Margaret Verrall 11/2/1907:

> [Drawing of three arrows]

Leonora Piper 12/2/1907:

> [Hodgson states he has given Arrow to Margaret Verrall]

Helen Verrall 17/2/1907:

> [Drawing of an arrow]

Leonora Piper 25/2/1907:

> (Hodgson) 'Got arrow yet?'

Margaret Verrall 18/3/1907:

> [Drawing of a bow and arrow, an arrow, and a target]

Note: Margaret Verrall did not know till 4/6/1907 that arrow had been the subject of a cross-correspondence experiment. Margaret Verrall's scripts were written at Cambridge and Helen Verrall's was written away from home. Leonora Piper's sittings took place in London. Margaret Verrall saw Helen Verrall's script of 17/2/1907 on 20/2/1907.

Thanatos

Thanatos (Piddington 1908) was a good example of an intricate cross-correspondence, simple in theme, but with some indications of having been crafted by an external literate intelligence, and that intelligence aware of what was going on. Moreover, the timescale was short, giving much less opportunity for coincidence to generate the links.

Leonora Piper 17/4/1907, 23/4/1907, 30/4/1907, 7/5/1907:

> [I want to say Thanatos (or something very similar) on each occasion as she was waking from her trance]

Trix Fleming 16/4/1907:

> Maurice Morris Mors. And with that the shadow of death fell on his limbs

Margaret Verrall 29/4/1907:

> Warmed both hands before the fire of life. It fades and I am ready to depart. [She also drew the Greek letter Delta. She wrote in Latin Give lilies with full hands and then Come away, Come away, and in Latin pale death. Then she wrote You have got the word plainly written all along in your own writing. Look back.]

On one level this appeared well-designed. Leonora Piper had Thanatos (Ancient Greek for death: she knew no Greek). Trix Fleming had an English quotation and a reference to a young soldier friend Maurice who had died. Margaret Verrall had, appropriately, the most sophisticated allusions, to a poem by Walter Savage Landor (both hands before the fire of life), to Shakespeare (Come away, come away death), to book VI of the *Aeneid* where Anchises foretold the early death of Marcellus (give lilies with full hands), and pale death a reference to Horace (*Odes*, 1.4.13-14: pale death knocks equally at the door of pauper's hovel and king's tower). The whole cross-correspondence occurred within a reasonable timescale and there was clear evidence of intention to signal the common topic across the automatists.

Note: Margaret Verrall was in Cambridge, Leonora Piper was located in London for the sittings, and Trix Fleming was in Calcutta.

In addition to the stimulation of cross-correspondences, the investigators also tried to question Myers directly, through Leonora Piper, about topics the living Myers would have had detailed knowledge of. The success of the former was rather patchy and did not always bear any relationship to the confidence with which the communicators stated that they had achieved a cross-correspondence. The latter was also mixed — particularly with Myers' attempts to grasp the Latin Message. However, three very specific questions were asked of Myers (two by Margaret Verrall, and one by

Eleanor Sidgwick) to which interesting and persuasive, if at times indirect, answers were given. They were: which Ode of Horace's had entered most into Myers' inner life (Piddington 1908: 398), what did the phrase *autos ouranos aukomen* mean to Myers (Piddington 1908: 111), and what was the content of his last conversation with Mrs Sidgwick about Henry Sidgwick (Piddington 1908: 417)?

What was the Content of Myers' Last Conversation with Mrs Sidgwick about Henry Sidgwick?

Mrs Sidgwick deposited a memorandum in a sealed envelope with Piddington on 22/1/1907 and it was not opened till 17/9/1907. The gist of it was that she and Myers had had a conversation in the porch at Terling Place (her sister Evelyn's home) in August 1900 where Myers had gone to make his farewells to Sidgwick. Myers was keen to get the life story of Sidgwick written but because of his own work on *Human Personality* and his belief that he would die within two years, he wanted Mrs Sidgwick to persuade Henry's brother, Arthur, to undertake the task. There was much vagueness in Myers' answers, and he seemed aware of this himself but he did gradually inch towards the subject of the conversation.

Margaret Verrall put the question on 29/1/1907 but Myers' response was not on the topics in Mrs Sidgwick's memorandum. He said he would think the matter over more carefully. However, his next statement, through Margaret Verrall's own automatic writing, rather muddied the waters.

Margaret Verrall 4/2/1907:

> Tell Mrs Sidgwick...something about the Gurney Library which I think she will remember or a Gurney memorial which she was to take over

And his next communication through Leonora Piper seemed to be a mixture of vagueness, fishing, and red-herrings.

Leonora Piper 6/2/1907:

> ...I remember vaguely making a suggestion to Mrs Sidgwick regarding a certain document which I thought she would find necessary to be attend [sic] to...Besides I referred to matter pertaining to the College if I remember rightly; also a library matter which she will recall quickly

Myers appeared to be running two horses at once, and he wasn't helped by three investigators questioning him and Piddington forgetting some of the detail of the Margaret Verrall script of 4/2/1907. Myers insisted that, despite Piddington's denial in a session that they had together, he had actually provided relevant information (though it was not what Mrs Sidgwick wanted) and he stuck to his guns. Piddington apologised: 'You *did* mention Mrs Sidgwick's name, you *did* mention a library, and you *did* sign the message with your name.' In the same sitting (12/2/1907), Myers said: 'Do not give me too many things to do at one time will you?' And whoever, or whatever, he was, he was right. Piddington compounded the matter by having asked Myers on 12/2/1907 to give the name of the library next time, failed to pass that information on to Mrs Sidgwick who was confused when Myers on 13/2/1907 asked if she understood his reference to library (Piddington 1908: 56).

Not only were there too many cooks spoiling the broth, when Mrs Sidgwick sat with Leonora Piper, she blatantly led her with her line of questioning towards the desired conclusion.

Leonora Piper 20/3/1907:

> Can you remember what you said about writing his life?
> I do very clearly. I remember referring to some letters and collecting them.

The last point was absolutely true. Myers gave Eleanor Sidgwick copies of his own correspondence which, since it was usually meticulously dated (unlike Sidgwick's own), was a great help in establishing the narrative thread. At last he seemed to be approaching the nub of Mrs Sidgwick's memorandum.

Leonora Piper 23/3/1907:

> My advising you to see about...see about his life...(Rector, communicating) It sounds like Revnua of his life...(Myers, communicating) Yes. It was to write it.

Leonora Piper 2/4/1907:

> Do you remember my suggesting to you...photographs which I thought would be necessary? And I think I suggested Arthur...to assist...you.

Myers did eventually get the two main points in the memorandum. Mrs Sidgwick's verdict was that (Piddington 1908: 435) 'knowledge of which I believed myself to have been the sole living repository was shown'. But the information came out piecemeal and fishing/guesswork and/or telepathy could not be ruled out. Leonora Piper would have known that the life had been published and that it was the work of A.S. (Sidgwick) and E.M.S. (Sidgwick), the initials on the title page. One could argue that the selection of a simpler test question from a period before Leonora Piper's involvement in SPR matters might have yielded less ambiguous dividends.

Which Ode of Horace's had Entered Most into Myers' Inner Life?

The early 1870s was a bleak period in Myers' intellectual and spiritual life. His earlier faith, as reflected in his famous poem *St Paul*, had crumbled under the impact of scientific developments. As he put it: 'It must be remembered that this was the very flood-tide of materialism, agnosticism, —the mechanical theory of the Universe, the reduction of all spiritual facts to physiological phenomena.' He was left with 'an agnosticism or virtual materialism which sometimes was a dull pain borne with joyless doggedness, sometimes flashed into a horror of reality which made the world spin before one's eyes' (Myers 1961: 14–15). Horace's *Archytas Ode* (C.1.28), read during those years, deeply mirrored this sense of utter hopelessness as to humankind's ultimate destiny and Myers wrote during this period poems that expressed the same sense of futility.

Leonora Piper 23/1/1907:

> (Myers was asked)Which Ode of Horace entered deeply into your inner life?

Leonora Piper 17/4/1907:

> (after a reminder, Myers replied) I recall the question and I had an ode to nature on my mind; but as I thought I loved another ode better I did not reply until I could say it more clearly. Do you remember immortality?

Leonora Piper 10/3/1908:

> Ode Horace to Mortality

Leonora Piper 22/4/1908:

> (Dorr read out a general reference to Orion, son of Neptune and Myers replied)
> Do you recall an ode of Horace?

These partially disjointed responses at first seemed completely irrelevant. But the investigators thought they could make good sense of the fragments. The Horace ode expressed a pessimistic view of survival. Archytas, a great mathematician and astronomer, was now just a little bit of dust on the sea shore. Myers' poem *Immortality* expressed the same bleak feeling—extinction after death: 'Till nothing any more should still be I.' Myers' *Ode to Nature* continued the same theme: 'Let all in darkness end, as darkly all began.' The phrase 'Orion Neptune's son' was a direct allusion to two lines of the *Archytas Ode* which was the only Horace ode in which both Orion and Neptune were mentioned. George Dorr in Boston in 1908, who was overseeing the sittings with Leonora Piper, had no knowledge of the question that had been asked in 1907 or of the specific link to Horace. The reader was and is presented with the familiar choice of interpretations— either Myers had carefully selected fragments to get round the objection from telepathy or Leonora Piper was fishing in the dark, or the difficulty of communication created fragmentary almost surrealistic responses. Whatever the conclusion, the sophisticated allusion in the last script quoted was precise, clear, and not one that Leonora Piper was capable of creating (Sidgwick et al. 1910: 150–69).

Autos Ouranos Akumon
(the Very Heavens Waveless)

Margaret Verrall chose a question that would be completely unintelligible to Leonora Piper but well within Myers' knowledge and it was spelled out to her in the original Greek. The quotation was from the neo-Platonist philosopher Plotinus who, in his use of the phrase in the fifth book of his *Enneads*, was outlining the conditions necessary to access the ecstatic mystical state (Piddington 1908: 107–72).

Leonora Piper on 29/1/1907:

> [Margaret Verrall asked Myers what the above phrase meant]

Margaret Verrall 25/2/1907:

> The lucid interspace of world and world

Margaret Verrall 26/2/1907:

> I think I have made him understand (Rector, one of Leonora Piper's controls)…best references elsewhere…not Leonora Piper at all.

Margaret Verrall 6/3/1907:

> the calm, the heavenly and earthly calm…And in my heart, if calm at all. If any calm, a calm despair (In Memoriam)

Leonora Piper 6/3/1907:

> a cloudless sky beyond the horizon…Arthur Hallam

Leonora Piper 6/5/1907 (Mrs Sidgwick the sitter):

> Will you say to Mrs. V. Plotinus…My answer to autos ouranos akumon.

Some material relevant to the question appeared in Margaret Verrall's scripts, some of it apparently beyond her conscious knowledge but these are not quoted since they are potentially suspect. There was, however, a clear cross-correspondence on 6/3/1907 with Tennyson's *In Memoriam* which had been written in memory of the gifted Arthur Hallam who died young, and Myers, through Leonora Piper, did eventually provide the source of the quotation, and also a phrase approximating fairly closely to the Greek.

Light in West

Piddington (1908: 241–81), for the first time, began to suspect that wider and deeper meanings might lie hidden in the material. He argued that the

Myers persona in both cross-correspondences and his responses to the questions put to Leonora Piper was beginning to develop two important themes across a number of automatists which Piddington collated under the title *Light in West*. These were the identification of opposites and the union of East and West, and an example of the latter was illustrated by the story of Hercules. The links are too complex to summarise here involving, amongst other references: Martha, Mary, Leah, Rachel from the Bible; the monster Geryon who bore Virgil and Dante from the 7th to the 8th circle of Hell and the three-headed monster Geryon whom Hercules killed in the extreme West; the Lake District and Wordsworth; and Tennyson's *Maud* and *In Memoriam*. Piddington was to conclude several years later that these themes were integrated into the broader global message of the scripts; the creation of world peace, after long conflict, in which all differences of race, creed, and character, and all opposition and tension physically between East and West, would be reconciled. In fact, convoluted as the details of the cross-correspondences were, Piddington argued, the over-arching theme had already been simply and unmistakeably stated.

Trix Fleming 8/4/1907:

> Do you remember that exquisite sky when the afterglow made the East as beautiful and as richly coloured as the West?

Leonora Piper 8/4/1907:

> Light in the West

Margaret Verrall 8/4/1907:

> The words were from Maud but you did not understand. Rosy is the east and so on.

Note: *Trix Fleming was in India. Leonora Piper was in London. Margaret Verrall's script was written on the train from Matlock to Cambridge.*

The correct quotation from Tennyson's *Maud* was 'Rosy is the West' and just before it came the lines 'Blush from West to East/Blush from East to West/Till the West is East/Blush it thro' the West.' The lines could not make the theme of the complex cross-correspondence plainer. All three correspondences were on the same day.

Alice Johnson had identified a number of cross-correspondences that showed a complexity and interconnection beyond the simple repletion of a word or topic and now Piddington was beginning to suggest a much wider thematic unity beyond that. However, at this stage (though he revised his opinion later) his conclusions were more modest both with regard to the nature of the pattern developing and whether it actually provided convincing evidence for the survival of Myers. His provisional conclusion at the end of the first round of Piper experiments was (1908: 241–2):

'Between the subjects of most of them there really was, I believe, no connection; but some of them, which in preceding sections I have treated as disconnected, really, as I discovered only after those sections were written, belong together, and were, so to speak, links in a concatenation, or cubes in a mosaic of ideas which had been distributed among several automatists... The concatenation or mosaic of ideas which I am about to describe I regard not as the result of telepathic cross-firing casually exchanged between the automatists, but as the work of a single directing intelligence, or a group of intelligences acting in concert... On the problem of the real identity of this directing mind—whether it was a spirit or group of co-operating spirits, or the subconscious or subconsciousness of one of the automatists, or the consciousness or subconsciousness of some other living person—the only opinion which I hold with confidence is this: that if it was not the mind of Frederic Myers it was one which deliberately and artistically imitated his mental characteristics.'

On Mrs Piper's return to Boston, George Dorr, a friend of both Hodgson and William James, carried out a series of experiments with her. The other automatists did not know about his sittings or his objectives for those sittings. Dorr was deliberately trying a series of partially controlled experiments even if his methodology left something to be desired. Kelly (1910: 247–82) is partly incorrect in stating that the cross-correspondences were a purely spontaneous phenomenon. Dorr was attempting both to generate new cross-correspondences and also, as a second objective, keen to see if, through reading a variety of texts to Myers, he could help stimulate and revive Myers' literary knowledge and scholarship. This would be very significant in terms of establishing continuing identity since Leonora Piper had virtually no knowledge of the classics and Dorr's had become very sketchy since his time at Harvard. So limited was his residual knowledge that this led him both to missing and to misunderstanding some of the responses of Myers through Leonora Piper, and, Margaret Verrall later argued, failing to appreciate their subtlety and complexity (Sidgwick *et al.* 1910: 31–200).

Dorr was a wealthy man who had inherited a substantial sum from his Bostonian parents and was able, much to the irritation of some other potential sitters like Theodate Pope Riddle—the first major female American architect (Katz 2003)—to monopolise the medium for a time. Dorr was well educated. He had attended both Harvard and Oxford universities and travelled extensively in Europe. Apart from psychical research his other passion was environmental conservation: he was instrumental in creating Acadia National Park in the state of Maine.

In order to revive Myers' literary memories Dorr brought a number of books with him to the sessions. Amongst these was A.W. Pollard's collection of translations, *Odes from the Greek Dramatists*, which he had borrowed from the Athenaeum Library, an exclusive private library in Boston (therefore one to which Leonora Piper would have had no access). He kept the books for the readings in a hand-bag and did not remove them till Leonora Piper went into trance. Furthermore, 'During the trance Leonora Piper's head is turned away from the hand which writes, and therefore also from the sitter who is placed on the right, and her eyes are closed.' For some sitters, the strange humanlike behaviour of the hand would have been unnerving. At a sitting during which Dorr was trying to clear up confusion as to the difference between a Centaur and a Cyclops, 'the hand reached out and touched the sitter on both eyes, and then upon the centre of the forehead where it pressed heavily' (op. cit.: 55).

A straightforward example of Myers' success occurred on 31/3/1908 when Dorr said that he would read something by Myers' brother Ernest (from the Pollard book). It was his translation of the invocation to Zeus from the *Agamemnon* of Aeschylus. Dorr read it aloud and said, 'Now I want you to try whether you cannot give me later, in the waking-stage perhaps, the name of the old Greek play from which these lines are translated'. And in the waking stage there came '*Agamemnon*' (op. cit.: 46).

But the most interesting but also the most complex response was in reply to Dorr's questions on 9/3/1908 on the subject of the *Aeneid* (op. cit.: 59-85). 'Arma virumque cano' (the famous opening) was given to Hodgson for translation on 25/2/1908. On 9/3/1908 Hodgson said he had brought Myers with him to help and Myers suggested 'I sing of the feats of the exile who by fate' and then other words reminiscent of the first thirty lines of the poem. The name of the exile or the poem was asked for and the script faltered but finally produced 'Enoid-Eid–I did not get all the letters in..."Eiane Aenid"' and the curious later comment (quite often repeated in Piper) 'I hear with difficulty' (op. cit.: 72-3).

On 10/03/1908 Dorr asked Myers why Juno was angry with the Trojans. He expected an answer referring to the Judgement of Paris. Juno, Minerva, and Venus had each hoped that Paris would judge them the most beautiful woman in the world but Paris chose Helen of Troy. This helped provoke the Trojan War. However, Myers replied:

> No, she destroyed because she did not wish a better city than her own.
> Africa Africa

This was accurate. Juno did not want a rival to her favoured city of Carthage on the Mediterranean coast of North Africa. When tackled about this by Dorr on 16/3/1908, Myers then provided the expected, conventional answer:

> I remember, *let me think it over*, don't tell me. I remember it caused wrath because of jealousy. She was jealous of-because-because it-she was not *selected*.

But Myers displayed not only semantic and episodic memory (Fernyhough 2013). He demonstrated his linguistic skills as a classical scholar (procedural memory). On 17/3/1908 Dorr read out Dryden's translation of the opening of the *Aeneid*.

The lines were:

> For what offence the queen of Heaven began
> To persecute so brave, so just a man;
> Involved his anxious life in endless cares,
> Exposed to wants, and hurried into wars.

The original Latin was:

> Musa, mihi causas memora, quo numine laeso,
> Quidve dolens, regina deum tot volvere casus
> Insignem pietate virum, tot adire labores
> Impulerit. Tantaene animis caelistibus irae?

Margaret Verrall's translation was:

> Muse, tell me the causes, for what outrage to her godhead, or suffering what smart, did the queen of gods drive a hero, renowned for goodness, to pass through so many mischances, to undertake so many labours. In heavenly hearts can such anger be?

Myers' response was very sophisticated.

> Is there such anger in celestial minds?
> A hero for piety renowned — should suffer and toil

He produced his own version of part of the Dryden translation that had been read out and added the line from Virgil that would have come next. It was an excellent translation of *Tantaenae animis caelistibus irae*/Is there such anger in celestial minds.

On 17/3/1908 Dorr asked Myers 'what was the connexion between the Wooden Horse and Troy?' (*op. cit.*: 74-7). In reply he received:

> Fleet behind on island, — soldiers in Horse. Arrow in heel

He could make no sense of this but Margaret Verrall later pointed out that the elliptical statements implied substantial factual knowledge and grasp of the narrative. It was on the island of Tenedos that the main fleet of the Greeks hid to make the Trojans believe they were returning home while they waited till the Trojan Horse had done its work. Dorr had no idea that there was a shrine to Apollo on the island and that it was the god Apollo who brought about Achilles' death by guiding the arrow of Paris to Achilles' only vulnerable part, his heel. As Margaret Verrall clearly stated: 'Here, as elsewhere, familiarity with classical literature shows a coherence, where a first reading found only broken fragments, by supplying an association of ideas which may account for the otherwise arbitrary juxtaposition of unconnected allusions.'

Another problem, apart from Dorr's lack of detailed classical knowledge, was his methodology. Several times there were complaints that Dorr was giving Myers and Hodgson too much to do. Margaret Verrall commented: 'In this, the first set of experiments, too many topics were presented at a time to the control. A further element of complexity [was] the simultaneous effort at experiment along another line—the so-called cross-correspondences...' (Sidgwick *et al.* 1910: 40). Dorr also compounded the confusion by his habit of reading over the responses of the previous session before moving on to new tests for Myers, so it was not always clear what the particular current focus was. Despite this, Margaret Verrall pointed out that there were very few examples of persistent error as opposed to confusion in the replies, and in those cases that appeared to be 'disjointed' it was unwise to discount them. As Piddington demonstrated in the case of Lethe (see below), what appeared to be gibberish made sense once the appropriate context and source had been identified. Margaret Verrall concluded her assessment by making four points—considerable knowledge of the poem was demonstrated; the knowledge was presented in a way characteristic of a revived and stimulated memory; the answers were persevered with despite being sometimes opposed to the beliefs of the sitter and despite his criticism; and the errors seemed to be caused by confusion or forgetfulness rather than a lack of grasp of the subject.

Myers also proved competent in Greek. He successfully translated line 5 of the Odyssey which had been read to him in the original Greek. It was, as has been seen, a line of great significance to the living Myers: 'Striving to save my own soul, and my comrades' homeward way.' He had wanted it 'graven on some tablet' in his memory and, as has been seen, the line was on his memorial tablet in the Protestant Cemetery in Rome, and in Greek it headed Lodge's memorial address to Myers and in English tailed it. It was also on his tomb at Keswick. In theory, Leonora Piper might have matched the Greek with the English but it is very difficult to believe that she could, actually, have done so (*op. cit.*: 77).

In addition, though not as technically persuasive as some of the material already quoted, Myers' response to Dorr's reading from *Fragments of Prose and Poetry* (1904) on 10/3/1908 was both moving and carried an emotional resonance and response which seemed authentic:

> Oh! It is all so clear. I recall so well my feelings, my emotions, my joys, my pain and much pain. Oh! I am transported back to Greece. I recall it all... I remember before my marriage all my imaginations, my pain, my longing, my unrest. I lived it all out as few men did... And never was it complete. (*op. cit.*: 154)

The script clearly captured Myers' disappointment at the huge gap between the reality of his visit to Greece and his imaginative anticipation of it from classical literature. There was authenticity in this voice. One would naturally suspect that Leonora Piper had constructed this response from a reading of Myers' published *Fragments of Prose and Poetry*, but when Piddington made extensive enquiries of Leonora Piper's knowledge of the book (*op. cit.*: 109–10) she told him she had never heard of it. He then went further in his enquiries and eventually established, from Boston and New York publishing houses, that the book had sold very poorly, so the likelihood of it being the source for the above outpourings was extremely remote.

Nevertheless, Margaret Verrall was still cautious in her general assessment of the sittings. She carefully examined the range of possible alternatives to communication from the discarnate Myers: 'instances of direct thought-transference from the sitter'; hints and fishing; 'we must also allow for changes of tone and other involuntary indications'; and she accepted that much of the classical information could have been stored in the subliminal memory of Mr Dorr and also some, much less likely but still possible, in the subliminal memory of Leonora Piper, 'especially if an interval elapses between the question and the answer' (*op. cit.*: 42).

The Lethe Case, well summarised by Carter (2012: 234–56), was probably for him and other commentators (Murphy 1970: 214–52; Burt 1975) the most significant example of Leonora Piper's demonstrations of paranormal cognition. It was also part of a sophisticated later cross-correspondence between Leonora Piper and Winifred Coombe-Tennant. Myers provided allusive references to Lethe in Ovid's *Metamorphoses*. Dorr (*op. cit.*: 86–144) who had posed the question, on 23/3/1908, 'What does the word Lethe suggest to you?' had expected an answer on the lines: 'Lethe is a river that flows through Hades and the dead drink from it to wipe out their memories before being reincarnated again on earth.' Instead, he received amongst other items in the waking stage:

> Sybil, Olympus, water, Morpheus, Winds, Lethe, delighted, sad, lovely, mate, I shot an arrow through the air, (with instructions to put them all together. Then on the following day came): caves, banks, shore, arrow, C—YX.

The essence of the story in the Ovid was: Iris the goddess of the rainbow ordered Somnus the god of sleep to tell Alcyone of the death of her husband Ceyx. Somnus, from his cave of sleep (the source of the river Lethe), sent Morpheus to reveal this to Alcyone in a dream. She then tried to drown herself in the sea and the gods turned her (and later) her beloved Ceyx into kingfishers so they could be together for ever. The match between the Piper script and the Ovid text is clear.

Piper Script	Ovid *Met.* XI
Cave	Cave of Sleep
Female figure with half a hoop	Iris with bow (rainbow)
Sad lovely mate. Entwined love	Lines 733–8
Cave banks shore Flower banks	Lines 603–6
Iris Morpheus Latin for sleep	Iris—Morpheus—Somnus
Cyx	Ceyx
Pavia/poppies	Papavera

Note: Lines 733–8 described the miserable Alcyone (as a kingfisher) skimming the waves, and passionately wrapping herself round the corpse of Ceyx. Lines 603–6 described the Lethe flowing at the bottom of the cave with poppies blooming by its entrance.

Three other points also stand out from the original material: a) the persistence with which Myers and Hodgson tried to make Dorr grasp the references; b) the personal touch when Dorr asked, 'But can't you make it clearer about what there was peculiar about the waters of Lethe?' And Myers replied, 'Yes, I suppose you think that I am affected in the same way but I am not?'; c) references to Orpheus, Eurydice, and Pygmalion, elsewhere in the communications, as Piddington speculated, in order to indicate that Ovid's *Metamorphoses* was the source of the allusions and that their richness was such that they came from the original source and not summaries which Leonora Piper and Dorr may or may not have read like Bulfinch's *The Age of Fable*, Gayley's *The Classical Myths in English Literature*, or Lempriere's *Classical Dictionary* (*op. cit.*: 142–4). Piddington was exhaustive in his thoroughness on this point. He even asked Dorr to visit Leonora Piper after her move from the Arlington Heights house and 'to go through all the books at her flat'. 'He found no copy of Bulfinch or Gayley, nor did he find any book even remotely bearing on classical myths.'

Margaret Verrall was particularly encouraged by these preliminary evidences characteristic of the specialised knowledge and personal interests of Myers. In a private meeting read to Members and Associates at Hanover Square in July 1911, with Lodge in the chair, she argued (Verrall 1911: 98–100) that the investigators had established evidence 'of intelligent direction of the phenomena of concordant automatism'; and that there should be strenuous efforts to identify the characteristics of this directing intelligence. For, 'if there is present in the intelligence a factor not identifiable with any of the living human factors with which it is combined, it is reasonable to look for evidence of its possession of individual tastes, interests, or capacity,—for evidence, in short, of idiosyncrasy or personality'. In other words, it was worth looking more closely at the actual content of the cross-correspondences in terms of the particular topics chosen by Myers for communication, his knowledge of them, and the way he handled them.

In the same paper she pointed out that even more literate automatists than Leonora Piper had material in their scripts outside their normal range of reading and recall. For example, that there was a correspondence on Ruskin's *Sesame and Lilies* which was presented in a form that was beyond the conscious knowledge of Mr and Miss Mac and Margaret and Helen Verrall, and she particularly emphasised the Renan cross-correspondence between herself and Winifred Coombe-Tennant (only two days apart) in which the words 'Eikon Renam' led to the discovery in Renan's *Les Apôtres* that his rationalist explanation for the conversion of St Paul was based on St Paul seeing a visual image, an 'Eikon' which was not actually mentioned in the narrative of Acts on which Renan founded his statement. In other words, Renan hypothesised the incident in order to justify his thesis. It is worth remembering that Renan was the subject of one of Myers' *Essays Modern* (1897: 163–234) and Myers, while himself no defender of the unthinking acceptance of the Christian story and its associated miracles, criticised Renan for his, at times, superficially rationalist denigration of those elements in Christian faith.

Finally, one needs to consider the position and reputation of Leonora Piper herself. The debate about her has perhaps waged a little more furiously than some supporters of her phenomena would have it. As the only professional medium involved in the cross-correspondences she has faced the kinds of attacks and criticisms that the others did not. But many of these negative comments referred to sittings other than the cross-correspondences and, in the context of this book, one must concentrate on Leonora Piper's performance in respect of the latter, during which she was under the intensive scrutiny of a small number of investigators who were not judging her in the terms of a traditional sitting with a medium. In addition, others have pointed out the reliance of later critics like Martin Gardner (Taylor, G. 2015) on the negative and inaccurate criticisms of Hall and Tanner (1910) which were rebutted in detail by both James Hyslop (1911) and Eleanor Sidgwick (1911). However, a more subtle and historically informed critic, Munves (1997), has highlighted the psychological and emotional factors that may have led early investigators of Leonora Piper to over-invest in her trance speech and later automatic writing. This point particularly referred to Hodgson but it still, as will be seen, has relevance to the general assessment of this material.

The Life and Automatic Writing of Winifred Coombe-Tennant to 1919

The Death of Daphne Coombe-Tennant;
Early Paranormal Phenomena; Affair with
Gerald Balfour; the Story of the Palm Maiden
(May Lyttelton) and the Knight (Arthur
Balfour); the Wizard of Melrose (Francis
Maitland Balfour); the Peacock Lady
(Laura Lyttelton); and the Messianic Child
(Henry Coombe-Tennant)

A new and powerful automatist joined the SPR group in 1908. This was Winifred Coombe-Tennant, born 1/11/1874, the only child of George Edward Serocold Pierce-Serocold's second marriage (which was to Mary Clarke Richardson of Glamorgan). She had a disrupted formal education, living at various times in Stroud, Boulogne, Montreux, Wales, Bristol, Cherryhinton near Cambridge, and Naples, where the family stayed three years. Her father, an Old Etonian and a Royal Navy officer, was an obsessive traveller and often took his family with him. By the time she had reached her early twenties she had become fluent in French and Italian and had a breadth of perspective beyond many young women of her age and class. In 1895 at Bellagio on Lake Como she encountered the Tennant family who had an estate in South Wales at Cadoxton near Swansea, and a large town house in the heart of Whitehall, 2 Richmond Terrace. The head of the family was the widowed Gertrude Tennant, an intimate friend of Gustave Flaubert, and a renowned political and literary hostess of the 1880s and 1890s (Waller 2009). After a brief courtship the twenty-one year-old Winifred married Gertrude's son Charles Coombe-Tennant, who was twenty-two years older (Lord 2007: 6–20).

Winifred, through her marriage to Charles, became part of the glittering family circle that clustered around Charles' mother, Gertrude, whose daughters, Dorothy and Eveleen, shared their mother's interest in the literary and social world. Dorothy married the African explorer Henry Stanley, while Eveleen married Frederic W.H. Myers, celebrated poet and essayist, classical scholar, and a leading light in the Society for Psychical Research. Winifred, may well have felt inferior to her sisters-in-law. She was less impressive physically than Dorothy, who was statuesque and quite a flirt, both before and after marriage. Eveleen was a particular beauty when younger and had been painted by Millais. Both these women had established an individual creative identity. Dorothy, as a painter, attracted the attention of Ruskin, while Eveleen, after her marriage, became recognised as a very fine photographer and her portraits of Gladstone and Balfour by their austere presentation and lighting captured central aspects of their characters (Hamilton 2009). Dorothy and Eveleen had a tendency to look down on the slightly plump but immensely energetic Winifred, who did much to make herself useful to the family. She catalogued all Stanley's paraphernalia brought back from Africa (RMCA archive) and she was obviously on good terms with Myers' children, as a charming photograph of her sandwiched between Silvia and Leo around 1900 shows (National Portrait Gallery archives).

The Death of Daphne Coombe-Tennant

Because of Myers' influence she became an associate member of the Society for Psychical Research but resigned from it in 1905 as other interests supervened. However, her slightly distant interest in this area painfully quickened as she and Charles suffered the devastating blow of losing their daughter Daphne, at the age of eighteen months. Daphne died some time in the very early hours of 21/7/1908 and seems to have been a particularly lively, happy, and intelligent child. Winifred Coombe-Tennant was naturally absolutely distraught and, because of the family links with the SPR, wrote to the Society on 28/7/1908 (Verrall 1910a), only a week after Daphne's death, in tones of urgency, need, and almost command: 'I wanted to tell you at once—so that no allusion might be lost or misunderstood in any communication… If through any channel any word of her comes, you will tell me—for I am her mother… I knew and loved F.W.H.M.' This initiated a correspondence and eventual friendship with Margaret Verrall which had profound consequences for the future direction of the scripts and their interpretation. Margaret Verrall, one could argue, had been warned about this. For on her return from her Swiss holiday in July 1908 she received instructions to increase the volume of her automatic writing.

Margaret Verrall 27/7/1908:

> Write, write all this summer. F.W.H.M. There is to be a great effort in September and I want you at least to be ready to do the best you can.

Early in September, Margaret Verrall, writing outdoors, produced a poem which was in part interrupted by her husband also coming to sit in the garden (the occupational hazard of the automatist) but not before she managed to get down twelve lines:

Margaret Verrall 7/9/1908:

> The lengthening shadows on the dewy lawn
> And then the first faint splendour of the dawn
> Sat through the growing shadows of the night
> Saw the light fail, and saw relive the light
> Watched the faint gleam dim in the eyes of Death
> Watched the last throb of the fast failing breath
> Still was the starry night, but with the dawn
> Faint breezes stirred the leaves upon the lawn
> And for the watcher, with the morning light
> Hope stirred and broke the silence of the night
> Faith saw the promise in the dawn's faint breath
> Love was triumphant in the arms of death.
> F

The single initial F was not normally used by Myers in Margaret Verrall's scripts. He usually signed himself as F.W.H.M. or Tuus. But as a family member Winifred Coombe-Tennant had called him Fred, hence, possibly the F, to indicate that the message was for Winifred Coombe-Tennant and not Margaret Verrall.

The poem was sent to Winifred Coombe-Tennant who said it seemed to describe her efforts to cope with the immediate period at and after Daphne's death (Verrall 1910a: 12): 'It was only a question of a few moments... perhaps twenty breaths... the breath just stopped... In the silence of the night it sounded very loud and strange to me... I lifted Daphne slightly and looked into her eyes and saw "the gleam of Death".' Leaving her mother's flat in Chelsea, which was where Daphne had died, she returned to Cadoxton and, sleepless and grieving, at night used to go out into the garden: 'There was a balcony into which I could walk... and look out over a lawn. I was haunted by the sound of those throbbing breaths... always at dawn there came a rustle of wind in two large poplars that stood close to my window... It was that strange feeling of triumph which came with the dawn.' Margaret Verrall, worried that the description might be too general, discussed the matter with Mrs Sidgwick whose comment was that it was not unlikely there would be 'script appropriate to the loss of a child after you had heard from her', but the details, plus the links between the scripts (for reasons of space not all the material has been quoted here), do 'make a strong chain of appropriate associations'.

Margaret Verrall's poem encouraged Winifred Coombe-Tennant to take up the practice of automatic writing in a sustained fashion. On 8/10/1908 she wrote to Margaret Verrall that she had tried it when sixteen or seventeen but had given it up because there was no one to advise or help her and, when at the end of August 1908 she had started again, hoping to contact Daphne, she was suspicious of the writing which was signed Myers or F.W.H.M., and tore it up. She then went abroad for a while, hoping that travel would ease her grief, and was incensed to read there on 26/10/1908 Mrs Myers' statement in the British press that both she and her eldest son Leo had found nothing of value in the Spiritualistic messages purporting to come from her late husband (Lord 2011; Hamilton 2009). In fact, Winifred (after an initial friendship with Dolly) had an increasingly difficult relationship with her more glamorous older sisters-in-law and in later years some of her diary comments on them were scabrous: 'Lunched at Richmond Terrace. Dolly very fat and vulgar, Evie looking an haggard old woman, smeared with paint' (Lord 2011: 131).

She now began to to read more widely in the history of psychical research and about some of the individuals involved. By November she had received Alice Johnson's first report on the scripts of Trix Fleming and at the beginning of November was sent a copy of Piddington's report on the Piper sittings of 1906/07 which she noted carefully (Lord 2011: 19). And in January 1909 she read *Man and the Universe* by Sir Oliver Lodge, the first of his books she had tackled (Lord 2011: 18). On 31/1/1909 she obtained Henry Sidgwick's memoir from the library, having been told he was the principal communicator in the Macs' scripts (see below). She was, too, a reader of the *Hibbert Journal* (Lord 2011: 18, 19, 22), quite a demanding intellectual and cultural review. All this needs to be taken into account when assessing the paranormal content of her scripts.

As had happened with Mrs Raikes, Helen Verrall, and Alice Fleming, connections of various sorts began to be established between the scripts of Margaret Verrall and the developing scripts of Winifred Coombe-Tennant.

Margaret Verrall 9/12/1908:

> Try to describe two floating ribbons and a small square box with a sweet strange foreign scent. The box should be tied with the ribbons and then sent [there was a drawing of a box and two ribbons]. And in the box a single stone a carved gem. Surely she has not forgotten the association of that stone. It should reach her before this month is out to remind. Just say that. To remind and send the little box tied with its green ribbon.

On finding this in her automatic writing, Margaret Verrall was on first reading unable to see its relevance to her. But on the following day at 1pm she received, unexpectedly, a short memoir that Winifred Coombe-Tennant had written about Daphne. Winifred Coombe-Tennant had been told, in her own automatic writing on 8/12/1908, to send it to Margaret Verrall. Margaret Verrall knew that Winifred Coombe-Tennant was writing a brief memoir of Daphne but had thought that it was for herself alone. As she opened the parcel she saw a possible way (Verrall 1910a: 15–17) of explaining her own script—who the 'she' was and the 'her' and who was to receive the little box. Removing the brown paper wrapping, she noticed a small box inside and within it were the sheets of the typewritten memoir tied crossways with a narrow green ribbon. There was a sweet scent coming both from Winifred Coombe-Tennant's covering letter and from her enclosed script of 8/12/1908. Margaret Verrall carefully compared her own script above with the package sent to her. There were minor differences but the similarities were beyond doubt. The main weakness was the lack of a carved gem and Margaret Verrall could only come to the conclusion that it might be an allegorical reference to Daphne as a precious jewel. In March 1909 she handed the material over to Lodge to be stored as evidence.

Winifred Coombe-Tennant's scripts soon began to impute meaning and design to the suffering she and her husband had experienced.

Winifred Coombe-Tennant 20/1/1909:

> Gurney I want to say something. Former scripts should show that the coming of Daphne was no chance but a completely thought out & recognised event & so agree to suffer be willing because of the vast interests involved.

Any assessor of her scripts has squarely to face the central spiritual role that she claimed for Daphne and some of these passages in her scripts read as a heart-breaking exercise in making sense of something that is, for many people, part of the random cruelty of life itself.

Winifred Coombe-Tennant 30/4/1909:

> CC of a Literary kind per se could never reach a wide circle never impress any but a close student of already literary Culture Myers their necessity was this I had to devise some kind of Myers evidence that would first cause to be admitted the probability of an Outside Agent... The next stage was...conveyance of veridical matter under that guise... Observe I don't use my machine here for the utterly secondary important purpose of CC. I am using her as far as I can to beget new ideas.

Winifred Coombe-Tennant 3/7/1909:

> Daphne was going to have 'a sort of birthday soon', something was being arranged for her by F.W.H.M. 'quite like a birthday party'—the birthday being the day she came 'here' (i.e. July 21, 1908, the day of her death).

Winifred Coombe-Tennant 18/7/1909:

> Here is a message waiting from Daphne to her Grandmother to say she is to have something like a party really a very important Meeting of Various Workers this side but she is to be the Crowned Queen of it the Child I mean and it is to mark the third greatest date in the history of the Society…1882 and 1907 and 1908

Winifred Coombe-Tennant 27/7/1909:

> Among the persons present at the 'birthday party' was mentioned a lady 'belonging to' E.G. who had known him when he was 'quite a baby', and a 'funny old gentleman' who asked of 'what species' Daphne was to be, and said that a 'new name' would have to be found for her.

These scripts have been interpreted as referring to the founding of the SPR in 1882, the cross-correspondences with Leonora Piper and others from 1906–1908, and the role of Daphne from 1908 onwards in stimulating further important developments. One also assumes that the 'funny old gentleman' was Charles Darwin and that this introduced the spiritual eugenics/evolution theme which became an increasingly marked feature of her scripts. In essence, Winifred Coombe-Tennant was, though it was not fully appreciated at the time, beginning to shift the focus of the automatic writing away (as the script of 30/4/1909 indicated) from the literary devices of the cross-correspondences, to communication that focused more broadly on the nature of psychical processes and, eventually, revealed the hidden purposes of the scripts. In all this Daphne and later Henry were to have significant roles; Alexander less so, and there was curiously little mention of Christopher. This central role for some of her children in the later interpretation of the scripts presented the investigators with real problems. To what extent did her intense maternal ambition for her children colour and even warp the communications she was receiving?

On the other hand, in the scripts of Helen Verrall there were quite specific references, plus a number of indirect symbolic ones, which could reasonably be linked to the short life of Daphne, pre-dating her birth and before Margaret and Helen Verrall knew anything of any detail about the Coombe-Tennant family.

Helen Verrall script:

> 29/8/1906: Llangattock bay remember this name, they will write of it
> 20/1/1907: more sarn? [Outline drawing of a map] Winifred was the name
> 17/3/1907: Quinque et viginti annos post urbem conditam laurel leaves are emblems
> 22/11/1907: Once more ye laurels Llangattock was the place
> 25/11/1907: Llangattock looking westwards through a gap in the hills towards the sea

31/1/1908: Llangattock's St Peter's Church but not at Rome there is a font that has some connection
20/7/1908: the day of the feast with myrrh and frankincense a white bull for the sacrifice

The Welsh word sarn means causeway (Latin strata into Welsh sarn) and, it was suggested by the early investigators, indicated a lane near the Coombe-Tennant home; 6/1/1882 was the date of the first meeting to found the Society for Psychical Research (*Quingue et* etc. translates as 25 years after the founding of the city and could be seen as symbolic); Daphne in Greek means laurel/bay tree; Winifred was Winifred Coombe-Tennant's Christian name; Llangattock is Welsh for Cadoxton, Daphne's home village, and there is a view near there through the hills to the sea; Daphne was christened in the Cadoxton church, though it was not called St Peter's; and the last script links Daphne's birthday, 6/1/1907, with Epiphany (myrrh and frankincense, the Magi) and the idea of sacrifice. It was written a few hours before Daphne died.

While Myers appeared first as a communicator in Winifred Coombe-Tennant's early scripts, Edmund Gurney soon took an active part in them. This is a point of especial importance since she had never met him, knew little or nothing of his personality, and had to ask her husband what he was like as a man. Charles Coombe-Tennant had possibly first encountered him when Gurney vouched for Myers' qualities as a suitor for the hand of Eveleen in 1879 (Hamilton 2009), and Charles did not like him. He found him sardonic. In fact, Gurney, very early on in the scripts, demonstrated the kind of sharp, idiosyncratic humour that he had displayed in life. For example, Winifred started to write up a Daylight Impression (see below for definition) in the dark, which Gurney commented on sardonically.

Winifred Coombe-Tennant 3/3/1909:

> If Podmore ever gets hold of the records, he will prove your complete instability by triumphantly pointing to the fact that you solidly recorded receiving a Daylight Impression after having put your candle out. [Myers interjected] Don't. Gurney don't, you will confuse her.

Winifred knew Podmore existed but nothing about his reputation as the SPR resident sceptic.

These early scripts were received by her alone and sent to Margaret Verrall. But the communicators on 31/1/1909 expressed the wish that she should meet Sir Oliver Lodge. She was not initially in favour of this but Myers pointed out that there were wider purposes involved above and beyond her personal interests.

Winifred Coombe-Tennant 1/2/1909:

> Let others hammer at your scripts but remember they are not for you. Myers I wish to re emphasis this because there will naturally be a distrust of anything through you owing to the very fact of your connection with Daphne and myself...

And in the same script Gurney made the point that her automatic writing had given Myers fresh hope that good communication was possible and it was again urged that she sit with Lodge since sensitives should only sit with those in tune with them. There was, too, the point, echoing a similar statement in Trix Fleming's script, that she was not to worry about the detail of the content:

> ...what does it matter to the telegraph girl what the wire contains the only thing is that it should be accurate & dispatched to destination

This point was elaborated on in a later script.

Winifred Coombe-Tennant 3/3/1909:

> No one on your side yet does more than conjecture what the full meaning of the whole experiment is or its magnitude. But by degrees they will begin to see I have waited long & much denunciation here have I experienced over the whole thing but I wish to see now the fruits beginning to be gathered in

Piddington, as has been seen, had already begun to suspect, with *Light in West*, that broader symbolic structures lay behind the cross-correspondences. Here was the first emerging indication in Coombe-Tennant script that this was in fact so. The phrase 'much denunciation here have I experienced over the whole thing' is curiously interesting. At several points in the scripts there were references to the family of the Archbishop of Canterbury, Edward White Benson, who married Henry Sidgwick's remarkable sister Mary (Bolt 2012). Benson was something of a tyrant both domestically and with regard to Church procedure and doctrine. One can well expect a post-mortem Benson (he died in 1898 — much one imagines to the subconscious relief of his wife and family) to argue that Christian faith rather than psychical research should suffice the incarnate as hope and consolation for suffering and loss.

Like Margaret Verrall earlier, a number of spontaneous paranormal experiences occurred when Winifred Coombe-Tennant began regular automatic writing. On 28/2/1909 she awoke at 8.00am from a dream of Lodge reading a letter from Margaret Verrall about her and, checking later, she found that the dream closely matched the environment in which Lodge had read it. On 31/3/1909 at Cadoxton, she and her husband Charles experienced an odd event (and the point is the experience was shared):

> At 10 min. to 3 today we were in the hall just going out when as I opened the front door the oak grandfather's clock, which is not going and has not been going for years, suddenly struck 'one.' [My husband] and I stopped aghast.

They examined the mechanism carefully but could not account for it. However, on that date died General Palmer of Colorado Springs, the father-in-law of Myers' son Leo, and a powerful economic force in the opening up of the American West (Verrall, c1910c: 43-4).

On 21/5/1909 came the first witnessed Daylight Impression with Margaret Verrall sitting with her. This was the term that was used to describe the intense two-way conversations that developed between Winifred Coombe-Tennant and her communicators and which were to provide some of the most vivid and informative communications of all the cross-correspondence material. It was her 112th script, which sheer volume of script in such a short time certainly demonstrated the seriousness of her intent. The first script she had found acceptable was written on 9/10/1908 when in Venice. This meant in seven months she had produced 112 scripts at an average of 16 scripts per month.[1]

Margaret Verrall noted (Verrall 1914 vol 1: 60-4): 'Mrs Willett sat at some little distance from me near a table, over which hung a photograph of Daphne. She rested her elbows on the table and her face in her hands for a few moments; then lifted her head, keeping her eyes shut, and spoke as if in answer to some one, saying that she could hear, and would repeat.'

The Daylight Impression (D.I.) is too long to print. The key points are summarised here. Myers stressed that, though Mrs Willett's condition in a D.I. was trancelike, it was telepathic and not telergic (that is not physical possession), unlike that, for example, of Leonora Piper. The communicators did not want a traditional trance medium but someone who remained alert enough to communicate in a more effective and nuanced fashion. He stressed the importance of getting all the material together for the inner ring to study — Piddington, Lodge, Alice Johnson, Mrs Sidgwick, and Gerald Balfour, 'if he would like it'. A note by Margaret Verrall stated that she had suggested this possibility to Winifred Coombe-Tennant a couple of days previously. Myers stressed the importance and urgency of the matter:

> Remember the awful lesson of my own case: no one has dealt with the papers which I left. Do not let that happen again.

In response to Margaret Verrall's puzzlement that Daphne in the script of 10/5/1909 appeared to her mother to be a child of four, Myers replied that 'there is a growth here to maturity': a point that was frequently made in the

---

[1] In this book the term script is used for both Mrs Coombe-Tennant's automatic writing and her Daylight Impressions. Balfour (1935: 90-116) has a perceptive analysis of the different nature of these communications.

Spiritualistic literature of the time and later. He stated that Daphne was their first experiment with so young a child (whatever that meant), that the relationship between her and Gurney would have a real bearing on the whole, and that Lodge should have a D.I. with Winifred Coombe-Tennant since 'there is a certain similarity in colour with this machine'. Myers later reinforced the point about telepathic influence and how to make it effective.

Winifred Coombe-Tennant 10/6/1909:

> All telergic phenomena is clumsy and creaking creaking in comparison with telepathic medium

> Calm must precede easy communication...I am continually growing in knowledge in regard to importance of conditions conducive of success

One unflattering condition of success had already been stated in the scripts, when Mrs Coombe-Tennant was staying at Saunton Sands in North Devon.

Winifred Combe Tennant 9/4/1909:

> a large part of her potentiality as a telepathic machine is directly due to...her lack of sophisticated habit of thought...I have little to uproot and therefore less to contend with. The moment a machine begins to say Lord is it I that moment something rises between Machine and Operator...

Some Early Paranormal Phenomena

Lethe

Lodge, when he sat with Winifred Coombe-Tennant, though interested in the psychological processes involved, was also keen to encourage cross-references and cross-correspondences between scripts. Aware of the success of some of the Piper sittings with George Dorr, he asked Myers through Winifred Coombe-Tennant the same question that he had been asked through Leonora Piper: 'what does the word Lethe suggest to you?' Winifred Coombe-Tennant had no knowledge either of the previous question or of the content of the reply. The essence of the reply was as follows (see Carter 2012, Murphy 1970 for fuller details):

Winifred Coombe-Tennant 4/2/1910:

> Tu Marcellus Eris you know that line you I mean Write it nevertheless and add Henry Sidgwick's In Valle Reducta...Add too the Doves and the Golden Bough...add too, Go not to Lethe...there was the door to which I found no key...the shining souls shining by the river brim...but there is another more intimate link and connection...fluttering rose leaves like ghosts from an enchanter fleeing...

Just as Myers through Leonora Piper had used Ovid as the basis for his response, it was clear to Piddington that Myers through Winifred Coombe-Tennant had used *Aeneid* VI as the source material for his allusions to Lethe. Marcellus was one of the souls lined up on the banks of Lethe to be reborn. Doves led Aeneas to the Golden Bough which allowed him to descend to the underworld and to via a sheltered vale (Valle Reducta) Lethe.

There were two further interesting touches in this reply. First, there was a correspondence with Mac 8 (the Mackinnons from Aberdeen; see later) and Valle Reducta (the only automatic writing in which Sidgwick was the main communicator). Second, on the following day Myers seemed very keen to point up the link with Dorr (Winifred Coombe-Tennant knew vaguely of his name but nothing more).

Winifred Coombe-Tennant 5/2/1910:

> you felt the call...it is I who write Myers I need urgently to say this tell Lodge this word...the word is Dorr.

Lodge noted in his article on the matter (Lodge 1911: 165) that no confusion was ever exhibited by a Myers control 'between the rivers mentioned in the *Aeneid,* Book VI., namely the Styx, Cocytus, and other rivers of Hades on the one hand, and Lethe—a river washing the shores of the Elysian field...'. He pointed out the common error that the famous Virgilian line *tendebantque manus ripae ulterioris amore*/they stretched their hands out in longing for the further shore, did not refer to the souls clustered on the banks of the Lethe, swarming said Virgil like bees. It referred to the unburied dead on the banks of the river Styx not allowed to cross to the underworld in Charon's boat till their bodies had been buried. The souls by the Lethe waited to drink its waters to obliterate their memories and prepare themselves for rebirth. Their longing was for the material world.

Two points must be raised even if their significance is theoretical rather than actual. First, Lodge had sent his question about Lethe in a sealed envelope to Winifred Coombe-Tennant on 28/9/1909, leaving it up to her when she wanted to ask Myers the question (Lodge 1911). She later returned the opened envelope to him at his request, having written on the tongue 'Opened by me Feb. 4, 1910 at...' She was staying at Twalefa, Langland Bay, with her parents, and to her inner amusement her father started to discuss the cross-correspondences with her, not realising that she had become one of the group generating them (Lord 1911: 41). But, this aside, there was always the possibility, no matter how remote, that she had opened the envelope earlier and read up on the Lethe topic.

Second, the phrase *Tu Marcellus Eris* is iconic, and the subject of frequent allusion in painting and poetry of the classical tradition. Winifred Coombe-Tennant had a great love of art and there were two well-known paintings on this theme: Ingres' *Virgil Reading the Aeneid to Augustus* and a copy of it by Charles Simon Pradier in the Boston Museum of Fine Arts. Dante (and Winifred Coombe-Tennant had good Italian) alluded to it in the scene in the *Purgatorio* where Beatrice first appeared to him. It was the expression Anchises, Aeneas's father, used in the *Aeneid* when describing the spirit of Marcellus before his incarnation and short life. Virgil read his poem to Augustus and his sister Octavia, the mother of Marcellus, a possible heir to Augustus, himself (Hardie 2014: 117). He died before his potential could be fulfilled. So moving was the reading that she fainted. This is one of those cases where Winifred Coombe-Tennant's cultural and artistic interests, rather than an external source, might well have provided the content.

Margaret Verrall was well aware of this issue and she examined the scripts of February 1910 with her usual punctiliousness. She made 'a detailed examination of the probable sources of the quotations and allusive phrases of which Mrs. Coombe-Tennant's script largely consists' (Verrall 1911: 176-217). This was a daunting and laborious task but she identified forty-four key phrases from the scripts of 4/2/1910 and 10/2/1910 and managed to find forty-one potential sources for them that theoretically Winifred Coombe-Tennant might have accessed. However, it was the way these items were organised and their links with other scripts that really impressed Margaret Verrall. The most vivid and concrete example of this was probably the play and correspondence on the word Dorr, which she explored in detail. Lodge himself agreed with this conclusion and pointed out that even if Winifred Coombe-Tennant had opened the sealed envelope and researched the question beforehand, the deft, subtle, and allusive nature of the statements reflected an intelligence and reading much beyond hers: 'The one hypothesis which seems to me most nearly to satisfy that condition, in this case, is that we are in direct touch with some part of the surviving personality of a scholar—and that scholar F.W.H. Myers' (Lodge 1911: 175).

Dorr

Margaret Verrall (Sidgwick 1910: 193-204) in the *Proceedings* (and Alice Johnson (1916b vol 2: 101-3) in her edition of Fleming scripts) pointed out the systematic and sustained references to key/door from 1908 onwards. A number are given here:

Macs 12/9/1908:

> Tis not for every chance seeker after knowledge to obtain the key that unlocks the DOOR

Helen Verrall 23/9/1908:

> the open door

Winifred Coombe-Tennant 29/3/1909:

> ...when the Key slips in and opens the door of Truth the Key's work is only beginning

Diana Raikes 12/12/1909:

> openings of doors

Winifred Coombe-Tennant 4/2/1910:

> ...there was the door to which I found no key

Winifred Coombe-Tennant 5/2/1910:

> the word is DORR

Diana Raikes 6/2/1910:

> Oliver Lodge will be glad to know that the key we send it to open(?) be sure it will be opened by the seeker

Note: Helen Verrall was in Cambridge. Winifred Coombe-Tennant was at Saunton, Devon, for the first script and her parent's home, Tawelfa, Langland Bay, Wales, for the last two. The Macs were in Scotland. Diana Raikes was in Yorkshire. However, the Mac script of 9/12/1908 was seen by the Verralls on 26/9/1908 and by Winifred Coombe-Tennant on 6/5/1909.

Myers had obviously attached enormous importance to getting the links across, if the impact on Winifred Coombe-Tennant was anything to judge by. She gave Lodge (1911: 125) a description of her physical and mental state at the time. She found the script of 4/2/1910 the most scrappy she had ever received with its bits and pieces from other scripts and poems and she described the weird state she went into before the production of a short, explosive script the next day while staying at her parent's house, as mentioned above: 'I came downstairs from resting and suddenly felt I was getting very dazed and light-headed with a hot sort of feeling on the back of my neck... I felt my hands being as it were drawn together (she had been trying to read the *Times*)... I felt compelled to get writing materials and sit down... The enclosed Sc. Came...'

Winifred Coombe-Tennant 5/2/1910:

> You felt the call it it is I who write Myers. I need urgently to say this tell Lodge this word Myers Myers get the word I will spell it (scribbles) Myers yes the word(?) is DORR

Syringa

Winifred Coombe-Tennant also picked up in a script and D.I. the importance Myers attached to the syringa flower.

Winifred Coombe-Tennant 1/5/1910. Script and D.I. with Oliver Lodge present:
Script:

> (Note by Lodge. After about three-quarters of an hour of
> general conversation there ensued several minutes of silence, broken
> by her saying that she felt as if an impatient voice were saying
> 'What are you waiting for?' So we prepared for script; and,
> immediately we were ready, it began as follows)
> Myers. Syringa. Ask him if he understood.
> Lodge. No, I do not think that I have understood, — not yet
> Myers. There is a point in it. Ask Piddington.
> Lodge. I thought that perhaps it had to do with Piddington's
> No. 7 (see Sevens cross-correspondence)
> Myers. My own life. Not Piddington's Post Letter. My own life I
> myself. Let Pid think it over.
> Lodge. Then I understand that 'Syringa' is connected with
> something in your own private life, and that either I or Piddington
> may find out that something definite is meant by it.
> Myers. Precisely. Precisely. Precisely.
> Lodge. Then it is true that the word Syringa did come to
> me for some reason.
> Myers. Yes. Try for a D.I. and come back to Sc if I tell you F.

D.I.

> There is a reason why Syringa should be known to me in my
> own life. It came to you because of your question a little time
> ago as to whether I knew what you had been reading lately. You
> will see the point. Beatrice and seven circles.
> Lodge. I know that. That is Dante, but I was not reading-
> Dante.
> Myers. No, I know, but there is an analogy.
> Lodge. Very well. I do not understand at present.

As has been seen, syringa stood as a symbol for Myers and Annie Marshall and their love, and the description of that love in Myers' unexpurgated autobiography. In the D.I., Myers linked it quite appropriately to the love and support Beatrice gave Dante as he moved upwards through the circles towards Paradise, and the same symbol was used later for the Palm Maiden, May Lyttelton, spiritually supporting the Knight, Arthur Balfour. Winifred Coombe-Tennant did not see the relevance of the remark till she later read the unexpurgated autobiography for the first time on 9/10/1910, having been lent it by Lodge (Lord 2011: 56). In the stress of the sitting, Lodge did not appear to have picked up the importance and relevance of syringa. There were demands on sitters as well as mediums as the cross-correspondences developed and the maintenance of sustained attention was never easy.

By 1911 a substantial body of quite dense literary material had been accumulated and Lodge was keen to clarify with the communicators the value and purpose of this. In a sitting with Winifred Coombe-Tennant on 9/2/1911 he posed a question to Gurney which a number of students of the scripts have raised in later years:

> We have lately had long lists of quotations, so many and so widely supplied that it would appear as if cross-correspondences must occasionally occur by accident...We think that sceptics will claim that the cross-correspondences are accidental; also that the meaning is so obscure that we may miss it...

Winifred Coombe-Tennant 9/2/1911:

> Woven strands...
> Pick out the golden thread...Wait. To recall one beloved. Browning wrote of it...The flute and the breath and the music.

Gurney in his reply stressed the importance of selecting the key points in a script and, as an example, gave a quotation from Browning's *La Saisiaz* – 'But the soul is not the body: and the breath is not the flute' – which Winifred Coombe-Tennant had never read. These references were early allusions to the Palm Maiden story, the predominant focus of Winifred Coombe-Tennant's scripts.

In parallel with these complex scripts and Daylight Impressions with Myers and Gurney, Winifred Coombe-Tennant had to deal with the implications of a series of sittings with Leonora Piper which so disturbed her in their intensity and scope that much of the detail was kept very private. Her own scripts had urged her to sit with Leonora Piper: and she had a number of sittings under Lodge's supervision from late in 1910 to early 1911 (Lord 2011, Johnson 1934c). In them Gurney said he loved her (Winifred) and wanted her to have another child and one that in some way would be spiritually his. She was distressed by this since she had found giving birth very difficult in the past and she had no plans to have another child after Alexander, who had been born in November 1909. But the communicators seemed insistent that she have one, and one, the scripts later implied, who was destined to have a profound and positive impact on humanity.

It was becoming increasingly clear that Winifred Coombe-Tennant's scripts shared some of the characteristics of the other automatists' scripts in terms of their literary allusiveness, but, in general, they were more accessible and dramatic and began to provide clues which revealed that there were larger purposes than paranormal literary puzzles behind them.

It was also apparent that the communicators were deliberately using Winifred Coombe-Tennant's strong maternal drive as a central emotional energy or fuel to get these messages across. There is no doubt that she had a very strong maternal streak. This sense is caught in Evan Walter's painting of her and her two young sons, Alexander and Henry, playing dominoes on a pink carpet, her left hand on Henry's left shoulder and her gaze on him, intense, instructing, protective (Lord 2007: 61).

The Affair with Gerald Balfour

Gerald Balfour eventually expressed an interest in meeting Winifred Coombe-Tennant and possibly sitting with her. In February 1911 she paid her first visit to his house, Fishers Hill, Surrey. He went to see her at Cadoxton in July 1911 and the affair began (Lord 2011). One can trace the rapid deepening of the relationship not only in her diary and their letters but it also spilled over into her scripts. The affair seems to have been a classic case of *coup de foudre*.

From her letters in the Houghton archive at Harvard: 20/7/1911 'you help me just by being my friend'; on 27/7/1911 she wrote to him, 'I shall not mind you seeing all my scripts, or recording <u>anything</u> once I know it is for you only'; on 2/8/1911, 'How wonderful the world is — the world as you have made it for me'; on 20/8/1911, 'if I stretch out my hand very very far above my head I shall be able to reach to somewhere near your foot's resting place; on 29/8/1911 she wrote re the scripts, 'You have the Key to these latest scs, but you and I will do no explaining except to each other'; on 31/1/1912, 'Yes, Darling we must work them over together... for I am like an intelligent child given a message to deliver that I don't quite understand & know to be beyond me'. Certainly, the Balfourian sense of intellectual superiority came out clearly when he tried to explain, in a letter of 8/11/1913, the Messianic Child references in her scripts: 'How funny of you not to know that Virgil and Augustus were contemporaries.' Then he outlined Virgil's Messianic Eclogue (see Mayor *et al.* 1907) to her and how Augustus then and Augustus Henry now were represented as bringing back the Golden Age of peace, prosperity, and stability (see last part of appendix 4).

From the scripts: a private passage withdrawn from 22/7/1911, 'If he appoint to meet thee Go thou forth' (the biblical language gave it respectability but there was another meaning which it did not require a Freud to excavate); in her script of 13/9/1911 Gurney insisted, 'never abandon her — <u>never</u>.'; in another script of 5/3/1912 which contained an abstract discussion of the mind–body relationship which her conscious mind found tedious, there was in the eighteen pages of scrawled pencil in the original the phrase, 'Gerald, & let it be your policy <u>ever</u> to let sleeping dogs lie never explain and never <u>deny</u>' (Houghton archive). This was a characteristic saying of hers in daily life, particularly as she tried to prevent her secret lives, as the mistress of a married man, and as an automatist, from leaking out and discrediting her social position and her later substantial and responsible work as a magistrate and a political and community figure.

She had increasingly, as her diary entries showed, been finding her husband Charles dull and far too conservative in politics for her tastes, and he was becoming contaminated by his association with his two difficult sisters and their family in-fighting. Fishers Hill and the connections with the Balfour circle presented an exciting alternative, offering access to a richer and more intellectually flexible environment. Moreover, Winifred Coombe-Tennant was growing in confidence as to her own abilities even if she initially framed her early letters to Gerald Balfour in the conventional language of subservient female adoration.

The relationship with Gerald Balfour entangled her in an increasingly complex and dynamic web of emotion and paranormality. In some superficial ways Balfour was a late-Victorian pin-up. He was tall and good looking with a charming smile if and when he smiled. He came from a wealthy Scottish aristocratic background and had strong establishment connections (see Hudson 2003: 57–65). He had been a politician and his brother Arthur had been prime minister and was, at the time of Gerald's first meeting with Winifred, still leader of the Conservative and Unionist Party. Yet there was a remoteness about him and a cold intellectuality which did not endear him to all. At Cambridge he had been known as the Blessed Virgin Mary because, no doubt, of that combination of a fine profile and a certain ethereality which shyness or indifference might produce. There was a self-absorption about him which made him a not particularly good judge of character, and Lady Jebb in her sharp and amusing letters on Cambridge life in the 1870s and 1880s commented on the 'cold, emotional nature' of the Balfours and how her own niece after three weeks in Florence, where Gerald Balfour had a villa and was writing his philosophic treatise on the pre-socratic philosophers, exploded that he was the most conceited man she had ever met (Bobbitt 1960: 174–6).

In 1887, Balfour married Lady Betty Lytton (Hudson 2003: 65), by all accounts a charming, vital, and warm-hearted woman, and her friendliness and sociability, to some extent, softened the edges of his personality. Indeed, Betty Balfour proved remarkably accepting of the affair as it developed, though one could argue that that was part of the mores of her class, and that the alternative, divorce, would have been unthinkable. Betty Balfour had had a wandering life as the daughter of Lord Lytton, diplomat, Viceroy of India, and poet. Her mother was a lady-in-waiting to Queen Victoria. Her sister Emily married the architect Lutyens (who designed Fishers Hill) and her other sister Constance became a militant suffragette.

Constance's letters edited by Betty provide an interesting insight into the psychology of the time. For example, in a long letter to Constance, Betty gave a detailed and thorough account of Gerald Balfour's verdict on Tolstoy's novel *Resurrection*, which ironically, in the light of later events, concluded that regarding sexual desire Tolstoy 'enormously exaggerated the part played in life by this passion' (Lytton 1925: 104–6).

Winifred Coombe-Tennant began to visit Fishers Hill at regular intervals and became, if a little uneasily, a member of the wider Balfour family, and her diary entries (Lord 2011) revealed the combination of pain, passion, and possessiveness that seethed through her on these occasions: 'The agony of this home to me, I who have no lot or part in it and yet whom Gerald places first in his life.' At some time that year they consummated their relationship and she became pregnant in July 1912. This, coupled with her sense of the importance of Daphne and her role as a mother of remarkable children, was reflected in a script of 1/12/1912 labelled very private which referred to Plato's children of the mind and the body:

> and the Newer Biology of the metetherial Eugenics which is almost an unmapped field.

She almost certainly had little knowledge of the detail of the education intended for the ablest children in Plato's Republic who were to be the guardians of the state (Ryan 2012: 58–63). For Plato, citizens were to be taught the 'golden lie' that there was a hierarchy of talent—bronze (workers), silver (soldiers), and golden (the philosopher-kings)—and there was to be a disciplined education appropriate to each type. Henry Coombe-Tennant was very much in the third golden category—that rare individual who could see beyond the illusions of art and the illusions of the senses to the world of forms beyond, where true wisdom and spirituality resided.

That script was written at Langland Bay, Winifred's mother's home, where she and Gerald had a few days together with her mother as chaperon. She described their perfect communion (Lord 2011) as they sat looking out to sea and he showed her a letter in which Betty had written that she accepted the situation.

Their child Augustus Henry arrived at 11.45pm on 9/4/1913, so both Gerald Balfour and his son shared the same birthday, which may have further increased their sense of wonder about this child. They began to feel that they were in the grip of powers beyond their control and Gerald Balfour on 21/2/1914 wrote: 'Does Babe respond in some mysterious way to the very touch of Father's letters', before pulling himself up straight with 'or is all that mere fancy, psychometric rubbish?' (Houghton archive). They came to believe that this child had a special role to play in the future of the world and that this role had been hinted at in the earlier scripts of other automatists and was increasingly being revealed in hers.

However, immediately after Henry's birth, Gerald Balfour had practical problems to sort out. He and Arthur Balfour were beginning to invest heavily in the exploitation of peat bog deposits in order to convert them into alternative sources of energy and he visited Denmark in April to monitor the situation. He and his brother stuck with these investments throughout their lives, losing a considerable amount of money in the process (Egremont 1980: 311-12). One wonders if there was any psychological connection between the pig-headness with which Gerald Balfour stuck with this investment and his belief in the correctness of his and Piddington's interpretation of scripts?

As Gerald Balfour increasingly became her chief sitter, her scripts seemed to go up an intellectual gear with the initial appearance of the Dark Young Man, Francis Maitland Balfour, the embryologist. From the script of 21/1/1912 onwards came testing interchanges between Gerald Balfour and Edmund Gurney. Balfour (slightly younger than F.W.H. Myers) was at Cambridge with a particularly gifted group of men, almost all of whom were referred to in the scripts—his brother Frank, Leaf, Butcher, Maitland, A.T. Myers, Verrall, and Gurney. His interest in metaphysics manifested itself early on. As Leaf (Leaf, C. 1930) stated, 'Gerald was the most purely metaphysical of us all, and retired for a time to an almost eremitic solitude in a villa outside Florence in order to develop a complete metaphysical system... I spent three or four weeks with him in close communion there. After breakfast he used to retire to his thinking room, trying to work out his system of ultimate categories of thought...' Of Gurney Leaf wrote, comparing him to the historian Maitland, 'for wit and humour in conversation he was at least a good second to Maitland, and he shared with him a love of speculative inquiry which made him a master of subtle dialectic'. William James also greatly admired Gurney and thought that he would have done even greater things, 'some big philosophic achievement', had he survived (Skrupskelis 1998: 429-30).

It is not surprising, therefore, that the interchanges between these two should have had the strong flavour of a Cambridge tutorial of the late nineteenth century, and that reading the scripts one could easily forget that one of the participants was discarnate. As the intermediary, Winifred Coombe-Tennant complained in irritation, impatience, and puzzlement on a number of occasions at the abstract nature of these conversations. These interchanges, sometimes in automatic writing but mainly in Daylight Impressions, were in quality way beyond much though not all of the 'inspirational' channelling of the last hundred and fifty years, and yet they are almost unknown in comparison. The following is a characteristic extract.

21/1/1912 (Gerald Balfour present):

G.W.B. Is the subliminal to be
regarded as a number of distinct, or at all events distinguishable,
centres of consciousness?

He says, Ranges of varying depth. Tell me again, slowly.
(Question is repeated.)

It's One: and an enlightening point of view — I think it is —
is to conceive of it as allied and distinguishable...
grouped round one nucleus. He says, Your interpretation of centres of consciousness may not be mine

G.W.B. Are the centres of consciousness of the subliminal related to each other in a manner analogous to the relation of the subliminal to the supraliminal?

Wait. Something about centres of cognition. He says, Tentacles
of the star-fish. Interaction, he says, is right. The supraliminal
and the subliminal ebb and flow; and he says that the profundities
of the subliminal which grade right up and merge into what I've
spoken of as the transcendental self,...he says, if you are going to
confuse any of this with the whole question of secondary and tertiary
personalities and their respective memories of each other, you'd be
making a mistake.

Edmund, you do bore me so — (comment by Winifred Coombe-Tennant)

G.W.B. Are supraliminal and sub
liminal separate in a manner analogous to the separateness of
different human beings?

BOSH! (very loud and emphatic) different aspects of the
same thing.

G.W.B. I'm not putting forward a doctrine, but only asking
a question. How the same thing can be both one and many has
always given rise to difficulties. What I wished to know was
whether supraliminal and subliminal are distinct in a manner
analogous to the distinctness of different human beings?

Not in that sense. He says that's extremely important. I've
got your thought, G. My answer is, No, not in that sense. It's
very difficult, but he says, what is the relation between the human
being and the Absolute? He says, Answer me that.

G. W. B. That is the most difficult question in Philosophy.

He says, It's the Absolute on its way to self-consciousness...
...there **is** an analogy between the supraliminal
and the subliminal, and the individual rooted in the Absolute
and the Absolute. And he says, You've got it now, and he says,
No bones broken — and he says to me, Yon know, dear, I feel

sometimes I must appear to you like the Devil when he said,
Cast thyself down; but, he says, if only you'll go blindly there'll
be no pieces to pick up. And he says, I really got what I wanted
in answer to Gerald, and I believe he'll make it clear.

G.W.B. Is there any harm in asking questions like these?

He says, If you'll ask them realising the difficulties we have
got to encounter, and not mistaking a poor result for anything
more than a failure to inform, you'll do no harm, and help us to
break through.

It is important to note that Gerald Balfour was dissatisfied with what he felt was a lack of clarity in Myers' writings on the subliminal self which he, Balfour, expressed in his SPR presidential address (1906: 373–96). He here took the opportunity to explore the matter further and was roundly rebuffed by Gurney on a couple of points. Gerald Balfour hypothesised that the subliminal selves were separate selves and might communicate by telepathy. The script intelligence's response was subtle and cautious, hinting at a fluid and organic relationship between only apparently discrete centres of consciousness and distinguishing them clearly from the pathology of secondary and tertiary personality (in other words what is now called dissociative identity disorder).

In a later equally dense Daylight Impression of 11/5/1912, Gurney and Gerald Balfour discussed the three main theories of body/mind relationships current at the time, again, much to Winifred Coombe-Tennant's irritation. However, the philosophical positions referred to in the script—parallelism, epiphenomenalism, interactionism—were all examined in Gerald Balfour's article (1909) in the *The Hibbert Journal* and, as has been seen, Winifred Coombe-Tennant took that journal.

The Story of the Palm Maiden (May Lyttelton)

But, as well as the dense material on process, another set of compelling communications erupted in her scripts.

Winifred Coombe-Tennant 31/3/1912 (written on Palm Sunday at Eastbourne):

Gurney it is a new strand that I want you to grasp
to-day...
the message is not for you and is not from me through me it comes but I
am only a channel and you likewise are only a channel

Begin now
Day the day it is to which an allusion is wanted not the date
but the day It moves according to the seasons according to
the Moon but it is the day that is full of meaning the Entry
say that amid the throng who sang how fickle is the mob the

stainless years what is the quotation beneath the sky
Momento mori
Pass on
yes say that
Oh memory cast down thy wreathed shell the graves of
long ago

Piddington and Balfour realised later in the year that this and other scripts referred to May Lyttelton, Arthur Balfour's love, who had died on Palm Sunday in 1875, with its emphasis on the moveable date and the brief allusion to Christ's entry into Jerusalem riding on an ass. In addition, there were allusions to poems by Tennyson, Hood, Rossetti, and Wilde on the loss of a loved one. The Daylight Impression of April 14th furnished more indirect detail concerning the personality, appearance, and names of Mary (May) Catherine (Kate) Lyttelton. The name Catherine was played on in a variety of ways in the scripts: Catherine Coronaro in Browning's *Pippa Passes* (Hist! said Kate), St Catherine of Sienna, the Catherine Wheel, and so forth.

Winifred Coombe-Tennant. G.W.B. present. 14.4.1912:

> She's quite young. [Laughs] What amazing fashions!
> Oh, don't look so sad.
> She says, It was for him, it was for him. She says, not for
> them, it was for him.
> She isn't speaking to me, but I can hear those words, and they
> belong to her She is such a curious-looking figure—Her hair
> done—She's very attractive;—gentle-looking.
> Oh! [sighs.] Edmund says The Lily and the Wheel.
> [making a, circular motion with her hands] round and round
> like fireworks.
> Hist!—something about the dogs being fed. Hist! said Kate.
> 'tis only the boy carolling as he gives the hounds their messes.
> Do you know the dark young man? He says to me, Try
> Sienna. And he says, A variant of the wheel, but not a Highland
> Mary.

It was Piddington, in long and intense discussion with Gerald Balfour in the late summer of 1912, who finally began to crack the code of these scripts of March and April 1912. One can almost still feel the mounting excitement in his letters to Lodge during that period. On 3/8/1912 he wrote to him, with regard to the Palm Maiden case, 'there have been scores of references to it in Fleming, M.V. & H.V. (especially H.V.) scripts from 1903 onwards!' (SPR/35). And after further intensive study, he saw Francis Maitland Balfour as the prime mover behind the plan 'in all the scripts— M.V., H.V., Fleming, Coombe-Tennant, & Piper—the same symbols for F.M.B. are found... I believe Darwin is in it...'

The Palm Maiden, Mary Catherine Lyttelton was born on 26/5/1850 and died of typhus on Palm Sunday 21/3/1875. She was tall and slim with an interesting rather than beautiful face. She had brown eyes and glorious hair with golden lights in it. She was an intelligent and independently minded young woman and the young Arthur Balfour came to know her and her family well. There were plenty of points of contact. There were eight Balfour children and fourteen Lytteltons. The Balfour's country seat was Whittingehame in the lowlands of Scotland, and the Lyttelton's was Hagley Hall in Worcestershire, but both families had London town houses. Arthur Balfour's home was 4 Carlton Gardens and the Lyttelton's was in Portland Place. Most of the Lyttelton boys went to Trinity College, Cambridge, and Spencer Lyttelton was Arthur Balfour's great friend there. The families made music together in both houses. May Lyttelton was an excellent pianist and Spencer had a fine singing voice (Balfour, J. 1958–60). The direct and outgoing Lytteltons seemed to release something in Arthur Balfour who, as the eldest son, and brought up by an intensely evangelical mother, was on the surface initially a little more inhibited.

There was tragedy in May's life for both the young men she had loved before Arthur Balfour had died, but she gradually came out of the depression associated with this and began to see Balfour, whom she had originally thought bright but a little superficial, in a more serious light (Fletcher 1997). She wrote to her brother Arthur, later Bishop of Southampton, 'The more I know of him the more I respect his talent and character'. May was no lightweight. She had read many of the same books as her brother while he was studying for his moral science tripos. Her sister Lavinia believed that an engagement was imminent and heard May, in her delirium, talk of Arthur during her last few days (Roy 2008: 207–8). But he had left it all too late. Shattered by her death he gave Spencer Lyttelton an emerald ring that his mother, Blanche, had given to him, with instructions that it was to be placed on May's finger and buried with her. He later had made a silver bronze casket (engraved with flowers and a text from Corinthians XV: 53,54) for the lock of May's hair that Lavinia had kept: 'For this corruptible must put on incorruption and this mortal must put on immortality. But when this corruptible shall have put on incorruption and this mortal shall have put on immortality, then shall come to pass the saying that is written, Death is swallowed up in victory.' (See p. 108.)

The Knight (Arthur Balfour)

Winifred Coombe-Tennant heard from Gerald Balfour, in April 1915, that his brother would like a sitting with her having read some of her scripts and been very interested in them (Lord 2011). Staying at Fishers Hill she sat with him on 22/4/1915 just two days after he had made a swift visit by destroyer (45 minutes across the channel) to see the situation at the front

(Lord 2011). (Arthur Balfour had been invited by Asquith, despite their political differences, to make an active contribution to the direction of the war.)

The script was a lightly symbolic one.

Winifred Coombe-Tennant 22/4/1915:

> <u>Elsewhere</u>—not much can be attempted now but hints and previsions enough for the seeing eye to recognize…Arthur A circle a <u>wheel</u> thus a flaming wheel do you understand? I think a Palm

She had another sitting with him on 29/4/1915 at 4 Carlton Gardens where Gerald Balfour told her as a 'profound secret' that Italy was going to come into the war on the Allies' side (Lord 2011: 165-6). She went into the Long Room, formerly the Music Room, where some of Burne-Jones' Perseus cartoons were displayed. She entered before Arthur Balfour came in and she spent some time looking at the pictures. She wrote a script, 'mostly in trance conditions' the note stated. There were specific references to the Lyttelton coat of arms, the Moors Head, the scallop shells, the motto, and to Holman Hunt's *Light of the World* (kept at Keble College, Oxford, where Lavinia had been the wife of Warden Talbot). According to the script May Lyttelton walked in that room with children who had died, children who were unborn, and with Daphne. She walked with a candle (drawn in the script) and she was named La Madonna della Candela. Winifred Coombe-Tennant appeared to describe the room as it was in the early 1870s (one must remember that Winifred Coombe-Tennant was not born till 1/11/1874), as if she were sharing May Lyttelton's perspective and memories. As well as the symbolic references above which over the years became very familiar to Gerald Balfour and Piddington there were more precise and personal touches reminiscent of conventional mediumship:

> Did a lady with very long fingers make music in this room?…I feel music coming out of walls when there were fewer pictures in it…Wasn't there a man who sang here? A very tall man? But the music came from the lady

Could Winifred Coombe-Tennant have picked up this sort of information from the press or from society gossip at 2 Richmond Terrace? At first sight this message seems very impressive, but it is not watertight evidence. To his credit Gerald Balfour (1920: 181) noted that Winifred Coombe-Tennant might have read in the book *Memorials of Edward Burne-Jones* that the Perseus series were intended as 'as set of pictures to ornament a music room'. Whatever the source, Winifred Coombe-Tennant found Arthur Balfour a sympathetic sitter, and Gerald Balfour later told her that he 'was intensely interested and excited in the script I had had' (Lord 2011).

She visited 4 Carlton Gardens again on 15/7/1915. After Alice Balfour had shown her to the Long Room, and then left her alone, she began to sense a number of unseen presences and felt herself overshadowed by the Palm Maiden for: 'the only thing in the room that jarred on my sense of "remembered familiarity" was the loose covers on the chairs; also I felt there was more furniture in the room than belonged to *my* time' (Balfour 1920: 196). She seemed to be accessing May's memories as she did on a number of occasions with Francis Maitland Balfour's. Yet these shifts, or sharing of identities, powerful though they were, were limited and controlled. And she was able to switch from the dazed state of the trance script or the Daylight Impression within a reasonable period of time in order to cope with the strenuous and tiring wartime travelling that her local and national suffrage and war work required. She would sometimes make the round trip by rail from London to Cadoxton in forty-eight hours or less, on occasions after three or four hours of continuous committee work (Lord 2011).

She immediately posted the above script to Gerald Balfour and they discussed and went through it together the following day. This, of course, compromised their objectivity but it has to be stated that the symbols that occurred in this script were also to be found in the scripts of automatists outside the magic and intimate circle of Winifred Coombe-Tennant and Gerald Balfour. They were the familiar ones: Diana, Berenice, a candle, candelabrum, musical chords, allusion to Abt Vogler, Sursam [sic] Corda, Mont Auban, the snowy peaks, aes triplex, the Child of Destiny, St Francis, etc. (See appendix 4 for explanatory comments on the symbolism.)

The most impressive and significant sitting with Arthur Balfour was on 19/6/1916. It was particularly interesting both in content and context. Balfour had just come from an interview with the King—hardly far to come from 4 Carlton Gardens—and was, in general, under considerable pressure. As First Lord of the Admiralty he had to deal with the fallout after the Battle of Jutland. (He was strongly criticised for the depressing and laconic nature of the announcement of the outcome of the battle which seemed to give the impression that the Germans had triumphed: see Adams 2007.) There were continuing tensions in cabinet over Ireland after the Easter Rising in April; there was general dissatisfaction with the prosecution of the land war; the German submarine campaign was continuing to bite and threatened to expand; Kitchener had been drowned on his way to Russia; and there was some negative comment on Arthur Balfour's accepting the Order of Merit from the King in the Birthday Honours. Nevertheless, despite all this, he still found the time to lunch with Winifred Coombe-Tennant, have a sitting in the Long Room with her, have a detailed conversation with his sister Nora afterwards about it, and late at night to go through and check the written record (Lord 2011: 191; Balfour 1920: 332–9).

Winifred Coombe-Tennant 19/6/1916:

> A slender girl with quantities of hair worn in heavy plaits—I see her standing in the glade of a Park—over-arching trees…
> She is standing close to a young man with rather curly hair parted in the middle and small semi-whiskers—can you recognise him?
> …Berenice's vow. She cut the lock from her head…It has been said Ariadne and Berenice…The lock of hair—that is the link—is that clear…
> All these Classical allusions are scattered about and disguise a reality that touches the Blessed Damozel—is that clear? The stars in *her* hair were seven…The lock of hair Berenice The Symbol…

To Arthur Balfour it was clear that the script was referring to the grounds of Hagley Hall, May's home. There were references to Francis Maitland Balfour, the Talbots of Keble, and a description of the young Arthur Balfour himself. If one stands outside the romantic, aristocratic story, one might not find the above particularly impressive in terms of mental mediumship. There must have been many well-born young women with fine locks of hair standing in the grounds of their family estates; and pictures of the young Arthur Balfour with his hair parted in the fashionable way of the late 1860s/early 1870s would not have been difficult to access. However, the unmistakable reference to a lock of hair cut from a woman's head, linked to the general script symbolism of Ariadne, Berenice, and the Blessed Damozel, was particularly remarkable.[2]

Arthur Balfour then told Gerald Balfour after the sitting that he had made a silver box for a lock of May Lyttelton's hair which had been cut off either shortly before or at death. Lavinia Talbot had showed it to Arthur Balfour and 'He said "I know what I can do"' and then he had the silver box made. He took great trouble about it and suggested the design. He chose all the symbolic flowers to be engraved on it—Forget-me-not, Pansy, Passion flower, Rosemary' (Balfour 1920: 8). Gerald Balfour's wife, Betty, though knowing of and accepting the affair between Winifred and Gerald, was still prepared to research on their behalf. She saw the box in Mrs Talbot's (née Lyttelton) sitting room. The hair rested on a lining of purple velvet and was unchanged, a rich auburn. As mentioned above, the Palm Maiden had been known for her wonderful hair in the family: naturally wavy, very fair in childhood, later becoming dark brown, thick and with 'golden lights'. The investigators were aware that hair references were important in the scripts but the episode of the cutting off of the hair and placing it in the silver box was barely known till 1916.

---

2 Berenice's hair taken from the temple became the constellation Coma Berenices. Ariadne's Crown placed in the sky by Dionysius also became a constellation.

Thus far the symbolic structure had a certain romantic appeal. It seemed designed to illustrate the Palm Maiden's role in providing spiritual support and illumination for the Knight (Arthur Balfour) as consolation for her loss and to help him in the late renaissance of his career. But the obvious question the independent observer must pose is why there was any need for this complexity at all. According to Piddington and Balfour, that would be to mistake the purpose of the communicators. In life they had been acutely aware of the difficulties involved in disproving that evidential material from mediums about the dead had not been obtained by telepathy or clairvoyance from the living. Therefore, expanding and elaborating on the Alice Johnson thesis, it was argued that Myers, Gurney, and Sidgwick were encoding their messages in a cryptic structure to which no one would have the key until they provided it. In other words, it was almost like a sealed envelope test. The early scripts remained hidden in the envelope of symbolic complexity till the discarnates through Winifred Coombe-Tennant provided the key, or keys.

But what did Arthur Balfour, the main focus of a large number of the scripts, really feel about it all: that a dead lover, brother, and Cambridge University friends, and an intimate friend from the Souls' coterie that he had led, were trying to make contact with him and with Gerald? He was certainly sceptical about the wider aspects of the Plan (Roy 2008: 498), but his views on the more personal elements referring directly to him were probably more nuanced and complex. His latest biographer (Adams 2007) has played down the May Lyttelton story and rather cynically suggested that he used it to avoid entanglements in later life. This certainly does not accord with the actions he took at the time or his continuing involvement with the Lyttelton family both with regard to the ring and the casket for May Lyttelton's hair and that, for many years, he regularly spent the Palm Sunday anniversary of her death with her sister Lavinia, and that on the eve of Alfred Lyttelton's marriage to Laura Tennant he wrote, 'you know, dear old man, that I always think of you as a brother; as I used to hope you would be not alone in thought but in name also' (Balfour, J. 1958–60).

Gerald Balfour in old age told Jean Balfour that his brother was rather incredulous when first informed of the Story but he believed him to be more moved than 'he allowed himself to appear' (Balfour, J. 1958–60: 121). Gerald Balfour also suggested a reason for Arthur Balfour's psychic imperviousness to her presence (Balfour, J. 1958–60: 122). 'It is permissible to conjecture that a solution to the problem is to be found in the distinction between the subliminal and the supraliminal consciousness—that the subliminal self of the Knight may always be open to the Maiden, but that she cannot get even into one-sided touch with his *normal* self except through the mediumship of some person still in the body...' Yet any speculation about Arthur Balfour's inner thoughts was and is pretty fruitless. As Jean

Balfour stated (1958–60: 169–70): 'He was intimate with no one, he was extremely reserved, and he left no private papers beyond a small photograph of M.L. in a locked box.' And when it was mooted in middle age he marry a certain lady 'for the sake of the family inheritance' he said: 'But she must understand that I have no heart to offer her—nothing but ashes.'

He was not the least antagonistic to psychical research. He was an intellectually curious individual, interested in the arts, literature, certain kinds of music, philosophy, science, and technology. He did not seek the assurance of survival through psychical research, his own Anglican upbringing and intuition gave him that, but he was interested in the light it shed on human personality and on the strengths and weaknesses of the scientific methodology. There had been séances at his home, 4 Carlton Gardens, in the 1870s, but it is not clear how much he was involved in them, for he was travelling abroad with Spencer Lyttelton during part of that time (Young 1963: 37; Egremont 1980: 50). He was quite happy to succeed Sidgwick as president of the SPR in 1893 at the very time he was leading the Conservative opposition to the Liberals in the House of Commons. As has been seen he met Trix Fleming and was much interested in her, and in July 1911 he had Annie Besant, the Theosophist leader, to supper where he and Gerald Balfour discussed matters Theosophical with her (Egremont 1980: 250).

Arthur Balfour thought that men of science should not ignore what he called 'well-attested facts which did not naturally fall into the framework of the sciences or of organised experiences as they conceived it'. He asserted in his presidential address (1894) that unshowy, even boring, experiments in telepathy were more likely to convince the scientist rather than the more startling phenomena: 'If we could repeat very definite and very simple experiments, which do not fit in with hitherto accepted conclusions sufficiently often and under tests sufficiently rigid, it would be impossible for physicists to ignore our results.' He had the Mrs Sidgwick/Alice Johnson tests with George Albert Smith in mind (Gauld 1968: 359) and his words appeared to be anticipating the later experimental methods of J.B. Rhine (1937).

He also wrote on the philosophy of science and its relationship to religion, pointing out that science could only take one so far and that there were grounds to be cautious about the objectivity and ultimate reality of both its fundamental premises and its methodology: for example, the law of universal causation and the uniformity of nature were beliefs and not in strict truth provable; and that even the theory of evolution (almost by its own premises) might be discarded when it was no longer of evolutionary value! He had articles published in the philosophy journal *Mind* (1881, 1884) and produced three major books: *A Defence of Philosophical Doubt* (1879), *Foundations of Belief* (1895), and *Theism and Humanism* (1914), based on his earlier Gifford lectures. He was no 'dabbler': the Gifford lectures, for example, were prestigious, and the Gifford lecturers included amongst their number William James and Henri Bergson, and his arguments were in the sophisticated and sceptical tradition of David Hume (Root 1978; Gray 2011: 66–70).

The Wizard of Melrose (Francis Maitland Balfour)

But if the most passionate communicator in the scripts was May Lyttelton, the strategic mastermind behind it all was Francis Maitland Balfour. He had been intellectually and emotionally very close to two of his brothers, Arthur and Gerald. These three had less in common with the wilful Cecil and the more mediocre Eustace. He showed outstanding promise as a morphologist and his death in 1882 in a climbing accident was mourned not just by his family but also the wider scientific community. Again, the familiar pattern was identified by Balfour and Piddington—symbols with meaningful links to him were spread across the scripts of the automatists He appeared most vividly and explicitly as the Dark Young Man (there was a photograph of him suggesting a dark thoughtfulness) in Winifred Coombe-Tennant's scripts and another frequent highly appropriate symbol for him was Michael Scott, the Scholar/Wizard from Walter Scott's *The Lay of the Last Ministrel*. For, as has been seen, it was claimed that Frank Balfour's 'wizardry' in 'spiritual eugenics', in conjunction with Gurney, helped to shape and mould the Messianic Child (see appendix 4 for further symbols and their explanation).

The Peacock Lady (Laura Tennant/Lyttelton)

An intimate friend of both Arthur and Gerald Balfour's, Laura Tennant, was also identified as a communicator in the scripts. Her marriage in 1886 to Alfred Lyttelton, brother of May and also a close friend of Arthur Balfour's, was seen by many in society as a perfect match. Lyttelton already had a public image as an aristocratic sportsman of legendary prowess, and Laura Tennant had a reputation as a highly intelligent and charismatic young woman who was a renowned breaker of hearts. Laura and her sister Margot (later the second wife of Asquith the Prime Minister) were daughters of the fabulously wealthy Scottish industrialist Sir Charles Tennant (no relation to the Tennant family that F.W.H. Myers married into). They were brought up with an unusual degree of freedom for the time and their entry into society in the early 1880s caused a sensation. They became part of a small group of largely aristocratic friends that eventually became known as 'The Souls' (Ellenberger 1982). Laura had many admirers and Gerald Balfour actually became briefly engaged to her. A.C. Benson met Laura Tennant at a lunch given by Myers at Leckhampton in July 1884 and thought her brilliant and witty. Edward Lyttelton (Alfred's brother and an Eton Master) wrote in his diary with unreflective fraternal pride: 'a social triumph... the cleverest (as I believe) young woman in England to marry the finest specimen of man' (see Newsome 1980). Sadly, she died, on Easter Eve 1886, shortly after the birth of her son Christopher, who himself was to die in early childhood. The glamour of her life and the tragedy of her death were well known in society and, to some extent, in the press. This must be borne in mind when one tries to assess the references to her in the scripts.

Winifred Coombe-Tennant, 12/4/1914:

> L that's the first letter A then the next is like this U RA. NO that's an O BILI then there's that S...I am the Resurrection. The tomb where no man had been laid. The Eve of the Feast...The door set wide to every wind of pain (a reference to Murray's translation of the Medea). Some one said he couldn't say it in the Greek words because I shouldn't know them,— and it's very hard to get. Oh, what an odd funny word! Is there such a word as <u>glossolaly</u>, or something like that? Oh, I can't understand. Somebody said to me Lady Elcho It's very confusing. It's a little slumber song—a sort of little crooning song—a sort of hush-a-byesong. M

There is in the above a strong if indirect reference to the Peacock Memorial of Burne-Jones to Laura in Mells Church, Somerset, and to the reading by Margot Tennant of Laura's will (Lady Elcho was bequeathed a cradle), but both these items were in the public domain.

Perhaps more subtle and persuasive is Piddington's assertion (in his comment on a Margaret Verrall script of 15/7/1911) that, with regard to the symbols that had been used to compare and contrast the personalities of the Palm Maiden and the Peacock Lady, the former had symbols that emphasised love, devotion, and service, and the latter those that suggested a capacity merely to enchant. Many of the symbols eventually identified for her seem to play on this theme: Peacock Lady; Cleopatra; Rosamund; a Siren; a Mermaid; Circe; Dolores; Helen of Troy; a Will o' the Wisp; a Wizard of Delight. There is some evidence for this from their lives. May was an intense and passionate individual, strongly committed to the individual she was in love with at the time, and Laura was much more 'flighty'. In her book *Edwardians in Love*, Anita Leslie (1973) described the way she 'shamelessly' flirted with A.G. Liddell while Alfred Lyttelton was paying court to her, and, as has been seen, Gerald Balfour was so taken with her that he proposed marriage.

The Messianic Child (Henry Coombe-Tennant)

Winifred Coombe-Tennant began to find emerging in her scripts predictions that her youngest child Henry was to be both remarkably gifted and to have a truly remarkable destiny. She had been led to expect this, as has been mentioned, from the Piper scripts of 1909–10 (well before she met Gerald Balfour). So, she monitored Henry's development, looking keenly for signs of the outstanding intellectual and leadership qualities that would be necessary for the high calling anticipated for him. She meticulously collected examples of Henry's precocity and a number of them remain in her archive at Harvard, including a thin rectangle of card with sharpish criss-crossed lines. It was headed, The Wise One Dec 19/14, with the comment that it was superior to most children's of that age owing to the firmness and detailed nature of the marks. But her private adoration was matched by her public concern that nothing about these strange matters should leak out. She had real concern, as time went by, about the discretion of Oliver Lodge, who had been given a copy of the highly significant third volume of her scripts: ' — I fear he will now lend his copy to various cronies — his want of proper reticence disgusted me'. She felt he had considerably declined since she first knew him (Houghton 2/4/1914).

The need for discretion was understandable given the outrageous messages in the scripts. According to Gerald Balfour and Piddington, as has been briefly outlined, symbolic messages in the scripts described a process of spiritual eugenics, the development and shaping of spiritually advanced individuals who would benefit humanity and eventually bring about world peace. It would be a long and arduous task, and there would be much pain and sacrifice on the way. That meant that not all the individuals with promise would necessarily survive and that those that did might face war, struggle, and hardship. But the precise nature of the struggle was never clearly and fully spelled out in scripts, or why the deaths of certain children—Daphne, Antony, and Christopher Lyttelton— should have been regarded as sacrifices. One could hazard a guess, in terms of psychological comfort and motivation for the automatists who had lost young children, that their deaths could in some general way have been seen as contributing to the good of future humanity, but the specific idea of psychological eugenics, that in some way they were not up to standard and so should be discarded, was morally absolutely abhorrent. Margaret Verrall, who had lost a young daughter, found that aspect of the scripts too much to stomach.

8

The Later Scripts and Last Years of Margaret Verrall

Post-Mortem Communication from A.W. Verrall; and Interpretive Disagreements with Gerald Balfour and John George Piddington

Margaret Verrall's later scripts continued to be a mixture of clear and cryptic material with some scripts contributing to the Messianic theme of the Plan, even though at the time of writing she had absolutely no conception of that underlying purpose. Take, for example, a script of April 1907 which was begun at 8.30am in the train from Cambridge, and which was, despite its humble suburban context, a very clear expression of progressive evolution leading to the Golden City of God at some unspecified date in the future. The script was finished at 9.50am, with the train drawing into the station, and none of the other passengers any the wiser:

Margaret Verrall 29/4/1907:

> But I mean a wider thing, a universal country, the mother of us all...Not O fair City of Cecrops But Oh fair city of God...The city of Cecrops is violet and hoary look back at that. The Universal City is all colours and no colour but best described as a golden as a golden GLEAM.

Cecrops was the first King of Athens. Athens eventually moved towards a form of democracy. Rome and Jerusalem added other particular virtues: order, peace, spirituality, and wisdom. But the world city, the world civilisation was located in no one country and was for the benefit of all humanity.

As Margaret Verrall grew older her scripts also reflected more personal concerns. On 21/6/1911, which was a Wednesday, the day of the week often set aside for their writing sessions, she particularly thought of Trix Fleming and wondered what had happened to her. No doubt, through Alice Johnson, she would have been informed about the deaths of her parents and Trix Fleming's mental collapse, but it would certainly not have been possible to approach Rudyard Kipling or Colonel Fleming directly without making matters worse for Trix. Her script on that day was a poem (just the first of the two verses is quoted here).

Margaret Verrall 21/6/1911:

> The old dim oracles are half forgot
> The god himself if questioned answers not
> No smoke of incense rises to the sky
> The sacred fount of Castaly runs dry

One could argue that this referred to the end of Trix Fleming's mediumship. Castaly was a spring at the Oracle of Delphi, and Trix, quite possibly, was the Sybil who, it was indicated in early scripts, would come to join Margaret in the work.

Another example, and one involving both her scripts and Winifred Coombe-Tennant's, was linked to the death of her husband's great friend, Henry Butcher, on 29/12/1910. A Margaret Verrall script of 11/1/1911 stated that she would receive a message from someone else soon and that even she would have to believe.

The message came through Winifred Coombe-Tennant. It was late evening on 21/1/1911:

> Last night after I had blown out my candle and was just going
> to sleep I became aware of the presence of a man, a stranger,
> and — almost at the same moment — knew it was Henry Butcher.
> I felt his personality, very living, clear, strong, sweetness and
> strength combined. A piercing glance. He made no introduc
> tion, but said nothing. So I said to him, 'Are you Henry
> Butcher?' He said, 'No, I am Henry Butcher's ghost.' I
> was rather shocked at his saying this and said, 'Oh, very well,
> I am not at all afraid of ghosts or of the dead.'
> He said, ask Verrall (or A.W., or Dr. Verrall, I can't remember
> which, but I think it was 'Verrall' if he remembers
> our last conversation (or meeting) and say the word to him
> Ek e tee
> He said it several times. I said, 'Very well.' He seemed
> only to want to give that message and then he went in a hurry.
> I never heard the word Ek e tee in my life and don't know
> what it means but record this. He was alone to the best of my
> knowledge. I never felt a greater sense of vitality and strength
> than that which seemed to flow from him.
> P.S. I hadn't been thinking of him at all.

A.W. Verrall could not remember the conversation but Butcher had been staying with him shortly after he, Verrall, had published a paper in the *Classical Review* which partly discussed Hecate. One should note, in the above, Winifred Coombe-Tennant's palpable ignorance of both the name and the significance of Hecate and that, as well as appearing directly to

Winifred Coombe-Tennant, Butcher later communicated in a Margaret Verrall script.

Margaret Verrall 15/7/1911:

> Now go on It is a message from Henry Butcher that is attempted there Arthur would recognise we two read at the same time and talked together of an English book—put down the word Antony that is what I tried to say before a pearl dissolved Ask Arthur whether he cannot find the record of what I am trying to say in a composition book.

Margaret Verrall did some investigation (a composition book was a book containing material that could be used for translation exercises in the tripos) and found that Verrall had translated parts of Dryden's *Antony and Cleopatra* into Latin, but he could not remember ever discussing it with Butcher. However, her scripts encouraged her to expect more good quality evidence in the future.

Margaret Verrall 1/1/1912:

> The beat of those unseen feet which only the angels hear
> There is a point about the moon which you have not seen
> Perhaps I can make it clearer later on—Try now regularly
> to write. I think later on when you see what has been said
> to [Winifred Coombe-Tennant], it will help you but you
> are not to see her script for some months—remember that.
> See her when you
> can—
> Yours F W H M

The first part of this extract referred to symbolism that is explained in Part 2 (Shelley's poem *The Cloud*), and the second part suggested that there was good evidence to come through Winifred Coombe-Tennant. This, indeed, happened. After the death of Arthur Verrall in June 1912, over the next few years precise, dramatic, and vivid communications highly characteristic of him appeared in Coombe-Tennant scripts. Margaret Verrall knew that her husband had moved from a friendly but neutral attitude concerning psychical research towards a growing willingness to take it seriously. The Piper sittings with George Dorr and the classical knowledge therein displayed had been a major factor in this. Therefore, given his survival, and the extreme closeness and harmony of their marriage, one might expect Verrall to make every effort to prove his survival. In scripts of 6/7/1912, 13/8/1913, 17/8/1913, and 8/9/1913, an A.W. Verrall-like communicator manifested who set the investigators a large-scale cryptic puzzle to solve, reminiscent of the earlier cross-correspondences in some ways, except that the fragments of information were all contained within the scripts of the one automatist, Winifred Coombe-Tennant.

Verrall used several techniques to confirm his identity. First, he referred to a passage where a traveller hesitated to cross a torrential river and in the last script gave a reference to Dante which would make things clear. This turned out to be an essay of Verrall's (1913), *Dante on the Baptism of Statius*, in which Statius, a late first-century Latin poet, was metaphorically described by Dante as reluctant to declare his Christian belief (hesitating to cross the river). Second, he alluded to the one-horse dawn episode (in itself, because of its celebrity within SPR circles, of no evidential value) and linked it ingeniously to material he was working on at the time of his death. He referred to Gray's poem *The Progress of Poesy* in which the phrase a two-horsed charioteer was deployed comparing Milton and Dryden as poets. Third, the phrasing of the scripts, their slightly impatient, but amiable jossing, their theatrical stylishness, their love of comic songs and phrases, were all highly redolent of Verrall's speech patterns and interests.

Some extracts from Winifred Coombe-Tennant's scripts now follow.

6/7/1912 (Margaret Verrall's husband had died only a week before on 30/6/1912):

> Does she remember the passage in which there's a reference
> to a river? A traveller looks across it, and sees the inn where he wishes
> to be; and he sees the torrent and is torn both ways, half disliking
> to battle with the current, and yet desiring to be at his destination.
> Should it be possible to identify this passage, the matter would
> prove interesting.

13/8/1913 (note that this next script was over a year later and Verrall waxed indignant at the delay):

> HAS THE PASSAGE been identified about the traveller looking across a stream…Have this seen to, for he swears he will not here exercise any patience whatsoever. Not even about Lavender or Lub.
> Not a one-horse dawn, but a two-horsed chariot, though one-horsed in a way might fit, because as compared to another charioteer's exploits <u>his</u> were but a one-horsed affair. It is a poem I am alluding to—a man who drove two horses in a less ambitious manner. His predecessor—Does God exact day labour, light denied? <u>That</u> <u>ought</u> to make it clear.

And he continued again on 8/9/1913 with:

> He of the little patience demands now this third time (whether the references have been understood)…Dante makes it clear.

In addition to the reference to Verrall's essay on Statius, the phrase 'Lavender or Lub' was also highly characteristic of Verrall, who had been tickled by this phrase in *Punch* and changed it into 'Tavender or Tub' and used to chant it before taking his bath—a process which, of course, given his severe arthritis could ease his considerable pain.

This interpretation of the scripts was strongly challenged by the experienced psychical researcher Hereward Carrington, who argued that Balfour was just reading what he knew about the character and interests of Verrall into the scripts, and that he was making the blunder of a novice researcher. One could just as easily interpret the scripts, he asserted, as referring to Bunyan's *Pilgrim's Progress* and Christian's fear at crossing the deep and billowing River of Death before entering the Kingdom of Heaven. Carrington was a severe and trenchant critic of Gerald Balfour and M.A. Bayfield's assessment of the Statius material. Bayfield was a member of the SPR and an intimate friend of the Verralls. Carrington, in effect, accused them of wishful thinking and a predisposition to believe in A.W. Verrall's survival and that the evidence just did not support this. He argued that the scripts, rather than evidence of personal survival, 'represent... the piecing together of disjointed fragments of subconscious knowledge and subconscious memories; they have no systematic connection, and point to no "spirit" as their author'. Much of what was seen as evidence of character and personality was really the 'dramatic play' that planchette and automatic writing often displayed and which was mendacious and without substance, as Flournoy's work (1911 and translated by Carrington) had demonstrated. This was a weakness with the cross-correspondence evidence generally and the investigators should return to the scrupulous examination of high quality individual mediumship. (See Carrington 1914-15: 458-91; Bayfield 1914-15: 244-9; Balfour 1914-15: 221-43 on these issues.)

Carrington was particularly without mercy on one central weakness in Balfour's position. There were impatient references to Hair in a Temple and to the Pilgrim and these were privately interpreted by Gerald Balfour and Piddington as referring to the Palm Maiden's hair via the story of Berenice's hair, and to her love for Arthur Balfour, for whom pilgrim was another symbol. This information could not be revealed at the time, much to Carrington's slightly contemptuous irritation: 'Mr. Balfour says it has a hidden and very intimate and subtle connection with Dr. Verrall—too intimate and subtle, unfortunately, for publication!'

The second clutch of scripts highly characteristic of Verrall and also his co-communicator in this instance, S.H. Butcher, has been called the Ear of Dionysius case (Balfour 1918a: 197-244). The scripts were those of 26/8/1910, 10/1/1914, 28/2/1914, 2/3/1914, 2/8/1915, and 19/8/1915. Over the period of these scripts there were references to (Saltmarsh 1975: 106-23): the Ear of Dionysius, the stone quarries of Syracuse where prisoners were kept and where their conversations could be overheard because of the acoustic properties of the stone; the story of Polyphemus and Ulysses; jealousy; music; something to be found in Aristotle's *Poetics*; and satire. These individual allusions were not particularly difficult to spot but the problem was what was the point of them and what bound them together, and of whom was such a puzzle characteristic?

In the last script the key words Cythera, Cyclopean, Philox enabled the investigators to identify the satirical poem by Philoxenus of Cythera who, becoming too close to the tyrant Dionysius's mistress Galatea, was imprisoned in the quarries (the Ear of Dionysius). In revenge he wrote a satirical poem, *Cyclops or Galatea*, lampooning Dionysius (who was blind in one eye) as Polyphemus the Cyclops outwitted by Odysseus (Philoxenus).

As in the Statius Case there was a challenge to Gerald Balfour's interpretation, this time by Miss Stawell who, like Margaret, was a Newnham classicist (Wyles and Hall 2016). She asserted that, starting from the premise that survival was antecedently improbable (given, ironically, all the negative evidence scrupulously collected by the SPR including the failure of the Myers' sealed envelope experiment), the more probable explanation was unconscious telepathic leakage from Margaret Verrall. She also pointed out 'an astonishing lapse of memory on Dr. Verrall's part' with him stressing on 28/2/14 and 2/3/14 that his wife was not to hear anything yet about the matter and yet expressing surprise in the sitting of August 1915 that she had been told nothing (Stawell 1918: 260–9). She also pointed out that *Greek Melic Poets* (Smith, H. 1900), in which the above story was told, was quite well-known to Newnham students and she found it difficult to believe that Margaret Verrall had never come across it.

Again, as with other material, Gerald Balfour (1918b: 270–86) argued that the information communicated had been shaped and designed in a way suggestive of an external intelligence rather than the subliminals of either or both Margaret Verrall and Winifred Coombe-Tennant. Indeed, as Gauld (1982: 97–101) pointed out: 'The information which it gives... would need to be supplemented by an informed classical scholar before the Ear of Dionysius puzzle could be constructed from it... and deployed in the manner of persons who were masters of their subject...' And he quoted part of the script of 2/8/1915 to exemplify this:

> The Aural instruction was I think understood *Aural* appertaining to the Ear
> And now he asks HAS the *Satire* satire been identified
> The man clung to the fleece of a Ram & so passed out surely that is plain (i.e. Ulysses escaping from Polyphemus's cave) well conjoin that with Cytherea & the Ear-man...
> There is a satire
> Write Cyclopean masonry, why do you say masonry I said Cyclopean
> Philox He laboured in the the stone quarries and drew upon the earlier writer
> For his Satire jealously
> The story is quite clear to me and I think it should be identified

> A musical instrument comes in something like a mandolin thrumming...
> He wrote in these stone quarries belonging to the tyrant

This was not the vague, crafty rambling of much automatic writing. The intelligence communicating had a donnish love of precision and feeling for the right word—stressing *Aural*, avoid confusing with oral; using thrumming with mandolin; and signalling specific links between particular topics which together neatly assembled into the story outlined above.

During these years, Margaret Verrall, for her part, continued to produce material that fitted in ways of which she was only partially aware into the over all symbolism of the scripts.

Margaret Verrall 29/6/1911:

> Swan wing's beating–the swan's nest...
> A was once an apple pie...

For Piddington (1921: 109–17), these apparently innocuous lines were replete with meaning and significance. He argued that in this script there was a clear reference to John Ruskin's *Fors Clavigera* Letter XXVIII. In that letter Ruskin mused in his usual intense and breathless way on an old Florentine engraving of Theseus and Ariadne, incorrectly titled Abberrinto, the engraver having missed off the L which would have made it *Laberinto* (labyrinth). This stimulated Ruskin to a little aside on education: 'You miss the first letter of your lives; and begin with A for apple-pie, instead of L for love.' This, then, was seen by Piddington as another symbolic allusion to the Knight/Theseus/Arthur Balfour and the Palm Maiden/Ariadne/May Lyttelton story. Piddington also asserted that the swan references in scripts were often linked to these symbols since swans represented loyalty and were thus highly appropriate to that story. Hans Christian Anderson's *The Wild Swans*, Elizabeth Barrett Browning's *The Romance of the Swan's Nest*, and Wagner's *Lohengrin*, were all drawn on for allusive references (Piddington 1919: 294–8).

Margaret Verrall continued to be able to write almost wherever she was —in the train from King's Cross to Cambridge, at the seaside, and abroad. While at Pierre-a-Voir, on holiday, she was thoroughly told off by Edmund Gurney for writing verse:

Margaret Verrall 13/8/1912:

> I don't know why you will write verse—it would be much easier for both you & us if you wrote plain words that represent our thought. Remember it is not words we give you, thought is what we send to you, & you have an odd trick of translation which reproduces the thought in some form not natural to you—Try to drop this trick & put our thought in the simplest form.

She occasionally went to stay at Fishers Hill and to produce and discuss scripts there while Piddington and Gerald Balfour tried to convince her of the broader symbolic code that lay embedded in the writing of all the automatists. She had been told something, though not all, about this background early in October 1912, but she still felt she was not receiving the full story and that much remained fanciful. For example:

Margaret Verrall 12/10/1912:

> Fire and water Vinegar and Oil — these pairs do not mix yet both have their uses, and Fire and water may generate steam and [also] move the world — Don't try to interpret [sic] — just write only Greek fire and Roman water

This was seen by Piddington as a reference to *Aeneid* VII where Latinus King of the Latins had been told by his father's oracle not to marry his daughter Lavinia to Turnus or any other Latin, 'for foreigners shall come to be thy sons whose blood shall raise our names to heaven, and the children of whose race shall see... all the rolling world swayed under their feet' (Piddington 1919: 375). Lavinia married Aeneas and so initiated the line of Roman leaders which led in time to Augustus. Hence this script was seen by Piddington and Gerald Balfour as referring to the birth of the Messianic Child.

On the other hand, another script at Fishers Hill was pleasantly uncryptic and was just a description, in plain prose, of some of the conditions in the afterlife. As with many of the scripts, was the origin subconscious metaphysical speculation on her part, or a genuine but unverifiable description by the discarnates?

Margaret Verrall 17/10/1912:

> Never the place and the time And time is the first of
> your modes of thought to be forgotten by us — but it is
> recoverable by effort — And the disappearance of time does
> not prevent there being a sequence — but we do not have to
> project our thought into space which is the reason for no,
> which is what happens when we enter into relations with
> the world of action, & it is that that makes the time relation
> necessary —
> I can't use your pencil to record my thoughts on abstract
> subjects — I expect that you have greatly misunderstood
> my meaning — but the experiment was new & worth making

As Piddington and Gerald Balfour increasingly managed to map, interrelate, and understand the scripts, Margaret Verrall felt both irritated at her exclusion from the process and what she saw as the over-sophistication of their interpretations. Her diary entry, 17/7/1913, clearly indicated this: 'Yesterday I sent JGP an "ultimatum" saying that I could not work at SPR without knowing his conclusions concerning recent scts — up to a date to be arranged, — & that if I could not work at SPR, I should take to classics or English literature as I must have some literary occupation: practical work is so distasteful to me that it causes disproportionate fatigue.' She noted a little later that they had responded positively to her 'ultimatum' and were prepared to provide her with more detail (Salter A/3/5).

John George Piddington

Although Gerald Balfour had a very strong personal interest in interpreting the scripts in a particular way, he was fully supported and helped in this by his close friend and SPR colleague, John George Piddington. Who was he? What was he like as a man? And what were his qualifications as an interpreter of the scripts? These questions are as central to the understanding of the scripts as is knowledge of the relationship between Gerald Balfour and Winifred Coombe-Tennant, since Piddington worked out the methodology on which interpretation of the scripts was based and did by far the lion's share of the detailed assessment.

John George Piddington was originally John George Smith. He changed his surname in order to to avoid confusion with other Smiths who were members of the Society when he became heavily involved with the SPR. He came from a comfortable middle-class background. His family were carriers of letter and parcel trade to the continent (and across it) before the First World War — the company was called Continental Daily Parcels Express and also Vitesse Express (Ellis 1949). Piddington came up from Eton to Magdalen College Oxford in 1888, gaining a Second in Classics Mods in 1890 and a Third in Greats in 1892. The record was not distinguished but he had the family business to go into, and the results may have reflected the particular strengths and weaknesses of Piddington's cast of mind. According to the Magdalen archivist (Darwall-Smith, personal communication 2014): 'Until the 1960s, Classics at Oxford was taught in two very distinct chunks. In one's first five terms, leading up to Mods, one was taught nothing but Latin and Greek language and literature (mainly language at this date). For one's remaining seven terms, leading up to Greats, one left language and literature behind, and was taught ancient history and philosophy. There are cases of people who sailed through Mods, and then came seriously unstuck in Greats because they were not especially good at history or philosophy. The most notorious such case was A.E. Housman, who got a first in his Mods and actually failed Greats first time round. So it could be at least possible that Smith was not very good at either history or philosophy.'

He joined the SPR in 1890, becoming a member of the Council in 1899. On Myers' proposal he became Hon. Secretary, a post from which he resigned in 1907. As a successful business man he was particularly effective in building up funds for research, and from 1917–1921 acted as treasurer of the Society (Salter 1952: 708–16). In 1901 Piddington was living in Sloane Square with his wife Pauline and their daughter Leonora and four resident servants (Demarest 2014: personal communications). In 1911 he was living in Holy Well, Hook Heath, Woking, with his wife and daughter and he had five servants. His 1911 address was fairly close to Gerald Balfour's and they met regularly for golf and SPR business, and at some stage Piddington separated from his wife and, after the First World War, came to live with Balfour and Mrs Sidgwick at Fishers Hill. For almost twenty years the three were in regular contact about the cross-correspondences and the general policy and running of the SPR. They were particularly vigilant in guarding against the infiltration into the Society of the more credulous aspects of certain forms of Spiritualism. Given the ages of Gerald Balfour and his sister Eleanor (and the private nature of much of the material), the heavy responsibility for interpreting and organising the scripts, seeing the later volumes of *Notes and Excursuses* into print, and securely storing the bulky results increasingly fell on Piddington's shoulders (Roy 2008: 408–11).

In his overview of Piddington's life and work, Salter (1952) emphasised that, despite his intense interest in what to most people must have appeared rather a bizarre and esoteric activity, Piddington was not an eccentric or unbalanced individual: 'Apart from psychical research, he conformed very closely in manner, opinions, and interests to the typical Englishman of his age, and education.' He played golf regularly, and also the piano, with enthusiasm if not subtlety. He occasionally took European health cures for his poor digestion. He had a sympathetic manner, once one got past his initial shyness and reserve, and a good sense of the ridiculous, something he shared with Lady Betty Balfour to whom he was close (Roy 2008). He did not accept communications from trance mediums hook, line, and sinker. He could be quite irreverent about them and took particular glee in stirring up one control, Nelly (a child of Mrs Thompson's who had died), to make teasing and critical remarks about Mrs Cartwright, another control (a former teacher of Mrs Thompson), who was pompous and dogmatic (Holt 1914 vol 2: 602–28).

In December 1912 Piddington was informed of Winifred Coombe-Tennant's pregnancy (Lord 2011: 111). This fact, for a variety of reasons, had been concealed from Margaret Verrall. Gerald Balfour, commenting on the script below, stated: 'This script probably alludes to the birth of Augustus. Mrs. Verrall had no reason to anticipate any such event.' But there is a caution worth making here. The interpretation of the scripts had become such an intense private amalgam of the cryptic and the dangerously personal by this stage that no thought, and this can apply to much of the material, had, or perhaps could have been, given to getting independent and objective outside views. What would an intelligent stranger have made of the script—was it just preaching patience for the good things to come eventually, or was there a specific fertility reference in it?

Margaret Verrall 23/10/1912:

> Not when the hearth fire dimly burns
> Nor when wind blows cold
> Not when the hand of Autumn turns
> The falling leaf to gold
> But with the promise of the May
> The budding of the rose
> When twilight passes into day
> After the nights repose
> Wait for the coming of the spring
> The quickening of the year
> Then look for what the Hour will bring
> Then, listening, you shall hear—

As has been seen, Margaret Verrall herself still remained pretty down to earth, and the script written on 1/11/1912 very strongly reflected her own attitude to matters psychic.

Margaret Verrall 1/11/1912:

> The more you automatists can live like other people,
> the better for your work. Too much introspection and
> brooding develops, over develops the subliminal—If you
> would take things more simply everything would be easier,
> our work & your life. Of course I know you must have
> peace and times of solitude, but so must all human beings
> if they are to live, really to live—Automatists don't want
> special conditions. And above all they ought not to be
> only automatists—There are other things to be done &
> learnt, even by the oldest of you
> And don't make claims on us—

Margaret Verrall never really believed in the full and intricate design in the scripts as delineated by Balfour and Piddington. She tended to chaff them for this and saw the scripts much more as individual units or units with a limited range of meanings and, therefore, argued Piddington, there were things that she missed. She was of a practical and rational turn of mind, disliking needless and silly fantasy, and her conscious mind tended to interfere with the flow of the scripts. She had been criticised by the communicators for this. As Piddington (1919: 1–10) stated: 'Her critical and rationalistic temperament was not favourable to the development of her automatic faculty.' However, he recognised an advance in the quality of her scripts in the last four years of her life and he believed there were two reasons for this. First, she came to think that some of her later scripts, and Winifred Coombe-Tennant's in the *Ear of Dionysius* and *Statius* cases, were inspired by her husband after his death. Second, she had a semi-mystical experience at Vermala in Switzerland in June 1913 (where she and Piddington spent time while he tried to persuade her of the symbolic significance of the scripts). The summer sunsets and the sense of contact with her husband had a deeply spiritual effect on her and she returned to Vermala in 1914, writing script on the hotel balcony while watching the setting sun and admiring the afterglow.

Margaret Verrall 4/8/1914:

> Dear rest in the thought that care and love prevails and that beyond these voices there is peace. Don't take a personal view keep the large issues before you and don't don't take a side Dear city of God — be a citizen of that city and no lesser

Margaret Verrall 22/8/1914:

> But now I want you to remember and kep[sic] a firm grasp on the peace that came in the Alps remember what I said then The afterglow has a real significance...

She believed these scripts to be from her husband and the advice to try to transcend crude nationalism was typical of their family values. On the outbreak of World War I, though she found it difficult to comprehend or forgive the German destruction of Reims Cathedral, she tried to be a citizen of the wider world rather than a narrow nationalist. She worked hard, as did the Newnham community generally, for the Belgian refugees who came to Cambridge in 1914, and she became the chair of the University Committee set up to allow Belgian students, not fit to fight, to complete a course of university training.

She had been suffering from stomach problems for some time and eventually a diagnosis of cancer was made. She told Mrs Sidgwick this on 17/5/1916 in a letter which fully demonstrated her courage, her practical abilities, and her sense of duty: 'I learnt on May 10th that there is malignant disease & nothing to be done... I hope I am not leaving much work unfinished. I can't manage anything involved or that needs consideration, but if there are any questions which should be answered I will do my best. As to papers, I think I have made all proper arrangements... Perhaps A.J. [Alice Johnson], if she is well enough, could come and do up parcels for despatch... I have had a full and happy life, and with Helen's happy marriage my last responsibility ended... only those of us who have been at Newnham know what we feel for you and Mr Sidgwick. It is beyond all expressing' (Roy 2008).

Winifred Coombe-Tennant was staying at Newnham College with Mrs Sidgwick in the middle of June. On 17/6/1916 she sat in the garden of Leckhampton House and went to 5 Selwyn Gardens to see Margaret

Verrall for the last time. They admired the spray of syringa that Winifred Coombe-Tennant had previously sent round and Margaret told her it was her wedding anniversary (Lord 2011). She passed away 2/7/1916.

9
The Life and Automatic Writing of Helen Verrall/Salter

After the death of her mother and the rift between Gerald Balfour and Winifred Coombe-Tennant (see below) Helen Verrall/Salter was the only one of the major automatists who continued to write regularly. It is, therefore, appropriate at this stage to provide an overview of her career and a general description of her writing. On 10/4/1903 Mrs Raikes' script (Verrall 1906: 253-4) had the phrase 'A grower of flowers one year will be sower of seed' with the initials E.G. (Edmund Gurney), and the script urged Helen to take up automatic writing. When told this Helen said that it probably referred to a discussion she had when recently staying with a friend who had just employed a new head gardener who was 'particularly skilled in raising plants from seed'. Helen tried planchette writing with her mother but when it proved unpromising she started to write, sometimes with her mother, much later on with Piddington or her husband present, but often alone. So began an automatic writing career which produced 625 scripts and did not end till 1928 when Piddington, overwhelmed with the volume, asked her to stop.

Helen Verrall found it easy to produce automatic writing of a crisp, staccato, and allusive type but, though intellectually interested, she did not feel the burning personal need to allow Myers to communicate that her mother had, and she did not have the kind of traumatic personal events in her life, unlike Trix Fleming or Winifred Coombe-Tennant, that might conduce to an interest in Spiritualism or the practice of automatic writing. She never really reflected in detail on the processes of her automatic writing and just seemed to be able to turn it out in what she called a steam roller sort of way (Piddington 1929: 611). This could mean that her scripts were merely the product of a highly educated sensibility which allowed her mind to roam free in the pastures of literary and classical associations. Nevertheless, a number of them, particularly in the period before the First World War, contained veridical material and also the symbolic structures noticed in the writing of the other automatists. Piddington argued that this detachment and lack of emotional investment in her scripts allowed the communicators to get some of their most convoluted materials through without too much interference from her conscious mind (Piddington 1930: 1-8).

Her childhood was singularly protected and fortunate. She was educated at home by her classicist parents. There is a very vivid account in Sheila Mann's biography (2013) of Aelfrida Tillyard (the novelist and student of occult and religious matters), of how she, Helen, and Myers' daughter, Silvia, were all educated together in the schoolroom at the top of the Verralls' house. Helen was a very dutiful and hard working child (more than the other two one suspects) and her parents were 'as cultured as it was possible for anyone to be'. She then went on to Newnham College in 1902, gaining the equivalent of first class honours in both parts of the classical tripos. Because of her parents' connections she came to know a number of the most gifted Cambridge people of their generation and her own. For example, the letters of Rupert Brooke (Keynes 1968: 120, 153, 207) mentioned his encounters with her: he took part, as she did, in the 1908 performance of Comus to celebrate the tercentenary of Milton organised by Christ's College; in December as a member of a winter sports party in Switzerald he composed a burlesque melodrama with her which was put on at the hotel. The following year they and others wrote and performed an opera, also no doubt of the comic variety.

There was also a connection with the emerging psychoanalytical world through her first cousin Joan Riviere (she was the daughter of Arthur Verrall's brother, Hugh, a Brighton barrister), later a prominent expositer and amplifier of Freudian ideas, which she first became acquainted with through the work of the SPR. In these years the links and crossovers between the emerging fields of psychoanalysis, psychology, and psychical research were quite strong (Hinshelwood 1991, 1995), and Helen, herself, later studied psychology, becoming a demonstrator in psychology at King's College London for three years, and also a member of the British Psychological Society in 1915.

As a child, Helen had taken part in telepathic experiments with her mother in November 1890 (*Proceedings* XI: 192) and had contact with some of the founders of the SPR, particularly Sidgwick, Myers, and Gurney. This should be kept in mind when assessing her scripts. She had a vague memory of Edmund Gurney (she was born in 1883 and he died in 1888) and that he had given her a doll. Her father told her that he had had a quirky, fantastic sense of humour. She saw Sidgwick often and once encountered him in the road near Newnham College shortly before his death where 'something in the brooding calm of his face struck my imagination'. She found Myers 'a vivid and occasionally formidable character' who mixed a capacity for fun and entertainment with brief flashes of anger and irritation when displeased (Salter, H. 1950a: 29–41). She was impressed by Myers' beautiful house and garden, and his extensive social connections through his wife's family, including the African explorer Stanley and the most celebrated male actor of the age, Henry Irving. She remembered having to entertain Eusapia Palladino, the physical medium, 'an almost illiterate peasant woman, ill-tempered and egotistic', and being highly annoyed at the way she would cheat at games. She liked Richard Hodgson, who came back from America to investigate Palladino. 'Wherever he went, Hodgson made friends with children.'

She seems to have been a remarkably self-composed individual. Winifred Coombe-Tennant met her for the first time in April 1910, no doubt at Hanover Square, around the same time that she met Alice Johnson ('very kind though rather new womanish', she wrote in her diary; Lord 2011: 45). She described Helen Verrall as tall, feminine, with the suspicion of a charming lisp (Lord 2011: 44). She kept in touch with her over the years, largely through the cross-correspondence links, and there seemed to be none of the irritabilities that affected some of Winifred Coombe-Tennant's relationships with women and men. She lunched with her and her cousin, Miss Merrifield, in 1917 and had regular contact with her as an officer of the SPR, though an aside in her diary suggests that she found Helen's self-control and detachment a little off-putting at times (Lord 2011).

Helen began to work for the SPR in 1908 and became Alice Johnson's research assistant in 1910. She has left a shrewd but touching portrait of Alice Johnson, describing her as shy, frail, but intellectually formidable, and a strong believer in the need for proper training in psychical research (Salter and Newton 1940). In 1915 Helen married W.H. Salter, who had a first-class degree in classics, had studied under her father at Trinity, as has been seen, and later became heavily involved in the SPR and the cross-correspondence phenomena. They did not leave Cambridge till 1916 after the death of Margaret Verrall. In that year she took over the role of (Honorary) Research Officer and Editor of the *Journal* and *Proceedings* from Alice Johnson. She continued to work for the Society in various capacities until a couple of years before her death in 1959 (Broad 1959: 129–30). Apart from her own substantial work as an automatic writer, she made a number of considerable contributions to the research of the society, including a study of one of Leonora Piper's more evidential cases, studies of mediums, some of whom she found fraudulent, and studies of Mrs Leonard, some of whose evidence she found impressive. She was seen at her best in her careful examination of these cases but less so in her assessment of the spectacular direct voice mediumship of George Valiantine. It is perfectly true that Valiantine was caught out in fraud on a number of occasions but she swept some of the more startling material aside, on the grounds of his record of fraud and the inadequate nature of the records, without really engaging in detail with the phenomena (Salter, H. 1931-32: 389-410).

In later life she participated vigorously in community affairs. She was a member of Saffron Waldon District Council from 1925-49 and a Justice of the Peace from 1937-49, and she was a governor and then chair of governors of Saffron Walden Teachers' Training College for many years. She also played a substantial part on county-wide local government committees. She was an impressive and equable individual of good judgement and active social conscience. She died in 1959.

As has been seen, some of her early scripts had quite specific references to the importance of Cadoxton and indirectly Daphne Coombe-Tennant; others made a significant contribution to the early cross-correspondences (Hope, Star, Browning, etc.); and many contained condensed allusive references to the Story and the Plan and the personalities involved several years before Balfour and Piddington had discovered the underlying structure. For example:

Helen Verrall 25/3/1908:

> Caller herrings W? a jug of water a golden ewer for the washing of hands and a sprinkling of sweet odours The feast of the purification
> [Drawing of a cross over the sun and of a bishop's staff]
> The pastoral staff
> He himself had given his name to the city he founded and he always the same
> [Drawing of a cherub] the fiery hosts the burning glory when the trumpet shall blow?

For Piddington and Gerald Balfour the symbolism was clear. Caller herrings (Scottish fishermen) and cherubs and the quotes from Milton's *At a Solemn Music* all stood for Frank Balfour/F.M.B./the Dark Young Man/St Francis. The Feast of the Purification was known as Candlemas (candle symbols for the Palm Maiden) and the date of the script, March 25th, was the day on which the Palm Maiden was buried. The jug of water and a golden ewer referred to the washing of the disciples' feet by Christ which occurred on that day. The drawing of a cross against the sun and the naming of a city were seen as references to Constantine who in scripts stood for Arthur Balfour, the constant and faithful knight. The wider point was that Constantinople was a symbol for one of the great cities, along with Athens, Rome, Jerusalem, Venice, which would lead to the uniting of East and West and the founding of the spiritual city on earth and the eventual reign of peace.

Her later scripts were quite baffling in parts, and Piddington, in his edition of her third volume of scripts, complained feelingly about the difficulties of interpreting them, compared even to the cryptic scripts of the other automatists (Piddington 1930: 1-8). She could give the source of the familiar quotations she quoted but had no idea of the reason for the associational links: 'Unlike other automatists, it is exceptional for her to form any idea — correct, suggestive or false — as to what the script is driving at.' Her scripts sometimes stimulated Piddington into almost unbelievable intellectual and interpretative acrobatics. For example:

Helen Salter 17/10/1916:

> Sabrina — ever fair — the translucent wave — a nymph — Sabrina is important — we want to call P.'s attention to this — particularly now — we wish this borne in mind — it may not be understood at once, but the meaning is there — we wrote years ago about Sabrina & we wrote with a purpose

George Dorr had instigated a successful Sabrina cross-correspondence eight years before (Johnson 1910b: 253). Did this 1916 nudge mean that the communicators had not had adequate feedback on its success, or was there an extra layer of symbolism to be uncovered? Such was the complexity of Piddington's explanation that part of the modern reader's reaction must depend on what evidence they believe exists for the enormous selective and organisational power of telepathy and clairvoyance that the discarnates must have possessed for his interpretation to be the right one.

Piddington (1929: 96-7) suggested that 'Sabrina, through an out-of-the-way literary allusion, stands for the supposed date of the Palm Maiden's death and for her symbol the Candle.' He quoted from Galt's *Annals of the Parish* (an 1821 novel of Scottish country life) concerning the death of a Miss Sabrina Hookey: 'for Dr. Tanzey had told me in the winter that he thought the sharp winds of March would blow out her candle, as it was burnt to the snuff; accordingly, she took her departure from this life, on the twenty-fifth day of that month, after there had, for some days prior, been a most cold and piercing east wind.' The communicators had thought that March 25th was the date of the Palm Maiden's death till they were disabused of this on 16/8/1915. (It was in fact the date of her burial.) Piddington argued that this was probably an acknowledgement of the fact that the puzzle had been set up with regard to the old date and that they now recognised the new situation, hence the stress on Sabrina in 1916. This all seems rather feeble.

After wading through the intimidating, tersely phrased Helen Salter's scripts and trying to follow the almost desperate ingenuity of Piddington's efforts to make sense of them, one longs to read the transcript of a high quality 'traditional' medium. Helen Salter certainly knew at least one. She had some involvement at one stage in organising, for the SPR, the sittings of one of the most remarkable trance mediums of the twentieth century, Gladys Osborne Leonard (Ormrod 1984; Souhami 1998; Salter 1955a).

Through this work, Helen met and became friends with the controversial novelist Radclyffe Hall and her partner, Una Troubridge. They were looking for evidence of the survival of Radclyffe Hall's deceased lover, Mabel Batten. They received good survival evidence at the Leonard sittings and they wrote them up in thoughtful and careful detail (Hall and Troubridge 1918-19: 339-554). They were also given a sitting with Helen Salter and must have found it by comparison a meagre and disappointing experience.

Helen Salter 12/7/1919 (Chip Chase, Hadley Wood, the home of Radclyffe Hall and Una Troubridge):

> Days beyond—the palm trees—when the day dawns—the cup of the sacrifice
> —the lantern—the colonnade—footsteps following along the way—a strange
> Light in the heavens spreading slowly—light from above [drawing of an Illuminated cross]—thus—it was seen at midnight in a clear sky opposite
> The sun—a cloak—the symbol [drawing of a fish]

It was as if the communicators were determined to stick to their last and not allow their automatists to become conventional mediums and give the usual standard messages. In her script, symbols for the Palm Maiden (palm trees, the lantern) and for the Dark Young Man/Christianity (drawing of a fish) seem to be combined with the Emperor Constantine's vision of the cross and the idea of sacrifice: all familiar elements in cross-correspondence scripts, but of no value to Radclyffe Hall in her efforts to contact her dead lover. This pattern seemed to occur as a rough general rule throughout the cross-correspondences. When sitters not connected with the Story and the Plan sat with the automatic writers, almost invariably the material that was produced referred not to them but to the circumstances and intentions of the communicators and the central figures in the scripts, living or dead.

Though she disappointed them as a medium, Helen Salter staunchly defended Radclyffe Hall and Una Troubridge in the vicious attacks on them for their 'immorality' as a lesbian couple, telling Fox-Pitt, their main antagonist, that it was a dangerous word to use, and offering the help of the SPR's solicitor in dealing with the matter. She was rather more sympathetic to them than Winifred Coombe-Tennant, who met Radclyffe Hall in conjunction with a Leonard sitting (Lord 2011) and found her an 'uncongenial manly creature'.

Winifred Coombe-Tennant
The End of the Affair with Gerald Balfour; Her Later Scripts and the Last Years of Arthur Balfour; the Education and Career of Henry Coombe-Tennant

The End of the Affair with Gerald Balfour

With Margaret Verrall's death, Winifred lost a valued friend and counsellor at a time when, as her diary entries reveal, the pressure of her various roles (automatist, mistress, wife, public servant) was really beginning to take its toll, and, apart from Margaret Verrall, she did not seem to have any intimate women friends of her own class, no one perhaps in whom she could confide problems concerning her automatic writing or her intense relationship with Gerald which inevitably had its tensions and difficulties. An intimate, trusted friend might have helped her cope with her fury and distress when she learnt that Betty Balfour was expecting a child. Winifred felt completely betrayed by Gerald but eventually forgave him. However, she always resented the child, Kathleen, and her dislike was noticed by the other Balfour children (Roy 2008, Lord 2011). She complained at the thought of Kathleen in that house which 'should be ours by right' as she, Winifred, was his, Gerald's, real wife. She also thoroughly disliked the idea of Denzil Stanley (the adopted child of Dorothy her sister in law and Henry Curtis) usurping the inheritance she thought should go to Alexander and Henry (she never seemed to have given a thought to the position of Eveleen Myers' children Leo, Harold, and Silvia). Through all this, Betty Balfour, remarkably, remained calm and warm, welcoming Winifred and her children (first Christopher and then Henry) into her home. She was the unsung heroine of the whole affair.

A further complication was the highly different sensibilities of Winifred and Gerald. She had already lost one child and she was dreading the involvement of her eldest boy, Christopher, in the war. He became a lieutenant in the Welsh Guards and was killed at the front in 1917 on September 3rd. He had only been in the trenches for two days. As she wrote in her diary, she tried very hard to think of him and his new conditions rather than dwell on her own grief and she was comforted that he would be with Daphne, Myers, and Margaret Verrall (Lord 2011). She had discussed with him what should happen if he died in battle, how he should behave and whom his spirit should seek out (Lodge 1918). It is easy for a more materialistic and hard-bitten age to mock this, but by this time Winifred had been convinced, by her own experiences and the wider evidence of the cross-correspondences, of survival after death. But she was shocked by Gerald Balfour's reaction to Christopher's death. He was slow to write or make contact and when he did write he seemed to be more concerned with SPR matters (Lord 2011; Houghton archive).

To compound matters, he was reluctant to write a suitably laudatory introduction to the memoir of Christopher which Winifred put together (Lodge 1918). Such volumes were not uncommon during World War I amongst the upper and upper middle classes with the cultural and financial resources to do this, but it appears that Gerald Balfour did not think that Christopher was in the same golden boy class as some of the others so memorialised. He had icily high intellectual standards and was not prepared to compromise them even for his lover. She complained bitterly in her diary (Lord 2011) of the emotional coldness of the Balfour/Cecil family (the Balfour children's mother, Lady Blanche Cecil, had been a sister of the 3rd Marquess of Salisbury). That was both fair and unfair. Unfair in that the Balfours were not a demonstrative family. They took an intellectual and detached approach to life. On one famous family occasion, Frank Balfour went missing, and they discussed whether or not he had drowned in his boat. Looking at it logically they decided he had not and so did not bother to search for him or enquire further (Balfour, F. 1930). However, the criticism was fair in that this was the second child that Winifred had lost and an immediate sympathetic response to that loss would have been the reaction of the vast majority of people who had contact with her.

Winifred had managed to attract Gerald Balfour by her youth, her energy, her natural intelligence, and her obvious admiration for him, but as the years went by each saw the weaknesses (from their perspective) in the other's character. These incipient tensions were made particularly painful by their different approaches to the interpretation of automatic writing. She had been buoyed by a script from Edith Lyttelton (who had started automatic writing after the death of her husband, Alfred). She saw it on 16/10/1917. The message was full of Childe Roland references which were symbols of particular meaning to her and Christopher (they used to read the poem together). On 18/10/1917 she finished her first rough draft of Christopher's memoir, working intensely and quickly as she had done with Daphne's. On 24/10/1917 she received a memorandum from Gerald commenting on her notes on the Lyttelton script: in essence he could see nothing referring to Childe Roland in it. She replied remonstrating, and he, wounded by this, sent back what she called an 'infamous letter'. She received it on 31/10/1917. He complained that 'love for you and for our son was the biggest thing in my life, and that till now I had thought it was the same with you' (Houghton archive). In that fortnight the grand passion foundered as suddenly as it had begun.

But Gerald Balfour rather missed the point. It was no time to apply strict SPR standards at this period of great grief. Depending on the position one takes, one can either see Balfour's reaction as a mark of acute insensitivity to the woman he had addressed in letters for a number of years as his real wife, or, on the other hand, as an adherence to the highest objective standards of the SPR, no matter how personal the circumstances. It was quite clear that she no longer considered him to be an appropriate helper for the book. On 15/12/1917 Oliver Lodge wrote to Winifred Coombe-Tennant asking if there was a message from Myers for him (he had been prompted to this from another mediumistic source). She then produced script which, conveniently ignoring her previous distrust of Lodge, stated that Myers requested that Lodge write a forward to the book and co-operate in its final production. Her diary recorded that Myers had already been bombarding her with requests of this nature (Lord 2011: 236-42).

All this was against the backdrop of some of the darkest days of the war. The Russians had collapsed, allowing the Germans to transfer troops to the Western Front. Winifred Coombe-Tennant bitterly felt 'the intense misery, waste and criminal wickedness of it all. Down with all armies, all kings, all diplomats, all wickedness in high places' (Lord 2011). Her mood was lifted a little by the passage of the suffrage clause through the Lords, by Lodge's full involvement in the book, by his suggesting a title that she thought wonderful, and by impressive sittings with Mrs Leonard on 8/2/1918 and 11/2/1918 at which her beloved Christopher came through.

And there was the continued undercurrent of tension and bickering at Richmond Terrace to be dealt with as well. Mrs Tennant still clung to life while brother and sisters squabbled over the potential spoils (Hamilton 2009: 291–2). Winifred knew Dolly and Eveleen were devious and avaricious and feared that Charles was being outmanoeuvred by them. Particularly galling was the fact that all the family china, pictures, and possessions were left only to Dolly (Lord 2011).

By the end of the war Winifred Coombe-Tennant's scripts became far less frequent. The rift with Gerald Balfour meant that he had no sittings with her for almost two years after September 1917, and she produced few scripts indeed between then and 1922. She began increasingly to concentrate on practical, social activity after Christopher's death and she thought about standing for Parliament. One of the few scripts during this period indicated that the communicators had encouraged her to do so and that they restricted script communication because there would be too great an inner and outer pressure on her. However, script production flared briefly again into splendid life late in 1922.

The context of this was the expansion of her political ambitions. Lloyd George thought highly of her and supported her attempts to get into parliament, at which she was unsuccessful. In addition, he offered her the opportunity to become the first British female delegate to the League of Nations Assembly in Geneva. She went there in September and was based at the Hotel Metropole where she worked energetically on the 5th Commission dealing with Opium, Russian Refugees, Women and Children, and the White Slave Trade. This, combined with the proximity of Arthur Balfour (whom she found very impressive in the sessions of the Assembly) as the leader of the delegation and the emotional impact of revisiting the scenery of Caux and the surrounding area which she remembered from her youth, led to a sudden almost overwhelming resumption of her mediumship, in which the Dark Young Man, Frank Balfour, was heavily involved. Rarely, if ever, could automatic writing have been produced in such unusual circumstances. There is a photograph of Winifred, by the lake, in wide-brimmed fur-lined hat, stole, long dress with a fringe of Welsh lace, and bright buckled shoes, looking slightly uncertainly at the camera, as if trying not to reveal that inner life (Lord 2007: 67).

She actually managed to have a sitting on 26/9/1922 with Arthur Balfour which dramatically recapitulated the themes of earlier years. It was remarkable that they found time for this given the vivid picture of continued activity at Geneva described in her diary and other documents and the physical toll on her: 'I was so tired this morning after a heavy week's work [I never clear up my papers until 1.a.m., having the whole of the Vth Commission on my hands and no Secretary]...' (Balfour 1928: 395).

Winifred Coombe-Tennant 26/9/1922:

> There are two who are in all this Both young a man & a woman & hers is the influence of which you feel the pressure...A young and very gracious lady...I hear the word Perseus & she draws for me the letters BJ (a reference to the Burne-Jones pictures in the Long Room at 4 Carlton Gardens) She has been able to get very near him much nearer much much more nearer because of your presence here...He is quite unaware of this as he is always unaware of her presence...

The script of 26/9/1922 was the only one written while the conference was taking place but after it, in the euphoria of the experience and the release from tension, and the chance to visit the neighbourhood and travel on the lakes and see the mountains—'Oh, how I love mountains and how they comfort me' (there is an implication for script symbolism here)—there was a flurry of scripts in early October, with the Dark Young Man very much in evidence. It is no surprise, given the political context, that these scripts should have been full of the Story and the Plan.

Winifred Coombe-Tennant 3/10/1922:

> ...The whole story goes much further back than the first man (of the Triumvirate F.M.B., G.W.B., A.J.B.) but it is on so vast a scale that we can only give little bits of the pattern at a time—the weaving has arrived at a most interesting stage There has been a glowing excitement over here as we have seen the circumstances fall into place tell Gerald this This script should make things clearer also for him Destiny the 7 stars Mary's crown The Mother & the names Wonderful and Councillor In this thing is also the Blessed Damozel who leans across the Bar of Heaven the unforgetting

Winifred Coombe-Tennant 4/10/1922:

> ...An octave was the answer I wish I could get you to write about the age of Peace A Roman Emperor Pax Romanum

The Arthur Balfour she renewed contact with at Geneva had had a remarkable war career and was to have an exceptional post war one also, and the scripts, according to Piddington, both reflected and predicted this. Before World War I many would have written Arthur Balfour off as a successful Irish secretary and a very mixed Prime Minister and Leader of the Opposition, seeing his resignation in 1911 as the end of politics for him. Yet, he was appointed to the War Council, became First Lord of the Admiralty and then Foreign Secretary in the war coalition, to which he made noted contributions: indeed, as he also did to the peace conference at Versailles, the League of Nations, and the Washington Naval agreement, and the work with the British Dominions. And as Mackay (1985: 354-65) has put it: 'To the end, in 1929, of his prolonged career of service in Baldwin's Cabinet, he remained a uniquely sophisticated and clear-thinking minister in the sphere of defence policy.' Piddington saw all this expressed in the *One Crowded Hour of Glorious Life* cross-correspondence (Piddington 1928: 345-75). But, as he stated, 'In the original version as read and published I treated the phenomena discussed in it merely as a cross-correspondence of the literary kind, and I did not in any way hint that they were concerned with a living person and with real events' (Piddington 1934: 304-5). He wrote, however, that Gerald and Nora knew, and that Lodge had guessed. 'Everything in this group of scripts... seemed to point to "one last act of kinghood" done at the very end of life and to a dramatic finale of the Knight's political career', giving examples from Greek mythology and British history of those who had ended their lives in this glorious fashion. In very broad terms there is some truth in this, though there may also be more than a touch of wishful thinking, and the glamour associated with the Balfour reputation, shaping this conclusion.

The other cross-correspondence written up in the *Proceedings* (Piddington 1928: 472–505) that had this dual meaning was *The Master-Builder*. According to Piddington, Ibsen's Master-Builder and Milton's Satan were both presumptuous defiers of God, as was the Palm Maiden in her rejection of the 'normal' post-mortem progression and her tenacious insistence on remaining close to the borders of terrestrial life in order to communicate through a medium to the Knight, Arthur Balfour. The Palm Maiden fell from the highest sphere (or refused to ascend there), the Master-Builder fell to his death from the top of his house, and Milton's Satan fell from the highest point on the Temple. Piddington argued that the communicators used such bizarre and forced symbolism 'on the ground that the very strangeness of the imagery, especially when not confined, as is rarely the case, to the scripts of a single automatist, tells against its having its source in the minds of the automatists' (Piddington 1935a: 580–1).

At last in February 1923 Winifred Coombe-Tennant was able to visit Whittingehame for the first time, a house she called her dream house since she was sure she had already visited it in sleep. There had been plans that she might have gone there much earlier in her relationship with Gerald Balfour but he had put her off since the society ladies, Lady Elcho and Lady Desborough, were likely to be present (Houghton archive) and he was very worried (they were worldly members of the Souls' group) at their ability to detect the slightest possibility of a liaison. However, by the 1920s their relationship had become more of an old friendship and was based on a common interest in Henry and so there was much less in their behaviour to give them away.

She made notes of the impressions she received on first visiting the house.

Winifred Coombe-Tennant 8/2/1923:

> This is my dream house…I came up to the front door from the wrong side—I always come from the left…I know the inner hall—never remember a billiard table there…Big room with books…the covers on the chairs are not *my* covers—my colours are much darker…When I go into my room *I nearly* shout—there is my striped furniture

She seemed to be seeing the house much as Francis Maitland Balfour would have experienced it and her impressions were broadly correct—there was no billiard table then, there was a room called the Zebra room (from the striped wardrobe in it), and there were darker covers on the chairs at that time (Balfour 1928: 152–63).

These impressions lasted three days as she was shown over the house by Nora Sidgwick, and finally she saw a picture of the Dark Young Man in

Alice Balfour's room. Yet she never seems to have associated him with Francis Maitland Balfour or to have been told that that was a picture of him. Most people would find it impossible to believe that she could not make the connection, and Gerald Balfour's comment was: 'The identity of the Dark Young Man is still withheld from Mrs. Coombe-Tennant's normal self... it seems impossible to account for her ignorance except by supposing that it is artificially maintained either by "designed inhibition from the other side"... or by auto-suggestion.'

She had two scripts while there, with Gerald Balfour as sitter on both occasions, one on 9/2/1923 with familiar symbols — the Catherine Wheel, the Blessed Damozel, the drawing of an Ice Axe — but the one on 11/2/1923 was more unusual. It contained words that she said she did not understand 'Hypnosis? Is that a word?' 'Infiltration? What does that mean?' And the language was very uncharacteristic of her and rather like the intellectually complex script of 21/1/1912.

Winifred Coombe-Tennant 11/2/1923:

> There is nothing outside law — and you can only tentatively adumbrate a hypothesis by studying processes...He says he was accustomed to research work with infinitely delicate structures — but as he saw them they were material structures. But when you're carrying through a great work in embryology
> (Here she said: '"Embryology"? What is that?')
> on a human plane, then you have a mass of unmapped phenomena and incalculable x quantities, which are part and parcel of the deciding factors in the result

The sitting was then brought to an end by a loud rattling on the locked door, which jolted Winifred Coombe-Tennant out of her semi-trance condition and shocked her badly. All the automatists, perhaps Winifred Coombe-Tennant the most severely, suffered from the effect of sudden noisy interruptions. The second point to comment on was, as Gerald Balfour himself noticed, 'We have here perhaps the plainest intimation to be found in the Scripts' of the role that F.MB.'s technical knowledge was to play in the production of 'the Messianic Child'.

Arthur Balfour does not seem to have been present or to have been given a sitting in February 1923, but Winifred Coombe-Tennant and he were together at Fishers Hill in March 1925, and he, sitting in the study around 6pm with Nora, Gerald, and J.G. Piddington, asked if there was any chance of getting script from her since she was sitting on her own in the drawing-room nearby. She obliged. The script contained the familiar symbols but was noticeable for her stressing that she was not in trance. It is difficult to find the correct term for her state: intense absorption in the experience and concern to render the communications clearly and accurately while still retaining a core of self-awareness and executive capacity.

Winifred Coombe-Tennant 9/3/1925:

> 'Lord Balfour, I'm not in trance. You might think I was because my eyes are shut' and at the end 'The worst of this kind of thing is you never want to come back. You get loosed-free. Yet I wasn't a bit unconscious.'

The next visit to Whittingehame in 1926 stimulated another burst of script which started the night before her arrival. She sent a letter to Gerald Balfour explaining the context. The letter was interesting in that the force seemed to have come from outside her at an inconvenient time and, yet again, she appeared to have had no idea as to whom the lovely lady might have been, even after all the volume of script. Also worth commenting on was the use of the word 'heavy' as if it was a kind of metaphorical pregnancy. Her scripts were saturated with references to birth, death, the coming of children, their illnesses and destinies, and to the unfulfilled longings of the Palm Maiden for what might have been.

Note on script of 6/2/1926:

> Heavy with Sc. All day—& finding no uninterrupted time…until 9.30 p.m. when I felt an absolute *rush* as if someone were literally dragging me…my bad arm making writing a trial…Have been profoundly moved by this unknown 'lovely lady'.

Winifred Coombe-Tennant 6/2/1926:

> She has been trying to send a message by you it is very important She has been wringing her hands because she could not get a message sent to him She kept saying to me Oh if only she had been there—there where he is—It is like seeing an open door & then a chasm of distance between Try for her tonight she is very urgent there is a meaning She says—this for identity the Saxon Jewel and the flashing sword—flashing in the moonlight Gerald will understand…she knocks and knocks at the door of your mind crying out for you to send a message Surely surely they will find the reference—I, I too have written swift iambics…Hist said Kate—crumbling the hounds their messes

There were several particularly valuable features in the script (Balfour 1928: 257–63). First, the longing for a message from Arthur Balfour. Has anything, of her presence, come through to him? Second, the standard symbolism, Excalibur, Kate, and the reference to Alfred Lyttelton (King Alfred—the Saxon Jewel). Third, the gnomic and quite outside Winifred Coombe-Tennant's normal range of reference, 'I, I too have written swift iambics'. The rest made moving sense but what was the point of the last? Gerald Balfour argued in a note that it made a correspondence twenty years back with a Margaret Verrall script of 15/3/1905, and that the point in quoting the line which originally came from Horace, C.I. 16 – 'me quoque... in celeres iambos/Misit furentum' – was to refer to the whole Archytas Ode matter and ultimately to Myers' rejection of the pessimistic view with regard to survival expressed in that ode and his own poem *Immortality* (discussed above).

Arthur Balfour wrote a letter to Nora Sidgwick in response to the script, which one assumes was read at a later sitting with Winifred Coombe-Tennant. In it he stressed that he knew 'Death is not the end... [But] During all this time he has had no access to her mind except through the rare intervention of others, no intuition of her presence though he does not doubt its reality' (Balfour 1928: 266-7).

The Last Years of Arthur Balfour

In the period shortly before Arthur Balfour's death there was a brief late outpouring of scripts comparable to those stimulated by the League of Nations events of September 1922. (On this sequence of scripts see Balfour 1938: 1-32.) In his preface to these last scripts Gerald Balfour stated that he and J.G. Piddington still believed that the script material was best interpreted as suggesting that the communicators 'are really what they claim to be, and that they had genuinely been engaged in an effort to bring about the birth of a child of Messianic order', but there was no conclusive proof of this. And, was there any evidence 'apart from the assurances held out in the Scripts, for anticipating a successful conclusion to the experiment?' In other words, was Augustus Henry Coombe-Tennant beginning to make his mark? The conclusion was modest:

'The central figure round whom the Scripts turn is now a young man of twenty-five; but signs and wonders are still to seek. Here we can but wait and see. Meanwhile it is well to put on record that the individual in question has not the faintest idea of the destiny foretold for him... Up to the present he has been kept in complete ignorance, not only of [Mrs. Coombe-Tennant's] identity, but even of the fact that his mother posseses any automatic faculty whatever.'

Winifred Coombe-Tennant was staying at Fishers Hill shortly before Arthur Balfour's death and on 16/10/1929, she was sitting quietly in his sitting-room while he was lying on a couch. She suddenly sensed, as she told Betty Balfour later, that the room was full of presences.

Winifred Coombe-Tennant 16/10/1929:

> I asked 'What sort of presences?' She said one figure there – Things coming out of that figure – The profound unchangeableness of it all. It was a woman's figure – quite young – dressed in old-fashioned dress. Lovely quantities of hair gathered up round her head. Her head was turned from me, but I saw the side of her neck. Impossible to describe

all the things that seemed coming from her — the mass of sureness, tenderness and power. It made everything else in the room appear dead, while every form of life you can imagine radiated from her. Her hand was upon his arm. She never took her eyes from his face...

Gerald Balfour's own account of the incident was written up the next day (for he was in the room and she whispered what she was experiencing to him):

Her whole attention was
concentrated on a single figure, — that of a lady in an old-fashioned dress, young, and with thick and beautiful hair. A brilliant light streamed round, or from her whole figure; she was standing by the side of A.J.B.'s pillow, resting her hand on his arm, and gazing down on him with a fixed look of infinite tenderness.

The two accounts closely match.

On 18/10/1929 came the last sitting of Winifred Coombe-Tennant in Arthur Balfour's presence, while outside in the hall a gramophone was playing Bach. Winifred Coombe-Tennant said that the lady of the other night was there (the Palm Maiden), the Dark Young Man (F.M.B.), and also 'the lady of the picture in your little room' (Arthur Balfour's mother, Lady Blanche).

Winifred Coombe-Tennant 18/10/1929:

...she knows that you know all about her, and she's not troubling about evidence now — that's done with — it's just companionship, deep calling to deep...She's leaning down and stroking like that (*the automatist was stroking A.J.B.'s hand*) and saying — And suddenly she tells me the most important thing she has to say — Tell him he gives me joy.

Arthur Balfour died on 19/3/1930 with Gerald Balfour and Nora Sidgwick at his side. Shortly after his death Winifred Coombe-Tennant wrote Gerald a letter in which she described the apparent post-mortem condition of his brother who seemed to be in a state of some confusion (quite a common situation according to many of the standard Spiritualist accounts in the literature).

Winifred Coombe-Tennant 2/4/1930:

He (the Dark Young Man) said that when AJB was <u>here</u> he was in touch with some reality over there <u>through me</u>, & since his death it has been necessary for them to bring him into touch with me when I am asleep in order to re-connect him back to a reality he grasped in life...[in order to help with] the process of 'finding his feet' over there [which] involves this drain on my vitality...

On 8/6/1930 she sat with Gerald Balfour at Fishers Hill to see if she could make further contact. At this sitting she said that Arthur Balfour was present with the Dark Young Man, who was explaining the process (one assumes of communication) in which he (A.J.B.) was frightfully interested. On 15/8/1930, in a dream, she had a most vivid impression of him: 'His eyes were of extraordinary brilliance, his whole frame the embodiment of strength and energy, as of a man in the full zenith of his powers.'

On 5/9/1930 while at Whittingehame again there came another script. (For these last scripts see Balfour 1938: 72–150.)

Winifred Coombe-Tennant 5/9/1930:

> The shining waters of peace the peace that is among
> the lonely hills Pax vobiscum Peace & Plenty a
> good motto note the connection The victories of
> Peace not won by shock but by the slow process of
> evolution to evolve a background Power write that
> Power in stillness the stillness of the central sea
> a harmony...

It seems strange that her script should have focused so strongly on the general topic of peace and not on evidence of Arthur Balfour's post-mortem survival. For her, of course, the great theme now was not Balfour but the destiny of Augustus Henry Coombe-Tennant, and the part he would play in the coming of world peace. In early 1932 Gerald Balfour reminded her that March 19th was the anniversary of Arthur Balfour's death, and begged her to try for script that day, or at least to bear him specially in mind. She, accordingly, tried for script early in the morning but without success. Then in the evening before going to bed she managed to produce something.

Winifred Coombe-Tennant 19/3/1932:

> Caesar perhaps why write when script is wanted
> this side it will come but the pause is intentional
> Only this word East meeting West the desert tree
> & the hawthorne in blossom the May blossom
> White and the rising star the morning star an
> efulgence of light radiating pulsing a sense of
> waves & rhythm the music of the spheres the merry
> world is round A star danced at his birth The
> pillars of the house the Star moving to follow the
> star starshine brilliant day the light of perfect day

One notices the emphasis on scripts being generated by the discarnates 'when script is wanted'. Successful, meaningful contact required the full co-operation of the communicators. The symbols for the Palm Maiden (May blossom, etc.) and the Messianic Child (a star danced at his birth, etc.) were combined with the reconciliation of opposites theme (East meeting West)

The Education and Career of Henry Coombe-Tennant

and were part of the movement eventually towards world peace (the light of perfect day).

How did Henry develop under the weight of the concealed expectations on him? What did he know? And how did he turn out? As has been seen, in Winifred Coombe-Tennant's published diary and in the archive at Harvard, there was an intense emphasis on Henry and the eager, speculative search for evidence that might suggest the prediction was being fulfilled. Henry stayed on at Eton, where he had glowing tutorial reports, till he was 19. A little long one might have thought. Piddington and Balfour, both Old Etonians, visited him there. On one visit Gerald Balfour wrote back to Winifred Coombe-Tennant, using the embarrassing term that the group, and even Henry himself, made use of in letters, that the 'Wise One' (Houghton archive: 1/12/27) had his mind full of metaphysics and solipsism. Philosophy and music became Henry's main intellectual and creative pursuits. He went up to Trinity College in 1932, took a first in part 1 of the moral sciences tripos and then another in part 2 in 1935.

On her visit to Cambridge just after Henry had gone up, Winifred experienced a very powerful sense of communion with the Dark Young Man, as if he were there to look over his spiritual creation.

Winifred Coombe-Tennant 28/11/1932 (extract from letter to G.W.B. of 2/12/1932; Balfour 1938):

> I went to Cambridge on Sunday [Nov.] 27 to see the Wise One… was with him from 2 pm to close on 10 pm.
> He had lectures next morning so — having slept at the Bull —
> I sallied out alone — an incredible morning of warm sunshine & blue skies.
> I went wandering through Kings — & Clare — & stood on the bridge with its stone cannon balls, idly watching the water flowing below me — the lovely tints of the weeping willows Trinity-ward — & the distant leafless branches of tall trees in Trinity Fellows Garden.
> Suddenly — there was the Dark Young Man. He said nothing to me in words — nor I to him — but our minds met. He was young, gay, very vigorous, radiating some strange sense of satisfaction.
> For a long time — it must have been quite 10 minutes I judge — we were there on that bridge together — he with his back to Trinity — I facing towards it. Sometimes he seemed standing over the water, always his face level with mine. We were quite happy, quite silent — the silence of familiar companionship. I was basking in the sun — lying fallow, the whole of me, & he was timeless — but quite solid & real.

Both Winifred and Gerald were delighted by Henry's academic success and saw this as the start of his march towards future predicted greatness. They were worried, however, when he became like so many of his generation, temporarily attracted to left-wing politics and ideas and showed a real sympathy for the long-term unemployed. In *Stalin's Englishman*, Downie (2015) describes the intellectual atmosphere of Cambridge in the early 1930s, consequent on the depression, the rise of the Dictators, and the apparent impressiveness of Stalin's Russia. It was little wonder that Henry was influenced by this. But he always remained his own man and may well have found much of the left-wing activity too intense and conspiratorial, and though aesthetically more attracted to men than to women (Roy 2008) he would probably have found the milieu of Burgess and Blunt distasteful. In fact, his tutor, C.D. Broad, assured his mother that his flirtation with left-wing politics was only temporary and that he would make a fine scholar (Kremer archive). That was not to happen. Quixotically, given his academic gifts and achievements, Henry decided to go into the army, joining the Welsh Guards. He added another entry to his establishment portfolio when, partly through Gerald Balfour's influence, he became a member of the Athenaeum.

The closest and shrewdest observer of him during these years was Jean, Lady Traprain, the wife of Gerald Balfour's son and heir, Ral (Roy 2008). She found him charming and highly intelligent, but lacking in positive initiative and energy, and somewhat sexless. She believed that his rather domineering and possessive mother had had, psychologically, a negative impact on him. She wrote that all the Balfour children knew of Henry's predicted greatness and that she believed that Betty Balfour told them this so that it might explain the fuss that was always made of Winifred and Henry when they came to stay at Fishers Hill, and so that they would not guess that Henry was Gerald's child. She stated that the future Messianic status of Henry did not appear quite as bizarre to them in the 1920s and early 1930s as it would have done later. The world was crying out for spiritual saviours, and indeed one of them, Krishnamurti, the protégé of Betty's sister, Emily, came to stay at Fishers Hill, only to be compared rather unfavourably to Henry, Jean was amused to find, by Gerald Balfour (Roy 2008).

Henry had a very distinguished war, and the old men Balfour and Piddington might have thought, with the need for a new political and social settlement, a new Jerusalem, after the Second World War, that perhaps his time was about to come. But he remained in the army and then moved to work for the Foreign Office and MI6. So he never pursued the political career which alone from 1945–51 would have given him appropriate access to the national and international stage.

He showed a considerable interest in psychical research and often discussed the subject with Jean. Jean urged Winifred to tell him that she was Mrs Willett, but she refused, probably because it would have led eventually to the revelation that he was Gerald's son. And, much to Henry's frustration, she was never prepared to discuss psychical research with him and never appeared to have achieved that intimacy with him that she had had with Christopher (Roy 2008).

However, after her death Henry and his brother Alexander were fully prepared to co-operate with Geraldine Cummins (1965) in the experiment that led to the book *Swan on a Black Sea*, one of the most interesting, fluent, and persuasive examples of automatic writing in the canon (Fontana 2005: 185-9) and, on the surface, of evidence for Winifred Coombe-Tennant's post-mortem survival. With regard to the cross-correspondences themselves, he found little time, in his army and later his diplomatic life, to study them in depth, but he appreciated and understood the method, though fully aware of the capacity to over-read meanings into such a rich texture of material. He illustrated this, for example, by identifying certain sections in some of the earlier scripts that could have been predictive of aspects of his later military career (Roy 2008).

His final choice of career, that of Benedictine monk, effectively ended any possibility of a charismatic impact on world events. He worked at Downside, and, temperamentally, found the teaching of groups of boys unappealing, though on an individual basis he could provide valuable guidance and support. But it was far too late, and impossible from his position, to move up the Church hierarchy and establish a power base in the Vatican, which was probably the only other way apart from politics that he might have been able to make the kind of world-wide contribution that the scripts predicted.

The career progression of his life suggested someone who found it easy and attractive to adapt to institutional life—Eton, Cambridge, the Welsh Guards, the Foreign Office, the Catholic Church—all organisations with codes and cultures to follow and structures that provided an appropriate mix of intellectual authority, freedom, and security, provided one entered at a level commensurate with one's ability and class. He was gifted, charming, and multi-talented, but at his core there was the fatal Cecil/Balfour detachment that Winifred had complained of in Gerald Balfour. On the other hand, this quality of distance and apparent lack of warmth should not make one overlook evidence of his great personal kindness to certain individuals (Roy 2008).

11

The Minor Automatists
The Mackinnon Family from Aberdeen; Dame Edith Lyttelton; Kenneth and Zoë Richmond; and Mrs Wilson

There were a number of what one might call minor automatists who in varying measures contributed to the development of the scripts. The Mackinnons (the Macs in the literature) were a family of brothers and sisters from Aberdeen: three girls — Lilias, Esther, and Doris — and two brothers — Alan and Lachlan. They played a brief but significant part in the cross-correspondences. They, all five, produced material, using the Ouija board and a planchette, but the best results came from Esther and Alan working the planchette together. There was a fair amount of silliness and disjointed verbiage, but the two most effective communicators appeared to be Henry Sidgwick and someone called Reynaud Carson. The most valuable feature of the relatively small number of Mac scripts was that the first ones were sent unsolicited to Margaret Verrall (1910: 264–318): 'On September 26th, 1908, when I was away from home, I received a letter from a complete stranger in Scotland...' It was also of value that, though the Mackinnons had read Myers' *Human Personality* and some SPR publications, they did not move in the same circles as the Cambridge automatists and investigators, and they had no investment whatsoever in the cross-correspondence 'project'. Their scripts seemed to focus particularly on the death of a young female and there was some debate by Piddington as to whether that was Daphne Coombe-Tennant, May Lyttelton, or both, and there were some interesting correspondences particularly with Margaret and Helen Verrall (Salter 1963: 13–17, for example).

Another minor automatist was Mrs Stuart Wilson, who was the American wife of a British Brigadier General, and, with him, spent much of her time abroad. On his retirement in 1923 Brigadier General Wilson was appointed, by the Grand Lodge of England, District Grand Master of Free Masons in Egypt and the Soudan. (Piddington seemed to think it was particularly significant to record this post.) Mrs Wilson knew only Helen Salter, of the SPR group, and she and Helen became involved in telepathy experiments from 1915 onwards (Piddington 1938a). From these early experiments emerged material which seemed relevant to the wider pattern of the scripts. Mrs Wilson adopted the procedure of lying on her bed in the evening in a state of self-induced light hypnotic trance in order to pick up telepathic messages. She later changed this to a wider, more passive focus and made the interesting comment (Piddington 1938a) that 'better results are likely to be obtained when I leave my mind completely free and do not try to direct it towards any particular subject or person'. She would write up her impressions and experiences afterwards. This was Piddington's description of the process: 'Mrs. Wilson's procedure is as follows: having provided herself with pencil and paper, she lies down in the dark and lapses almost at once into a light stage of hypnosis. In this condition a series of very vivid mental pictures present themselves to her... [sometimes] visual hallucinations... [sometimes] auditory hallucinations... [she] makes brief notes of her impressions at the conclusion of the experiment.'

W.H. Salter (1948) rated her records highly because of their apparently clear references to the Story and the Plan of which she knew nothing. Also, like the other automatists, she occasionally got a sense of Myers, Gurney, and Sidgwick as communicators.

Mrs Wilson 22/7/1917:

> I had a dream later on that three men who sometimes seemed to be talking to me about the experiments were regretting that I knew no Greek. I can't describe them except to say that the principal one has a kindly, rather whimsically gay manner.

One record seemed particularly apposite to the cosmic themes of the scripts and combined references to the St Francis symbol for F.M.B. (with possibly a coded reference to the early death of Laura Lyttelton, one of whose symbols was the laurel) with the Messianic Child.

Mrs Wilson 29/2/1916:

> St. Francis of Assisi in his monk's robes. Laurels covered with snow, and the words 'There is always snow on their laurels'. The next picture, of a family group,...looking with awe rather than affection, at a baby in a cradle,...who will someday rank among the saints is not altogether their own, but in some sort a changeling.

Another self-hypnotically induced impression linked to the Plan theme: the change from a world order based on savage physical authority to one, after many, many vicissitudes, founded on civilised and ethical principles.

Mrs Wilson 24/3/1916:

> The light took the form of gigantic warriors leaning on their great two-handed swords and watching something intently. The expression, awe-inspiring, describes the feeling they gave me. I think they were the old

Norse Gods. In front of them the Christ child lying in a little manger and radiating a more golden light.

One must, however, be careful with Mrs Wilson's scripts. By the time Piddington came to work through them he already had a well-formed view of the symbolism of the Story and the Plan and there must always be the suspicion that he was manipulating or massaging the data to fit this framework. The fact that Mrs Wilson's scripts were generated by scenes which she visualised as she was falling asleep (hypnagogic images), and her comments on those scenes, may also have contributed to this. Her scripts lacked the intricate precision of the best automatic writing and were susceptible to the charge of easily being read into.

The Richmond and Lyttelton scripts must, for different reasons, also be treated with great caution. The Richmonds became involved in the SPR towards the end of the First World War (Gaythorpe 1950), and were soon friends with both Betty Balfour and Edith Lyttelton. Their scripts were assessed by Piddington and Gerald Balfour but, like Edith Lyttelton's, for whatever reason (lack of time, resources, variable quality) were never printed in book form. Kenneth Richmond's scripts were of two types—the early ones which seemed to be continuous prose statements from Myers and the later ones with his wife that had more of the allusive tangential nature of the main body of cross-correspondences. Zoë Richmond described the process thus: 'My husband, Kenneth Richmond began to discover something odd was happening to him when we moved from London to Cornwall in 1915. He started turning packs of playing cards over and over from a shuffled pack, and found he knew beforehand a remarkable number of times what card was going to turn up. He spent several mornings doing this. I took a poor view of it. Then he suddenly gave it up, and began to take down messages in clear "printed" writing, and they were signed F.W.H. Myers. When these began we knew nothing of Psychical Research, and had not even heard of the Society for Psychical Research, and the name of Myers therefore did not mean anything to us in this connection. Shortly after the messages began we met Lady Betty Balfour at a Conference, and so "The Work" started: and still goes on' (Gaythorpe 1950).

Richmond had had a difficult early life, brought up by a clergyman and headmaster father, Canon Wilfred Richmond, who did not treat him well. This may have been the source of his alcohol problems later in life. After the war he established a psychoanalytic practice at 15 Devonshire Terrace near Lancaster Gate where he treated a number of patients with a variety of mental problems, including the young Graham Greene. Greene rewarded Richmond, if that is the right phrase, by portraying him unflatteringly in his novel, *The Ministry of Fear*. Zoë Richmond attributed the origin of their interest in psychical research to her mediumistic contact with her brother who had been killed in the war and the use her husband made of this discarnate aid as a diagnostic tool in his work with patients. Kenneth Richmond practised, without formal qualifications, as a psychoanalyst in the Jungian school and West (1998), one of Graham Greene's biographers, virtually called him a charlatan and quack. However, Greene's official biographer painted a more nuanced portrait (Sherry 1989).

Richmond was well read in both literature and the classics, and his range of content was wider than his wife's or Edith Lyttelton's. Piddington argued that these and other allusions still continued to spell out the main symbolic messages of the earlier scripts. For example, Richmond was plagued by references to the 'brindled cat' (a Macbeth allusion) and could not understand the frequency and persistence of these phrases. Piddington noted thirty-five references to the 'brindled cat' and he confidently stated 'I believe that the Brindled Cat is a symbol for the Palm Maiden; and I may add that I think that the Palm Maiden is one, or all, of the Three Witches, and also Hecate the mistress of the Three Witches'. The expansion of the symbolism in this fashion makes the modern observer uneasy: it casts doubt on the integrity of the interpretation and also increases the likelihood of chance creating the pattern (Piddington 1935b: 1487).

Kenneth Richmond 15/6/1929:

> ...Now be patient if you get the brindled cat again...(KR) Yes: I have heard enough of her, and I don't know what she is mewing about...

Richmond's scripts were a mixture of trance speech and automatic writing. Two of the trance scripts were spoken in the presence of Arthur Balfour and one wonders what he made of them.

Kenneth Richmond 26/10/1929:

> Life is a repetition...[but] every smallest circle completed is a gain on which other gains are built. The purpose in things does not return upon itself and bite its own tail; nor does the purpose in any single soul.

Kenneth Richmond 27/10/1929 (again in Arthur Balfour's presence):

> ...Argonauts and Alchemy comes next. Golden Fleece seems to be the association of ideas, and transmutation and the Golden Branch in the Aeneid.

The third of these scripts contained another Palm Maiden reference. Piddington argued that the auricomi fetus (golden leaved/golden haired fruit) of the Golden Bough/Golden Branch meant the Palm Maiden's hair and 'There is good evidence to show that the Golden Fleece sometimes means the hair of Portia, and therefore the Palm Maiden's hair...', and he quoted from *The Merchant of Venice*: 'her sunny locks/Hang on her temples like a golden fleece' (Piddington 1934: 149-50). It is worth repeating Gerald Balfour again: 'The Palm Maiden was remarkable for the wonderful beauty of her hair. Her sister described it to my wife as the most irrepressible hair, growing in natural waves like the sea, very fair in childhood, but later becoming a rich dark brown with golden lights, amazingly thick though not very long—"it was the most alive hair, a very great beauty in her."'

Kenneth Richmond's scripts were curiously ruminative and self-aware at times. This suggested that his state of dissociation was very slight indeed (E.L. was Edith Lyttelton).

Kenneth Richmond 13/4/1930:

> That brindled cat again. I should like to drown it. Even the weariest pussy wends somehow safe to sea—with a brick on a rope round its neck—I hope. Creeks and inlets again—Clough—I had this quotation at our last sitting, or last but one with [Arthur Balfour]...and he lit up with appreciation of the poem. I know that E.L. has more than once had this reference in her script when I have been present...

Zoë Richmond's scripts also had symbolic references to the Knight, Arthur Balfour, and the Palm Maiden, May Lyttelton.

Zoë Richmond 14/6/1929:

> I see the picture of the hand holding the sword...The Knight of the Round Table...a crest with a arm holding a sword...your crest cast aside in the stable...

Zoë Richmond was, of course, well aware of the details of the Lyttelton crest but knew nothing of references to it in the scripts of the other automatists unless, as Piddington on one occasion suspected, Edith Lyttelton was the leak (Roy 2008).

The role of Edith Lyttelton needs to be examined in particular detail: to some extent on account of the quality of her scripts but also because of the range and depth of her social and political connections. Dame Edith Lyttelton (née Balfour but no relation to Arthur and his family) was a thoroughly establishment figure. She lived close to Westminster Abbey and Westminster School. She was the widow of Alfred Lyttelton, the Colonial Secretary, and was part of the Souls. She had joined the SPR after the death of her son Antony in 1902, and she began to practise automatic writing after Alfred's death in 1913 (Jalland 1996: 365-70). She became one of the SPR group of automatists, but was never absolutely central, since both Balfour and Piddington had suspicions about her discretion and thought the quality of her automatic writing very variable. As a member of the Souls she knew of the May Lyttelton and Laura Lyttelton stories and she had lost a child who appeared to figure symbolically in the scripts. Both these factors seriously prejudiced anything she wrote on these topics.

Balfour and Piddington judged that, though she had many admirable qualities (she was intelligent, energetic, warm, and supportive to her friends), she could be something of a loose cannon in matters psychical.

She was a well travelled, well read, and resourceful woman. She visited France, Ireland, South Africa, Japan, China, Korea, and Canada at various times in her life (Lyttelton 1917; Bush 2000). When Alfred Lyttelton was ill in 1903 she spoke frequently for him on the hustings and was instrumental in saving his seat. She was active in public service. She helped establish the Victoria League after her visit to South Africa, was chair of the Personal Service Association (a voluntary body designed to help deal with unemployment in London), she followed Mrs Coombe-Tennant as a female British delegate to the League of Nations, and she campaigned strongly against sweated labour in the clothing industry.

As a well-known social and cultural figure she was sufficiently trusted by the security services to become a member of the front organisation, the Joint Broadcasting Committee (which may never have met formally), which masked the start of Britain's secret propaganda broadcasts to Germany in the 1930s. The members of that committee were seen to be 'biddable' (West 1987: 115). There is no doubt that she was a patriot and believed strongly in the civilising mission of the British Empire. But she was no simple-minded upper-class jingoist. She was a strong critic of many aspects of society and wrote vigorously about this in her plays and journalism. She campaigned for a National Theatre which was eventually founded some years after her death, and she was a friend of a number of literary and artistic figures including George Bernard Shaw and Mrs Patrick Campbell.

Her writing was notable for a number of predictive statements she made about events in the First World War. Piddington (1923) in his analysis of her scripts had an interesting section on predictions. He identified four types: general, those dealing with the imminence of war, specific incidents, and the future of the world. Those dealing with the imminence of war seem to this writer to be the kind of predictive platitudes that the period of rising international tension from 1905–14 would psychologically generate.

Edith Lyttelton 27/7/1914:

> Great trial and tribulation but in the end peace and light.

The same applied broadly to the 'general' and the 'future of the world' categories. What was much more interesting and worth evaluating was the material in the specific incidents category. The names Pathfinder (in German), Lusitania, and Fenchurch given in her scripts, before the outbreak of war, could all be linked to individual events in the war: the torpedoing of HMS Pathfinder on 5/9/1914; the sinking of the Lusitania by a German submarine on 7/5/1915; and the bombing of Fenchurch St on 13/6/1917. Other scripts had an even more eery element with their reference to Bechtesgaden (Berchtesgaden, Hitler's mountain retreat) and the phrase 'the Munich Bond', which could be a prevision of the diplomatic mistakes of 1938 and the appalling consequences of those events. Mackenzie (1968: 27-49) has produced a very useful summary of the main predictions, and a general assessment of them, as well as providing background on Edith Lyttelton and the nature of her automatic writing.

Edith Lyttelton 20/2/1914:

Lusitania, foam and fire — mest [sic] the funnel — in broken arcs —

Edith Lyttelton 14/5/1914:

...open your ear to the unknown — fear is the arch enemy. Lusitania...

Edith Lyttelton 25/4/1914:

The Pathfinder. Die Pfadfinderin cut out a new way for the spirit the flight — take heed to that, take heed Many waters cannot quench love nor the floods drown it — The dark...Now — the trumpets blow the bugles sound and all the world is in the war

Edith Lyttelton 14/4/1914:

Crossing the Bar. Some are crossing now — Fenchurch St. the underground. In the boat are many — The Teuton, the bandaged eyes

Edith Lyttelton 4/6/1914:

Fenchurch Street — the deluge — the noisome pestilence that walketh by night — courage he said and pointed to the dawn...the frightened feathers in the wind blown here and there — Shelter O God shelter...this is a bad business — if we can do anything we will but it's a bad business

Edith Lyttelton 31/1/1915 (this was written at Hackwood, Lord Curzon's home, another example of the breadth of Edith Lyttelton's connections — see Mackenzie 1968: 37):

The nemesis of Fate nearer and nearer — No respite now nearer much nearer than you think and once it begins there is no stay — no one knows — the leaves of the autumn — they will fall in quiet — the fugitive armies — the overshadowing of fear the price of peace. Nolens Volens. The Munich Bond remember that — you will see strange things.

Edith Lyttelton 24/5/1915:

In the western fields carnage — marching — the vines on the hills the vintage — flight — now mark this — behind the curtains of blackness there is light never doubt it — be of good cheer. The hand stretched out to stay Bechtesgaden — Markovitch.

It is superficially intriguing that one Aleksander Markovitch (Lipiansky) in the 1930s and 1940s was, from a Catholic and spiritual perspective, urging a European federalist approach to prevent the horrors of further European wars (Hellman 2002). But one could probably identify many Markovitchs at the time in Europe who had diametrically opposed objectives.

Mackenzie's overall verdict with regard to the predictive elements in her scripts was that the statements did forecast air raids in Fenchurch Street and its vicinity and that 'these references to Lusitania are very odd. In my opinion, they must refer to the ship.' In the Pathfinder case, he believed that the word was ambiguous, possibly linked to the sinking of the ship but more than likely it was a memory of a story that Edith Lyttelton had once translated from the German (Die Pfadfinderin). Those interested in the detailed arguments, and the claim that the Munich crisis was also referred to in her scripts, can consult Mackenzie. These predictive scripts do have a certain persuasiveness but, in general, Edith Lyttelton was just too inextricably linked with the Lyttelton and Balfour families story for her scripts to have substantial value. Therefore, scripts like that quoted below needed to be handled with care.

Edith Lyttelton 23/10/1915:

> Ring out wild bells—no—yes, that's right [or eight] bells. The plaited crown of hair. She waits in tenderness for the time when she can help. Beatrice, L'amore che muove—l'altre stele. That's it. The gladsome May. (At this point the automatist says: 'I know what you are talking about, don't bother to pile up identity.')

This script formed part of a series of symbolic correspondences with a Winifred Coombe-Tennant script 13/8/1913, and a Helen Verrall one 4/3/1915: the Dante line was common to all three; the wheel (not quoted) was common to Coombe-Tennant and Helen Verrall; and the *In Memoriam* bell reference was common to Helen Verrall and Edith Lyttelton. Yet some of these items had appeared in a paper read by Balfour to the SPR in March 1914 and Edith Lyttelton knew the story of the Palm Maiden's hair (Balfour 1927: 477-8). One should note the time gap between the first and the last of these scripts. In addition, Edith Lyttelton's scripts were often vitiated by her 'insider' position. For example, one can give no credence to the following references to Arthur Balfour.

Edith Lyttelton 22/11/1913:

> Tell Arthur that nothing venture nothing have he is bound to try he is the only man who can

Edith Lyttelton 22/7/1914:

> We have this to say to Arthur that he must reign

In this one can see a member of the Souls calling for action by their leader, even though Balfour himself had said in 1911 that he believed at his time in life he no longer had the drive or energy to re-enter government. There is no need to posit any kind of discarnate imperative.

The Balfours: From top left clockwise; Arthur; Francis Maitland; Eleanor (who married Henry Sidgwick); and Gerald.

The Verralls: From top left clockwise; Helen Verrall (who married W.H. Salter); her mother Margaret Verrall; and Margaret's husband, Arthur Verrall.

The Friends: From top left clockwise; Oliver Lodge; Edmund Gurney; Richard Hodgson; and Henry Sidgwick.

The Myers: From top left clockwise; the mature Myers; the young Myers around the time of his trip to Greece; Myers' wife, Eveleen (National Portrait Gallery); and Leckhampton House, their Cambridge home.

The Mediums (also see Helen and Margaret Verrall above): From top left clockwise; Leonora Piper (National Portrait Gallery); Rosalie Thompson; Winifred Coombe-Tennant; and Trix Fleming (The Keep/Sussex University Special Collections).

The Script Interpreters (see also Margaret Verrall and Winifred Coombe-Tennant above): Top left J.G. Piddington (Mary Evans Picture Library); mid-left Alice Johnson; right side group photograph of five SPR presidents—from left clockwise: Hans Driesch; Gerald Balfour; J.G. Piddington; Lawrence Jones; and Eleanor Sidgwick (Mary Evans Picture Library).

The Messianic Child, Henry Coombe-Tennant, and the Palm Maiden, May Lyttelton. According to the scripts, Henry was in some spiritual sense her child as well.

Burne-Jones' Peacock Memorial for Laura Lyttelton. He kept a personal, gilded version in his home and it is now in the Victoria and Albert Museum. The original, in white gesso, is in St Andrew's Church, Mells, Somerset, under the tower.

Part 2

Assessing the Cross-Correspondence Automatic Writings

In Part 1, evidence was presented that the cross-correspondences, whether specific or symbolic, had a strong claim to be recognised as paranormal and that there were a number of examples of paranormal cognition in them. How is one to rigorously test and challenge these claims? One can address this issue by posing a number of specific questions as assessment criteria (repeated for the readers' convenience from the introduction): were the cross-correspondences, whether literal or symbolic, unambiguous, consistent, and meaningful; did they demonstrate a capacity for paranormal cognition; might not the cryptic nature of the cross-correspondences be merely a psychological artefact (the dreamy, ruminative activity characteristic of much normal subliminal mentation); was the process interactive and was it clear that the 'discarnates' both initiated and signalled cross-correspondences and understood and accurately responded to messages and requests from the investigators; did the cross-correspondences occur within a reasonable time frame and above chance expectation and were they distributed sufficiently widely amongst the automatists; had all normal avenues for acquiring the information been ruled out; had the correspondence been tweaked by wishful thinking or over-subtle interpretation or deliberate selection; and were the alleged aims, intentions, and long-term predictions of the 'discarnates' fulfilled? It should be stressed, for a variety of obvious reasons, that conscious collaborative fraud is ruled out in this context and that in order to make a sound and reliable assessment judgement all the appropriate criteria for each specific case need to be covered. Underlying all this was the fundamental question as to what extent the Story and the Plan really were in the scripts of the main automatists. And, most crucially of all, did the communicators succeed in their overall purposes: the ambitious plans, led by one or more remarkable individuals, for world peace at some indefinite future date; and the production of survival evidence invulnerable to alternative telepathic explanations?

12

Were the Cross-Correspondences Unambiguous, Consistent, and Meaningful?

Five types of cross-correspondences (to some extent they can merge and blend) have been identified in the scripts: simple, intricate or complex, symbolic, ideal, and progressive. They are largely verbal (though there are occasional drawings that are relevant to the communicators' purposes) and they are scattered across the automatists often at around the same chronological period but also over a longer timescale, appearing, disappearing, and then resurfacing years later. The content itself could be highly fragmented both in terms of its allusiveness, terseness, incompleteness, or appearance in a script with no obvious link apparent to what went before or came afterwards.

The simple cross-correspondences are easy to assess—the same word or topic was clearly expressed in two or more scripts. The problem is more difficult in the case of intricate cross-correspondences. In essence, a series of clues, disguised in a variety of ways (this provides the intricacy or complexity) were scattered across the scripts of two or more automatists. The investigator has to identify the underlying theme or topic from the limited information available. As seen above, Alice Johnson argued that this method was devised to surmount the objection that telepathy from the living was the source of so-called mediumistic messages. There is much to be said for this argument but the approach has disadvantages.

For example, it has often been argued by supporters of the cross-correspondences that when the key phrase or clue was identified in the script it made the whole intricate cross-correspondence fit together like a jigsaw. This is a misleading metaphor. A traditional jigsaw is cut so that one and one only picture/pattern can emerge from the small physical elements into which the jigsaw has been dispersed. The fit is geometric. There can be no argument about it. It is a physical fact. However, the script material was densely literary and historical and required literary and historical judgement and sensitivity to evaluate it. Therefore, unambiguity in this context means best fit based on a considered and informed assessment of the scripts and not the absolute unambiguity of the jigsaw. While some intricate cross-correspondences just seemed to click into place (Thanatos for example), in others there was room to challenge the interpretation and to suspect bias or the over-ingenious interpretation of large convoluted bodies of data.

Saltmarsh (1975: 34–5) argued that there were a number of intricate/ complex correspondences between two automatists that were beyond dispute, but that ideal examples, conforming to the Latin Message type, and involving at least three automatists, could not be found. The very fact that Alice Johnson claimed to have identified several emphasises the problems with the jigsaw metaphor mentioned above.

In addition, when assessing symbolic cross-correspondences one needs to look at the spread of symbols across the automatists and their first independent appearance in each script. It should be stressed that the symbolism referred to in this case was the internal symbolism that the interpreters stated was created by the communicators. It should not be confused with (even though it may draw some of its power from) the wider world of esoteric and occult symbolism. The symbolism can work in the revelatory and participatory ways that Main (1907: 57–62) suggests it can often do in a spiritual context, but in the cross-correspondence scripts its main rationale was more pragmatic. The progressive cross-correspondences raised the same issues as the other types with the additional consideration that as they occurred within the scripts of one automatist it was more difficult, though not impossible, to argue for an external design.

There are certain generic tests one can apply to the cross-correspondences. Operationally, this means a) estimating whether the cross-correspondence was or was not a fortuitous platitude derived purely from the automatist's own cultural resources. One must look closely at the nature of the link, the precision, complexity, vagueness, or generality of the phrase, and the frequency of its use or recurrence in scripts in order to be able to do this; b) mapping the extent to which the key phrases and topics were distributed across the writings of the automatists before they had, if ever, access to the other scripts involved in the cross-correspondence. This is particularly important with regard to the symbolic cross-correspondences since Gerald Balfour (1927) and Piddington claimed the symbols lay concealed in the earliest scripts until the communicators decided the time was right to reveal the clues that liberated them; c) checking whether the automatist consistently used the same symbol in the same way to stand for the communicator, or another symbol. Using other symbols increased the sense of complexity and design but it also increased the likelihood of chance generating the link. One must interrogate the rationale for assigning a particular symbol to a particular individual. Did it connect directly or indirectly to something in their life history, or was the association a more tenuous one, a desperate attempt to create a cohesive meaning?; d) looking at the rest of the script from which the cross-correspondence (of whatever type) came. Was the rest of the script unintelligible? Was there anything in the script to indicate that the cross-correspondence had been signalled or intended? This last point is part of the wider issue of incarnate/discarnate interaction and will be explored in greater detail in a later section.

Given the sheer volume of the scripts, the actual number of cross-correspondences worth identifying and examining was comparatively small and they mainly occurred in the period before 1916, even though technically the scripts went on into the 1930s. There were two main reasons for this. First, under the influence of Winifred Coombe-Tennant's scripts, Piddington and Gerald Balfour shifted their main focus from cross-correspondences pure and simple (if that is the appropriate phrase) to gathering evidence for the broader purposes that underlay the scripts—the Story and the Plan. Much of this later material, with some exceptions, was rather repetitive, even static, adding little new, except extra layers of possibly imagined complexity. Second, the number of individuals available to map and assess the whole body of material contracted. Margaret Verrall died in 1916. Alice Johnson had increasing ill health. Oliver Lodge was out of favour for some time and Mrs Sidgwick was getting older and was engaged in her massive Piper study. Moreover, the private nature of the material prevented the obvious solution—the introduction of young and energetic research assistants to help with the assessment.

A small selection of examples in each category is given to see how they measure up to the criteria outlined above and only, because of time and resource constraints, a limited demonstration of the application of the criteria can be provided. Note, too, that just the basic structure of the cross-correspondence is sketched out.

Simple Cross-Correspondences

The Blue Flower

Trix Fleming 24/10/1906:

> (Drawing of a flower) The Blue Flower.

Margaret Verrall 24/10/1906:

> Where others see the flowers blue... The misty blue veiled flower. Let him that has eyes see.

The cross-correspondence was very simple and clear and pointed up. The timing was tight: in fact the same day. There was nothing cryptic. However, the lack of complexity increased the possibility, with such a common adjective and phrase, of mere coincidence. Obviously, this objection was weakened if other cross-correspondences were discovered between these automatists in the same scripts. Two other examples were very similar in format. Again, in these other two, notice both the closeness of the dates and the unambiguity of topic (see Piddington 1908: 145, 177–8; Johnson 1910a: 207–8, 215).

Note: Trix Fleming was in India. Margaret Verrall was in Cambridge.

Violets

Leonora Piper 11/3/1907:

> Violets. Dr.Hodgson [said] violets

Margaret Verrall 11/3/1907:

> With violet buds their heads were crowned…The city of the violet

Note: Margaret Verrall was in Cambridge. Leonora Piper was in London.

Yellow

Trix Fleming 6/8/1906:

> yelo…yellow ivory

Margaret Verrall 8/8/1906:

> I have done it to night y yellow is the written word…Say only yellow

Note: Margaret Verrall was in the UK. Trix Fleming was in India.

Intricate Cross-Correspondence

Euripides

Margaret Verrall 4/3/1907:

> *Hercules Furens* Ask elsewhere for the Bound Hercules

Margaret Verrall 25/3/1907:

> …the clue is in the Euripides play if you could only see it. Bound to the pillar.

Leonora Piper 8/4/1907:

> Do you remember euripedes(?)…I meant to say Harold

Trix Fleming 16/4/1907:

> Lucus. Margaret. To fly to find Euripides. Philomen.

Note: Margaret Verrall was in Cambridge and then Matlock. Leonora Piper was in London. Trix Fleming was in India.

Browning had translated the *Hercules Furens* and it was a central feature in a poem of his, *Aristophanes' Apology*. Lucus was one of the characters mentioned. Another was Philomen who cried, 'I'd hang myself — to see

Euripides'. Often the name Margaret (Verrall) was used to signal a cross-correspondence. Piddington also argued that the Christian names of Myers' children—Leopold, Silvia, Harold—had also been used in this way in scripts. Trix Fleming had not read the poem and wryly commented that 'it was one of the peaks in the Browning range which I still wait to scale'. The clue could possibly have referred to the wider sacrifice theme of the scripts. In his madness (*furens*) Hercules murdered his children. It is interesting that the simple idea Euripides appeared in Leonora Piper's script; classical allusions in Margaret Verrall's; and literary references in Trix Fleming's (Piddington 1908: 210-20, 244-8, 251-9). Much the same approach as with the Thanatos cross-correspondence.

Piddington was fully alive to the objection that one could read into Leonora Piper's often faint and disorganised automatic writing what one wanted. In this case 'Mrs Sidgwick sent me a tracing of the original, and I have no doubt Euripides is the true reading'. In the case of the name Lucus, which was indistinct: 'I asked Mr Bickford-Smith... to say how he read the word.' He confirmed Piddington's interpretation.

Ideal Cross-Correspondence

Prometheus

Leonora Piper 31/3/1908:

[Dorr suggested Prometheus as a cross-correspondence]

Margaret Verrall 23/9/1908:

In a casket was hidden the fire by which Prometheus made men unto like God. There is something wanting to make this complete

Helen Verrall 19/11/1908:

Time's hour glass whose sands never run out—Time and Eternity

Trix Fleming 30/12/1908:

We bear Time to his tomb in Eternity (from Shelley's Prometheus Unbound)

Note: Leonora Piper was in the United States. Helen Verrall was in Cambridge. Margaret Verrall was in the New Forest. Trix Fleming was in the United Kingdom. Neither Helen Verrall nor Trix Fleming saw Margaret Verrall's script.

For Alice Johnson this cross-correspondence, like the Medici Tombs, was a fulfilment of the Latin Message (Johnson 1910b: 255-61). The Margaret Verrall script had a clear allusion to the story of Prometheus and to concealment and a statement that something was wanting; the Helen Verrall script had a specific reference to the relationship between Time and

Eternity; and the Trix Fleming script brought them together by linking Prometheus in Margaret Verrall's script with Time and Eternity in Helen Verrall's, using the quotation from Shelley's *Prometheus Unbound*, Act IV.

Symbolic Cross-Correspondences

Sevens

One of the most difficult problems for the modern assessor is that the scripts have to be assessed on two levels at the same time. Two examples are discussed here, 'Sevens' which was the subject of Piddington's sealed envelope test (see above) and Shelley's *The Cloud* (see below). Piddington's experiment seems to have been hijacked by the discarnates for their own purposes as part of the evidence for the plan to produce the Messianic Child (like Arthur Verrall's one-horse dawn). It was also an impressive cross-correspondence (Johnson 1910a: 222-53).

Helen Verrall 6/8/1907:

> A rainbow in the sky
> Fit emblem of our thought
> The sevenfold radiance from a single light
> Many in one and one in many

Helen Verrall 11/5/1908:

> The seven branched candle stick it is an image
> The seven churches but these not churches
> Seven candlesticks united in one light and
> Seven colours in the rainbow to
> Many mystic sevens all will serve
> We are seven who F.W.H.Myers

Leonora Piper 8/5/1908:

> We are Seven. I said Clock! Tick, tick, tick.

Leonora Piper 12/5/1908:

> We *were* seven in the distance as a matter of fact.

Helen Verrall 16/5/1908:

> A seven stringed lute the lute of Orpheus

Mrs Frith 11/6/1908 (a minor automatist):

> Pisgah[1] is scaled the fair and dewy lawn
> Invites my footsteps till the mystic seven
> Lights up the golden candlestick of dawn

---

[1] Pisgah was the mountain in Jordan from which Moses viewed, but never reached, the Promised Land.

Trix Fleming 23/7/1908:

> There should be three at least in accord and possibly seven

Mrs Home 24/7/1908 (Cheltenham trance medium, Myers communicating):

> Seven times seven and seventy seven
> Send the burden of my words to others

Note: Helen Verrall was in Cambridge. Leonora Piper was in London. Trix Fleming was in India. Mrs Frith's location is not known.

On the level of a cross-correspondence these seemed to be pretty remarkable, as also were the links with Piddington's sevens letter. A further layer of complexity was that Alice Johnson believed that some of the content which formed the sevens cross-correspondence came from Cantos 27–31 (*Purgatorio*) of Dante's *Divina Commedia* (Salter 1961: 177). Dante had a vision of seven candlesticks whose trailing flames were like the colours of the rainbow and then he encountered Beatrice, with her wonderful emerald green eyes. Piddington and Balfour later came to believe that Dante and Beatrice were symbols for May Lyttelton and Arthur Balfour, and Gerald Balfour, particularly (1927: 67–71), added a richly esoteric layer connected with the Messianic Child: 'The blending of the seven colours of the rainbow to form white light symbolises the perfect combination of elements to be looked for in the Messianic Child. White light is the *unity* of the rainbow colours. So in like manner the Octave (diapason) was conceived to be in some sort the unity of the seven notes of the scale.' There was also the implication in 'We are seven'. Balfour and Piddington later concluded that all seven of the discarnate individuals identified as communicators were referred to in this cross-correspondence and, in different ways, were supporting the development of Henry Coombe-Tennant. They based this partly on the statement in the Winifred Coombe-Tennant script of 22/4/1915: 'The seven stars and the seven pillars in the House of Wisdom'; and the clustering of symbols for the Angel of the Annunciation, and for the Palm Maiden and the Knight. However, while one can see reasons for regarding the cross-correspondence elements as persuasive, the wider claims for the symbolism seemed to be based purely on the emotionally charged Winifred Coombe-Tennant scripts and on the general resonance of seven as an important magical number.

Shelley's The Cloud

As Gerald Balfour stated (1927: 83): 'There are few passages in poetry more frequently referred to in the scripts than this stanza of Shelley's.' It was an easily intelligible example of what Piddington called the scriptic method: the challenge being to find the source that made sense of a number of statements spread across the automatists' scripts. In this case at least eighteen references could be found as quotes from or allusions to the stanza. The stanza runs:

> That orbèd maiden with white fire laden
> Whom mortals call the Moon
> Glides glimmering o'er my fleece-like floor
> By the midnight breezes strewn;
> And wherever the beat of her unseen feet,
> Which only the angels hear,
> May have broken the woof of my tent's thin roof,
> The Stars peep behind her and peer.
> And I laugh to see them whirl and flee
> Like a swarm of golden bees,
> When I widen the rent in my wind built tent, —
> Till the calm rivers, lakes and seas,
> Like strips of the sky fallen through me on high,
> Are paved with the moon and these.

Of the eighteen or more references in scripts to this poem, the first four by Helen Verrall and Trix Fleming were almost certainly uncontaminated by knowledge of the other automatists' scripts. Both Margaret Verrall and Winifred Coombe-Tennant as joint writers/researchers with access to the scripts of the others could have obtained the phrases normally. Just a selection is provided here but the range is sufficient both to indicate the way the script intelligence persisted with a particular phrase and the manner in which it could draw attention to its significance.

Helen Verrall 3/12/1908 (Margaret Verrall present):

> Wherever the beat of her unseen feet

Trix Fleming 1/4/1909:

> Charonic the staircase for the unheard unseen feet of those returning

Helen Verrall 26/8/1910:

> and wherever the beat of her unseen feet

Trix Fleming 23/6/1910 (Fishers Hill: Eleanor Sidgwick, Gerald Balfour present):

> Orbèd maiden with white fire laden

Margaret Verrall 15/7/1911:

> And ever the beat of those unseen feet

Margaret Verrall 1/1/1912:

> The beat of those unseen feet which only the angels hear—There is a point about the moon which you have not seen—Perhaps I can make it clearer later on—

Margaret Verrall 8/1/1912:

> And ever the beat of those unseen feet

Helen Verrall 7/4/1913:

> a swarm of golden bees

Note: Due to considerations of space just the location and content of the first four scripts quoted above are considered here. Both automatists were in the UK, probably Cambridge in Helen Verrall's case and Tisbury in Trix Fleming's. The only potential source of leakage was Trix Fleming's visit to Fishers Hill on 23/6/1910.

In all cases the references to the poem were absolutely unmistakable. But above and beyond this, the question, of course, is what was their symbolic purpose and what did they combine with in the particular script that they appeared in? Piddington and Gerald Balfour argued that Shelley's *The Cloud* was used in a strategic sense across the scripts to act as a symbol for the continuing illumination and support—sometimes hidden, sometimes blazing forth in dreams or the passionate mediumship of Mrs Coombe-Tennant—that May Lyttelton gave to Arthur Balfour. The image of the moon emerging from behind the clouds was, therefore, very appropriate.

The examples were so clear that the modern parapsychologist might point out that they appear to have avoided the trap of subjective validation: that is, searching for verbal associations that combined to build a general meaning for the reader, and discarding the rest.

To test this one has to look at the remainder of the scripts from which the allusions came. The other parts of Trix Fleming's two scripts contained a further reference to the poem, an allusion to the value of suffering in producing great achievement, as in the *A Musical Instrument* theme, a possible comment on the Cadoxton coalmines of the Coombe-Tennants, and Delta, the symbol for Daphne, some comments on the difficulties of communication, a possible communication from Lady Mount-Temple concerned about the illness of her daughter Juliet (this was later confirmed as accurate), and a prediction that at the SPR meeting the following day there would be a brief announcement which would later become of significance (this was the first mention of Mrs Coombe-Tennant's mediumship and the Lethe Case). Therefore, the Shelley references were embedded in scripts which contained other material that was relevant to the overall structure of the scripts and the individuals involved.

The same patterns continued with the other scripts, though as stated above one cannot be sure that the automatists had not, by this stage, read material in which the Shelley *The Cloud* symbolism appeared. Each of the Helen Verrall scripts, as well as the Shelley quotation, had familiar symbols in them for the main personalities — in one Arthur Balfour, in another Frank Balfour, and in the third there was an interaction with Piddington clarifying the nature of some of the communications. Most of the *The Cloud* references were in Margaret Verrall's scripts and they clustered around the crucial period 1912-14 and the revelation of the key messages in the scripts — the relationship between Arthur Balfour and May Lyttelton and the coming of the Messianic Child. The scripts themselves stressed the importance of these quotations as well as providing symbolism relevant to the deaths of Laura Lyttelton and her child Christopher. There was also an apparently evidential communication from S.H. Butcher, Arthur Verrall's great friend. The Winifred Coombe-Tennant scripts, as with most of her automatic writings, were easily understandable with their references to May Lyttelton (Madonna della Candela) and Frank Balfour (Il poverello — St Francis), and the last in 1923 linked *The Cloud* reference to symbols for the Messianic Child, which in this case were the Orb and Sceptre.

To sum up: an examination of these scripts certainly does not prove survival but it does demonstrate that there was a pattern in them and that the pattern was not the product of wishful thinking or a kind of verbal pareidolia. It should be stressed that Trix Fleming never saw any of the scripts of the other automatists (except possibly one reference to the charonic staircase: Johnson 1910b: 273) and that Helen Verrall did not see any of the Margaret Verrall scripts referring to *The Cloud* or the Trix Fleming scripts before her early scripts of 1908 and 1910 were written. On the other hand, Margaret Verrall and Winifred Coombe-Tennant, as part automatists/part investigators, saw many scripts.

Progressive Correspondences of a Single Automatist

Two examples of this type of cross-correspondence have been given earlier: Statius and the Ear of Dionysius. A less familiar one is presented here (Johnson 1907-09: 312).

Theseus

Margaret Verrall 19/2/1906:

> Ask for the volume bound in green with a swan upon the cover. She will know…

Margaret Verrall 21/2/1906:

> The green book must be found with the swan upon it, there is verse inside. The swan is gilt and quite conspicuous

Margaret Verrall 14/5/1906:

> Ask for the fragment about the snake and bowl — your friend will know

Piddington took this to mean a nudge towards (a friend of the Verrall family) Gilbert Murray's (1904) *Euripides translated into English Rhyming Verse*, which contained in its appendix a number of fragments from his lost plays. The book was bound in green and it did have a swan on the cover. The last fragment in the book was the *Theseus* (the snake and the bowl referred to another fragment in the book that Murray had translated) and Piddington particularly noticed the shepherd's speech announcing the arrival of fresh victims for the Minotaur, one of whom was Theseus whose intention was to slay the monster. The shepherd was illiterate and could only describe the letters on the prow of the ship which spelled out Theseus's name in capitals (Murray 1904: 351–2). Piddington spotted that the descriptions of the s's, the sigmas, were described as 'curled like curling hair' and that they had frequently appeared in early Margaret Verrall script and played a dual symbolic role with their reference both to the Palm Maiden's hair and the labyrinth of the Minotaur.

The direct quotation from the play was:

> ΘΗΣΕΥΣ (THESEUS)
> First, a perfect round, through the heart of it one prick
> The second, two posts, one rail midway
> The third curled like curling hair
> The fourth one standing stave/three lying stiff
> The fifth two separate lines into one trunk
> The last was like the third

Piddington also concluded that there was a richer symbolism involved, since references to Theseus and Ariadne fitted neatly in the scripts in terms of the relationship between the Knight and the Palm Maiden; in terms of symbols of loss and separation; and in terms of a metaphor for solving a complex problem like the automatic writing scripts: 'Ariadne gives the clue', 'A long clue to unwind in a maze labyrinth'. (See Piddington 1919a: 208; Balfour, J. 1958–60: 214–15.)

One can therefore see that a number of the cross-correspondences did stand up in terms of the accuracy of the link between scripts and that this was not a mere imposition of meaning onto vague generalities. Yet, these symbolic cross-correspondences required an additional form of assessment: that is, a mapping or tracking exercise to see how the symbols were used in the scripts of other automatists. Was there a consistent rationale across all three thousand plus scripts (see appendix 1) for their selection and deployment? The task was and is an enormous one and only a limited demonstration of the process can be given here. One symbol has been selected for three of the main protagonists: May Lyttelton (the candle), Frank Balfour (Naples), and Arthur Balfour (Excalibur).

Candle/Candlestick

There were at least 47 candle/candlestick references in the scripts of the four main automatists, and the number increased if references to taper, chandelle, and candela were added, or if the symbol was broadened to include all lamp/lighthouse references that metaphorically suggested the Palm Maiden's role in providing the Knight with guidance and illumination. The candle/candlestick references were distributed fairly equally across all four writers. Helen Verrall and Trix Fleming had a small number of unmistakable ones, including allusions to *Macbeth* and *The Merchant of Venice*. They were written at a time when they had no access to other scripts in which the candle symbol was used and they had no sense of its symbolic role. The Lady Macbeth references particularly emphasised the death of the Palm Maiden—'Out, out brief candle', etc. In many cases other relevant symbols, statements, or descriptions occurred in the same script and there was only a moderate amount of incomprehensible material.

Margaret Verrall had access to the other scripts but her one candle reference was not Shakespearean but from a children's rhyme, *Oranges and Lemons*, which contained two symbols for the Palm Maiden—the candle (here comes a candle to light you to bed) and bells (The Bells of St Clement's)—and which was used on a number of occasions for that purpose in the scripts. It was only in Winifred Coombe-Tennant script that there was a specific allusion to the Lady in the Photograph (the picture of May Lyttelton with the candle).

Trix Fleming 15/3/1905:

> To-night she did not read herself to sleep the candle has not been lighted

The candle phrase was embedded in a script which had references to Laura Lyttelton and her death and to a woman with long fingers and a turquoise ring; and the clear statement, 'Make no apology for anything that may be written—What is very vague now may be revealed some day'. It is tempting to see this as an allusion to Arthur Balfour having his mother's ring placed in May's coffin. But one must be careful on several counts. The descriptions were too generalised. There was some ambiguity. Was the description of the woman a reference to May Lyttelton or to Margaret

Verrall? Finally, the candle reference seemed part of a simple narrative and not, except, by some straining, a symbolic reference.

Helen Verrall 12/8/1906:

> Mrs. Macalister and the broken candlestick

This was the first sentence of a script which might easily have been dismissed as meaningless. However, the line actually came from a work by R.M. Ballantyne, of Coral Island fame, and extracts from it, mentioning the candlestick, were in children's annuals as early as the 1860s (Routledge 1865: 457). The rest of the script was partially relevant in that it contained a reference to Berenice and her constellation, *Coma Berenices*, but it also had some apparently random names and a gnomic comment in Latin.

Trix Fleming 3/12/1906:

> Nowell—'So doth the Greater Glory dim the less'.

This is a *Merchant of Venice* quotation a couple of lines on from Portia's statement, 'How far that little candle throws his beams!/So shines a good deed in a naughty world'. The rest of the script had an apparent link with the Hope, Star, Browning cross-correspondence and a reference to, without much substantiating evidence, the death of Everard's brother, Basil. For Piddington, the first part of the script had a punning link to Roden Noel (Nowell) and in the middle of the script there were several lines of advice but, irritatingly as often in Fleming, one was not given the context—from whom to whom and why?

Margaret Verrall 7/1/1907:

> Jacob's letter [ladder?] was wanted...Diana is pleased...Here comes a candle to light you to bed.

The three phrases referred to Palm Maiden and Knight symbols: Jacob's Ladder to Heaven for their reunion after death; Diana Goddess of the Moon and the Candle for her spiritual guidance and illumination to the Knight in dreams. Here comes a candle to light you to bed from the *Oranges and Lemons* children's rhyme continues the illumination theme and to the bell symbolism linked to her; and after his death it was also used to indicate A.W. Verrall as a communicator because of the references to the Bells of St Clement's lines (St Clement Danes) close by the Inns of Court where he studied Law for three years.

Trix Fleming 16/1/1907:

> To-morrow—and to-morrow and to-morrow/Out out brief candle.

This was written the day before the anniversary of Myers' death (which date Trix Fleming knew). The rest of the script seemed to have been a subliminal reference to Trix Fleming's recent reading, Bram Stoker's *Reminiscences of Henry Irving*.

Helen Verrall 27/10/1910:

> Sleep Duncan sleep

This was a clear allusion to the murder of Duncan and the sleepwalking scene of Lady Macbeth with the candle, and occurred several times in script. The rest of the script was a series of short apparently disconnected phrases (all in English) which Piddington argued fitted in with the wider symbolic structure and message of the scripts.

Helen Verrall 1/2/1911:

> out, out brief candle

This phrase continued the Macbeth theme and the script had allusions to some symbols for the Knight—'flashing swords' (Arthur Balfour)—and to the Palm Maiden again (Adonais).

Winifred Coombe-Tennant 20/8/1911:

> How far that little candle sheds its beams

The statement occurred at the end of a script which was both curiously abstract and poetic at the same time. It was on the nature of individual consciousness and its relation to absolute or cosmic consciousness, using the metaphor of spray and the 'Abiding Ocean of Vital Force'. Again, as in some other Coombe-Tennant scripts, the ideas and the language seemed quite alien to her and, in fact, more reminiscent of the philosophical preoccupations of William James who had died the year before. James had speculated that the individual consciousness might, post-mortem, become part of the mother-sea, or World Soul, of consciousness, while possibly still retaining aspects of individuality (Kelly *et al.* 2015: 119). In this context, the little candle may have been both a symbol for the Palm Maiden and a metaphor for the relationship of individual consciousness to the World Soul. Again, a little caution is required. It is known that Winifred Coombe-Tennant had been given a copy of James's *Varieties of Religious Experience* at the beginning of their relationship (Lord 2011: 75).

Helen Verrall 25/8/1911:

> How far the little candle sheds his beams

The script also contained Francis Maitland Balfour symbols (snow and ice), Arthur Balfour symbols (the Horace reference triplex aes, the Ancient Mariner), and the Eumenides topic (Orestes) which was part of the major theme in scripts—the move from pagan savagery to civilised peace. The breast enclosed by triple brass was a symbol of courage and its appearance in the Horace ode was as part of his prayer for the protection of Virgil on his travels. Virgil in scripts stood for Arthur Balfour (see p. 237).

Winifred Coombe-Tennant 15/7/1915:

> Diana Here comes a candle to light you to bed & Berenice too the Candelabrum

Again, familiar Palm Maiden symbols were combined and this time with the Candelabrum which was a symbol for the Messianic Child (seven candles/seven discarnate influences). These symbols occurred in the lengthy script Winifred Coombe-Tennant wrote on her own after Alice Balfour had shown her to the Long Room at 4 Carlton Gardens containing the Perseus pictures. This triggered in her a sense of peace, belonging, and homecoming as reflected in both her diary entry and the script itself.

> How familiar this room is to you like a homecoming is it not You have a strange close link with it not only in the past but in the future...Sursam [sic] Corda

The phrase *sursum corda* (Lift up your hearts/part of the mass/and quoted in the *Little Flowers of St Francis* which Sidgwick was reading before his death) was a symbol for Francis Maitland Balfour. It was suggested that in some way the Palm Maiden, possibly through Henry Coombe-Tennant (a strange close link), was to be connected to the Balfour family in the future. Interestingly, on the following day she wrote (Lord 2011) that she met Gerald Balfour in London and they went through the script together and she annotated it for him. This tends to contradict some statements of Gerald Balfour's about her involvement. However, the circle can be squared if her comments were seen as purely the sources she was aware of for the material and not suggestions as to the symbolic Palm Maiden interpretation, of which she never appeared to have any knowledge. But, whatever the wider issues of interpretation, it was quite clear, that the candle reference was embedded in a body of relevant material, and not the only understandable fragment in vague nonsense.

Naples

Naples in the scripts was one of the symbols for Francis Maitland Balfour. As part of his zoological research he was based at the Stazione Zoologica at Naples for the study of marine animals and he regularly collected specimens from the Bay. There were at least ten allusive references to this across the four automatists including an indirect reference via a painting by Turner and a poem by Browning. Again, other relevant symbols occurred in the scripts from which the Naples symbol is taken, and much of the rest of the material was comprehensible. Two examples are given.

Trix Fleming 17/3/1908:

> Oh heaven and the terrible crystal etc

This was a quotation from Browning's *The Englishman in Italy*, a poem set in Piano di Sorrento on the south side of the Bay of Naples. This was seen as another reference to F.M.B. The script also included a number of Palm Maiden symbols—the hawthorn/may and reference to Dante's Beatrice.

Helen Verrall 7/7/1911:

> Labor improbus you have not understood that phrase look back
> A pine tree that is somewhere in the picture/Turner should help

This was a fairly explicit nudge in the direction of one of a number of paintings and sketches by Turner of the Bay of Naples, which also included pictures of pines and views of Vesuvius (therefore another indirect symbol for Francis Maitland Balfour). In addition, the phrase *Labor improbus* was also strongly pointed up. It came from Virgil's *Georgics* Book 1 and referred to the effort required in farming—toil overcomes all obstacles/*labor omnia vincit improbus*—after the end of the Golden Age, the Golden Age that first Augustus the Roman Emperor, and later Henry Augustus, the child of Winifred Coombe-Tennant and Gerald Balfour, were to restore. Again, the symbols were linked to each other.

Excalibur/Sword

There were at least twenty-four indirect references to the sword Excalibur in Margaret Verrall, Helen Verrall, and Winifred Coombe-Tennant scripts, including a number of sword drawings. In early Margaret Verrall scripts (from July 1901) these often occurred alongside drawings of a lock of hair (a symbol for the Palm Maiden). The early Margaret Verrall scripts were particularly interesting since she was the only one of the main automatists writing at the time and no one, at that stage, had any concept of the future design and development of the scripts. Other relevant symbols and descriptions also clustered round these Excalibur references though there was some incomprehensible material. See example below which clearly linked the Excalibur/sword symbolism with the hair symbolism (Knight and Palm Maiden).

Margaret Verrall 12/9/1901:

> In the long dull room with candles lighted...Scallop shells along the edge and marigolds—a funny little garden...sigma [drawing of a curl and drawing of a sword]

As Gerald Balfour stated (Piddington 1921: 159): 'Candles, a long room, and the rhyme "Mary, Mary, quite contrary" are all associated in the scripts with the Palm Maiden.' As has been seen, the Long Room was the room at 4 Carlton Gardens which served as a Music Room in the time of May Lyttelton and later the room in which the Perseus figures of Burne-Jones were displayed. Note the date of the script and that it was a script that Winifred Coombe-Tennant never saw and from which she could not have derived the candle references or the links with the Lyttelton family in her script of 15/7/1915 quoted above.

The link between the Sigma (Palm Maiden hair) and the Sword/Excalibur (Arthur Balfour) was particularly clear in the scripts and the point was made again and again.

Margaret Verrall 30/7/01:

> [drawing of a sword] This is the sign that helps and the snaky [drawing of a coil]

Margaret Verrall 17/10/1901:

> drawing of curly sigma and a sword I can't get it...But you are on the right track

Margaret Verrall 6/9/1902:

> Sigma is a riddle. Sigma will signify to your mind things not understood but to be understood some time. Only use intelligence and connect things of the same sort, even if they seem dragged in...

The Complexity of the Symbolism

But even though one can demonstrate that in a number of cases the same or similar symbols, or symbols with a clear rationale for the particular person referred to, were deployed across the scripts, this is only the start of the complexity. The tracking of a symbol could be made even more difficult depending on which particular aspect of it the communicator selected for transmission. Take the candle/illumination symbol. It was associated through the 'Oranges and Lemons' rhyme with the bells symbolism in scripts which, when followed through, led the reader on another convoluted journey.

As Piddington (1935b: 1065) put it: 'Thus there are Birth Bells (a peal of eight bells); Wedding Bells; and Death Bells; and in a great number of instances Bells are connected in one way or another with Light-houses. Then there are Tinkling Bells, and these include Sheep Bells, Sledge Bells, and Temple Bells. The epithet "tinkling" is, I think, important, for it may be intended to link these Bells on to the Golden Bough and its leafy gold, the foil (*bractea*) of which tinkled or rustled (*crepitabat*) in the breeze, and also on to the extremely thin *simulacra rerum* which Lucretius compares to cobwebs and to gold-leaf (*bractea* or *brattea auri*). Besides real Bells there are Bell-flowers, particularly the "Siver bells" in the garden of Mary, Mary, quite contrary, and the "white bells" of Tennyson's *Sea-Fairies*.' For

Piddington, these associationally related symbols were all meant to refer to — depending on context — the reunion of the Knight and the Palm Maiden, the death of the Palm Maiden, or the death of the Knight.[2]

The Peacock Symbol and Laura Lyttelton

Symbolic references to Laura Lyttelton displayed a similar rich allusiveness. According to Piddington, they could be traced as far back as the panoptican sphaerae/volatile ferrum references in very early Margaret Verrall scripts. Beyond its function as a cross-correspondence between Margaret Verrall and Leonora Piper, Piddington argued that the phrases had very strong connections to Laura Lyttelton, one of whose symbols in the scripts, he concluded, was Dido, Queen of Carthage. In the *Aeneid* Virgil had described Dido wounded with love for Aeneas as a deer is wounded with the spear of the hunter ('volatile ferrum'). The panopticon (all-seeing) element referred to the myth which explained how the peacock got its many-eyed tail (the story of Io and her guardian the hundred-eyed Argus) (Piddington 1943b: 726-7).

In addition, Piddington asserted that there were many references in early Margaret Verrall scripts to a real-life event connected with Laura which he finally identified as her Peacock Memorial in Mells Church. He made a detailed analysis of a number of the statements which seemed to refer tangentially to something being cut in hard stone with a knife.

Margaret Verrall 14/3/1901:

> hieroglyphema sane marmario glyptato non sine caelato
> quid dicam stellato cultellario.

Margaret Verrall 8/4/1901:

> Hieroglyphemata...Stellato cultellario...inscriptione porcellina
> in marmoreo topho glyptata...more pavonis.

Margaret Verrall 28/8/1901:

> cut on grey stone glyptatus in marmoreo lapide cultellario.

Glyptatus is from the Greek *gluptikos*, and the English adjective glyptic refers to carving on precious objects. The stem *hiero* means sacred. Glyphe means a carved character, from the Greek *gluphe*. *Cultellus* is a knife. *Stellatus* is starry. *Inscriptio* is inscription. *Porcellana* is the Latin for porcelain. Sky is *caelum*. *Sane* is certainly or truly. *Tofus/tofo* is tufa, a kind of limestone easy to work with. Marble is *marmor*. *Mos/more* in the manner

---

[2] Piddington (1935a: 933), based on his reading of Anatole France's *Vie de Jeanne D'Arc*, saw St Catherine of Alexandria's role as the Patron Saint of bells as further support of these links.

of a peacock, *pavo/pavonis*. *Lapis/lapidis* is stone. It is quite clear in their mongrel Latin/Greek fashion the scripts were referring to something carved on a durable white or off-white substance. Gesso is such a substance — a long-lasting primer applied with several, sometimes many, coats on which sculptors carve: and there are hints as to what was inscribed — the peacock and the starry tail.

There was also an interesting script by Helen Verrall of 13/4/1903, written on Easter Sunday (Laura died on Easter Eve 1886), which mentioned a peacock's feather connected with someone, with the instruction *to remember it since time will show the connection*. For Piddington the allusion was to Burne-Jones's memorial to Laura in Mells Church, Somerset: eight foot high in white gesso, in the shape of a peacock on a laurel tree, the laurel bursting out of the tomb. The peacock was a symbol for the Resurrection. Its most remarkable feature was the long tail, with its distinctive eyes, running down the length of the memorial. Burne-Jones made it at the request of an intimate friend of Laura's, Francis Graham (whose brother had been May Lyttelton's betrothed before his death), later the wife of John Horner, the owner of the estate at Mells. Burne-Jones, deeply affected by Laura's death, kept a painted cast of the memorial (now in the Victoria and Albert Museum) in the entrance hall of his home, The Grange. There was a further small detail to add, not picked up by Piddington, who was puzzled by the reference, in another part of the Margaret Verrall script of 28/8/1901, to a font. A visit to Mells in 2015 revealed that the bapistry with its Norman font was only a few yards away from the Peacock Memorial.

Burne-Jones also painted a mermaid picture, *The Depths of the Sea*, which he associated with the siren-like qualities of Laura, and the symbol of the mermaid is frequently repeated in scripts. Burne-Jones, who described himself as an 'occasional Soul', was greatly attracted to several of the young women who were part of that group, and Laura's death was memorialised in a variety of ways in his art. Burne-Jones inscribed the words 'In Memoriam L.L. Easter 1886' in the bottom left-hand corner of his picture *The Morning of the Resurrection* which was exhibited at the Grosvenor Gallery in 1886. Burne-Jones also had the phrase *habes tota quod mente petisti* (you have all that your heart desired) from *Aeneid* IV added to the frame (this original frame was later replaced) of *The Depths of the Sea* after her death. That phrase was quoted in Margaret Verrall's script of 14/3/1901.

At the time in 1901 Margaret Verrall and her colleagues had absolutely no idea of the potential meaning of these phrases, as was patently obvious from the way she treated them in her report of 1906. Her husband, Arthur, translated as much of the garbled Latin as he could but he and she were baffled by the phrases which Piddington later found so significant. For example (Verrall 1906): 'On March 14, 1901, in an unintelligible passage apparently concerned with an inscription, occur the words: "hieroglyphema sane marmorio glyptato non sine caelato quid dicam stellato cultellario." Little can be said of this incomprehensible medley except that it clearly contains a pun on the two meanings of the Latin word *caelum*, "chisel" and "heaven"; the first meaning was apparently intended, then the second meaning seems to occur to the scribe and produces the allusion to the "starry" knife, or whatever he may please to by *cultellario*. The play upon the word is marked by the regular classical phrase, *quid dicam*? "may I say?"' However, Piddington saw that this phrase could, very roughly, be translated as 'a hieroglyph/memorial definitely with marble sign not without chisel, or may I say, with starry knife.'

These fragmented statements did carry a certain intelligibility if worked at, and were given greater weight in that they clustered together and reinforced each other. Margaret Verrall script of 14/3/1901 linked the *habes tota quod* quotation with a memorial inscription; Margaret Verrall script 17/3/1901 alluded, through the word *recordamini*, to a quotation from the Vulgate, Luke xxiv (on the risen Christ), carved on the memorial tablet (*Non est hic sed surrexit recordamini qualiter locutus est*/he is not here but arisen remember how he spoke); Margaret Verrall script 8/4/1901 written on Easter Monday (Laura died on Easter Eve 1886) had a reference to Dido's sister Anna (Anna soror), to a cut inscription, and a peacock; and, as mentioned above, Piddington traced allusions in other scripts to Ovid *Metamorphoses* I 583–750, which told the story of how Juno put the hundred eyes of Argus into the feathers of her own bird, the peacock. There were two books that might have contained relevant information from which Margaret Verrall's scripts were built up: *Edward Burne-Jones, A Record and Review* by Malcolm Bell, 1893, which had a reproduction of the memorial in it and the Latin inscription; and Lady Burne-Jones *Memorials of Burne-Jones*, 1904. There is no evidence that Margaret Verrall had read either and she was scrupulous about recording such items. It should be noted that Lady Burne-Jones's book was not published till three years after the early Margaret Verrall scripts. Much of this material was highly complex and tedious to read and unravel but, for those with the patience to wade through it, it seemed to have had a solid base (Piddington 1943c: 1096–106, 1486–518).

Later scripts by other automatists were, thankfully, much more open and moving about Laura Tennant/Lyttelton, but because already in the public domain, their emotional content was probably more powerful than their paranormal evidentiality, particularly in Trix Fleming's scripts. She had references to Lady Elcho (a member of the Souls and and an intimate friend of Arthur Balfour) and her friendship with Laura and Alfred Lyttelton. There were eleven references to 'Annette' as Laura was disguised in the scripts ('George' was Alfred) published in the *Proceedings*

(Johnson 1907–09) between January 1904 and August 1905: to the date of her death, her house, her sisters, her child who died young (erroneously referred to as a girl), and to Laura's cradle. This was an item in Laura's will, which was read out loud by Margot Tennant (Laura's sister) to a highly embarrassed company shortly after Laura's death (Asquith 1920): 'I leave Mary Elcho my Chippendale cradle… She gave me the lovely hangings, and I think she will love it a little for my sake, because I always loved cradles and all cradled things.'

There was another script that had links with Laura. Trix Fleming was staying with Edward Tennant, Laura's brother, at his house in Wiltshire and on Easter Eve 10/4/1909 her script began: 'The Eve of All. The Great Token-Noli me tangere.' Laura died on Easter Eve 24/4/1886 and *noli me tangere* was an umistakeable allusion to Burne-Jones's picture *The Morning of the Resurrection*. There were also Laura Lyttelton references in Winifred Coombe-Tennant scripts, as has been seen, but she had a passionate interest in the arts and would have known the Pre-Raphaelites well, though her specific knowledge of Burne-Jones and his links with Laura is difficult to estimate.

From even this limited examination of a small selection of symbols, it is quite obvious that there was purpose, consistency, and organisation in the manipulation and deployment of the script content. The symbols were not vague. Their rationale was understandable, drawn as it was directly from the lives and environments of the main communicators, even if the allusions to those lives and contexts were indirect, terse, and in a mixture of Greek, Latin, and English. Some of the symbolism in scripts was of the kind against which the charge of loose generality could be levelled and sustained (roses, lilies, etc., the stock poetic repertoire) but the symbols examined above were clearly not of this sort and they appeared in and across the body of the scripts with other material that reinforced the overall intentions and purposes. The intricate and sustained hair symbolism was only the most high profile example of this central feature of the scripts.

The Plan

When one considers another major feature of the scripts — the prediction of a new Golden Age ushered in by a new Augustus — two further questions present themselves. First, were the references to a new Golden Age sufficiently clear, sustained, and reliable to be called messages? Second, was there any evidence beyond the scripts of Winifred Coombe-Tennant that the new Augustus was to be Henry Coombe-Tennant?

One of Margaret Verrall's early scripts stressed the importance of Virgilian references (largely though not excusively from the *Aeneid*). The main sections in the *Aeneid* referring to the Golden Age occurred, quite naturally since they were both classicists, in her scripts and in Helen's. The most significant were made long before Winifred Coombe-Tennant became involved in the automatic writing. These were:

In Margaret Verrall scripts 21/12/1901, 13/1/1902, 29/1/1902, and 3/2/1902, clear references in Latin to people of the toga, which meant those wearing the toga, the symbol of Roman citizenship and the Pax Romana, and came from *Aeneid* Book 1 257–296, a section which also predicted the coming of peace under Augustus.

In Margaret Verrall script 21/3/1901, Helen Verrall script 2/12/1907, 10/2/1909, 29/8/1904, 16/8/1907, 6/5/1909, there were clear references in Latin to the Sibyl of Cumae who prophesied the future greatness of Aeneas and his line leading to Augustus and the death of Augustus's nephew Marcellus, who was regarded as a sacrifice to the future destiny of Rome. These allusions clustered round the famous scene in Book VI when Aeneas descended into the underworld and visited his father, Anchises, who showed him his descendants, including the unfortunate Marcellus.

And there were further relevant allusions in Margaret Verrall scripts, 19/3/1903 and 12/12/1910, to *Aeneid* Book VIII and to the shield of Aeneas made by Vulcan, the craftsman god, decorated with great events in Roman history with at its centre the future victory of Augustus over Antony and Cleopatra at Actium. However, these references were rather sparse and fragmented and it is very important to look at the remaining information in these scripts to try to deal with the charge that the material was not just cherry-picked from unintelligible free-associating automatic script. For example in Margaret Verrall 21/12/1901:

> Marigolds and Cockle shells—Find the key for the lock and keep it close…gens togata

One can see script symbolism, later very familiar to the investigators but at this stage completely unknown to anybody, being introduced, and there was the hint with the lock/key reference that the matter was significant. For in this script were brought together Knight and Palm Maiden symbols which in their turn were connected with the theme of peace.

It is also important to examine whether or not the Plan was just a piece of consolatory interpretation grafted onto the scripts by investigators working on them during the dark days of World War I and the economic and social difficulties postbellum. But such references occurred long before the War and seemed to have had a crafted structure to them and they were not just found in Margaret Verrall's writing. For example, Helen Verrall (who did not see any of her mother's early scripts on this theme till 1912) expressed the Messianic theme, in a nuanced and indirect fashion, combining sources from two different Latin poets.

Helen Verrall 6/5/1909 (Margaret Verrall present):

> ...tu Marcellus eris that was said
> tanta erat moles Romanam condere gentem many sacrifices to
> the purposes of Fate that was the thought it is in Horace
> too Do you U.D?
> Margaret Verrall.Yes. Is the word or idea in Horace?
> *Idea* jam satis and elsewhere in Horace

Jam satis (already enough) referred to the second ode in Book One of Horace's *Odes*. The poet argued that only Augustus could bring to an end the suffering and ghastly portents that afflicted Rome after the murder of Julius Caesar. Which God, the poet asked, would restore order? Not Mars the God of war but Augustus in the guise of Mercury the God of poetry. In scripts Augustus stood for the Messianic Child. Equally specific was the Virgilian reference *in tanta erat moles* etc. above (so great a struggle it was to found the Roman Race). This statement and references to it cropped up throughout the scripts and Myers himself alluded to the phrase at the end of *Human Personality*, adapting it to the spiritual struggle of humanity as it strove for spiritual development both incarnate and discarnate. Note that Helen Verrall was not told the details of the Plan till the 1930s. Margaret Verrall was not informed of the Plan till 1912. Therefore, it was a truly independent reference to one of the two main themes in the scripts.

Two further aspects of the Messianic theme need to be stressed. First, that the Messianic element was much more than the Pax Romana which was based on the triumph and power of Roman arms. It was to be the establishment not only of world peace but also of a world civilisation, as has been seen.

Margaret Verrall 29/4/1907 (quoted before):

> But I mean a wider thing, a universal country, the mother of us all...Not O fair City of Cecrops But Oh fair city of God...The city of Cecrops is violet and hoary look back at that. The Universal City is all colours and no colour but best described as a golden as a golden GLEAM.

Second, this Plan could not be achieved without a considerable amount of suffering and sacrifice. A number of cultural allusions were used to express this: the Thyestean banquet and Medea killing her children, for example. However, a particularly accessible one was the role played in scripts by Elizabeth Barrett Browning's poem, *A Musical Instrument*.The theme of the poem was a stern and challenging one: that great art and achievement sprang from toil and suffering:

> This is the way laughed the great god Pan
> (Laughed while he sat by the river),
> The only way, since the gods began
> To make sweet music, they could succeed.

> Yet half a beast is the great god Pan,
> To laugh as he sits by the river,
> Making a poet out of a man;
> The true gods sigh for the cost and the pain—
> For the reed which grows nevermore again
> As a reed with the reeds of the river.

Gerald Balfour argued that directly or indirectly elements from this poem were used in ten Helen Verrall scripts and that Tennyson's *In Memoriam* was also used in a sophisticated way to get the theme across, particularly in the Helen Verrall script below.

Helen Verrall 22/1/1909:

> The river—by the river. What is he doing the great good Pan? E.D.B. what initials are those? I sing but as the linnet sings Trix Fleming wrote it too.

There was the slight error in Mrs Browning's initials (really E.B.B.) and one senses a deliberate mistake in good for God, hinting that the pain was for ultimate benefit. The phrase 'as the linnet sings' led to *In Memoriam* xxi:

> I take the grasses from the grave
> And make them pipes whereon to blow.

Two immediate points are worth comment. Trix Fleming did not write anything from that part of *In Memoriam* though she frequently quoted from or alluded to the poem. In addition, it is interesting that, on one of the occasions that he sat with Helen Verrall, Piddington was asked to make sure that he traced and understood the references to this topic; and in Helen Verrall's script of 10/11/1910 there is no vagueness or ambiguity about this:

> I take the rushes from the grave and make a pipe whereon to blow—that is better—It is something of the same idea in Mrs Browning the great god Pan—the living man and the dead—the heart of a man—that is what we wanted to say here and elsewhere—I think it should be traced.

In Mrs Browning's poem the tall reed in the river was hacked down by Pan, its pith (like the heart of a man) removed so that Pan could blow into it and make sweet music, and the same process was alluded to in the Tennyson quotation. Tennyson described himself singing like Pan to 'him that rests below', namely the dead Arthur Hallam: 'I take the grasses of the grave, And make them pipes whereon to blow.' He had been accused by critics of making poetry out of private pain, and ignoring the great issues of the time, but his defence was 'I do but sing because I must, And pipe but as the linnets sing'.

The whole point, Piddington and Balfour argued, was to link the idea of pain and sacrifice to ultimate gain and achievement both for individuals and civilisations. Just as Hallam's death led to Tennyson's greatness as a poet, so to war and sacrifice would lead to spiritual growth and social and international reform, and the early deaths of Laura and Edith's children would lead ultimately to the development of an individual (Henry) and a group of spiritually influenced young people working to establish the new world civilisation. There can be little doubt that these themes of sacrifice and the coming of a new Golden Age did appear in the scripts, but there does not seem to have been any explicit linkage of a persuasive nature to one individual, one Messianic Child, except in the scripts of Winifred Coombe-Tennant.

13
Did the Scripts Demonstrate Paranormal Cognition?

It is very important in this connection to consider the different backgrounds and personalities of the automatists. The demonstration of classical knowledge, unless really sophisticated, would not be impressive coming from Helen or Margaret Verrall. In terms of knowledge of society, both Trix Fleming and Winifred Coombe-Tennant, in different ways and at different times, moved in circles that could have provided them with a lot of social and cultural information which their dramatic imaginations might have reworked and represented as paranormal.

Trix Fleming's scripts present a particular difficulty in this respect. It was seen in Part 1 how impressive some of her scripts were in their descriptions of people and places apparently beyond her ken. But other material was less clear cut owing to her social contacts and wide reading. For example, because of her family connections with the Burne-Joneses and the fact that her parents moved to Tisbury, not far from the Wyndham family at Clouds, Trix Fleming had occasional contact with the Souls. Arthur Balfour still was and Laura Lyttelton had been a member of that group. Trix Fleming had visited Clouds in 1895 when the first 'Laura' scripts were produced and she was invited in 1906, as has been already mentioned, to the annual April/Easter house party that the Wyndhams threw.

This was a major social occasion and one which Arthur Balfour regularly attended through his life, as did Sir Oliver Lodge in later years. He and Arthur Balfour would often drive off for a game of golf during the stay, a game nicely enlivened by the hamper of cold food and bottle of Chateau Yquem prepared for them by Mary Elcho, Balfour's lover, and the daughter of their host, Percy Wyndham (Jolly 1975). On that occasion, at Clouds, Lodge talked freely to Trix Fleming, showing her part of the proofs of *Proceedings* XX (Margaret Verrall's report on her own scripts) and forgot to tell Alice Johnson about this. Arthur Balfour himself was incorporated into a script written by her while they were both there and so one must very carefully probe any Arthur Balfour references in her later scripts.

Trix Fleming 15/4/1906:

> Make no blunder over this for it is important.
> Tell him the family history will not repeat itself in this case.
> Older than the mother was and even more beautiful a passing.

Both Balfour's parents died relatively young. Trix Fleming possibly knew this from reading a memoir about his mother, Lady Blanche Balfour. However, one should point out that Balfour did live to a good age and the account of his death in the associated cross-correspondence literature is moving.

One also has to be very cautious about all references to Lady Mount-Temple in Trix's automatic writing. One of the leading patrons of Spiritualist ideas and alternative beliefs in the late nineteenth century, she was well known to Myers and Gurney, who first met Stainton Moses at Broadlands (her Hampshire estate) and whose accounts of his mediumship encouraged their (particularly Myers') early ventures in psychical research (Burd 1982; Hoare 2005). Again, uncertainty as to Trix Fleming's normal knowledge of Lady Mount-Temple made scripts like the one below difficult to assess. She said that she had only met Lady Mount-Temple once when she visited a friend in Torquay who took her to Babbacombe where Lady Mount-Temple moved after leaving Broadlands. But she occasionally frequented circles where she might have picked up some background material either through gossip or reading which, dramatically reshaped, could have appeared in her scripts.

Trix Fleming 28/2/1906:

> It was first started when we were all sitting under the cedars at Broadlands. While the sunset flared crimson on that noble window.

This script seems to have been derived from *Fragments of Prose and Poetry* (Myers 1904b: 38–9): the sunlight, the lawns, 'the immemorial forest-trees'. A later script on 4/4/1906 linked the Mount-Temples with Henry Fawcett, who worked with Lord Mount-Temple for the preservation of commons and open spaces, especially the New Forest. Henry Fawcett, the blind postmaster general who hunted and stood for parliament, had a reputation for courage and a certain sort of manliness in some intellectual circles (Collini 1991). Trix Fleming did not know the Fawcetts and Fawcett died in 1884 when she was a child, but as an avaricious reader she may have picked up some details from the press and books (or via the work of Fawcett's wife, Millicent, who long outlived him and who was the high profile leader of the Suffragists). In another part of this script, obvious symbols for Fawcett were provided: dark glasses, a letter, and the whip. This seems somewhat more convincing than Trix's Arthur Balfour script above and it was wrapped in a complex cross-correspondence with other automatists on bearers of the name Fawcett and its meaning (see above).

Another example of paranormal cognition that was difficult to assess was the message from Constance Wilde (who had died in 1898), a close friend of Lady Mount-Temple, to her son Cyril via Lady Mount-Temple's adopted daughter Juliet.

Trix Fleming 7/1/1904:

> I want Juliet to go to Cyril — he is needlessly miserable — someone has been talking very unwisely to him.

Trix Fleming did not know the name Cyril at the time and she was not sure if she had known that Lady Mount-Temple had been kind to the Wilde family and was an intimate of Constance's. The Wilde children certainly suffered in later years because of the Wilde trial and its repercussions, and Constance changed her name after Wilde's conviction and took the boys to Switzerland.

Lady Mount-Temple may have contributed unwittingly to the Wildes' miseries (Moyle 2012: 213–16). She had lent Constance her house at Babbacombe, near Torquay. It occupied a fine position overlooking the bay and was full of Pre-Raphaelite treasures, including Rossetti's *Beata Beatrix*. Lady Mount-Temple named her favourite room Wonderland (referred to as the Paradise room in the scripts). Oscar Wilde and Lord Alfred Douglas stayed at Babbacombe while Constance went abroad and the fateful relationship developed. Some of this information might have been known to Trix Fleming. She did once meet Wilde at the Burne-Joneses, disliking him, and describing his sluglike lips in a letter of 18/3/1882 to Rudyard Kipling (Birkenhead 1978: 107). She skewered Wilde very effectively. 'To look at he is like a bad copy of a bust of a very decadent Roman Emperor, roughly modelled in suet pudding.' The writing is very sharp. She was only thirteen at the time. In addition, her friends, the Wyndhams of Clouds, were distantly related to Lord Alfred Douglas and she may have picked up gossip from them (Dakers 1993).

Establishing prior knowledge and estimating the precision or the generality of her descriptions can be (though an issue with all the automatists) a particularly tricky problem in her automatic writing. In three scripts, 1/3/1905, 15/3/1905, 20/3/1907, a woman's physical appearance was sketched. Initially, Alice Johnson claimed it for Margaret Verrall. Much later, Piddington suggested that some features could refer to May Lyttelton. One of them seemed to fit quite well with those photographs of May Lyttelton that still exist: the length of face, the expanse of skin between nose and upper lip, the slight hollowed outline of the cheeks, the abundant dark hair knotted at the base of the neck, and the long fingers. It seems both a good illustration of the problems involved in identifying individuals from insufficiently precise descriptors, *a priori* desires to make things fit, and the discarnate Gurney's point that the communicators did not have complete control over the process of communication. Piddington, to his credit, was alive to these issues, and, painstakingly, phrase by phrase, identified the similarities and differences between the scripts that contained these descriptive features (Piddington 1921: 402–7). His conclusion was that aspects of the appearance of both of them were successfully outlined but the descriptions were blurred because of the mistakes the automatist made in the process of communication. On the other hand, the description of Winifred Coombe-Tennant's house at Cadoxton, the appearance, environment, and personality of Hodgson, and the catching of Myers' warm appreciation of Lodge all had a sharpness and vivid specificity about them.

The most impressive evidence for paranormal cognition occurred in the Piper, Coombe-Tennant, and Fleming scripts where they displayed classical knowledge, expertly deployed, completely outside their knowledge and capacity. The clearest examples of these were the Lethe case, Margaret Verrall's two questions to Myers (the Archytas Ode; the phrase *autos ouranos akumon*), and Dorr's quizzing Myers on the *Aeneid*. These were discussed above but they still need to be seen in the broader context, generally, of paranormal cognition and the difficulties involved in establishing its authenticity.

In the case of Leonora Piper, the assessment of paranormal cognition was superficially straightforward—it was by direct questioning of the discarnate who was communicating. But there was a real issue with the other automatists unless someone else was sitting with them at the time. The ownership of, the reflection on, and the interrogation of one's own memories demonstrably from one's own perspective is a key identifying test for psychological individuality and it can be explored in a Piper-like situation by direct interview. But when memories presented in automatic script are examined, without a sitter present, it is difficult both to attribute them to a particular individual and have that individual own and demonstrate that ownership. In the scripts of Margaret Verrall, Helen Verrall, and Trix Fleming, sometimes there were only voices, disconnected, abrupt, fragmentary, urgent, demanding, wistful, elegaic. To which communicator did these memories belong? Sometimes other detail in the scripts helped the identification. But there was often uncertainty as to whom the particular memories belonged—the discarnate communicator, a 'passing' discarnate, or the automatist herself?

There were plenty of examples of different types of memories in the scripts: some demonstration of the procedural memories of the classicist, the semantic memories of the philosopher, and a number of autobiographical and episodic memories. However, with autobiographical and episodic memories, the unambiguous attribution of them to the discarnate individual concerned varied according to the amount of information available to verify that the incidents and episodes referred to actually occurred and that it was absolutely certain that the automatist had no prior access to the information displayed in their script. There is probably no cast iron example to put forward. Some of the most moving and apparently convincing communications—like the Laura Lyttelton communications in Trix Fleming script—must be discarded on these grounds. On the other hand, some material does stand up to sustained scrutiny, as does the evidence for intricate design that ran through many of the scripts which inevitably required the capacity to access a specialist body of knowledge for its creation.

As well as statements that seemed to reflect individual personality and identity, there were also a number of predictive statements seeded across the scripts. By one standard, of course, these communications were exemplary in that they were written down in advance. But that does not always work in their favour. Trix Fleming, perhaps reflecting her own history of mental ill-health, seemed almost obsessively concerned with issuing warnings or predicting illness and recovery to a wide variety of known and unknown characters in her scripts. Moreover, a number of the predictions would not meet the test of non-inferential predictions (that is, predictions that could not reasonably be inferred from the current situation of the individual(s) concerned: see Irwin and Watt 2007). Good examples of this were prophecies concerning the coming of war and the veiled references to Arthur Balfour's important political role later in life. The former, no doubt, could be explained by the international tensions before 1914, and one has to ask, re the latter, how many of them occurred during Balfour's lean political period from 1906–1914 and how many at the time of the revival of his career during and after the First World War?

Llangattock in Helen Verrall script (the Welsh for Cadoxton, the home of Winifred Coombe-Tennant) had, as has been seen, precision, signalling, and other verifiable details clustering round it. But something can be both highly specific and commonplace at the same time. Roy (2008) makes play of the name Winifred mentioned in Fleming script, stating that it is precognitive. But Trix Fleming could have equally been referring to her good friend Winifred Holt (daughter of the publisher Henry Holt who wrote on the cross-correspondences and knew both Myers and William James). Llangattock, particularly its frequent repetition, deserved serious attention, but names like Winifred, Florence, Ethel (these latter two also occurring in scripts), with their Edwardian flavour, did not, unless they were well supported by contextual detail.

In more general terms, there were some impressive examples of paranormal cognition concerning the lives and personalities of the ostensible communicators and some of the automatists: Myers' unexpurgated autobiography and his love for Annie Marshall, the characters of Myers and Gurney (Sidgwick featured but with less élan than his friends), the character and appearance of Mrs and Professor Verrall, the Lyttelton family and descriptions of their home at Hagley Hall, and Winifred Coombe-Tennant's home at Cadoxton, for example. But verifying such descriptions took and takes much time and labour, and the picture that emerges can sometimes be less clear cut than appears at first sight.

Take the references to syringa. In Myers' life syringa flowers, as has been seen, were symbols for his intimate moments walking with Annie Marshall, before her death, in the valley/gardens at Hallsteads in the Lake District. In one of her early automatic scripts (5/2/1904) Margaret Verrall had:

> Five syringa flowers I tried to say that before like white stars in the dusk. you will find that written.

Winifred Coombe-Tennant, as stated above, wrote on 1/5/1910: 'Syringa... Something in his own life and that Syringa implies it all.' Winifred Coombe-Tennant had not seen and did not read Myers' unpublished autobiography with its syringa references till 9/10/1910.

It all seems very convincing, but Margaret Verrall had already learnt from Hodgson early in 1904 (see below) the importance Myers attached to syringa, though she did not read the poem in his autobiography, stressing the link between syringa and Annie Marshall, till the end of the year. And by the time Winifred Coombe-Tennant came to write the script of 1/5/1910, Margaret Verrall, Oliver Lodge, and probably both Piddington and Alice Johnson all knew of its significance. The potential for leakage, telepathic and/or social, existed.

On the other hand, after she had understood the full significance of syringa, Margaret Verrall looked back in her own scripts to search for other references to the flower and found:

16/5/1902:

> The crown of flowers will soon be plain L. florum corona mox tibi plana erit.

18/5/1902:

> in the woods it will be found the sweetest flower that blows — then you will know that I sent you this message, all in a month of May.

24/11/1902:

> Try other flowers yourself to send — white with a scent — that helps

And the evidence came from multiple sources. There were the cryptic references in early Margaret Verrall scripts: on 9/9/1903 the word coronaria; on 17/9/1903 you have the key word '...Berenice's hair'; 5/10/1903, 'this is the sign and name: send'; 20/1/1904, Hodgson wrote Mrs Verrall that coronaria suggested the plant syringa (philadelphus coronarius). Mrs Verrall realised that Berenice's hair (she was the daughter in law of Ptolemy Philadelphus and cut off her hair in order to ensure the safe return of her husband/his son from the wars) was also a coded reference to syringa. Finally, Mrs Verrall read in Myers' unexpurgated autobiography (Piddington 1943: 513) the poem that described Myers walking with Annie in the valley at Hallsteads in intimate spiritual communion: 'When in late twilight slowly thou hast strayed/Thro' wet syringas and a black-green shade.'

The mediumship of Winifred Coombe-Tennant, as has been seen, provided some of the most powerful evidence for paranormal cognition but here one must be very careful to distinguish between that material semi-consciously acquired through reading or social interaction, then imaginatively reworked and presented in a highly persuasive manner, and those scripts that clearly contained information that went beyond what was in the normal knowledge and understanding of the automatist. Into the former category must fall some of the references to Laura Lyttelton, who was extremely well-known in upper-class social, cultural, and intellectual circles in the 1880s. Into the latter fall the Ear of Dionysius/Statius cases and the philosophical discussions between Gurney and Gerald Balfour (though even here, as mentioned earlier, one must exercise caution given that it is known that Winifred Coombe-Tennant read the *The Hibbert Review: A Quarterly Review of Religion, Theology and Philosophy*).

There was frequent reference in the scripts of other automatists to the difficulties of communication, but it was only in Winifred Coombe-Tennant's scripts that the matter was explored in depth and the process analysed and, while acknowledging the caveat above, if one compares the language of Winifred Coombe-Tennant's diary with the sophisticated nature of her philosophical scripts (ably analysed and written up by Gerald Balfour 1935: see also Broad's lucid and perceptive account 1962: 287–314) they seemed way beyond her range. A summary of some of this content now follows.

The discarnates, particularly Gurney, stressed that there were three main methods of communication — telepathy, telaesthesia, and telergy, though the balance between the methods and the precise relationship and blend between communicator and medium was as infinitely variable as the nature of individual personality itself. Under the generic heading of telepathy, Gurney identified three subsets. The first was the bullet-like transfer from one mind (incarnate or discarnate) to another of words, images, impressions, and intuitions. The second was the allowing of the medium into the communicator's mind by a deliberate opening of selective parts of that mind, partially lifting the shutters as it were. The third was accidental leakage from the communicator's mind.

Gurney also distinguished telaesthesia from telepathy. Telepathy was the communication of thought but telaesthesia was 'knowledge, not thought, acquired by the subliminal when operating normally in the metetherial'. This distinction, however, needs further unpicking. Myers defined telaesthesia in terms of clairvoyance, but in the sense used in the Coombe-Tennant scripts it referred more to the access of the contents of another mind rather than the usual definition of clairvoyance which was the direct perception of objects/events in the physical environment, other than through the normal senses. In truth, the terms may shade into each other, as acts of clairvoyance or telaesthesia in the sense that Myers defined it (and which Myers himself recognised) may in fact be acts that access the contents of other minds — it is merely that the mind, living or dead, cannot be identified. The problem is that, as Tyrrell (1961) pointed out, such a faculty in its widened sense could undercut the apparent accuracy of mediumistic communications. As a communicator, Gurney himself recognised this: 'What I am saying may be used to cut at the spiritualistic hypothesis, but it doesn't... who selects what of the total telaesthetically acquired knowledge shall externalize itself — shall blend with those elements received by direct telepathic impact?'

The essential preliminary to all this, whether the communication was telepathic or telaesthetic, was the process of excursus. (This should clearly be distinguished from its use in *Notes and Excursuses* where the term was used in the sense of an expanded and detailed commentary on something.) This required entering a condition of active passivity or meditation, and again and again across all the automatists that state of calm and alert tranquility was emphasised. Piddington, following scriptic clues, called it the 'native element', the metetherial environment in which communication could take place. It was through a stratum of the subliminal of the medium that this communication took place. By a process of mutual selection the communicator could take matter from any part of the medium's mind but the medium could only access part of the communicator's mind (unless there was accidental leakage). Both paranormal knowledge and the cross-correspondences themselves were created by this process. Communication was not perfect because it was constrained by the resources available in the medium's mind and the instability of the discarnate/incarnate interaction. Gurney distinguished three strata in the subliminal mind of the medium which he labelled $H/0$, $H/1$, $H/2$, and it was at the third stratum ($H/2$) closest to consciousness (which Gerald Balfour roughly identified with Freud's preconsciousness) that the message was actually bound into language for transmission. Broad (1962: 312) wrote with characteristic dry humour: 'At any rate, it may be fairly said that the Gurney-persona is pellucidly clear, even in his darkest utterances, in comparison with, e.g., Hegel or Whitehead at their not infrequent worst.' It is obvious from an examination of her published diary that the above philosophical and psychological content was not part of Winifred Coombe-Tennant's daily intellectual activity. There was, almost certainly in these scripts, a marked qualitative difference in cognitive style and capacity.

There is another interesting contrast between her scripts and the published diary. In the scripts there were barely disguised references to the Balfour, Lyttelton, and other upper- and upper-middle-class families of the period. Given her position in society and the importance of these individuals in the political and cultural elite of the time, and the fact that her mother-in-law (Gertrude Tennant) was a renowned society hostess, one would have expected her background knowledge to have been considerable. Yet, her diary for the period does not reveal either a wide social acquaintance with these families or any sense that she was researching them or fascinated by them. The full diaries of Winifred Coombe-Tennant are not yet available to researchers and when they are it may be possible to have greater clarity on this question.

Trix Fleming is also rather difficult to read in this connection. She produced three levels of statements: knowing, often inaccurate, references to people's health and what might happen to them; sometimes surprisingly impressive and apposite descriptions of people and places; and, finally, a small number of specific items that clearly transcended her own knowledge and capacity. She, too, like Winifred Coombe-Tennant often seemed unaware of the references in her scripts and also, like Winifred Coombe-Tennant, had (though more sporadically) access to aristocratic circles.

There were at least two examples of access to information beyond her own background and experience, and both are worth exploring in some depth.

The first was the use of the words *eidolon* and *simulacrum*. *Eidolon* and *simulacrum* occurred in her script of 7/1/1904:

> I want to make it thoroughly clear to you all that the eidolon is not the spirit-only the simulachrum [sic]

Alice Johnson stated that this theory as to the nature of a ghost or phantasm was probably derived from pages 3–10 in the second volume of *Human Personality*. Yet the actual words *eidolon* and *simulacrum* were not used in that section, and, as Margaret Verrall pointed out, they were used in Trix Fleming's script in the way that a classical scholar would and one who was familiar with them in Homer and Lucretius. In the *Odyssey* (XI 601) Odysseus met the phantom (*eidolon*) of Heracles in Hades while the real Heracles himself (*autos*) 'rejoices amid the immortals...' The *eidolon* or *simulacrum* is the phantom image of the individual projected by them but not the individual themselves. See Trix Fleming's script of 8/1/1904 where the same point continued:

> The appearance of the simulacra [sic] does not necessarily imply that the spirit is consciously present. It may project the phantasm from a great distance.

In *Human Personality* Myers wrote (1904a vol 1: 296-7): ' Of all vital phenomena, I say, this is the most significant; this self-projection is the one definite act which it seems as though a man might perform equally well before and after bodily death.'

The phrase *pars casiam*, perhaps even more sharply, demonstrated classical knowledge beyond Trix Fleming's education and background. She knew no Latin or Greek and was always eager to point out when a Latin tag occurred in her script and where she might have got it from, but this was more than a cultural Latin tag like *eheu fugaces*. It occurred as part of a cross-correspondence on the Proserpine/Persephone myth.

Trix Fleming 2/3/1910:

> Pars thyme — pars casiam — melifontes (a mistake for meliloton) Plurima lecta rosa est et sunt sine nomine flores — crocus liliaque alba
> (The Latin means: part thyme, part cassia, part clover, many picked roses and many flowers without name and crocus and white lilies)

The Latin is virtually a direct quote from Ovid's *Fasti* IV 393–620, the description of a scene in which Proserpine and her friends were picking flowers before she was snatched by Dis and taken down to the underworld. Margaret Verrall checked the script quotation against two editions of the *Fasti* and found that in the earlier edition (one probably accessible to Myers as a schoolboy) was the phrase *pars casiam* rather than the more usual *pars rorem* (part roses) of the later edition. Apart from Myers, the only potential telepathic source Margaret Verrall could identify was herself. She had published, the day before Trix Fleming's script was written, an article on 1/3/1910 in the *Classical Review* in which she discussed passages in Virgil where white lilies were mentioned and she named cassia and thyme among low-growing plants favoured by bees. Yet she did not quote or allude to the Ovid reference though she knew it well. Trix Fleming stated that she had not read the *Classical Review* before writing her script (Johnson 1910b: 242-8).

There are also some remarkable examples of paranormal cognition in Helen Verrall scripts, in addition to those referring to Daphne. One example was the detail she produced about Hagley Hall, May Lyttelton's country home, including the park, the church, the house, and walks in the area. There were some mistakes — no mullioned windows, no carved gateposts, or marble staircase. But quite a lot fitted, including references to 'a carved an ornamented chimneypiece, a relic of the original black and white house of the Elizabethan age'. The specific statements in her script of 14/3/1916, 'a lozenge—diamond shaped—and a bird on the shield', were easily identifiable in two of the three panels of the chimney piece, since Piddington had appended a photograph of it to the volume containing the relevant script (Piddington 1930: 44-47). Again, Helen Verrall, of a younger generation, did not know the Palm Sunday Story or move in circles that might have.

Probably the most remarkable overarching paranormal characteristic of the scripts was the nature of the cross-correspondences themselves. They seemed to be unique in the literature, and the question naturally arises, was there anything in the life and work of Myers himself that might suggest an intention to use such a complex method of post-mortem communication? There is no doubt, in general terms, that Myers believed in co-operation between the two worlds and in devising experiments to furnish evidence for survival. What is more problematic is whether one can find any evidence from his life to suggest that the allusive and cryptic approach to survival evidence based on classical literature might have been a methodology that would have appealed to him? There was no direct statement of such a methodology. But elements of it can be identified in his life and writing. On the question of the living and the discarnate working together there was much emphasis on this in *Human Personality*. In the 'Scheme of Vital Faculty' in that book (vol 2) there is an extensive section on the interpenetration and co-operation of the two worlds—a kind of cosmic dualism. On the question of transmitting the same message through different mediums, there is evidence from James Hyslop that Myers and Hodgson were trying to do this before Myers' death, though not specifically the creation of complex cross-correspondences (Johnson 1907-09).

Yet, there is evidence from Myers' life that the manipulating, fragmentation, and recombination of literary material held a particular interest for him. Myers' winning entry, while an undergraduate at Cambridge, for the 1863 Camden Medal for Latin verse was a notorious and spectacular example of appropriating classical literature and fragmenting it and recombining it to create new form and content. It cost him dear in terms of reputation in some quarters. He had taken some Latin poems from students at Oxford and synthesised the best lines from them into one superior poem. He was accused of plagiarism and resigned the prize. He put forward a sophisticated theory of poetic aesthetics to justify the manipulation of existing content in this manner (almost anticipating, in terms of verbal collage, literary developments in the first third of the twentieth century), taking from Virgil the classical ideal of imitative allusion to enable the poet to get 'his purchase of larger meanings and to evolve the finer resonances of poetry' (Stein 1968). It is perhaps not too fanciful to state that the cross-correspondences were full of these two concepts — first, the breaking up and distributing of larger units into smaller units across the automatists, and second, the frequent quoting of certain key phrases in Virgil, Milton, Shelley, Browning, Tennyson, and others with occasional changes of individual words to enrich and refocus their meaning. It is as if the classical tradition of allusion, imitation, and ornamentation had been co-opted into the service of psychical research.

As has been seen, the other overarching example of paranormal cognition was the stress in the scripts on the co-operation between the two worlds, as well as the co-operation between the automatists. For Myers, this lay at the heart of his concept of evolution. It was partly terrene (and in this aspect he broadly accepted Darwinian evolution) but it was also cosmical. This was in two senses. There was, he believed, an endless process of spiritual evolution beyond the grave. As Lodge stated (1930): 'Infinite progress, infinite harmony, infinite love, these were the things which filled and dominated his existence: limits for him were repellent and impossible.' He also believed, in a wider sense, reminiscent of the great esoteric schools, that the mutual co-operation of the discarnate and the incarnate led to the evolutionary growth of the whole universe itself. 'Perhaps, indeed, in this complex of interpenetrating spirits our own effort is no individual, no transitory thing. That which lies at the root of each of us lies at the root of the Cosmos too. Our struggle is the struggle of the Universe itself; and the very Godhead finds fulfillment through our upward-striving souls' (1904a vol 2: 274–7).

14

Could One Be Sure that the Cryptic Nature of the Cross-Correspondences was not the Product of a Psychological Artefact?

Psychological artefact is used in two senses in this section: first, that the scripts were the product purely and simply of the psychological and psychodynamic needs of the living rather than sustained and significant messages from the dead; and second, that the apparently cryptic and allusive nature of many of the scripts was really a function of the automatic writing itself as the automatist accessed the confused and dreamlike nature of their own subconscious.

For many people automatic writing can be easily dismissed. It may appear to be involuntary or caused by some kind of external agency and it can be argued that that is an illusion, as some simple psychological experiments appear to have demonstrated, or, if produced via the Ouija board or planchette, the product of ideomotor action, as William Carpenter asserted in the nineteenth century (Wegner 2002: 120–1). It could also be the result of imitative behaviour. A platform medium or a medium in a general séance faces certain sociological pressures to behave in a particular way, so too some automatic writers may have read about automatic writing and subconsciously moulded their writing to conform to that norm.

One notices two contradictory things: first that there has been an enormous amount of automatic writing produced, and second there has been very little contemporary research into it compared with that, say, on hypnosis or dissociative identity disorder. This has led to occasional uninformed public enthusiasms and fads for it, as Stevenson has pointed out (1983), but with little advice and guidance for those who get carried 'far out in waters beyond their depth'. And, at the other end, it has led to an assumption that all the material is drivel, which might mean that occasional examples of high quality may be unfairly denigrated.

There is a very rich history of automatic writing, painting, drawing, composing, playing, and speaking, barely acknowledged by the academic community, and some of it of considerable quality. Some of the most famous historical examples are: Stainton Moses, Pearl Curran, and Geraldine Cummins in the Anglo-Saxon world, Alan Kardec's mediums from France, and Carlos Mirabelli and Chico Xavier from Brazil, and from

Sweden the automatic paintings of Hilma af Klint which, in some ways, prefigured the abstract work of Kandinsky and Mondrian (see Hastings 1991; Klimo 1998 for overviews). Indeed, high quality creative writers and academics have sometimes used automatic writing as a stimulus to their imagination (Platt 2015; Lurie 2001; Knight 1975). More recently, the automatic drawing of Matthew Manning and the painting of Luiz Gasparetto are also of great interest. Incidentally, one notable feature of the cross-correspondence writings was that, regardless of automatist, they were austerely verbal, the few drawings and diagrams in them were generally of poor quality and, one could argue, reflected the interests and capacities of the communicators themselves. However, the Manning material does share one characteristic with the cross-correspondence scripts, particularly those of Trix Fleming: that is the way stray communicators sometimes wistfully, sometimes almost desperately, broke into the main communication.

To assess this material is difficult and, in the same way that Myers and his brother Arthur (1893) stressed that medical experts should always be involved when examining the miracles at Lourdes and similar phenomena, so too individuals with experience of the particular content base of the automatic writing to be assessed should should also be consulted. Otherwise, superficial verdicts, either way, may be delivered. Some recent automatic writing is very impressive in terms of its access to precise information and skills way beyond those of the automatist. See particularly the Rollans case where a discarnate Hungarian chess player Maróczy (Rollans could not play chess) put up an excellent fight against the world number 2 Korchnoi and gave extremely accurate and consistent information about a number of events in his life (Eisenbeiss and Hassler 2006).

One looks in vain for a detailed, balanced, authoritative modern text on automatic writing. As Wegner (2002) states: 'There is simply not enough systematic research on automatic writing to allow a full understanding of its nature and causes. What we have at present is a collection of observations that point to the possibility that some people can lose either conscious awareness of what is written, or the feeling of doing, or both when they try to do so as they write. We don't have enough collected observations of the effect to have a strong conception of when and why it happens.' His chapter on automatic writing clearly reflects the thinness of the research in this field.

His comments on automatisms (99–144), at first glance, do not easily fit the context, conditions, and behaviours of the cross-correspondence automatic writers. They did not require a simple psychological trick, like *movement confusion*, to get them going; they sometimes had a very strong sense of external agency and personality, often accompanied by tension, pain, or headache, before the writing; they had sufficient control and awareness to interrogate the writing as it continued; the quality of the writing was often high and contained information sometimes demonstrably beyond the knowledge of the automatist; and the automatist did not, in life, display the attributes of a dissociated personality but contributed fully, even outstandingly, to the social environment around them. In the jargon, the mediums had non-pathological spiritual and psychic experiences, a characteristic that many contemporary gifted mediums and psychics share.

However, one must explore the question in a little more detail. Dissociative identity disorder is characterised in various ways: the manifestation of two or more distinctly different and discrete personalities; dissociative amnesia; depersonalisation; and sometimes somatoform disorders like temporary blindness or deafness; and the cause being usually some kind of trauma (Lilienfeld *et al.* 2015: 113–52). One cannot link this list in any comprehensive sense with the cross-correspondence group. The only obvious candidate for this interpretation was Leonora Piper, the trance medium. And Helen Dallas wrote to Hyslop, who took over the detailed investigation of Piper after Hodgson's death, to ask for his views (Dallas 1910: 69). His reply was: 'As secondary personality is known to the Scientist it has no traces of the supernormal… We must remember that the term secondary personality is not a name for any special power of mind other than the normal, as many people have supposed, but is as I have defined it… Mrs. Piper shows no traces of secondary personality as defined and recognised in psychiatry or pathology.' However, the SPR investigators, by and large, would have partially disagreed with this interpretation. Mrs Sidgwick (1915) in her massive study of Leonora Piper argued that she did share, in trance, certain common features with those suffering from multiple personality disorder. On the other hand, genuine, verifiable information came through these bridging sub-personalities and in her daily life Leonora Piper did not display such characteristics. She was able to contain them within the social role of mediumship and lived a normal life, as her daughter and biographer stressed (Piper 1929).

All the automatists abhorred anything connected with conventional Spiritualism and the idea (even probably subconsciously) that they would wish to imitate the conventional automatic writing medium would have been extremely distasteful to them. Trix Fleming, as has been seen, made a particularly explicit statement to this effect. Margaret and Helen Verrall would occasionally practise using the planchette with friends, but Margaret Verrall was very abrupt and sharp with any sensational behaviour by the planchette—the stupid thing, as she called it. Outside the SPR circle, the only medium Winifred Coombe-Tennant respected (Lord 2011) was Mrs Leonard, and when after Christopher's death (much of her best automatic writing pre-dated this) she occasionally sat with a new medium she usually found the process distressing and objectionable, and the activity petered out.

The cross-correspondence automatists had a variety of responses with regard to the agency involved and there was considerable initial reluctance to ascribing the source of the writing to an external source. Both Margaret Verrall and Helen Verrall were familiar with Myers' work and methods of classification and would have been alert to the nature of trance and its potential for deception. Moreover, the main communicators themselves exhibited consistency of focus and purpose and not the instability of a fugitive temporary personality, providing, and it is a big provide, one is prepared to attribute errors and vagueness to the difficulties of communication. Certainly, the discarnates displayed particular irritation at times with the way the automatists distorted their messages.

Trix Fleming 22/2/1905:

> If one could only find a *stupid sensitive* but the very quickness the impressionability that enables the brain to perceive an influence from afar renders it an ever present danger to the message that is trying to be impressed.

And they were equally annoyed when the investigators failed to respond to their efforts. They had an agenda and they stuck to it, in exactly the way Myers and Gurney did at psychical research during their lives. They were also a little unfair to the investigators at times. It should be repeated again and again that Piddington particularly had a huge administrative task in collating, printing, and indexing the scripts and the complex material they contained, and that this took many years. It was a major task to identify patterns and puzzles and respond to them within a reasonable timescale.

There was also a consistent emphasis by the communicators to all the automatists for the need to create the right conditions for the activity — calm, rest, no overwork, yet at the same time no complete withdrawal from the world as that would lead to self-deception. There was absolutely no sense here of the sudden 'switching' associated with the individual suffering from multiple personality disorder. The changes in awareness and perspective were much more varied and subtle. Indeed, the remarkable thing about the cross-correspondence automatic writing is that the consciousness of the individual automatist, particularly Winifred Coombe-Tennant, appeared to fluctuate between several levels of awareness: dream/trance with little or no awareness; automatic writing consciously aware but little control of the writing; and writing that was highly interactive (Balfour 1920: 2–3). In fact, one reading of the cross-correspondences is that of a massive exercise in individual training and development for each of the automatists except for the full trance medium Leonora Piper, where the emphasis was on handling her better and not giving the communicators, through her, too many complicated tasks at one time. But it must be acknowledged that, though some of the best evidence came from

Leonora Piper, some of the silliest (if divorced from its narrative context) did as well.

Trix Fleming worried away at her writing and was continually reflecting on what might or what might not be the product of her recent reading. She did not like to recognise real names in her scripts and, as has been seen, also had a particular distaste for the sugary automatic writing in vogue in certain circles. She had too much critical intelligence to be deceived, as her letters to Alice Johnson clearly demonstrated. Margaret Verrall, though largely unaware of the gist of her communications when writing them, had a healthy disregard for them and was quick to pounce on the silly and confused elements. Her daughter Helen remained detached from the whole process and seemed to rattle out short, cryptic scripts with only an occasional sense of effort. In later years she tried trance writing and speaking but found some of it difficult and stressful.

Apart from Leonora Piper, the traditional trance medium, all the other automatists had a very strong sense of their own identities and, while trying to put themselves in a passive and receptive state to facilitate the writing, would always react against matter and experiences they found unpleasant or distressing and intensely disliked any indications of the beginning of the full trance state. Winifred Coombe-Tennant was a partial exception to this in that the communicators stated that they could bring her to the edge of trance but allow her to remain sufficiently self-aware to act as an intermediary between the worlds in terms of question and answer in a way the other automatists could not.

Myers (1893b), himself, provided a useful classification for trance utterances which can also be applied to the cross-correspondences. This classification was based largely on the psycho-physiological origin of the behaviour. 'Trance is a name given to a form of motor automatism, whether healthy or morbid, in which the automatist appears to be in some way altered, or even asleep, but in which he may speak or write certain matter of which his normal personality is ignorant at the time, and which it rarely remembers on his return to waking life.' He identified five classes or categories into which trance could be grouped. The classes were: simulated fraudulent trance utterance based on prior research or fishing as was 'usually the case with professional clairvoyantes'; genuine trance but morbid and degenerative even if some statements showed 'memory or accuracy greater than the normal'; genuine and healthy and coherent but 'no actual fact unknown to the automatist'; genuine and healthy with facts not known to the automatist but to others present or existent elsewhere and known possibly through telepathy or telaesthesia; genuine and healthy with facts not known to the subject or the observers but verifiable and 'might probably be included in the memory of certain definite deceased persons from whom they profess to come'. 1 was false; 2 was hysteria; 3

could be created by hypnotic suggestion; 4 could be telepathy or telaesthesia; 5 could be 'a temporary substitution of personality'. One should note the double stress on 'genuine and healthy'. For Myers these powers could be a sign of health and growth, not disease and degeneracy: 'Telepathy is surely a step in evolution... To learn the thoughts of other minds without the mediation of the special senses, manifestly indicates the possibility of a vast extension of psychical powers.'

In a second classification he focused more directly on the source and quality of the information. He (Myers 1904a vol 2: 119) identified four potential sources. In A) the contents may come from the automatist's own memory, subliminal memory, and be dramatised as from another mind. Some of Trix Fleming's script fit very appropriately here. In B) '...we may place messages derived telepathically from the mind of some other person still living on earth... that person being either conscious or unconscious of transmitting the suggestion'. In C) 'the message may emanate from some unembodied intelligence of unknown type...' benign or malicious. In D) 'from the mind of the agent—the departed friend—from whom the communication does acrually claim to come'. Myers admitted that 'the great majority of such communications represented the subliminal workings of the automatist's mind alone'. He stressed that a very small portion of messages contained supernormal knowledge. Even after these alternative explanations had been discarded, one was still not home and dry: 'Parallel with the possibilities of reception of such knowledge from the influence of other embodied or disembodied minds lies the possibility of its own clairvoyant perception, or active absorption of some kind, of facts lying indefinitely beyond its supraliminal purview.'

The first investigators of the cross-correspondences worked cautiously with this classification of Myers and used his language, challenging, as Myers himself did, the physicalist approaches of Carpenter, Maudsley, and Huxley, which asserted that mind and behaviour were, no matter how apparently sophisticated, ultimately the products of highly complex and intricate physical reflexes and that it was not possible to access information other than through the normal channels of sensory communication. Examining the cross-correspondences one hundred years later one has to ask whether this theoretical framework and the language in which it was couched is still relevant.

A number of years ago Myers' terminology would have been dismissed out of hand given the climate of behaviourism in mainstream psychology and the colonisation of the territory of the subconscious and unconscious processes by Freudianism. However, there has been some recognition in recent years by parts of the psychological community that unconscious processes occupy a larger part of the executive and decision making activity of mind and body than was previously thought. Given this, using

Myers' conceptual framework does not appear as bizarre as it once might have, provided one points out where it treats of content and processes that the modern psychologists would not accept. For example, the cross-correspondence investigators' use of the term subliminal is much richer than the conventional modern one which tends to define it in terms of below conscious threshold perception of stimuli, though this concept in certain circles is now broadening. Second, there is the general minefield, reflecting different theoretical perspectives, as to how one should generally apply the terms unconscious and subconscious.

One thing is clear, regardless of terminology (Hassin *et al.* 2005: 82), subconscious/unconscious processing of sensory information is vastly superior to that of conscious processing: '…our senses can handle about 11 million bits [of incoming information] per second' but, depending on the task, consciousness processes it at 45 bits per second or less. This continuous unconscious activity can lead to high quality outputs when it emerges into consciousness. That has increasingly become recognised as has the fact that it is not just exhibited by the insultingly termed 'idiots savants'. This development of what has been called 'the new unconsciousness' vindicates much of the pioneering work of Myers on the subliminal mind. However, suggestions that this new unconsciousness could access or create paranormal phenomena would certainly be beyond the pale for the vast majority of modern psychologists. But whether they accept the origin of the phenomena or not, it exists, and the best of it is very sophisticated. However, the mere fact of a crafted and refined product should not lead one to attribute, prematurely, or necessarily at all, a discarnate origin.

Thus, though it is increasingly being recognised that much human behaviour and decision making is based on processes that one is not fully or even partially aware of (Wilson 2002; Mlodinow 2012; Eagleman 2015), the crucial question is to what extent do these developments help one explain and assess the kind of high quality automatic writing studied in this book and mentioned in other sources? Is it a product which is a combination of suppressed creativity and longing, and does it capture authentic paranormal information? Two credible and substantial books of collaborative authorship by a number of academics across a range of disciplines have argued, in a robust but scholarly fashion, that Myers' framework is relevant now more than ever. That is, both in terms of the richness of the unconscious/subconscious it delineates and the evidence accumulated since the time of Myers to support his assertion of the powerful part the subliminal plays in the perception and production of paranormal phenomena (see Kelly, E.F., Kelly, E.W., Crabtree, A., Gauld, A., Grosso, M. & Greyson, B. 2007; and Kelly, E.F., Crabtree, A., Marshall, P., *et al.* 2015.) On the other hand, the specific phenomenon of contemporary automatic writing is still under-researched in parapsychology (let alone psychology), as has been seen. There appear to be only scattered examples in the literature (see, for example, Palmer 2001; Palmer 2017; Krippner and Friedmann, 2010) and the classic text on it is over eighty years old (Muhl 1930).

One must not be gullible. A strange enchantment can sometimes descend on the producers and consumers of automatic writing. Much of the drive for the production of sophisticated and persuasive communication may stem from the psychodynamic imperatives of the automatists themselves. This point needs to be taken very seriously indeed with regard to two automatists particularly: Winifred Coombe-Tennant and Trix Fleming. Winifred Coombe-Tennant wove a certain amount of anxiety concerning her children into her scripts and usually Gurney was able to reassure her. She had lost Daphne in 1908 and Christopher in 1917 so her anxiety was completely understandable. One might argue that in her desire to make sense of these tragedies she elevated in her scripts the personalities, achievements, and potential destinies of all her children. Sometimes one can see this inappropriately overpowering a script. For example, in Winifred Coombe-Tennant's script of 18/6/1916, the birth of a child (Myers' daughter Silvia was pregnant) was described in Messianic language. Gerald Balfour's only explanation, a lame one he admitted, was that at this stage thoughts of a coming child triggered the Messianic vocabulary through association (Balfour 1920: 325–6).

There is also the very important matter of Winifred Coombe-Tennant's relationship with Gerald Balfour. It was not the height of scientific control and objectivity to have medium and chief sitter conducting a passionate affair in conditions of considerable secrecy, which may itself have heightened the emotions. Taken in this light, aspects of Winifred Coombe-Tennant's scripts and sittings in their most important period between 1911 and 1916 resembled less an act of independent mediumship and more the classically intense relationship a patient might have had with Freud or Jung, with all the obvious symptoms of transfer. The example of the relationship of Hélène Smith to Flournoy (1910/63) is also relevant in this context. But this should not be pushed too far. Winifred Coombe-Tennant produced evidential sittings with Margaret Verrall and Sir Oliver Lodge and was always prepared to co-operate in the provision of non-paranormal interpretations of her material. Moreover, she was a sturdily independent character who had a strong sense of her own position, values, and goals in life. Jean Balfour (Roy 2008) made a clear distinction between Mrs Willett the medium ('I felt I could love and almost worship this one') and the rather bossy and possessive Winifred Coombe-Tennant whom the children of the Balfour household did not really like.

Trix Fleming was another candidate for a psychodynamic explanation. She had suffered the traumatic experiences of the *House of Desolation* and she had a long and unhappy marriage with a depressive of limited means with whom she was not physically or intellectually compatible. She had literary and creative gifts which were never fully developed or recognised. Because of her sense of conscience and duty and lack of an independent income she could not leave him. It could be argued that her writing was a form of fantasy or escape or compensation, were it not for the nature and quality of much of it. Such items can be found but they constitute a fragment of the total production. And, as has been seen, Alice Johnson, who knew her well, stressed both in conversation and in writing that she was happiest during the period 1903–1910 when she was doing automatic writing, when she was in the company of intelligent, civilized, and supportive people, and when she had long periods of time away from her husband. In addition, there is evidence (Lee 2004) that the origin of her psychic and mediumistic gifts were powerful and genuine and partly inherited, and that she saw their exercise as natural and not created by frustrations in life.

On the other hand, Trix Fleming's scripts sometimes expressed opinions in a tone and voice that hovered ambiguously between her talking to herself and the communicator reflecting on her condition, her state of mind, and her psychic receptivity. In such passages the source of the statement was by no means clear cut.

Trix Fleming 29/7/1909:

> I am anxious that she should avoid any approach to hypnotism. Even unconscious self induced hypnotism would be undesirable in this case — The difficulty is to prevent the reflections of other minds near at hand to be a good channel for the further influences.

Elsewhere there were comments in scripts that she was generally too psychic, that she would pick up any number of stray communications from the recently dead, or psychometric impressions generally. These sorts of statements may well have reflected her constant worry about her husband's mental state and her parents as they grew older and also about the physical and mental ailments of people generally. There was a fussiness and anxiety in the scripts at times with regard to this. She was possibly the most naturally gifted of the automatists but never had the support that the Verralls and Winifred Coombe-Tennant had.

Helen Verrall, it could be argued, as a loved only child in a highly civilised and protected environment, just wished to please her parents and meet their very high academic standards. There appears to have been very little discomfort in her life. She had a pleasant childhood in an environment of comfort and status and met many highly educated and creative people. Her marriage was a partnership between equals and was long and collaborative. She seemed to be easily able to switch the writing on and off and without distress except on the occasions when she experimented with deeper trance. She easily tapped into the rich literary nexus that her education and environment had furnished her with. Whoever the sitter was the symbolism always seemed to swing back to the central themes of the scripts. Take that of 4/3/1914 written at SPR headquarters 'to amuse a stray American lady who called at 20 Hanover Square'. Woodland green, Beech woods, shamrock, lotus, Bacchus, and Ariadne all popped up. Was that an example of the tenacious focus of the script intelligence? A disapproval of sittings for purposes outside the vast cross-correspondence project? Or was it just the facility with which Helen Salter accessed subliminal mental processes and her subconscious desire to please? Bacchus and Ariadne certainly figured in script symbolism but, though Piddington claimed a consistent rationale for the other items, as symbols drawn from nature, they could be seen as too vague to impress.

In the case of her mother, Margaret Verrall, the main motive was scientific and intellectual curiosity and there seems to have been no other subconscious driver apart from that. She had lost one child but had reconciled herself by 1900 to the probability that there was no survival. She, too, had a long and deep marriage. She had a strong sense of loyalty to her friends and to her university colleagues, and particularly to Myers and his work, and one could argue that this might have warped the content of her scripts. Yet, she fought very strongly against any indications of discarnate identity in the scripts (for which the script intelligences often scolded her) and for a long time she saw the material as subconscious fabrication drawn from her general knowledge.

She, and the other investigators, was very familiar with Myers' research and his co-ordinating work on automatisms. The idea that messages would arise automatically from the subliminal (subconscious) and find the most appropriate vehicle of communication depending on the individual physiology and psychology of the automatist writing was a given to them all. As was also the idea that the message might take some time to emerge or be altered on its way to the supraliminal (normal consciousness). This became the language in which they talked about and approached the writing.

This, of course, presented the researcher with considerable problems of interpretation and explanation. Was it possible that the cryptic nature of the more complex cross-correspondences might be simply a function of telepathic communication between the living, or very similar to the random dreamy associational state that occurs just before sleep (hypnagogic state) or just after waking (hypnopompic state), which sometimes seem to have flashes of the paranormal in them? Or, was it a product of the difficulties of communication from the discarnate to the incarnate, much complained of in scripts, and which further exaggerated the gnomic character of the writing? Or was it, in fact, as Alice Johnson argued, that the cryptic method, while superficially looking like the product of the factors mentioned above, had been deliberately shaped by the communicators to circumvent the argument from telepathy and/or clairvoyance. Cryptic fragments could be telepathically transmitted but the design behind them was in no incarnate mind and so could only be accessed after the transmission of the final fragment, the clue or key. Gerald Balfour extended this argument by pointing out that, owing to the extreme ambition of the communicators and the delicacy of some of the arrangements, the cryptic method when applied to the Story and the Plan had been designed to reveal information in driblets and only as and when it was appropriate and safe to do so. There was almost a cultic element to this. To quote Balfour (1927): 'In like manner it is only natural to suppose that the communicators on their side should desire to restrict the number of the initiated within the narrowest limits.'

A.C. Pigou, a Cambridge economist, sharply challenged this position in an article in the SPR *Journal* of 1909. He asserted that evidence already published by the SPR itself—the telepathic experiments of Miss Ramsden and Miss Miles and the One-Horse Dawn episode involving Margaret Verrall and her husband Arthur—clearly demonstrated that the cryptic element was an illusion. It was created by the imperfect and inaccurate nature of telepathy. He gave a number of examples from the One-Horse Dawn case that showed that telepathic fumbling around a particular signal could create the illusion of complex design (Pigou 1909: 300-1). There was no plan behind it all but just attempts of variable quality to access the central phrase or idea. It might be yellow dawn, one horse, alone, a crowing cock, but nothing more. He stated, too, that when Miss Miles tried to transmit Sphinx and Miss Ramsden received Luxor in Egypt, that was a parallel example that supported his case. Braude made a similar point in his paper on telepathy (1978: 269): 'For example, there is evidence suggesting that a person's mental state can be causally efficacious in producing a *similar* mental state in someone else, independently of channels of communication involving the five senses. Thus, A's thought of the Queen of Spades might produce in B the thought of the Queen of Spades, or the Queen of Hearts, or Queen Elizabeth.'

Certainly, there were examples in the scripts of connections between different automatists that are more easily explained on this impressionable and associational basis than on crafted cross-correspondences. Take Eheu Fugaces and Electra (Johnson 1907-09: 313, 363-4).

Eheu Fugaces

The phrase comes from Horace C.2.14 line 1. Ah me, Postumus, Postumus, the fleeting years are slipping by (*Eheu fugaces, Postume, Postume, Labunter anni*).

Trix Fleming 11/4/1906:

> A great black shadow and the sound of a wailing wind — Eheu fugaces

Margaret Verrall 11/4/1906:

> Bells and a whip...they drive together over frozen roads Something fluttered and was gone — and the black bat night has flown — There is an effort to have the same words this time. On bat's wings rides Queen Mab

Note: Both Margaret Verrall and Trix Fleming were in the United Kingdom. The former probably in Cambridge and the latter probably at Tisbury.

The Latin quote would have been known, as a tag, by any literate person then, even if they didn't speak Latin. The impression of blackness and flight was common to the two but the link was purely impressional and the intention about getting the same words was not realized in practice. Coincidental but of impression and not of specific phrase: an impression picked up on the same day.

Electra

Trix Fleming 28/2/1906:

> *No* not in the Electra. M. will know better

Margaret Verrall 28/2/1906:

> Be sorrow sorrow spoken, but let the good prevail

The quotation comes from Aeschylus's *Agamemnon* and Trix Fleming just seemed to pick up from Margaret Verrall an impression of a quotation from Greek Tragedy.

It is notable that both these cross-correspondences occurred on a single day. In the former the impression of rapid flight was communicated in two different ways. In the latter the deep inexorable nature of Greek tragedy was caught but through different associations.

Pigou therefore concluded that what Alice Johnson called the complementary element (the clue that made sense of the cross-correspondence: the item from which one could infer purpose and design) in a complementary cross-correspondence was an illusion. There was clear evidence of telepathy between the living but anything more was the product of over-ingenious interpretation. He was strongly supported in this by Anna Hude

(1913: 46–58): 'This is the simple explanation of the complementary correspondences — a systematized "reading " of impressions, which only because it took place while the percipient was writing automatically differs from that of Miss Ramsden and other sensitives experimenting in a conscious state.'

If that was true the whole edifice of Alice Johnson's theory of the cross-correspondences and Gerald Balfour's and Piddington's elaborate tracing of symbolic connections in the scripts had all been based on the shaky foundations of a psychological quirk. This led to an arcane debate between Lodge and Pigou in the letter pages of the *Journal* in 1909, where Pigou stressed that he was stating 'not that a complementary correspondence, but that the complementary element in a correspondence, can originate in subliminal activity'. Lodge accepted, with his characteristic generosity, that he had originally misunderstood Pigou but that there was, with regard to the phenomena in scripts, a distinction between the accidentally fragmentary and the purposive complementary (Pigou 1909; Lodge 1909c; Lodge/Pigou 1909d).

This debate, virtually unnoticed in the general literature on the cross-correspondences, was crucial for the team investigating and assessing the material, and in 1911 Gerald Balfour produced a paper in the *Proceedings* which attempted to settle the matter. He accepted Lodge's distinction of 1909 and stressed the way in which the best cross-correspondences explicitly signalled intention and purpose (as in the Thanatos and Ave Roma cases) and that Pigou had not proved from the examples he gave that 'the production of complementary correspondences of the best type is within the known capacities of the subliminal self'.

This was an ever-present tension and uncertainty in the work of the investigators who would have accepted Pigou's position with regard to some of the simpler phenomena. They knew from Gurney's and Myers' pioneering work on hypnosis and automatic writing of the subtleties, indirectness, and confusion of the subconscious mind. As Mrs Sidgwick, as President of the SPR, in 1908 pointed out (and also in her later paper on telepathy in 1923): 'Hypnotism, chiefly because it enables the experimenter to communicate with the subconscious strata of the mind in a definite way, is one of the most effective means we have of experimentally investigating automatism and the relation of the subconscious to the conscious mind.' And this work had clearly shown the way that the subconscious or subliminal mind distorted both what it received and what it communicated. In his work on the Ganzfeld, Adrian Parker has much more recently demonstrated this process at work (in Storm et al. 2003: 65–89).

At a later date, Gerald Balfour (building on Piddington's enormous and persistent industry in trying to make sense of the scripts) would have given a much more confident answer. He would have said it was clearly not a by-product of the subliminal activity of the automatists; that the correspondences were marked by specific signs of purpose through precise instructions and signalling in the very best cases, by the intricacy, ingenuity, and aptness of their design and expression, and by their, at times, displaying ideas and information beyond the range and capacities of the individual automatist concerned. However, two fundamental questions remained. Was such purpose and design also evident to an objective and independent student of the scripts? Was such purpose and design beyond the capacities of the subliminal minds of one or more of the automatists or possibly the creation by a general psychic factor or force unknown and unidentified by any of the investigators? These issues will be taken up in a later section.

There are certainly examples in the scripts of intention by an external source (of whatever origin) to transmit something, of the automatist only partial picking up the message and possibly distorting this, and of that external source picking the distortion up and correcting it and trying to get the message through the most appropriate sensory modality. Take what Saltmarsh called the Spirit-Angel case (1975: 81-3; Piddington *et al.* 1908: 227-30).

Margaret Verrall 3/4/1907:

> Write three words—something about their serried ranks...wings or feather wings...[drawing of a wing with feathers]...long pointed rainbow wings...Of man's first disobedience—no that is something else... The hosts of heaven...[drawing of an angel with wings]...F.W.H.M. has sent the message through—at last!

Leonora Piper 8/4/1907:

> Spirit and Angel...with reference to messages I am trying to give through Mrs.V.

It seems a perfectly feasible interpretation based on the evidence (the complete Margaret Verrall script was on the same theme) to argue that Myers had done what he intended, had spotted Margaret Verrall wandering off into the wrong Miltonic associations (Of man's first disobedience), had corrected this verbally, and used a visual image as the best way on that occasion of getting the message across. The angel drawing in the original script was quite unmistakable.

One must also include the investigators in this examination of possible psychological and psychodynamic motives behind the cross-correspondence phenomena. Of the investigators, Lodge became a convinced believer in survival through sittings with Mrs Piper and the death of his son Raymond in 1915, and his sittings with Mrs Leonard just reinforced this. Margaret Verrall was more cautious and only gradually moved towards some form of acceptance of survival. Piddington and Gerald Balfour were also initially non-committal, as was Mrs Sidgwick. However, Balfour (as had Arthur and Eleanor) had lost a beloved and gifted brother and, as the cross-correspondences developed, began an intense affair with Winifred Coombe-Tennant. For twenty years he and Piddington (who had separated from his wife, partially disengaged from his business interests, and who suffered intermittently from a number of possibly psychosomatic stomach problems) shared the same house, Fishers Hill in Surrey, working indefatigably on the inner meaning of the scripts. Maybe this alone gave Piddington's life meaning? Did *folie à deux* or *trois*, group confabulation/ group thinking (call it what one will) cloud his and Gerald Balfour's judgement?

And there is a further more general sociopsychological point. World War I started in 1914. There was vast loss of life, and a particular burden, in terms of proportions of casualties per social group, fell on the 'officer class' from which the Souls and their friends came. This has been movingly examined in Jeanne Mackenzie's *Children of the Souls*. Bradley (1910) in his commentary on *In Memoriam* had argued that Tennyson used the convention in which the singer is supposed to be a shepherd as method of masking and controlling his much deeper grief. In the same way one can see that the use of the symbolic structure in the scripts helped the interpreters to handle the individual and collective grief that they and the wider group of the Souls faced at the loss of so many remarkable young men in the war (of all classes). Yet, the loss of Hallam turned Tennyson into a great poet and, commenting on Helen Verrall's script of 10/11/1910, Gerald Balfour hoped that there might be a parallel spiritual growth collectively and that this theme—suffering and sacrifice that produced the final flower of achievement or perfection—referred to the 'establishment of a "Universal City" and the reconcilement of nation with nation'. Though many scripts were written before 1914, much of the interpretation of the scripts came during the horrors of the war and the difficulties and consequences of the post war settlement. To work in a methodical fashion on complex literary problems may well have helped Gerald Balfour and Piddington to position and distance themselves from the sufferings and partial collapse of their world and their class.

There is one final point. The cryptic nature of the cross-correspondences might be explained by the difficulties of communicating telepathically between the subliminal minds of two or more automatists. Might not the errors, inconsistencies, and partial truths displayed in the scripts also be a function of the difficulties involved in communication between discarnate minds and the subliminal minds of the living? There were frequent complaints from the communicators about the complexities of this and the obstacles to be overcome. This was also reflected in the wider Spiritualistic and mediumistic literature, particularly that of Drayton Thomas who made an extensive study of Mrs Osborne Leonard. Minds seemed to meet and meld in a dark and shifting zone of great sensitivity where the clarity and cohesion of normal consciousness (whether incarnate or discarnate), of memory, purpose, and identity, was fragile, making erroneous and misleading messages and responses highly likely. Regardless of one's own views on the credibility of all this, the literature on this, from a phenomenological perspective, in the cross-correspondence scripts and other sources is broadly consistent. (See Crookall's survey of psychic communications 1961; also Fontana 2005: 142–4).

15

Was the Process of Communication Interactive and was it Clear that the Discarnates Both Initiated and Signalled Cross-Correspondences and Understood and Accurately Responded to Messages and Requests from the Investigators?

On this point care must be taken not to dismiss out of hand the superficially inaccessible or pompous. Take for example Margaret Verrall 21/3/1901 translated from the Latin:

> I should like to say but you deny. Oh if you cannot weave together, write pertinaciously. Consider all that is known. Soon will come the inviolate light of the Sibyl. Either one of the two receiving will choose. Do not fail her who asks...the best master for he himself said if you want anything, I do not hinder...It is of advantage to collect jewels at great expense...ask, ask, he says, do not despise the chords of the pure flute-player(?)...do you understand? Oh, ungrateful delay. To you I will sing. m..s Himself a mystic.

Despite the flowery and stilted language, one can sympathetically construe this, at a very early stage in the development of the scripts, as an exhortation to keep trying to understand, to put things together, the rewards metaphorically will be worth it (jewels at great expense), and not to despise the work of 'the pure flute-player' himself, m..s (Myers).

There was plenty of evidence that the communicators initiated and signalled cross-correspondences. They did this both with regard to short-term specific cross-correspondences and the wider long-term symbolic purposes of the scripts. As Alice Johnson (1910a) commented on the former: '...in most of the cases which I have here counted as cross-correspondences, the passages in the scripts are marked out by some phrase which seems to call attention to them, such as, "Remember the word and the date"; or by some device such as the repetition of a word, or its being written in specially large letters... [this] greatly reduces the probability that the coincidence is only due to chance'. For example:

Margaret Verrall 19/8/1908:

> 'You will have to wait some time for the ends of this story, for the solution of this puzzle'

Alice Johnson asked Margaret Verrall to compile a list of references in her scripts to these sorts of instructions (Johnson 1907-09: 378). She found twenty in the period from March 1901 to 30/1/1903. Many were general and sometimes in Latin or Greek: 'In mysteries I weave riddles for you and certain others for whom it is right'; 'Only use intelligence'; 'weave together perpetually things which hang together, even if they seem dragged in'. It should be remembered that these were general statements. They did clearly suggest the importance of putting material from different automatists together and interpreting them. However, the only really valuable statements were the precise ones. Sometimes, as in the Hope, Star, Browning Case, and with regard to the meaning of Sigma, they stood up. Sometimes, however, precise statements that this or that had been sent to a particular automatist were just not true. See below.

This raises the question to which one has to return at regular intervals in the assessment—what was the source of the voice? Was it wishful thinking on the part of the automatist, telepathic infiltration from another living automatist, or genuine discarnate intervention? Time, date, historical material that helped identify a particular discarnate, and an examination of the contemporaneous scripts of other automatists, were all required in order to evaluate this. But whatever the source, the scripts were not passive inert structures that did not answer back. They co-operated in their own assessment. They were interactive—sometimes there was an external sitter there (always with Leonora Piper) asking questions and sometimes there was an interior dialogue between automatist and communicator. The script intelligences offered clues as to how the material should be interpreted. They chided, supported, encouraged, and exhorted.

Take, for example, the cross-correspondence on the name Diana (Piddington 1908: 193-208).

Diana

Margaret Verrall 27/2/1907:

Dianam tenerae dicite virgins (Sing Diana youthful maids)

Leonora Piper 19/3/1907 (R.H. communicating):

Good Morning Mrs Sidgwick I said DIANNA—I tried to impress it on her mind (Margaret Verrall's).

Leonora Piper 4/4/1907 (Myers communicating):

I should be glad if you could tell me if she wrote about Diana...it was that I was impressing on her mind.
(Mrs Sidgwick replied) 'I think she wrote something like it, but not quite Diana'

Leonora Piper 29/4/1907 (Margaret Verrall sitting, Myers communicating):

> I referred to the word Dianna—I thought you wrote it...I told her (Mrs Sidgwick) so, but she said no.
> (Margaret Verrall) I've written the word Diana...some time ago.
> (Myers) We must try to do better and she must be sure of what you do write

Note: Margaret Verrall was in Cambridge. Leonora Piper was in London.

This seems to have happened on far too frequent a basis and to have been far too specific to be considered as chance. Indeed it suggested a scriptic intelligence and memory that was monitoring the situation and could exist in the same conscious narrative space as the automatists and interpreters. For example, Balfour and Piddington, in their earlier investigations, were not aware of the wider implications of the flower references (the flowers that decorated the silver-bronze box that Arthur Balfour had made to contain May Lyttelton's lock of hair) and had to be nudged towards them.

Helen Verrall 12/2/1909:

> You have not understood its full significance and the passion flower too is all part of the story

It was not till the Hair in Temple clue that Gerald Balfour, after discussion with his wife, realised that this referred to the flowers carved on the silver box in which the Palm Maiden's hair lay. Other comments stressed the importance of particular bits of symbolism. See another part of the above Helen Verrall script:

> Sigimund and Siegfried a legend of the Norse the forging of the sword the shield of Achilles should be compared in likeness and in difference

This referred to the consistent underlying theme of the scripts—the gradual march of history from savagery towards civilisation. In addition, there were the many comments repeated over and over again, as has been seen, phrased in different ways and using different metaphors, to weave things together to identify the missing pieces, to make things whole. And Myers sometimes was very blunt and explicit about the process, as in:

Winifred Coombe-Tennant 10/6/1910:

> Give me more opportunities I have to condense to the point of obscuration...Myers today I want only allusions which others will shift

Another example, one might say, of indirect signalling was to make use of the key anniversaries and significant dates of the communicators, automatists, investigators, and sometimes, more widely, dates associated with individuals mentioned in the scripts; and, though this was more contentious, as has been seen, the use of Margaret Verrall's, Arthur Verrall's,

Myers' children's Christian names as markers when there was a specific cross-correspondence or a thematic link between scripts to be noticed and assessed. Certainly, interesting scripts occurred around the time of the anniversary of Myers' death, as well as Laura Lyttelton's and May Lyttelton's.

And again, as has been seen, the insistent stress on the importance of the sign sigma and its various associations was impossible to miss.

Margaret Verrall 25/5/1902:

> The desire for Sigma, making use of intellect, will find out something true...You have not understood the Sigma...it would explain much.

The Greek letter for S could be written in a variety of forms and this was deftly exploited by the communicators. It was, first, the symbol that Myers used in his private diaries for his sitting with mediums, especially those at which Annie Marshall came through. Second, another variation of sigma, M, could refer to May, a further variation, C, to Catherine, and the twisted curl version, to her locks of hair: therefore, all symbols for Mary Catherine Lyttelton. For example, Margaret Verrall's script of 9/9/1903 had the M version of sigma, an indirect allusion to syringa, and Ariadne's crown in the sky. References, therefore, to both Annie Marshall and to the Palm Maiden, May Lyttelton.

Many of these allusions in scripts to the Palm Maiden and her hair were highly persuasive and long pre-dated Winifred Coombe-Tennant's arrival as an automatist. Balfour (1927) stated 'the real "Maid" is the individual called in these notes [volume 2 of *Notes and Excursuses*] the *Palm Maiden*: and what the communicators have done in the scripts is to weave round her a number of literary associations in such a way as to establish a connection between the various associations themselves... an allusion to any one of them readily brings up an allusion to any other.' Obviously, if one accepts the rationale of the scripts, this was a useful way to disguise direct references to May Lyttelton before the communicators were ready to reveal her identity.

Because of the particular nature of Winifred Coombe-Tennant's gifts both Lodge and later Gerald Balfour were able to interrogate her and 'hold' conversations with the 'discarnates' directly. They tried to get her to clarify the symbolism — for example, did Ariadne stand as a symbol for the Peacock Lady (Laura Lyttelton) or the Palm Maiden (May Lyttelton)? Helen Verrall (Salter) was also asked on a number of occasions to elucidate the symbolism in her scripts. With these two automatic writers and the trance medium Leonora Piper there was a considerable amount of two-way interaction between medium and investigator.

And there were explicit instructions to take a wider and deeper perspective on the scripts. The task was more than just the unravelling of specific cross-correspondences.

Winifred Coombe-Tennant 10/9/1911:

> Gurney. I want first to speak of Scripts and emphasize the word *Layers* of meaning...superficial or obvious meanings...the interconnection between the Scripts of various automatists...The next strata of meaning can only be tapped by the Holders of the Key to the non-obvious whole to which the Scripts are contributing.

The key, of course, to the scripts being, first, the importance of the death of Daphne as enabling the communicators to access the great natural mediumistic abilitites of Winifred Coomb-Tennant; second, the story of Arthur Balfour and May Lyttelton long in the past; and third, the planning for the coming of the Messianic Child in the future.

All this might seem very impressive and many of the cross-correspondences and much of the symbolic material summarised in this text did and does stand up to interrogation. But the scripts were not perfect and it is important to draw attention to failures, inconsistencies, and errors. There was on occasions an over-confident assertion that material had been delivered but often it hadn't or something approximating to it had been delivered to another automatist and not the one promised. A striking example of this occurred in one Coombe-Tennant script and was not publicised in the *Proceedings.* When Winifred Coombe-Tennant first started writing there was a veritable clamour that Myers would give crystal bars as a cross-correspondence. This phrase had a powerful meaning for her since it referred to a poem that she associated with the death of Daphne. The poem was *A Child's Grave at Florence* by Elizabeth Barrett Browning, and the relevant lines were: 'The crystal bars shine faint between/The souls of child and mother.' It was stated in the scripts of Oct 9/16/26, Nov 2/3/19/20/21 in 1908 that it had been given to Margaret Verrall. Yet it never appeared in direct and unambiguous form.

Mrs Sidgwick (Sidgwick *et al.* 1910: 193), when mentioning cross-correspondences between Piper script and other automatists, commented on the curious specificity of some of the correspondences in contrast to the inaccuracy as to who had or would receive them: 'Neptune, which is spoken of as to be written in the future by Mrs.Verrall, had, as a matter of fact, been written by Helen Verrall before it was mentioned by Mrs. Piper's trance-personalities at all; and we have no reason to think that it was written by any automatist we are acquainted with afterwards. Pharaoh's daughter, on the other hand, which is spoken of as written by Mrs. Verrall months before, is not written till months after, and then by Helen Verrall. Troy and Joy, Exile with Moore, are neither of them written till some days after it had been asserted in the Piper script that they have been got through.'

This, the absolute certainty of the statements, is a common feature of automatic writing. One can only speculate about the conditions under which the communicators operated that impeded communication or the authenticity of the communicators themselves. Certainly, from Mrs Sidgwick's massive study of the Piper phenomenon (1915), one knows that mixed in with veridical material there were assertions clearly the product of self-suggestion and subconscious dramatic impersonation.

On the other hand, there could be very little doubt that when Myers, through Leonora Piper, on a suggestion from Piddington, agreed to communicate a Triangle within a Circle, he, very largely, performed what he had promised.

Leonora Piper 16/1/1907:

> JGP. Myers when you send a message to, say, Margaret Verrall, and then a similar message to Trix Fleming, could you not mark each with some simple but distinctive design...you might put, say, a triangle within a circle...
> Myers. I can yes I shall be very glad to try this...It would be evidential

The triangle within a circle certainly appeared in Margaret Verrall's script of 28/1/1907, linked to the Hope, Star, Browning cross-correspondence, and a partially successful attempt at it appeared in Trix Fleming's script of 8/5/1907, though her script did not figure in the cross-correspondence concerned and was rather disjointed. Nor was the same sign drawn in Helen Verrall's script which was, in fact, a central part of the cross-correspondence.

It helped greatly when the communicators expressed an intention to create a cross-correspondence, particularly when some of the the phrases in a cross-correspondence were rather general and commonplace and there seemed to be nothing to tie the statements together. The famous Medici Tombs cross-correspondence, on the surface, was weakened in this respect.

In July 1912 Alice Johnson (1914: 50–76) spotted a clue in a Coombe-Tennant script of two years earlier that appeared to make sense of a number of references going across the scripts of five automatists altogether. The main statements were these:

The Medici Tombs

Leonora Piper 26/2/1907:

> Morehead...I gave her that for laurel.

Helen Verrall 17/3/1907:

> Alexander's Tomb...Emblem laurels for the victor's brow

Trix Fleming 27/3/1907:

> Alexander — Moors Head — Antres vast and deserts idle

E and A Mac 7/10/1908:

> Dig a grave among the laurels [drawing of a laurel wreath]

Winifred Coombe-Tennant 10/6/1910:

> Laurentian tombs. Dawn and Twilight.

Note: Leonora Piper was in London. Helen Verrall was in Cambridge. Trix Fleming was in India. The Macs were in Scotland. Winifred Coombe-Tennant was in Wales. Only Winifred Coombe-Tennant would have seen the other scripts.

Alice Johnson's research into the Medicis tied all the pieces neatly together. In the Sagrestia Nuova of the Church of St Lorenzo at Florence (which Myers had visited, as evidenced from his diary 14/2), Alessandro de Medici (called the Moor because of his appearance and seen as highly disreputable for a variety of reasons) was buried beneath the other tombs of the Medici family, the most famous being Lorenzo the Magnificent, whose emblem was the Laurel. The tomb with two Lorenzos in it has a seated helmeted statue on it and two recumbent figures, Dawn and Twilight. The other tomb of Giuliano has a seated statue labelled *Il Pensieroso* (the thinker or meditator) and two recumbent figures, Day (a man) and Night (a woman) on it. The tombs were designed by Michelangelo, as was the nearby Medici Library. In addition, Alice Johnson looked through a number of other scripts and came to the conclusion that there were descriptive references (dark, dawn, shadow, sleep, meditation); an ingenious play in Fleming script on George Herbert's *A Wreath* — 'A wreathed garland of deserved praise' altered to bays to refer to bays/laurel; and a piece of original poetry — 'Since Life had grown more pale than death/Waking more hushed than sleep', all of which could refer to the statues on the tombs.

What is perhaps more compelling is that the correspondence had been openly pointed up in 1909. On 9/2/1909 Helen Verrall was table tilting with a friend, Ethel Pye, and in Italian came the name Lorenzo de Medici and a reference to the family tombs. Margaret Verrall asked, 'Why about the tombs? Explain.' 'As you have not seen them I thought it would be evidence.' Ethel Pye on the same day had been thinking of Lorenzo, was familiar with his history, was contemplating visiting Italy, and knew about the tombs (Johnson 1916b: 132–3). On 10/2/1909 Helen Verrall had, 'the white moonlight gleaming on the white marble tombs and heavy shadows across the slabs black and white', and 11/2/1909 Winifred Coombe-Tennant received an impression which she conveyed to Margaret Verrall the next day: 'which I shall not go into now, but it leads me to think

"Alexander" may be a password.' But without the table tilting there was no real indication that a cross-correspondence was being attempted and one is tempted to put it all down to Alice Johnson's ingenuity.

These issues must be raised. First, the table tilting evidence strongly suggests two things depending on whether one privileges the telepathic or the discarnate communicator source. If the first, Miss Pye would seem to be the immediate source or stimulus; if the second, it is an example of the communicators signalling a possible cross-correspondence but fearing it had not been adequately pointed up in the actual scripts. Curiously, the evidence from Miss Pye was not quoted in any of the discussion of the cross-correspondence in the *Proceedings*. Second, many of the descriptive phrases allegedly referring to the tombs were vague, general, and stock poetic phrases. Third, the more specific ones—laurel, laurel wreaths, Moorhead/Muirhead, Alexander's tomb—still had alternative attributions and explanations. Fourth, the timescale was over three years, rather too long by the investigators' own initial standards for a cross-correspondence; and fifth, two of the automatists had visited Florence and would probably have been to the Medici tombs. They were on the tourist circuit. Winifred Coombe-Tennant had a Medici clock in her London flat with a number of the features mentioned in the scripts, which again might suggest a telepathic source. Sixth, the selection of individual statements from a range of scripts to create an overall theme might lead one to suspect cherry-picking, though a reading of the full scripts from which the extracts were taken does not indicate that the rest of the script was meaningless. These points in no way invalidate the cross-correspondence but they do need to be taken into account when making a judgement, and point to the need for caution even in the most celebrated cases.

It is quite possible that an investigator could be carried away by the sensational or highly emotional content that appeared to form a cross-correspondence and it might have happened (only might) in this case. The recent development of Reception Studies (the different way each distinctive historical period treats the literature, culture, and events of the past) can be helpful here. Fletcher's book (2016: 251–60) on Alessandro de Medici, *The Black Prince of Florence*, discusses these issues and perhaps provides a clue as to why Alice Johnson may have been drawn into the content: the sensational and exotic behaviour of the 'other' may have given the apparent cross-correspondence an invalid salience.

Finally, the statements were sometimes so insistent and convincing, persuasive, and clear that the researchers could have been encouraged to dig deep and always to have expected the treasure to be there. Take the script below.

Margaret Verrall 2/12/1907 (in train, after Hitchin):

> Castanette cast a net That is the type — There have
> been 3 little words given separately, — they should be put
> together by someone else and they will make sense. I am
> not sure how to describe them, but this is certain — Each
> single word has been given to a separate friend, & has been
> recorded — I know that, but I cannot say who has the first
> syllable — The whole word has also been recorded by one of
> the three friends — and we had great difficulty in keeping it
> out of the record of one of the others — that would, you see,
> have spoilt the exp*. For the whole point is that only one
> should have the whole word, but that the syllables should be
> distributed. And each syllable makes sense by itself so that
> it can be written about as well as written.
> Let me make it clear — Thus: cast a net — then one
> says cast, and one says net, but the one who says cast, writes
> about net, & the one who says net writes about cast — so
> that you get c.cs — of the complex type, & by putting together
> the words that are subjects of successful cross correspondences
> you get an intelligible. word — See ? Now ask Piddington
> to try if his ingenuity can't understand what I mean —
> And he ought also to be able to find the record where
> the complete word was, very nearly given again to the second
> writer — But we just stopped that in time.
> This is good — go on
> yours — and another writer also — one signature here, the
> other on her paper
> F W H M.

Despite their best efforts, Gerald Balfour and J.G.P. never discovered a cross-correspondence of that type. In this case one suspects that it might just have been one part of the highly literary and articulate Margaret Verrall talking to another.

16

Did the Cross-Correspondences Occur within a Reasonable Time Frame and Above Chance Expectation and Were They Distributed Widely Amongst the Automatists?

West (1954/1962) has stated that 'even the elementary question how far the cross-correspondences could be attributed to chance coincidence cannot be answered with certainty, owing to lack of control experiments and lack of precise information as to the volume of scripts from which the "coincidences" were extracted'. A scientist and numerate herself (as were Lodge and Mrs Sidgwick, of course), Alice Johnson addressed this point directly when she developed the theory of the cross-correspondences. She argued that it was not possible to assess the cross-correspondences as if they were experiments in telepathy using playing cards. The probabilities could not be calculated nor was there absolute clarity as to whether a cross-correspondence was successful or not, given that some of the material could represent ideas gradually emerging from the subliminal to the supraliminal. Therefore, it meant that all allusions to a particular topic at different times had to be compared together. In other words, the skills of literary, linguistic, and historical scholarship were the skills needed to assess the cross-correspondences.

This approach, putting forward a literary rather than a statistical methodology for assessing the cross-correspondences, did, however, make the argument against chance more difficult since stretching the correspondence to include related associative connections, alternative phrasings (as has been seen), and emergent attempts at the message greatly increased the possibility of random meaning. Margaret Verrall (1906: 206) put these points with her characteristic clarity and caution in her introduction to the non-experimental cross-correspondences she identified in her scripts: 'To the discussion of these references I shall not apply any statistical method. Where all is tentative and undetermined it might be misleading to classify.' In fact, the only attempts to quantify hits and misses occurred in Piper script from 1906–1908, but the approach was abandoned as the increasing complexity of the scripts was realised. In essence, the SPR investigators eschewed randomised controlled testing which systematically examined and isolated a number of variables, in favour of a rich narrative of individual bodies of evidence whose paranormal connections were to be validated in various ways by a largely post hoc analysis.

Part of the uncertainty centred around the way they thought the telepathic process might be operating. Alice Johnson distinguished the messages in the scripts from discrete experiments in telepathy because they were not isolated units but part of a continuous process with the content emerging gradually from the subliminal to the supraliminal in the writing of a number of automatists. And, as it was embedded in complex cultural and literary material, it required those kinds of skills to assess it: not in terms of aesthetic quality but with regard to its inner meaning (Johnson 1914–15). And, as Myers himself had speculated that subliminal action between automatists could be greatly stimulated by telepathy from one or more discarnates, this meant that the assessment problem hugely increased in difficulty. Who and when was transmitting what to whom? As Myers put it (1904a vol 2: 55), 'I conjecture that a current of influence may be started by a deceased person, which, however, only becomes strong enough to be perceptible to its object when reinforced by some vivid current of emotion arising in living minds. I do not say this is yet provable; yet the hint may be of value when the far-reaching interdependencies of telepathy between the two worlds come to be better understood.' This was one of the reasons that Johnson (1910b: 262) deprecated the comparison of telepathy to wireless telepathy 'as it inevitably suggests the inference that the processes referred to are essentially similar'.

This points to a very real issue in the early and continuing debates in the SPR and elsewhere about the nature and behaviour of telepathy (Alvarado 2009). If the physical model of telepathy which Gurney discussed in *Phantasms* was adopted as a hypothesis, using the 'familiar phenomena of the transmission and reception of vibratory energy' as an analogy, one could attempt to calculate odds against chance in the sending and receiving of impressions and messages and just accept that there was some unidirectional physical base from source to receiver even though one had no idea of the actual mechanism.

On the other hand, in the cases studied by the SPR, there was rarely the direct transmission of an unmodified image or impression, making it difficult to estimate success or failure. As has been seen, Gurney, Myers, and Mrs Sidgwick all stressed the part which the mind's unconscious operations could play in telepathic phenomena. If one added additional variables (clairvoyance, precognition, and the possible agency of the discarnate) the situation was complicated in several ways. It made the measurement of telepathic hits and misses even more difficult if modification of the original sender target was allowed in the assessment of the recipient's response, and it introduced alternative explanations for either the success or failure of the attempted communication. Take the Medusa's Head cross-correspondence, for example.

Medusa's Head

Leonora Piper 13/04/1908:

> [Dorr suggested Medusa's head was sent as a cross-correspondence]

Leonora Piper 12/05/1908:

> Blood — Horse — Head [Trix Fleming] wrote that

Trix Fleming 19/05/1908:

> Perseus — The Fateful Head — Medusa — The mirrored shield and the winged sandals of swiftness...such rocks as Andromeda knew while she waited for the coils of the sea monster to lift curling among the slow ripples at the margin of sand

Note: Leonora Piper was in the United States. Trix Fleming was in the United Kingdom.

This was an interesting and successful correspondence. It is clear that the less educated Leonora Piper grasped the gory physicality of the event but its emergence in Trix Fleming's script took five weeks and was clothed in the wider, more literary, details of the story (the gifts of Pallas which aided the destruction of Medusa) appropriate to that automatist (Johnson 1910b: 277–9). In this case the modification was obvious but in some of the more extreme of Piddington's interpretations the associational links appeared to reflect less an automatist dealing with the same central message from her own subliminal resources, and more the post hoc construction of theoretical links. And given the nature of the material this was an ever present danger.

In addition, there was the mundane question of counting. In a cross-correspondence did the same theme or topic in two scripts just count as one cross-correspondence? What if there were more hits/points of contact in the scripts? As below (Johnson 1910a: 213–15).

Procession

Trix Fleming 17/10/1906

> The men with staves head the procession...The noonday sun has dimmed the torches flare

Margaret Verrall 3/10/1906

> The sun shone in the north at midday...The propomps wave their torches

Note: Trix Fleming was in India. Margaret Verrall was in Cambridge. She did not see the Fleming script before writing her own.

There were three clear points of contact here: procession, noonday, torches. Was this a triple or a single cross-correspondence?

Despite these reservations, there were some attempts to explore aspects of the role of chance coincidence in the generation of cross-correspondences. Helen Verrall (1911) set up an experiment in which six participants were invited to do some free writing based on the random stimulus from a literary work of their choice and to do this six times. Her conclusion was that, apart from a simple correspondence to do with moonlight, such writing, though often highly literary like the cross-correspondence scripts, did not generally share their characteristics. This experiment was repeated in a slightly different format by her husband after World War I (Salter 1928). He found 'fourteen members of the Society, who kindly consented to co-operate in the experiment, [and] who were given a certain number of phrases to choose from, and [who] were asked to write down any words or phrases that suggested themselves and to post the replies to me before a definite date'. The second task was further complicated by including two telepathic experiments, one from Piddington and one from Salter. Both exercises were resolutely literary and in neither case were the products like the scripts of the automatists with their characteristic features of hidden design or signalled purpose. Nor were Piddington's and Salter's telepathic efforts successful.

At this moment, well over a hundred years after Mrs Verrall's first scripts, it is virtually impossible to answer West's criticisms satisfactorily, as a brief illustration will demonstrate. Using the data from the Helen Verrall experiments and a list of the cross-correspondences in Alice Fleming's scripts based on the Clennell indices (1966, 1967), it is possible to give a very approximate answer to aspects of West's original question and, at least, to highlight some of the difficulties involved. An average of 250 words is assumed for each of the Verrall experimental scripts and 137,000 words have been broadly calculated for Trix Fleming's scripts once the surrounding notes and commentary have been removed. There was only one substantial correspondence in (36 x 250) 9,000 words in the Helen Verrall experiment; 53 correspondences in the Fleming scripts, so one cross-correspondence per 2,585 words. The automatic writing cross-correspondence did appear to stand out in terms of a ratio of more than three to one. But such comparisons depend on the security of two key variables. How accurate the word count is and agreement on what constitutes a cross-correspondence.

And is such an exercise really of any value? Scouring through the individual Fleming scripts to include the simplest topic links with other scripts and checking and re-checking the precise wordage of each individual script might produce an even more superficially impressive result, as would, in the other direction, allowing the smallest connections that Helen Verrall saw between her thirty-six scripts. In addition, with Trix Fleming, one would have to decide which scripts of the other automatists involved in the cross-correspondences, and over what period of time, would have to be included. Otherwise the wordage is too low and not generated from the total number of scripts across the automatists from which the cross-correspondences were drawn. It would be a costly and laborious task, even with computer technology, to do this right across all the scripts, and establishing a consensus about the level and quality of the cross-correspondences would, in addition, be very person intensive.

Moreover, there are issues to do with the conditions under which cross-correspondences were or might be generated. One must establish whether or not like is being compared with like. The Helen Salter scripts were clearly based on an external stimulus which guided them in a particular direction whereas, for the cross-correspondence automatists, working independently, in theory they could have started anywhere and gone anywhere in terms of content. It could be argued that a few really remarkable cross-correspondences exhibiting unambiguous design, intricate planning, and conscious purpose were of much greater value than a larger number of vague ones stemming from a common, contrived stimulus.

These issues emerge quite starkly in the more recent debate between Moreman (2002) and Keen and Roy (2002) on the matter of chance coincidence in the cross-correspondences. Moreman's work and the earlier experiments of Verrall and Salter clearly demonstrated that, whether through stimulus material or the selection of literary texts at random, data could be produced from which a certain level of correspondence might be extracted. This was never in dispute. What was, and still is, is the relationship of that type of material both with regard to the conditions under which they were created and their quality. With those in the scripts assessed by Johnson and Piddington *et al.*, Moreman listed 18 examples in Appendix B of his article. This appears substantial. But, one should remember the conditions under which the Moreman scripts were produced: the scripts were derived from a sample of just over six thousand books from the fiction section of a local public library. The list of topics forming the basis of those cross-correspondences seemed just what one would expect to emerge from the concerns and interests of novelists past and present, and would, in theory, increase the possibility of commonality and overlap of content. Moreman's five participants were an 'intelligent group of post-graduate students from the department of English Literature' who 'were encouraged to be as creative as possible'. Such a group could extract a coherent symbolic meaning from a shopping list. However, a serious point. They did try to strive for an objective, agreed consensual meaning and this central issue haunted and still haunts the interpretation of the cross-correspondences.

Moreman usefully summarises a number of the above issues and arguments. He asserts: that there wasn't sufficient control over the production of the scripts; that many of the simpler cross-correspondences were banal; that the more complex cross-correspondences could have been produced by a combination of chance, cherry-picking of elements of the scripts, and over-ingenious interpretation; that telepathy and clairvoyance were more 'straightforward' explanations for the phenomena; and, finally, that the investigators did not even bother to count successes and failures, so unscientific were they in their approach to this matter. These are fair but not new points and all had been considered in various ways and at various times by the original investigators. There is no doubt that his approach can generate cross-correspondences by chance, but whether they in any way have the characteristics of their more famous ancestors, as Keen and Roy have pointed out, is highly debatable. But Moreman's article remains useful in that it puts all interpreters of the scripts on their guard against misattributing to a discarnate intelligence what may be the product, singly or in combination, of the factors mentioned above.

The conflict between this literary approach and the statistical approach to the cross-correspondences was what lay behind an acerbic exchange between the experienced psychical researchers Michael Coleman and Montague Keen (1998). Coleman asserted: 'That there is no satisfactory method for deciding whether the correlations observed in the published material represent a statistically signifigant fraction of the whole.' But Keen argued that that was irrelevant given the large number of individually impressive cases contained within the scripts and that the real problem was 'whether such examples of paranormal knowledge can somehow be explained by avoiding the hypothesis of survival of human consciousness'. These are spontaneous paranormal phenomena. 'The evidential value cannot be assessed by any statistical method but only by common sense. The more highly specific the information the less likely it is to be guesswork or chance.'

On the other hand, one of the most valuable features of the cross-correspondences is that they were embedded in automatic writing which created a permanent record that could be examined over and over again and the amount of material that appeared inexplicable gradually reduced, and the rationale for that reduction openly debated. In terms of the inner pattern of the cross-correspondences, Piddington demonstrated, to his own satisfaction, time and again over the years that the automatic writings had a coherent symbolic structure, if enough work was put into them. This also applied and still applies to the issue of paranormal cognition. It is still possible to study and research the unrecognised names and descriptions in the scripts. Indeed, Lambert (1964–71), as stated above, has argued that he traced eleven names in the scripts 'which can, with reasonable certainty, be identified as or related to named individuals who were at Cambridge in Henry Sidgwick's time'.

Hindsight is easy, and one must continue to regret that, once one or more automatists began to join Margaret Verrall, the idea of joint control experiments was not systematically developed and a pool of disinterested and objective volunteers (assessors and automatists) not built up. But, on the other hand, the logistics would have been too formidable to overcome and in 1901 there was absolutely no idea how the writing would proliferate over the coming thirty years or so, or indeed that anyone else would contribute significantly to it.

All one can really do is to identify within the scripts such examples of precision combined with complexity as to make the objection of chance coincidence (particularly if such examples proliferate over time) almost farcical. If this is combined with a clear intention in the scripts to create a cross-correspondence, of whatever sort, and it occurs within a reasonable time period, so much the better.

There is more to be said on the time factor—in part supportive of the cross-correspondences and in part not. Some of the cross-correspondences were impressive in the way they satisfied certain basic criteria: a cross-correspondence was signalled; whether complex or not there was substance in the correspondence; and it occurred within a short timescale. For, the longer the delay and the vaguer or more opaque the reference, the more likely it was that the asserted connection was the product of chance and wishful thinking. Gerald Balfour (1927) stated that in the early years of the investigations no cross-correspondences were to count unless they were nearly contemporaneous (about a week), but in later years the links were seen as stretching over a long period of time as the hidden symbolic meanings became more important. To a twenty-first-century observer this creates a curious effect. There was a sense of momentum, development, even intellectual excitement with regard to the earlier scripts, but in the later ones this slows down. The messages become curiously static and repetitive, particularly in Helen Verrall's (Salter) scripts and Winifred Coombe-Tennant's, and though the Richmonds joined the team after the war, their scripts spelled out the same basic message but without a real sense of progression. Gerald Balfour argued that this emphasis on repetition was to drive the messages home, one of great personal importance for Arthur Balfour and one of wider significance for humanity. To a later reader it might sometimes appear that the communicators and their mediums had run out of steam and were almost literally just on 'automatic' pilot.

17

Have All Normal Avenues for Acquiring the Information Been Ruled Out?

Given the similarity of allusive content across the scripts, it is crucial to ascertain what knowledge the automatists had of each others' scripts and what knowledge they had acquired generally of the main events and personalities referred to in them. There were social networks that linked a number of the automatists together and these have to be explored. In the literature on the cross-correspondences there has been too much emphasis on the isolation of the mediums from each other and this, though often true, was not in fact always the case. For example, Carter (2012): 'The messages which became known as *cross-correspondences*, were received by mediums in England, the United States, and India during the period 1901–1932.' It is true that some of the automatists were sometimes so isolated but not all, and not always. As Alice Johnson recorded (1934a): 'She [Trix Fleming] was in England (or on the Continent) from April, 1904–July, 1906, then returned to Calcutta and spent two years there, and came back for good in July, 1908.' Leonora Piper was in England from 1906–07, and from May 1910 to at least February 1911 (Piper 1928). Margaret Verrall and her daughter Helen were often writing together (though separately) in Selwyn Gardens. Mrs Coombe-Tennant divided her time between London and Wales but had frequent close contact, particularly in the early years, with Margaret Verrall.

The automatic writers and their investigators shared a range of formal and informal networks which could potentially have provided them with normal sources of information that might otherwise be interpreted as paranormally acquired. All of the investigators and all of the automatists had some knowledge, slight or profound, (even Leonora Piper) of several or more of the communicators. The Balfours, the Verralls, Lodge, Piddington, and Alice Johnson were steeped in the history of the SPR. Gerald and Arthur Balfour knew the Tennant and Lyttelton families intimately through their involvement in the aristocratic coterie known as the 'Souls', as did Lodge in a more marginal way. Alice Johnson was a biologist like F.M. Balfour and became the director of the laboratory set up in his honour at Newnham College (Richmond 1997). Trix Fleming's parents retired from India to Tisbury, close to the Wyndhams at Clouds where they and their children Rudyard and Trix were welcome and where members of the 'Souls' met, including the Lyttelton, Tennant, and Balfour families.

Several of the automatists had London Clubs. The Verralls, their friend the classicist Jane Harrison, and Alice Johnson were all members of the Sesame Club, founded in 1895, with its civilised ambience and its programme of literary and educational interests. Winifred Coombe-Tennant and Edith Lyttelton also were members of London Clubs reflective of their particular concerns. These clubs, which began to proliferate in this period, were a sign of the greater mobility and independence of women. The Albemarle Club, founded in 1874, was particularly favoured since, like the Sesame, it was open to men and to women, and Gerald Balfour's wife, Betty, and Millicent Fawcett, the suffragist leader (who knew the Verralls) were both members (see Stewart 1959; Crawford 1999).

Another common link was an interest in suffrage, as suffragists rather than suffragettes, though Lady Betty's sister, Constance, was active in her work for the cause and went to prison for a period. They also had an interest in social reform even though their political affiliations and tactics might have differed. The only one partially outside this network was Trix Fleming, partly because of her geographical isolation in India for some of the time, and possibly because she did not possess the financial resources of the others.

There was certainly a link between Lavinia (Lyttelton) Talbot's husband, Warden (later Bishop) Talbot of Keble, and Sir Oliver Lodge and Arthur Balfour which might in theory have been a conduit for the Palm Maiden and the lock of hair story. Talbot was the first chairman of the Synthetic Society which brought Lodge, Myers, Arthur Balfour, Gerald Balfour, and others together, in the mid-1890s, to discuss the great metaphysical questions. It had been stimulated into being by the publication of Arthur Balfour's *Foundations of Belief* in 1895 (Lubenow 2005). It is unlikely but not impossible that some personal material may have mingled with the metaphysical. But, it should be stressed, the Synthetic Society was wound up before Lodge and Gerald Balfour had any inkling of the significance of the hair symbols in the scripts.

The Souls were very well-known in English society and were a close knit group, and, though not exclusive in the way that other aristocratic cliques were, they were certainly elite and establishment in background: '...none of the Souls attended a public school other than Eton or Harrow, or, with the exceptions of White, Cowper, and Windsor, a college other than Balliol or Trinity' (Ellenberger 1982). Arthur and Gerald Balfour were members (Arthur Balfour was the leader: Gerald more tangential) of this group as was Edith Lyttelton, and many references to the group can be traced in the scripts. The paintings of Watts, Rossetti, and Burne-Jones, artists particularly favoured by the group, also figured significantly as material for cross-correspondences.

Another clique, or coterie, was the Cambridge secret society known as the 'Apostles'. It was composed of a handful of gifted Cambridge undergraduates who selectively replenished their numbers each year from the incoming freshmen (Lubenow 1998). Gerald Balfour, Arthur Verrall, Frank Balfour, Richard Jebb, Walter Leaf, S.H. Butcher, who were all mentioned in the scripts, were members of this self-perpetuating elite, and all at some stage fellows or aspiring fellows of Trinity College. There is some doubt, however, as to whether Arthur Balfour was ever offered or accepted membership. As has been seen, there was also a more informal clustering of wives in the Cambridge Ladies' Dining Society (Shils 1996), of which Margaret Verrall was a key member, and another network was the Cambridge-based group of graduates of Newnham College, like Margaret and Helen Verrall and Alice Johnson, who admired the Sidgwicks' work for women's higher education and strongly supported and worked with Eleanor Sidgwick on both psychical research and educational issues.

The direct impact of networks on the scripts was particularly visible in the scripts of Trix Fleming in early 1906. She was in England at the time and met Arthur Balfour and members of the Souls on a number of occasions. For example, in describing her script of 18/2/1906, she wrote (Johnson 1916a Vol 1: 114): 'I think the political prophecy [this was that the Liberal ministry would last less than two years before an election: it lasted four] may be explained by my having met Mr. Balfour at dinner that evening. I "read" his hand and was cheered to see that the really brilliant part of his career lies between his 60th and 70th birthdays!' This led to her scripts during this period being sprinkled with references such as that Balfour should have a complete rest after his period as Prime Minister and should read only light fiction, to the famous old yew tree at his family home Whittingehame (linked to Darnley and Mary Queen of Scots), and to his mother, Lady Blanche Balfour. Items of no real evidential value. On the other hand the prediction had a certain element of truth in it with regard to his later service in the War Coalition. In 1919 Arthur Balfour was seventy and Foreign Secretary.

The most celebrated and romantic paranormal item in the cross-correspondences is the story of the silver bronze box Arthur Balfour made, in which was kept a lock of May Lyttelton's hair. In the light of what one knows about the formal and informal networks to which both automatists and investigators belonged, what was the likelihood that this material had been consciously or semi-consciously acquired (then forgotten) by one or more of those involved? Gerald Balfour stressed that the story was forty years old at the time of revelation in Coombe-Tennant script in 1916 and was unknown to any of the automatists. However, the story of Arthur

Balfour's love for May Lyttelton was not unfamiliar in upper class circles in the 1870s (Gladstone 1930: 95) and the *New York Times* referred to it on Arthur Balfour's death in 1930. It is, therefore, not impossible that other aspects of the story also circulated.

The central issue is: can one trace a specific connection from the limited circle of Lytteltons and Balfours to the automatists involved in the cross-correspondences? It has been seen that there was a theoretical Bishop Talbot/Oliver Lodge/Gerald Balfour link but this was highly speculative. The investigators to their credit did explore this issue as thoroughly as they could and Balfour and Piddington recorded what each automatist knew and when. Margaret Verrall knew nothing of A.J.B.'s story till June 1912. She was acquainted slightly with Lady Mount-Temple of Broadlands and the Balfours of Fishers Hill before becoming more fully involved in the later stages of her scripts. She had heard of Francis Maitland Balfour and his death. But that was all. Helen Verrall knew the Sidgwicks well but was told nothing by them of the Palm Maiden story. She did not hear the details till 1933, long after she had ceased automatic writing (on all this, see Salter 1948). As a child she had played with the children of May's brother, Arthur Lyttelton, who as Master of Selwyn College lived very close to her home, but that was the faintest of links.

There is a an interesting letter in the Salter archive from Mrs Goldney (Goldney 14/1/1966), a senior SPR figure, on the circulation of the Palm Maiden story over the years. This was in the context of what Geraldine Cummins might have acquired from normal sources in connection with her book *Swan on a Black Sea*. The letter revealed the gossipy and indiscreet nature of Edith Lyttelton and raises again her role in the possible leakage of information over the years, particularly to Winifred Coombe-Tennant.

After the revelations of the scripts of 31/3/1912 and 4/4/1912, Winifred Coombe-Tennant motored over from Eastbourne where she was staying and Gerald Balfour interrogated her about her knowledge of Arthur Balfour and private events from the past (Lord 2011). She seemed to show no knowledge or awareness of the individuals referred to symbolically in the scripts and of the events around Palm Sunday 1875. Nor was there any indication in 1916 after her script at Carlton Gardens with Arthur Balfour that she had any knowledge of the casket and the lock of hair story. It is clear from her diary (Lord 2011: 97–101) that she was in an intense and heightened state during these years, but there is no evidence in it of any attempts at fabricating a message or of concealing sources of information. Furthermore, there is no trace in her published diary (it is not of course impossible that the unpublished diary might have something of relevance) of concerted efforts by her to research the background of the Balfour family. It is true to say she may have learnt something about the Balfours from Edith Lyttelton when they met for the first time on war work in 1917. But by this time her most evidential scripts had been produced.

Neither Oliver Lodge, a close friend of Arthur Balfour, nor Eleanor Sidgwick, his sister, knew the story of the silver casket, and Arthur Balfour was highly reticent in intimate personal matters. Trix Fleming never knew anything about it all and her scripts stopped in 1910. Therefore, the only other possible source of information was via Mrs Talbot (May's sister Lavinia who married the Warden of Keble, later Bishop Talbot, as has been seen). It does appear, however, that Betty Balfour learnt of the story of the lock of hair and the silver box from Lavinia Talbot probably in the mid-1890s, but she never seems to have told Gerald Balfour or, if she did, he said that he had forgotten it (Balfour 1927). She was bringing up young children and he was actively involved in political life, first as Irish Secretary and later, in Arthur Balfour's administration, as President of the Board of Trade. So it is not inconceivable that the communication between them was poor at times.

The lock of hair in the silver bronze box may broadly, with some qualifications, stand up to scrutiny, but given the close connections and networks between a number of the individuals involved, many script statements are moving but not evidentially impressive. Take Winifred Coombe-Tennant's script of 1/5/1911 (she was planning to visit the Verrall's in Cambridge):

> I know Cambridge My Cambridge I shall be there with you Myers ask Mrs V whether she remembers a time in a garden a an enclosed garden Myers open to fellows

This was a reference to the Trinity College Fellow's Garden between Grange Road and Queen's Road, where Myers and Margaret Verrall had often walked, and Myers had had his iconic encounter with George Eliot (Hamilton 2009). Winifred Coombe-Tennant denied any knowledge of the garden but, given her occasional visits to Cambridge to see Myers and Eveleen, she was very likely to have picked up something about it or even walked round it.

The more one probes, the more potential opportunities for leakage can be identified. For example, it was assumed, perhaps wrongly, that Leonora Piper, poorly educated and a trance medium, would not have been in a position to pick up relevant material through normal channels. Yet she, and her daughters, were virtually made part of the Lodge family when they came to England. But sometimes too much can be made of these theoretical possibilities. The original investigators were alive to this issue and checked the normal avenues for acquiring or generating the information through printed material, gossip, and conscious fraud—and were, too, aware of the possible shaping of these sources through unconscious fraud, self-delusion, and cryptomnesia into something that appeared to have a strongly paranormal flavour. One example of this was the pains taken to investigate Leonora Piper both by a detective, by the investigators, and by an examination and questioning of the books she read (see above; also Baird 1949). She put up with it because she was treated well and because she was being paid. The other automatists voluntarily submitted to (apart from investigation by a detective) the same discipline, often a wearying clerical task. This was an important activity, then and now, since a very impressive example of paranormal cognition, like Trix Fleming's dramatic account of Gurney's death, as has been seen, was only properly evaluated when Alice Johnson (a fact that Trix Fleming had completely forgotten) realised that she had told Trix Fleming about it some time before.

But the most truly puzzling problem of all centres around Winifred Coombe-Tennant and what she might or might not have known. It almost beggars belief that in her account of the birth on 9/4/1913 of Henry and the help and support that the dark young man gave her through the labour that she did not ask the Balfours who he was, particularly as she had seen a photograph of him in Mrs Sidgwick's Cambridge house on her first visit there in January 1912. She was deeply in love and having her lover's child. Wouldn't she have wanted to have found out all she could about him and his family? Especially as she had an ambitious side to her which seems to have fitted rather uneasily with the strong liberal sympathies she expressed publicly throughout her life. But Gerald Balfour was very explicit on this point (Balfour 1928: 4): '[Winifred Coombe-Tennant's] persistent failure one might almost say, refusal—to recognise the identity of the Dark Young Man is very curious and noteworthy. Not only does she affirm both in script, and also in her normal condition, that she is ignorant of it, but she has no wish to be informed. For the matter of that I have never in the whole course of my experience known [Winifred Coombe-Tennant] express any desire to have her scripts explained to her.' This last statement contrasts somewhat with their private letters and her diary in 1911, and one can only reconcile the two accounts if one assumes that the earlier discussions of script focused on tracing literary and artistic sources rather than their deeper meaning.

Trix Fleming suffered from the same selective blindness or ignorance in her scripts. She initially had to have the references to Laura Lyttelton and Alfred Lyttelton pointed out to her by Alice Johnson. The investigators eventually came to the conclusion that in certain circumstances there might have been a discarnate telepathic hypnotic influence (a discarnate version of the living Gurney's experiments in the 1880s with George Albert Smith) in order to keep the automatist from contaminating her script. But this is not a hypothesis particularly congenial to a later researcher outside the nexus of influences in which the scripts were produced.

The general potential for social leakage has been well established but even more important was, and still is, ascertaining what knowledge each automatist had of the others' scripts and when they acquired it. It is impossible to state precisely at any one time from 1901 to 1918 where the scripts of each automatist actually were, and sometimes individual and small groups of scripts were shown to an automatist to stimulate further writing or for help with interpretation. But after the discovery of the Palm Maiden story in 1912 this process was discouraged and the scripts came securely under Balfour's and Piddington's control. Mrs Sidgwick then compiled a detailed list which set down precisely which automatist saw which scripts of the group and when. A study of this reveals that the statement that the automatists wrote in ignorance of each other's scripts needs considerable qualification. To roughly summarise Mrs Sidgwick's exhaustive list (Piddington 1921: 1–86):

- Trix Fleming was probably the most isolated of the writers under discussion. She saw some of Margaret Verrall's scripts, a handful of Helen Verrall's scripts, and no Coombe-Tennant scripts as far as can be established.
- Helen Verrall did not see the first three hundred of her mother's scripts till 1912, but she saw the remainder fairly soon after they had been produced. She saw a small number of Fleming scripts in 1907 and the whole of vol. 1 in 1912. She saw the first 27 Mac scripts and only around 35 of the Coombe-Tennant scripts.
- Winifred Coombe-Tennant saw only one of the first three hundred of Margaret Verrall's scripts but she was given access to the remainder in large increments over the years, from 1909 onwards, and she had access to many Helen Verrall, Fleming, and Mac scripts.
- Margaret Verrall saw all Helen Verrall's scripts shortly after production. She had seen well before her death all Fleming scripts. She saw the first two hundred or so Coombe-Tennant scripts shortly after production, though from January 1912 she received them at greater intervals. She saw all Mac scripts.

Given this greater access to each other's scripts than has previously been mentioned in the published literature, one has to hazard (but only hazard) a guess that the sense of common style and symbolism which so impressed Janet Oppenheim (1985) may not be an example of external design but of the subconscious stylistic influence of other automatist's scripts. A further complicating factor was that Margaret Verrall had, for a number of years, (as did Winifred Coombe-Tennant) a dual role as automatist and interpreter of scripts, and Helen Verrall, herself, became an active official of the SPR and later (though after her writing ceased) with her husband a trusted confidant of Balfour and Piddington. One cannot help but suspect the development of a common line or approach to the material which might have inhibited really robust assessment of the content, even amongst individuals as gifted and conscientious as they were.

A final note on cryptomnesia or source amnesia is relevant here. A wide range of theoretical possibilities for acquiring information that might otherwise have been ascribed to paranormal cognition has been outlined above. But a certain common sense and balance is required. Stevenson (1983–84) has laid down a very clear set of criteria to judge these matters. They can be summarised as follows: a detailed correspondence between the information 'paranormally acquired' and its availability from normal sources; evidence that the producer of the material did at one time acquire (or it was more probable than not that she/he did acquire) the information normally; and that all elements in the situation be considered.

Applying these criteria to the cross-correspondences one can clearly see that in many cases there is not enough information to rule on this issue and that it would be irresponsible and lazy to invoke cryptomnesia as a catch-all explanation for the apparently inexplicable demonstration of knowledge accessed beyond the range of the normal sensory channels. On the other hand it cannot be ruled out. And, finally, only by looking at all the evidence in the case of each automatist, in particular the chronological evidence, can one make a fair and sensible judgement. The fact, for example, that by 1916 Winifred Coombe-Tennant had become an intimate of the Gerald Balfour family should not be used to discredit her apparent knowledge in 1910, before reading Myers' autobiography, of the importance of syringa in his life.

18

Have the Correspondences (Including the Overall Story and the Plan) Been Tweaked by Wishful Thinking, Over-Subtle Interpretation, or Deliberate Selection?

There is always the suspicion when reading script extracts in the *Proceedings* that, no matter how discriminating and meticulous the commentary, information may have been manipulated or massaged, particularly when one comes across something like this in the volumes of the complete printed scripts:

Helen Verrall 1/1/1907:

> Mancilium travetone Ambrose the name was a clue a father of
> The church in olden times less wise than pious Shadwood Mentone
> Corun what was that to do with the peas there was no need
> For others to interfere
> Memorabilia silent voces opulentia incumbit pondere magno
> (scribbles) Xen (Things to be remembered The voices are silent Wealth weighs down with a great weight)

Or

Margaret Verrall 4/9/1908:

> Pettigrew and the forecastle and another word which you
> have not understood. Then look back in earlier writing for
> a distinctive word which will give you the clue to his identity,
> Rector's I mean You have not found all that is hidden in
> your writing yet, it is in an early writing…Nequiquam Deus prudens…

It is interesting to see the way Piddington dealt with these two scripts. The former he took as a reference to Arthur Lyttelton, May Lyttelton's brother and former Master of Selwyn College and later Bishop of Southampton. He also identified a possible allusion to the Lyttelton children who died young. He based this on the references to a father of the church and also to Mentone on the French/Italian border where the Bishop had died. He took Shadwood as a mistake for Sherwood. Piddington argued that one of the symbolic codes in the script was Robin Hood (Arthur Balfour) and Maid Marian (May Lyttelton) and that Antony Lyttelton was seen as Puck or Robin Goodfellow inhabiting the forest with Robin Hood and his merry men (see Piddington 1943c: 1178).He ignored the rest apart from pointing out that Xenophon had written (Memorabilia) a document on Socrates.

He also ignored, or did not trace, the Pettigrew reference in the latter script. There is nothing on it in the *Excursuses*. He would have argued in both cases that stray phrases and puzzling statements could sometimes just be part of the wave motion of subliminal flotsam and jetsam. Communication was rarely pure and unsullied. That may be true but there is a limit to the amount one can tweak in a script without it devaluing the rest. Sometimes, and who can blame him, he was unable to track a statement to its source. Myers, in fact, had been very interested in Nelson and wrote and lectured on him and this may well be an example of an encoded reference to Nelson turning a blind eye and disregarding an order to avoid action before the Battle of Copenhagen. Pettigrew (1849) had written a biography of Nelson. This would fit with what Piddington decoded as the main theme in the script—the dangers of sea travel as a metaphor/symbol for the difficulties of communication between the dead and the living (see below), and the need, as Nelson did, and as the Palm Maiden did, to take risks for success. This interpretation was supported by a later script of Margaret Verrall's on 18/3/1914 which referred to the Nelson touch in an appropriate context:

> The battle & the breeze—and the Nelson touch. Copenhagen and other victories, victories too of peace no less than war

Piddington argued that the communicators used Margaret Verrall's fascination with the real identity of Leonora Piper's controls (Rector and Prudens particularly) to get the link to the Horace quotation (C.1.3.21–26: *deus abscidit prudens* etc.), the gist of which was that God had wisely and deliberately separated countries from each other by means of the ocean but impious and audacious humanity still ventured on the waters. Horace's ode described the voyage of Virgil to Greece across the rough Aegean and Piddington connected this to another poem which was quoted or alluded to several times in the scripts, Matthew Arnold's *To Marguerite: Continued*, particularly the line 'the unplumbed, salt, estranging sea'. He saw both poems as symbols for the separation of the Palm Maiden and the Knight and her showing great daring in attempting to make contact with him. He argued that in Winifred Coombe-Tennant's script May Lyttelton's passionate and courageous determination to make contact with Arthur Balfour was made fully explicit.

Piddington's years of study of the scripts gave him the confidence to bring together these scattered fragments into a meaningful, thematic unity. He (1921) believed that he had discovered the central methodology that lay behind the process of communication. In discussing, for example, the way in which *Gray's Elegy* was treated in the scripts and the gradual, apparently muddled emergence of references to it, he stated: 'They start by being scrappy and disjointed; then, as years go by, the separate elements are gradually drawn together—never all of them together, but first, say, topics (a) (f) and (c), next (c) (d) and (e), and so on; until finally in Mrs. Coombe-Tennant's script come the clues which enable us to co-ordinate and interpret all the component elements.'

As has been seen, Margaret Verrall was always a little uneasy about this. The difference in viewpoint came out most clearly in Piddington's preface to Margaret Verrall's scripts Vol. III (1919: 1-10). Piddington stated that the first set of Margaret Verrall's scripts to be edited and published was volume II by him in 1912 and she edited and published volume I in 1914. This curious and muddled arrangement meant that both volumes were thinly noted. When Margaret Verrall edited volume I she took an approach which differed from his and when he, earlier, had prepared volume II he had had no comprehensive collection of her scripts at the time of editing, particularly her crucially important first scripts. Moreover, he had been editing volume II from a limited perspective. It was not till 6/7/1912 that the words in a Coombe-Tennant Daylight Impression—'Oh, she says, look back. She says, Helen's mother. Far back I came—years ago I've been beating at this door'—provided the basis for a fuller interpretation of all the automatic writing. Piddington also stressed that by the time Margaret Verrall came to edit the first volume of her scripts she knew about the Palm Sunday Case and she had been told about the new method of interpretation but, for various reasons, she neither fully accepted nor followed the method. This meant that many of the references to the Palm Maiden, the Knight, and the Peacock Lady were not commented on or fully brought out in her notes.

There were a number of reasons for this. Temperamentally she liked to get through tasks and have done with them. She tended to scoff at the slow and minute way in which Gerald Balfour and Piddington operated. She also was inclined to treat the scripts in isolation and in a literal way, often trying to pin them down to an event in her current experience. This led her to ignore the repetition of 'striking words or phrases when the repetition occurred in a group of scripts having nothing in common according to her view with a group in which these words or phrases had first appeared' (Piddington 1919: 4-5). This helped to explain why, even after her knowledge of the Palm Sunday Case, she did not fully pick up on the personalities or the generic themes of the scripts.

Yet, despite her partial disagreement, Piddington remained confident that the methodology he and Balfour had evolved was the correct one. He emphasised, as well, the enormity of the task, the difficulty of ironing out (if ever) all inconsistencies, the importance of getting all the scripts in print, and the production of separate volumes of explanatory *Notes and*

Excursuses because of the sheer complexity of the material. He also concluded in 1918 that during their five years work on the scripts since 1913 'our methods of interpretation are in the main sound, and that the scripts of all our automatists are a composite whole'.

He also made a very bold claim for the early Margaret Verrall scripts. He stated (1919: 5) that her scripts from March 1901 to the summer of 1903 'contain, I believe, adumbrations of nearly all the leading topics that have figured in the scripts of all the automatists subsequently'. He asserted that they were expressed by certain key words or literary allusions. They were embryonic and grew into the full expression of the theme much later on: something clearly seen in the early sword and sigma references and the cryptic references to the Peacock Memorial at Mells. In Margaret Verrall's later scripts the topics became more clearly elaborated and more easily seen as connected. He believed, as did Gerald Balfour, that the approach was deliberate, laying down the key themes very early on but not revealing their inner meaning till the appropriate time.

But do Piddington's assertions and conclusions actually stand up? Was the method of cryptic communication actually there? Did tracing the quotations and topics between scripts and across time lead to coherent and consistent results? Given the sheer body of material to be studied and the number of allusions and references to be explored, it is quite natural to raise questions about the methodology used and the objectivity of the interpretation. These issues have been rather ducked or ignored in recent years. Were the original investigators overly influenced by the cultural space and historical context they inhabited? (See, for example, Turner 1981: *passim*; Hardie 2014: 114.) This is not to say that they did not strive for objectivity, for their efforts in this direction were strenuous and admirable, merely that one needs to look particularly closely at the personal, social, and cultural climate within which they operated.

Were there any key ideas at the time which predisposed Piddington, Balfour, and the others to accept the enormous claims that seemed to be emerging from the scripts? Certainly, the view of Rome and its importance in the development of civilisation would have been a common theme amongst the Victorians who saw themselves as heirs to both Athens and Rome with the additional moral enrichment of Christianity. One could argue that this underpinned the progressive and predictive element in the cross-correspondences though there was also a strong emphasis on the unity of opposites, the union of East and West, the theme made popular by E. Arnold's book *Light of Asia* and Blavatsky's Theosophical Society. This reflects another emerging theme of the age, the gradually developing sense of a need for international solutions to problems, something which was well exemplified in the life and career of Winifred Coombe-Tennant herself. There was also the strange charisma which Arthur Balfour exercised in the public and private circles he moved in. He was called King Arthur among the Souls. He was sometimes caricatured as such in the media, and there were frequent references to Tennyson and the Arthurian legends in the cross-correspondences. And Balfour, as has been seen, whose political career seemed to be over in 1911, nevertheless saw it revived in the First World War and in the various international settlements after it. He became the British elder statesman at a time Piddington and Gerald Balfour were deep in the interpretation of scripts.

All the above influences and tendencies may have made the more outrageous elements of the scripts easier to accept and to suggest deeper layers of meaning. For Theosophy had already predisposed sections of the artistic and cultural elite to ideas of spiritual development across and beyond traditional religious boundaries well before the deaths of the communicators, and it also strongly emphasised the concept of the spiritual growth and progression of the human race which Myers himself expressed in *Human Personality* (Dixon 2010; Asprem 2014). The theme of the destiny of the race of man to become the race of angels ran through the scripts and this was clearly reflected in the Messianic scripts of Winifred Coombe-Tennant. These kinds of ideas were part of the zeitgeist during the first part of the twentieth century, with the ultimate battle between Good and Evil being predicted, and the search for new gurus and spiritual leaders like Gurdjieff and Krishnamurti eagerly underway (Owen 2004).

One wonders, too, whether even the critical and shrewd Alice Johnson was swayed by these heady considerations. Roy (2008) quotes a revealing letter of 5/3/1915 from her when she staying at Cadoxton with Winifred Coombe-Tennant:

'Dear Mr Balfour, You asked me to try to prevent Mrs Tennant from overworking, so I think you might like to hear a little about things here', and the letter shows her thoroughly integrated into the family, wheeling the smiling baby about the place, and doing her best to prevent the energetic Mrs Tennant from overworking. This was hardly the picture of a detached and objective researcher. The fact that Henry was Gerald Balfour's son was revealed to Piddington by Winifred Coombe-Tennant (Lord 2011: 203) in December 1916 but it is not clear when, if ever, the other investigators knew that, only that he was a child for whom the scripts had prophesied a great future.

One can also, perhaps fancifully, detect a strong semi-conscious and unexamined sense of Englishness in the scripts and the commentaries on them, reflecting the pride and angst of the upper and upper middle classes at this time. A growing emphasis on the legends of Robin Hood and King Arthur has been seen as a reflection of this (Barczewski 2000). There was a revival of heraldry in the nineteenth century associated with national pride after the defeat of Napoleon and certainly, in the scripts, coats of arms and their crests and mottoes figured quite significantly as symbols. In a slightly broader way, in some of the memoirs of the individuals mentioned in the scripts, and in Piddington's jovial asides (1916), one gets a slightly jossing sense of Anglo-Saxon superiority. The Americans and the French, particularly, were teased. However, this point should not be stressed too much. The standard of languages was generally high amongst the investigators and there was a very strong literary appreciation of other cultures. Moreover, in his work as senior partner in the postal and parcel carrier company that his family had founded (Ellis 1949), Piddington had a much wider direct experience of European culture than many of his contemporaries. There was also a much stronger appreciation of German culture and science than, alas, has been evident in later periods.

It is very important to bear this contextual material in mind when examining the bizarre matter of the Messianic Child or children, and the children who were failed spiritual experiments on the way. An enormous amount of energy and ingenuity was expended by Balfour on the Messianic Child interpretation and by Piddington on the children who died young, Daphne and the two Lyttelton boys. One can, perhaps, only explain it by their natural and unconscious assumption that, if such things were to take place, it was appropriate that it should be situated in the milieu of the Balfours and the Lytteltons, the core of the Souls who numbered in their ranks a Prime Minister, his brother the handsome and gifted scholar politician and philosopher, and members of the Lyttelton family with their wide establishment connections (Hynes 1968: 389).

Such unconscious assumptions and drivers may well have helped energise and sustain Piddington as he continued his largely solo interpretive task. And, increasingly as Gerald Balfour aged and withdrew from the process of interpretation, Piddington may have lacked the critical friend necessary to give him objectivity and balance. It is worrying, for example, that such a huge amount of time and erudition was spent on his, first, identifying Bacchus and his mother Semele with Henry Augustus and his mother Winifred, and then an equally enormous amount of time and erudition given to revising that interpretation and replacing the mother by Laura Lyttelton and the child by Christopher Lyttelton. In all, he had to cancel over one hundred and sixty pages of interpretation in volume one of *Notes and Excursuses* (1921: 4). There was also uncertainty as to whom the Dido references pointed. Piddington settled on Laura Lyttelton while Jean Balfour, who had access to the scripts and who empathised strongly with her situation, argued in unpublished papers that Dido was Betty Balfour, the neglected wife of Gerald Balfour (Kremer archive).

From the vantage point of the twenty-first century, the vaingloriousness in interpreting the scripts as of cosmic significance for one dead aristocrat, and for one elderly one and his child by one of the mediums, appears astounding. But did this ever occur to anyone at the time? Was a lack of perspective rather than anything more sinister the main weakness? Piddington was a shrewd businessman who mixed with a wide variety of people. Gerald Balfour, however, was much less worldly and, like Arthur, ineffective in commercial enterprises. Witness the brothers' disastrous involvement in the scheme to convert peat into fuel for commerce and industry. It almost ruined the family fortunes. Vanity ran right through the Coombe-Tennant scripts particularly, and others, perhaps, were subconsciously excited to be caught up in the dream. One notes a letter from Alice Johnson to Gerald Balfour: 'have you observed that Augustus' head is the same shape as Shakespeare's. It comes out beautifully in one of your photographs' (Roy 2008). The present writer much prefers the earlier comment on Shakespeare's head by Trix Fleming: that she enjoyed eating caramel walnuts 'because of their extraordinary resemblance to the bald head of William Shakespeare' (Lee 2004). In terms of vanity, one could almost postulate that Winifred Coombe-Tennant's scripts were a subconscious attempt on her part to integrate herself and her child into one of the great families of the United Kingdom which governed, in part and at different times, the greatest empire in the world.

There certainly seems to have been an element of this in the Coombe-Tennant script of 16/8/1915 (Houghton archive):

> it is <u>one family</u> A and PM A and Peacock Lady and A linked to third A Augustus 'Yes but not only supernaturally but in blood. (That is, Arthur Balfour, Alfred Lyttelton and Augustus Henry Coombe-Tennant.)
> G.W.B. I understand that
> Well you should 'None of the scripts can be understood apart from the Paternity of the Child' 'To the Palm Lady the Child is as it were the fruit of the House into which she would have been drawn' 'she has woven it all into the vicarious child of hers and his—Do you see' and 'the large share of the Frate Minore' [Francis Maitland Balfour] in all this and the child to be 'the whole race bloom in that perfect flower'(Henry Coombe-Tennant)

That is perhaps unfair and over-simple, for Winifred Coombe-Tennant had a very powerful sense of social justice and sympathy for the poor, and she had an intense dislike of the public school system and the insensitive, militaristic characteristics it developed in many men; though she did make use of it for her children. She also had a strong sympathy for small nations struggling to be free and was staunchly supportive of Michael Collins in Ireland. On the other hand, what is one to make of the Daphne script quoted earlier which put Daphne at the centre of the SPR in the other world and co-opted a discarnate Charles Darwin into the activity? Nevertheless, vanity, self-interest, enchantment, companionship, community of interests, all these factors may have provided the necessary motivation to sustain over many years both the hugely complex and often tedious process of matching, cross-referencing, and decoding a wide variety of symbols and associations; and in the case of the automatists, enduring the continuous and demanding process of the production of scripts and reflections upon them.

The language of the scripts and the references in them may well have contributed to this sense of elitism. Knowledge of the classics, for example, was a central underpinning assumption of many of the scripts and their interpretation. It was a status marker, both within the SPR and more widely, as a rapid increase in wealth derived from commerce and industry in the late nineteenth century led to greater fluidity in the social field and the rise of the non-public school educated entrepreneur and industrialist (Stray 1998). References to Horace figured prominently in a number of the cross-correspondences and knowledge of Horace was regarded as a special mark of the English gentleman. There is an amusing passage in Ronald Knox's novel *Let Dons Delight*: 'it seems to me quite certain that the whole legend of the "English Gentleman" has been built upon Latin and Greek. A meets B on the steps of his club and says: "Well, old man, *eheu fugaces*, what?" and B says "*Dulce et decorum est pro patria mori*", and the crossing-sweeper falls on his knees in adoration of the two men who can talk as learnedly as that.' J.W. Mackail (the Oxford classicist who married one of Trix Fleming's cousins and of whom Myers himself approved) compared the psalms of the Bible to the odes of Horace: 'But both, in their enormously different ways, are central and fundamental; permanent lights on life and aids to living' (Harrison, S. n.d.).

Two automatists were first-rate classicists, but even Trix Fleming and Winifred Coombe-Tennant (and to a much lesser extent Leonora Piper) would have had indirect access to the classics through general English literature, and major classical texts and myths would have been encountered in translation at school or in the home. For example, there were many references to Persephone (for obvious reasons) in the scripts and Ruskin, Swinburne, Pater, Tennyson, Hardy, Rossetti, Jean Ingelow, Dora Greenwell, amongst others, all used or adapted this myth in their work.

They all (except Leonora Piper) had a high general level of culture (whether or not they were classicists) and had been brought up on the great (and not so great) literature of the Romantic and Victorian traditions. Galvan (n.d.) has stressed that 'this literary essence is important, in turn, for thinking about how the scripts worked, conceptually and emotionally, on the investigators who studied them'. She argues that at the turn of the century 'these voices were still affecting enough to seem to evoke beings from another world'. She is virtually asserting that the communicating spirits were conjured out of the literature, that the literature the SPR investigators were brought up on conditioned and predisposed them to that belief.

One can see this particularly clearly in the scripts with regard to some of the symbols that were applied to Annie Marshall, Myers' love. Myers/Orpheus certainly searched desperately for Annie/Eurydice, going deep into the other world of Victorian mediumship in his quest. Myers may well have felt that though there was nothing dishonourable in their relationship he might have put too much emotional pressure on her and this could have been something that indirectly contributed to her suicide:

> 'I said Ophelia Myers did Hamlet seek to win forgiveness from the dead Underline that *forgiveness from the dead.*'

The script from which these lines came was written on 29/5/1910 with Lodge present and, as has been seen, according to Winifred Coombe-Tennant's published diary, Lodge did not tell her the story of Myers and Phyllis till 26/9/1910. But Piddington and Balfour had certainly read the unexpurgated autobiography and were fully alive to references to lost, thwarted, and abandoned lovers in literature and in the scripts.

One should also stress, regardless of the emotional impact of literature, the sheer high general literariness of it all, particularly when the Verralls, mother and daughter, and Trix Fleming were involved. The cross-correspondence below seems to have been just such a literary artefact (Johnson 1910a: 211–13).

Savonarola

Helen Verrall 6/10/1906:

> Remember the word and the date. Carthusians two and two the long black robes and the candles and the images the bright sun and the gaping crowd she will remember

Trix Fleming 8/10/1906:

> Ask his daughter about the dream—Grey monks of long ago—

Margaret Verrall 10/10/1906:

> Savonarola all wrapped in black in threes and threes they entered...

Note: Trix Fleming was in India. Margaret Verrall and Helen Verrall were probably both in Cambridge.

A.W. Verrall was frequently referred to in Fleming scripts so to take 'ask his daughter' as indicating Helen Verrall seemed reasonable, as was interpreting 'dream' as script. Margaret Verrall had read George Eliot's *Romola* and found a description in the chapter *Unseen Madonna* which described a long line of monks processing on a bright day—white, grey, and black, with Savonarola bringing up the rear. The Franciscans were in grey—a symbol for Francis Maitland Balfour.

In addition, the Bible, its stories and its texts, which was also freely used as a cultural resource in the scripts would still have had such a powerful emotional resonance for the automatists' and investigators' generation (even if they no longer had a conventional faith). So, one must suspect that not all the allusions made were carefully crafted from an external source but could easily have been produced by a dream-like free association. Larsen (2012) has looked at the impact of the Bible in his *A People of One Book: The Bible and the Victorians* and the way it affected the philosophy and actions of important Victorians right across society, including those like Huxley and Annie Besant who rejected its miraculous premises. A number of the symbols used for the Messianic Child, Moses in the bulrushes/John the Baptist symbols, references to out of captivity, to the promised land, the Babylonian exile, would all have been familiar to the automatists and might well have come virtually unbidden to their lips. Take for example:

Helen Verrall 11/9/1911:

> The promised land—he shall lead his people—the land of Egypt bondsmen to a strange race The chosen people the destiny of a nation— Ecce homo.

Helen Verrall never knew anything about the Messianic implications of the scripts till the 1930s. What, therefore, was the source of the phrases—her recent reading, random association, telepathy from another automatist, or the external design of a discarnate intelligence?

One should not, however, exaggerate the influence of poetic and literary language on Balfour and Piddington. They were absolutely clear that their interpretations were not literary in the literary appreciation or criticism sense. There was no effort to get at what Shakespeare, Shelley, or Keats or whomever actually meant unless the script intelligence seemed to think that relevant. For example, in the Hope, Star and Browning case, Gerald Balfour clearly and firmly distinguished between the scriptic meaning of the C Major of this Life and Browning's meaning. They might overlap but for him the key questions were distinct: what does it mean in the original poem? Has it the same meaning in the scripts? (Balfour 1921: 27-35). For him the crucial point over and beyond the celebrated cross-correpondence was the relevance of this and the other scripts to the prediction of a Messianic Child and the coming of a Golden Age. This applied to Balfour's and Piddington's treatment of all the literary and cultural references. Their use was purely utilitarian and for scriptic purposes, even if their combination, to the modern reader, could produce (as in Eliot's poetry) an aesthetic frisson, an emotional and imaginative synthesis, built on unexpected and laconic juxtaposition.

The investigators' elite status in society may well have predisposed them to look favourably on the positive and optimistic long-term messages in the scripts. However, later readers of the scripts may well boggle when examining the psychological eugenics theme in the automatic writings. But this would be to read later appalling associations of the word back into the Edwardian period. Before, and for some time after, the First World War, many middle- and upper-class people of different persuasions saw some intervention of that sort as necessary to prevent the continued decay and degeneration of the nation's human stock. Arthur Balfour was a member of the Eugenics Education Society and gave the 1908 Henry Sidgwick memorial lecture on the subject of decadence. He encouraged the establishment of a chair of genetics at Cambridge, addressed the First International Eugenics Conference (held at the University of London) in 1912, and supported the passing of the Mental Deficiency Act in 1913 (see Rose, J. 1986: 135–41; Searle 1976: 13–40, 72). Gerald Balfour seems to have shared his brother's views.

One could argue that there was more than a whiff of elitist hypocrisy in all this. In fact, Gerald Balfour (certainly) and Henry Asquith and George Wyndham (apparently) had children with women other than their wives. But that was quite different, they might have countered, from the feckless immoral activities of the lower classes. Curzon's behaviour well illustrated this double standard. He had a mistress in Westbourne Terrace. The liaison foundered. The mistress unwisely decided to blackmail him and sent letters to senior politicians denouncing him. These were stopped and destroyed. She confessed to Curzon that on the night he left England 'she went on the street and took a man' (Egremont 1977). Curzon's reaction was reflective of his class and the time: 'Treachery, betrayal, anger, abuse, revenge—all I have forgiven but coarse and vulgar sin never—no, not till I die.' The politician who sorted the situation out for him was, interestingly, George Wyndham, whom it was alleged was the real father of Anthony Eden (Thorpe 2003).

This fear of the immoral masses and the need to control them should not be overstated. Harris (1993) has pointed out the wide spectrum of views that the Edwardian eugenics movement contained, ranging from a non-interventionist policy of neglect to active 'policies of selective breeding and sterilization of the unfit'. And one of Arthur Balfour's great achievements was the Education Act of 1902 which introduced the public funding of secondary education from the rates (Searle 2004: 329–33).

All this has to be seen in the context of the lives of the investigators before and after World War I, the civilised douceur of life for the upper and upper middle classes which Joad (1949) outlined as a preamble to his biography of Bernard Shaw (though see Hynes 1968 for a corrective to this view). It is really difficult to put oneself back into the cultural and historical context that shaped these people and the general assumption even among many moderates and social reformers, including a number of the automatists and their wider circle, that the British Empire had a civilising role to play in the world (Bush 2000). Imperialism, eugenics, and the occult subculture created by Annie Besant and others (Owen 2004) could all have fused at a subliminal level in the investigators' minds to soften and make less unacceptable the outrageous claims made by the scripts. After all, if such things could happen at all, it would make sense for the child to have been fathered by a Balfour whose brother had been Prime Minister and who was a central figure in the War Coalition fighting the forces of darkness, the powers of the Old Gods mentioned in scripts, the Norse and Teutonic Gods of Wagnerian music and legend—thus might Gerald Balfour and Piddington have mused subconsciously.

They had to be very careful, therefore, as to what they could reveal about the true nature of the scripts and when. As has been seen, it was not till the summer of 1912 that the interpreters first began to treat the scripts as one potentially intelligible whole, discounting the artificial and misleading unity that selection and chance might give the scripts. Statements made in the *Proceedings* about methods of interpretation tended to focus, a little misleadingly, purely on the cross-correspondences and on elements of paranormal cognition like predictions. In that context, the methodology seemed too subtle for the result. Issues of privacy prevented, for many years, a fair estimate of the scale of the task Piddington and Balfour faced in balancing the delicate relationship between private intimacies and public interpretation. As Piddington said: 'We do not pretend to understand all the scripts, but we do understand enough to realise that they contain matter of so private a nature that it cannot be published for a long time to come...'

The privacy issue adversely complicated the wider publication and reception of the results of the interpreters' efforts. It prevented the best evidence being revealed and it established a secrecy and mystery about the cross-correspondences which a number of people, particularly if they themselves had had clear, positive evidence from direct sittings with mediums, found hugely irritating. The long prohibition on examining the original scripts and associated papers is the prime example of this. The Salter archive was not open till the late 1990s and Winifred Coombe-Tennant's four locked boxes deposited at Harvard were not available for inspection till 2008. Nor was the repository of materials from Jean Balfour (the Kremer archive) available till the early 2000s.

Nevertheless, Balfour and Piddington were content to work patiently on the scripts till the time was right to reveal their wider structure. Balfour (1927) outlined this pattern in his introduction to volume 2 of *Notes and Excursuses*. Period 1 was the accumulation of material which would provide evidence of post-mortem design largely through the cross-correspondences. Period 2 started with the scripts of Winifred Coombe-Tennant which from November 1909 onwards began to spell out the plan that a child was coming whose worldly impact would be considerable. The initial reference appeared to be to Alexander Coombe-Tennant but Gerald Balfour argued, through various bits of internal evidence in the scripts, 'that they had never looked upon Alexander (Henry's elder brother after the death of Christopher) as more than the forerunner of a more perfect being yet to appear'. Period 3 began on Palm Sunday 1912 with the 289th script of Winifred Coombe-Tennant, continued with the birth of Augustus Henry Coombe-Tennant on 9 April 1913, and culminated with her sitting with Arthur Balfour in 1916 that referred to the Palm Maiden's hair in the silver/bronze casket. Then came the long fourth period, which, Gerald Balfour asserted, was a period of repetition and consolidation in order to drive the main messages in the scripts home. It also continued the theme of current and future wars culminating in world peace and world civilisation, as well as predicting a future late flowering greatness for Arthur Balfour.

This overall structuring and ordering of the material seems problematic. One can see in the early scripts apparently disjointed statements that made plausible sense when the Palm Maiden story was revealed — or at least a good if not definitive case (because of the issue of cherry-picking, etc.) can be made for it. But the Plan rested, at least to this writer, on more fragile grounds. Each of Winifred Coombe-Tennant's children was seen as absolutely remarkable and the concept of psychological eugenics only really appeared explicit in her scripts. It is true that the return of the Golden Age was strongly flagged up in a number of scripts outside hers but these seemed to be more in the sense of a general development of the human race rather than one specific individual. The only evidence outside this, and it was dramatic evidence, was the series of sittings Winifred Coombe-Tennant had with Leonora Piper, and on Gurney's insistence in them that she bear another child which in some way would be strongly influenced by him, and would do great things (Johnson 1934c).

Alice Johnson summarised these sittings in a letter to W.H. Salter (1935): 'From the fourth sitting, on Oct. 23, 1910, onwards, E.G. through Mrs Piper asked Mrs Willett to bear another child... in some sense his child... The coming child is not indeed called a Messiah, but only a Genius... an exceptional kind of genius.' One can theorize that perhaps, as much with Leonora Piper's trance writing, she was picking up subliminal yearnings from Winifred Coombe-Tennant. But the sittings with Leonora Piper began both before the affair and also expressed views that strongly contradicted Winifred Coombe-Tennant's conscious wishes. She found childbirth extremely difficult and had no desire to experience it again. Her published diary (Lord 2011: 56–61) shows the overwhelming impact of these sittings (which were orchestrated by Lodge at Mariemont in Birmingham, where on two occasions she stayed for several days) on her. They clearly anticipated the Plan. Mrs Piper had sown the seed but, as has been raised before, what independent corroboration of this was there in the scripts of the earlier automatists, particularly Margaret Verrall?

After the physical affair with Balfour had ended, the original scriptic intensity declined and Helen Salter, Mrs Wilson, Edith Lyttelton, and the Richmonds became the keepers of the flame. But their writings may have been given an unwarranted authority since by this time Balfour and Piddington already had a pretty fully formed idea, from their vast reading, of what patterns they were looking for and the kind of evidence that would confirm them. This could well have been (though this is not certain) reinforced by the fact that the Richmonds and Edith Lyttelton were close friends, all intimately involved in the SPR business, and all hovering on the fringes of the inner mysteries so carefully guarded by Piddington and Balfour.

The value of these later scripts is questionable but they certainly added to the volume of material and to the scale of the interpretive task. Piddington recognised that few readers would follow him through the intricate processes of his argument and that the demands on them would be considerable. In his introduction to volumes three, four and five of *Notes and Excursuses* (1934) he referred whimsically to the gentle reader, the patient reader, and the long-suffering reader who had to wade through the scripts and a full-blown scholarly apparatus of footnotes, cross-references, and commentary. One could be tempted to see him and Gerald Balfour as a kind of British Bouvard and Pecuchet or a highly literate Don Quixote and Sancho Panza, were it not for the fact that their standards were very high, their industry (particularly Piddington's) prodigious, and their central questions — the survival of bodily death and the hope of world peace — hardly trivial.

On the other hand the clinging to this complex rationale and methodology may not just have created order and meaning where there was none but it may also have led them to miss genuine, more straightforward examples of paranormal cognition. Take, for example, the case of Bobby Palmer.

The Bobby Palmer Case

Gerald Balfour's family was concerned about the fate of Bobby Palmer (Captain, the Hon. R. Palmer) who was with the British Army in Mesopotamia and who died from wounds there at some time in the first half of 1916. Palmer had a romantic attachment to one of Gerald Balfour's daughters, and his father, Lord Selborne, was both a political colleague of Arthur's and Gerald's and a personal friend. The fate of Bobby Palmer seems to have been alluded to in two of Winifred Coombe-Tennant's scripts (she was aware that the family were worried about him) and in one of Margaret Verrall's (Balfour 1920: 283–5).

Winifred Coombe-Tennant 11/3/1916:

> On March 11, 1916, at 9.50 a.m. Mrs. Coombe-Tennant felt a rush of somebody else's urgency, and the words 'Pray, pray, pray' pressed on her mind. She waited a second or two; the impression was renewed; she felt frightened in a vague undefined way, and seemed to catch the sense of stress. She knelt down, and began to pray—in the sense of reaching out to some Power beyond things here. The sense of rest came to her at once. Very shortly afterwards she tried for automatic script; and in answer to her questions the script said there was no danger to her or hers : 'None what ever. But there are those needing help.'
> Question Is it something happening in the war?
> Yes simply pray—that is the message.

Margaret Verrall 17/3/1916:

> Consule Planco Palmam qui meruit ferat
> …there has been
> a special message awaiting record but I do not think you have taken it yet Palm Palmer Give me my scallop shell of quiet Look back at that—qua lambit Hydaspes Oh it all seems so muddled & yet it is a plain story I have to tell—
> Try Browning A death in the desert but nothing to do with the subject of the poem, only the words help—
> Dominus illuminatio mea—That comes in—
> …My mind to me a kingdom is…the last quotation has a special
> Point

Margaret Verrall did not know Bobby Palmer or that the Balfours were interested in him. Yet her script was particularly apposite. The first Latin tag was from a Horace ode which indirectly referred to a young man on active service, as was Horace in the consulship of Plancus (C.1.7), and the second Latin reference (let him who has won the palm bear it) was the motto of Lord Nelson. *Dominus illuminatio mea* was the motto of Oxford University and Palmer was an Oxford scholar. 'lambit Hydaspes' (a river) was an allusion to Horace C.1.22, an ode often used to symbolise Arthur Balfour in scripts. The last quotation was particularly pointed up as was the usual way with the scripts and Gerald Balfour later discovered (in 1918) that the line 'My mind to me a kingdom is' came from a poem by the Elizabethan Sir George Dyer and the sentiments of the first four lines were accurately reflected in another of Winifred Coombe-Tennant's scripts on

30/5/1916. In addition, she had a specific reference to the Selborne family in a script three days later.

Winifred Coombe-Tennant 2/6/1916:

> A pair of friends David & Jonathan that should be
> said a community of occupation links of friendship...And
> weep for Adonais
> He beckoned like a star from the abodes where the Eternal
> are A glistering star
> A man with two dogs in a leash dogs built for speed
> Greyhounds — but these are black long & clean limbed There
> is a point in these dogs which should be identified They
> have a meaning

There was a clearish reference to the Selborne coat of arms in the latter part of the script since two greyhounds sable formed the supporters of that coat of arms and, as has been seen, the Hon. Robert Palmer was the son of Lord Selborne. So, a fair case can be made out for some evidential material related to Palmer, but Gerald Balfour found himself briefly locked in a tussle with Lord Selborne over the identity of the second person referred to in the Coombe-Tennant script. Lord Selborne wrote:

> I am surprised that you think David and Jonathan in the W script of June 2/16 cannot naturally be interpreted as referring to Bobby and Purefoy Cawston. Knowing the romantic friendship between the two I have never taken it for anything else. David and Jonathan exactly and without exaggeration describes their relationship—'a community of occupation links of friendship', 'a brother in arms by ties united.' They never knew each other till they found themselves in the same regiment in 1914, and then they found a wonderful correspondence of tastes and opinions... then come the quotations from poetry about friends parted, all very apposite. When you see the Leonard script of my sitting last Wednesday you will see that Feda at once said that Bobby (not named but described) had with him another young man who was not with him before, and proceeded to describe Purefoy well. Again and again it was said how immensely happy these two were to be together, and finally he was named.

However, Balfour argued that the second individual was Charles Lister (who had died in 1915 after Gallipoli), because of the play on the name Lister in 'glistered', and that Lord Selborne did not know the way the scriptic intelligence worked through puns and puzzles. Certainly there was a good cross-correspondence between Coombe-Tennant and Verrall scripts predictive of the death of Palmer. But there was a definite clash over the evidence and its interpretation. Lord Selborne preferred the direct evidence from traditional mediumship, especially from the remarkable Mrs Leonard, while one senses a proprietorial element in Gerald Balfour's approach, and a lack of common sense, basing the identity of Jonathan largely on the scriptic pun 'glistered'. There is one further point. From her diary of 27/3/1916 when staying at Fishers Hill, it is clear that Winifred Coombe-Tennant knew of the concern for Bobby Palmer since Nellie Balfour and he had a relationship. Therefore, only the Margaret Verrall element in these scripts had a claim to paranormality (Lord 2011).

One wonders, too, whether the general reputation as psychical researchers that Piddington and Gerald Balfour had was fully deserved. Certainly Gerald Balfour was wheeled out on a number of occasions to pronounce authoratively on the subject. He was involved in the case of David Wilson, a chemist who had invented an electronic machine which he claimed could communicate with the dead. Unfortunately, since one of the messages was in German, Wilson was soon in trouble with the authorities and Gerald Balfour tried to help (Foster 2003: 80–1). He was also (admiring the detailed accuracy of their report on Mrs Leonard), supportive of Una Troubridge and Radclyffe Hall in the difficulties they faced when Radclyffe Hall took out an action for slander against Fox-Pitt, a member of the SPR, who accused them of immorality (Souhami 1998: 100, 105–12). Gerald Balfour was seen to have intellectual and social authority but his range was rather narrow. When he became President of the SPR in 1906 he had a philosophical interest in survival but no detailed field experience, and the bulk of his and Piddington's expertise through life was in the assessment of mental mediumship with mediums, by and large, who were part of their own circle. They had little experience of physical mediumship or ghost hunting and when asked to investigate the famous case of the apparition of the chimney sweep Samuel Bull (who was seen by several members of his family after his death) they arrived, for a variety of reasons, too late to make any direct observations (Mackenzie 1982: 171–5), and one speculates that they might have been secretly relieved.

In fact, they had more than enough on their agenda given the sheer complexity of the communicators' methodology. So convoluted was it that it almost defeated its own purpose. As Piddington stated: '...I cannot rid myself of a suspicion that in their attempt to invent a form of evidence that cannot be easily attributed to the automatists, the communicators have created a body of evidence so complicated that it will repel investigators.' Piddington was quite candid in the *Notes and Excursuses* both about the effort involved to follow their arguments and the puzzles and inconsistencies that still remained. Addressing his remarks to any future readers of the scripts, he suggested that the reader was not competent to pass judgement until he/she had read some of the volumes three times. He was acutely aware of the problem of false or misguided interpretation with regard to such complex material. He stated that 'In this connection I would add that I regard several of the interpretations that I have advanced in these and earlier volumes of *Notes and Excursuses* as no better than tentative. Some I believe to be right in the main; others to be partially right; while some are probably wrong in the main, and some further study has shown to be wrong' (Piddington 1934).

Examples of tortuous interpretation, false starts, and the discovery of deeper, more complex patterns abound. The Bacchus and Semele case has already been mentioned. Others include the layers of meaning discovered in the One-Horse Dawn case which was initially meant by Arthur Verrall to be an experiment in telepathy. Eventually it was believed that the discarnate communicators had hijacked this experiment: that the underlying purpose was to draw attention to Jebb's note on Sophocles' *Oedipus Tyrannicus* in which Jebb discussed compound adjectives whose first element was a word associated with number, that is, monopolon, etc. This was then expanded into references to Oedipus, the blind wanderer, who stood in the scripts for Arthur Balfour. The other element was reference to the herb moly and Milton's Comus, which led the investigators to Verrall's edition of *Medea* where Verrall quoted Comus in the context of a general discussion on the interpretation of corrupt texts. It was argued that the real point of the allusive reference was to point up the importance of the sacrifice of children in the *Medea*, as part of the general topic of psychological eugenics. So Piddington had ultimately added two layers of mystery to Verrall's telepathy experiment—the topic of psychological eugenics and a major symbol for Arthur Balfour, one of the two main protagonists in the scripts. The modern reader must continually wonder, perhaps merely through sheer exhaustion, whether the text could bear such weight placed on it. Was each link in the allusive associational chain sufficiently robust?

This dogged ingenuity plus his belief in the overall rationale behind the scripts led Piddington into Herculean efforts to bring apparently disconnected topics under general headings that fitted with and reinforced the Story and the Plan. With regard to Trix Fleming's scripts: 'I came to the conclusion that there are at least sixteen different topics in Fleming scripts which are clearly interconnected.' These are absolutely bewildering, at first sight, to the contemporary reader:

Lord Bute and Shelley's *Adonais*,
Everard Feilding and members of his family,
Lord and Lady Mount-Temple, their residence Broadlands, and their friend Stainton Moses,
Myers's death at Rome, and the date of it—Jan. 17, 1901,
Wireless Telegraphy,
Henry Fawcett, and other persons of the same surname,
Various people of the name Tennant,
The name Merrifield,
Sensitive Plants,
Eliot Norton,
Leslie Stephen,

F.W. Maitland,
Cordelia Marshall,
William James and members of his family,
Myers's birthday, his marriage, and his children,
Laurence Oliphant, members of his family.

Piddington concluded that the references to Henry Fawcett were really attempts to link the name Fawcett (see Fawcett cross-correspondence), which was Margaret Verrall's mother's maiden name, with Henry Fawcett who was initially rejected as a by-election candidate at Brighton because of his blindness, to the whole of the Broadlands topic. Henry Fawcett, as has been seen, was a friend of the Mount-Temples. He had worked vigorously with Lord Mount-Temple on the creation and preservation of open spaces for the public. Broadlands, the Mount-Temple's country house, stood in the scripts for two things, Piddington concluded: (i) the physical phenomena of Stainton Moses and the impact of Myers and Gurney meeting him there (Hamilton 2009), which quickened their interest in psychical research, and also (ii) the story of Myers and Phyllis which played a strongly evidential part in the earlier scripts. He asserted that references to the psychical researcher Everard Feilding were meant to contrast the dubious phenomena he investigated with the genuine phenomena of Stainton Moses. The name Henry Fawcett was a key link which bound these several topics together. This was yet another example of the way in which a cross-correspondence (Fawcett) had, according to the interpreters, layers of deeper symbolic meaning.

There is not space to explain all the other inter-relationships between Piddington's topic headings but one can easily see from the headings that there was considerable detail on the death of Myers, Lodge's role (Wireless Telegraphy), the Tennant family, and the Verralls. However, much of this was in the public domain and one has the uneasy feeling, at times, that the idiosyncratic style of Trix Fleming's automatic writing, plus her superb memory, and Piddington's ingenious sleuthing and synthesising skills contributed much to the creation of the product. In fact, Piddington sometimes argued that it was the way the material was combined, rather than the revelation of paranormal knowledge, which was the truly paranormal element in the scripts. Unfortunately this put a huge premium on other people being able both to follow the argument and also to verify the source material and the automatist's access to it.

One keeps coming back to the central question — why did some of the material have to be expressed in such an indirect and sometimes grotesque way? This particularly refers to the Plan, for in its essence one could argue that aspects of it were not bizarre or objectionable, indeed it could be seen as a fusion of the best of optimistic late-Victorian liberal progressive values with Myersian concepts of cosmic and spiritual evolution. And, if one accepts and acknowledges a spiritual world that can interact with the mundane world (Saints in the Catholic Church), is it that odd or illogical to assume that the discarnate world might wish to work with the incarnate world for its spiritual progress? But what was most difficult to take was the distasteful message expressed, through extremely odd and indirect symbolism, that Daphne died to act as a spur to get Winifred Coombe-Tennant involved in automatic writing, and that Antony and Christopher Lyttelton were failed experiments on the way to the Messianic Child, Henry Coombe-Tennant. One can detect a certain unease in the commentators' writings on all these matters, particularly the last element. Salter, in his introduction to the scripts and in correspondence with Piddington, preferred to stress the wider point — an emphasis on children of the spirit rather than one individual; and Piddington, for his part, produced a detailed handwritten paper trying to establish clarity on this point, particularly with regard to the way in which Winifred Coombe-Tennant's maternal predisposition may have coloured the scripts (Salter 1948, 1947; Piddington 1947).

C.D. Broad (1925: 542–6) has commented on the need for someone not connected emotionally, socially, intellectually with the cross-correspondences, either in their production or interpretation, to take an objective look at the materials. Even Mrs Sidgwick, renowned for her critical balance and insight, was not immune to this, particularly with regard to Arthur Balfour. As Oppenheim has put it (1995: 196–232), 'Mrs. Sidgwick's commitment to her husband muted her brother-worship during Henry's lifetime, but after his death in 1900, it re-emerged undiminished. Visiting Whittingehame in September 1906, Beatrice Webb commented on the way that Eleanor, Alice and their two sisters-in-law all paid reverence to "Prince Arthur"'. Broad's point was particularly with regard to the earlier complex cross-correspondences but it applies with equal, if not with greater, force to the hugely emotional issues of the Palm Maiden's love for the Knight, and the Messianic Child or Children theme. The judgement does not necessarily require the skills of a classicist since all the main references and translations were provided by the original investigators and very little interpretation rests on disputed issues of translation. But what has never been done is the application of assessment criteria to a broad swathe of scripts, not just to see if individual cross-correspondences stand up (some of them certainly do) but to test Balfour's fundamental assertion (1927) that the Story and the Plan were 'analogous to that given by a scientific hypothesis that brings into unity a multiplicity of phenomena apparently disparate', and that this could only be tested 'by a careful comparative study of a very large number of individual scripts': in other words that the scripts could almost be seen as one giant symbolic cross-correspondence.

There are additional ways of testing this in addition to those proposed under the general assessment criteria. One is to take an individual script of one of the automatists, Trix Fleming, who knew nothing of the overall pattern and meaning of the scripts, and see if this script has the almost holographic quality claimed for the scripts generally. The rest of her Ave Roma Immortalis script is a good test case (see appendix 2). Another method is to sample, using a random number generator, three hundred more scripts and see if they tell the same story and provide the same unity in diversity that Gerald Balfour claimed for the three hundred he used in volume 2 of *Notes and Excursuses*. This has been done by the current writer and the claim broadly stands up (however, it would require another book as a giant supplement to demonstrate this). The patterns are there. But only if one accepts the rationale and methodology of the interpreters. And this writer freely acknowledges that his judgements may have been too strongly coloured and conditioned by his extensive reading of the original commentaries, and one wonders how much someone coming new to those scripts would have seen and if equally plausible alternative narratives could have been created.

There can be little doubt that the more impersonal theme is relatively easy to identify: the gradual evolution away from the blood feuding savagery of the ancient world to a civilisation based on ethics and law. In the scripts this was frequently illustrated and symbolised by references to the House of Atreus and the treatment of it by the Greek tragedians. The narrative was that Thyestes seduced Aerope, the wife of Atreus the King of Mycenae. She then stole for him the golden lamb which gave the right to rule Mycenae. For this impiety Zeus temporarily reversed the movement of the sun (see One-Horse Dawn episode) and Atreus, in revenge, feigned reconciliation and fed Thyestes the flesh of his own sons at a banquet. Thyestes cursed the House of Atreus and so the bloodbath began: Atreus's son, Agamemnon, was murdered on his return from Troy by his wife Clytemnestra (because he had sacrificied their daughter Iphigeneia to obtain favourable winds for the Greek fleet to sail to Troy). Agamemnon's son Orestes, with the help of his sister Electra, killed Clytemnestra and the curse was eventually lifted when Orestes, pursued by the Furies, was tried for murder by an Athenian tribunal on the Acropolis, only to be saved from death by the casting vote of Athena. It was argued, by A.W. Verrall and others, that this was the beginning of a more civilised legal and social system, and that the Furies were changed from avenging into beneficent powers (the *Eumenides* of Aeschylus).

The scripts particularly referred to this by quotations from Aeschylus's *Agamemnon* (140–150). At the opening of the play the watchman in his tower was awaiting the return of the brothers Agamemnon and Menelaus from Troy. He recounted the story of the Greek army's prophet Calchas seeing two eagles tearing apart and feasting on a pregnant hare. These eagles were symbols for the two brothers who would defeat Troy, but there would be a terrible vengeance, 'Sing Sorrow, Sorrow, but let the good prevail'.

The concept of spiritual and ethical progress was further alluded to in the Virgilian references to the coming of Augustus and the return of the Golden Age, and to the Christian slant Dante gave this, since Virgil's work was later interpreted as a prophecy of the coming of Christ. Finally, as has been seen, there were a number of references (some via Wagner) to the old Norse and Germanic gods gradually becoming more civilised.

The scripts were full of such allusions and quotations but the special role allotted to Henry Coombe-Tennant in this process of gradual civilisation seems less clear. However, Piddington argued (with some reservations) that that was what the interpretation of the scripts pointed to. There is a huge paradox here. Both Piddington and Gerald Balfour were humane and civilised men of a certain class. Both were fully aware of the woolly thinking and foibles of humanity. Yet in this one area they lacked insight. Why should Henry Coombe-Tennant be the chosen one? Surely the process of psychological eugenics ought to be taking place all over the world continually? If the message was the evolution of humanity of which Henry was merely seen as a good example, a mark for all to aim at, that was less extreme and more acceptable, but it would still be a stretch too far for most people.

On the other hand, some of the evidence was fairly explicit with regard to one of Winifred's children: the linking of the murder of Medea's children through the Epiphany references of myrrh and frankincense to the birth of Daphne. She was born on 6/1/1907. This was in the script below just hours before her death.

Helen Verrall 20/7/1908 (with Margaret Verrall):

> Why tarry ye for the bridegroom when the hour is past? The day of the feast with myrrh and with frankincense a white bull for the sacrifice garlanded and with the horns goldtipped and a train of maidens therewith With song and dance the hours are sped/With rhythmic beat of holy feet/Honour the maiden newly wed Sullen Medea and horror heaped on horror till the senses reel Something flaps in the wind something white

One very final point. One has looked at those predetermining factors that might have predisposed Piddington and Balfour to interpret the scripts in a particular way, but what really made them stick at it for so long, particularly as the scripts in the later stages merely seemed to be recycling the same symbolic messages? One answer may well lie in the theory of cognitive dissonance developed by Festinger (2008) in *When Prophecy Fails*.

This theory developed from the remarkable case of Marian Keech, who through automatic writing was told by aliens that the world was shortly to end but she and her followers would be rescued. Two of Festinger's colleagues managed to infiltrate the organisation and monitored the various psychological processes the group used to excuse the continued failures of the prophecies.

There is only a partial fit with the cross-correspondence automatic writings since Henry was still relatively young when Balfour and Piddington died. There was, theoretically, still time for him to make an impact. But it could help to explain, particularly, Piddington's obsessive efforts in the *Notes and Excursuses* in the late 1930s and 1940s to fit as much corroborating detail as possible into the framework that they believed had been revealed in the Coombe-Tennant scripts. Taking a summary of Festinger's theory, point by point, how might this apply to Piddington? (Festinger: 4.)

1. The belief must be held with conviction and relate to what the believer does and how he behaves.

2. The believer must have committed himself to action that is very difficult to undo.

3. The belief must be specific enough and sufficiently connected to the real world for events to refute it.

4. Such refuting events must occur and be recognised by the individual holding the belief.

Some aspects of the intellectual behaviour of Balfour and Piddington fit this theoretical model. There was a commitment for the whole of the second halves of their lives in terms of intellectual effort and also of finance for the study and printing of the scripts (1 and 2). It could be argued that part of what fuelled the interpretive drive, apart from the elitism and vanity mentioned above, was the unconscious fear that they had wasted the years certainly from 1912 to 1945 when Gerald Balfour died (Piddington died in 1952). They were, however, spared the actual direct challenge to their beliefs (3 and 4) since they died while Henry was still in his mid- to late thirties. On the other hand, Piddington (Roy 2008) wrote to Gerald Balfour near the end of his life that he never regretted their collaborative efforts regardless of what Henry might or might not achieve, and in their *Notes and Excursuses* and articles in the *Proceedings* they were very willing, in a civilised fashion (as were all the core team investigating the scripts), to debate and argue through different points of view, scaffolding their arguments with the appropriate scholarly apparatus, even on occasions to an unbelievable nth footnote.

However, the subjective selection of content is not the only way the original scripts might have been manipulated, despite Piddington's scholarly dedication. In his preface (1934) to volumes 3/4/5 of *Notes and Exursuses* he stated that he and Gerald Balfour eventually realised that 'historical or legendary male persons serve as symbols of the Palm Maiden: Keats, Murena, Charles Diodati, Milton's Lucifer, Lycidas, Arthur Hallam, and others...'. One extravagant consequence of this was that Piddington took the silver crescent luna that a Roman senator like Murena wore (he fell as part of a conspiracy against Augustus), via references to A.W. Verrall's *Studies in the Odes of Horace* in scripts, to be a contributor to the Palm Maiden moon symbolism (Verrall 1884: 44).

19

Were the Aims, Intentions, and Long-Term Predictions of the Communicators Fulfilled?

The main aims of the communicators were:

- That Arthur Balfour should be convinced of the Palm Maiden's post-mortem existence and of her continuing love and support for him;
- That the incredibly complex structure of cross-correspondences and symbolism revealed in the scripts, plus the paranormal cognition displayed, would convince careful readers that telepathy and clairvoyance were inadequate to explain the phenomena. Only the hypothesis of survival would cover the full spectrum of evidence;
- By intensive efforts from the spirit world to promote world peace (which would be successful after considerable difficulties) through supporting the incarnation (the process quite naturally was opaque!) of a number of highly gifted and special individuals, amongst whom Augustus Henry Coombe-Tennant was the putative leader. No precise timescale was provided either for the initiation of the work from the spirit side or the date of its successful completion.

Was Arthur Balfour convinced that the Palm Maiden had actually contacted him? He was deeply moved by the Coombe-Tennant scripts, but that is not the same as conviction. He had a deep spiritual intuition of survival and mentioned this on a number of occasions during the First World War to women friends who had lost sons in battle. While interested in mediumship and the paranormal he appears to have undertaken no specific investigation of mental mediumship to contact May Lyttelton and to have relied completely on the initiative of others. To the outsider, the most obvious question to be posed is why Arthur Balfour didn't have a sitting, one to one, with a high-quality traditional medium like Mrs Leonard? This seems never to have happened and his own intuitive sense of survival emanating from childhood (a religious faith that never seems to have been shaken by his scientific interests) probably sufficed him in general terms.

Certainly, when he did sit with Winifred Coombe-Tennant and in his last years with Mrs Salter and the Richmonds, the results were mixed. Some with Winifred Coombe-Tennant were persuasive and moving and the one on 19/6/1916 was specific enough to remind him of the silver bronze casket he had had made for May Lyttelton's hair. But those with the others were less so and just repeated the standard symbolic formula. For example, on one occasion Piddingtton and Gerald Balfour knew that Arthur Balfour would be at Fishers Hill at the same time as Helen Salter and so they arranged for him to sit with her. It was a short twenty-minute automatic speaking trance at about 4 pm and W.H. Salter recorded it. Helen Salter was not in the least put off that Arthur Balfour, former prime minister, foreign secretary, senior politician, and diplomat, was to sit with her: 'As regards a script—I am perfectly willing to try. Knowing the steam-roller habits of my script, I hardly think it likely to be affected by any slight accident—like [Balfour]. But I will do my best.' Afterwards the Salters stated that Arthur Balfour, who was rather deaf by this time and couldn't hear her clearly, didn't seem much interested in it and 'couldn't make head or tail of it' (Piddington 1930: 603–12). But both Piddington and Gerald Balfour thought the script was an excellent one containing all the appropriate symbolism for the Palm Maiden and the Faithful Knight and quite distinct from Mrs Salter's other scripts of that period. In other words, the information from the sitting fitted in with the formal symbolism of the scripts rather than providing Arthur Balfour with personal, intimate evidence of survival. In fact, Edith Lyttelton wrote to Lodge (SPR MS 35) shortly before Arthur Balfour's death that he seemed to be a bit bewildered about it all and perhaps Lodge, of whom he was fond, could come over and make things clearer.

Nevertheless, as has been seen, in Winifred Coombe-Tennant's final sittings with him shortly before his death something seems to have got through, but how much of it did he really appreciate? And, to come down to earth, Winifred Coombe-Tennant had been Gerald's lover and then friend for nineteen years. No self-respecting and independent member of the SPR, trained in canons of evidence by Myers, Gurney, and the Sidgwicks, could possibly have accepted her statements as veridical.

Balfour's bewilderment about the evidence for survival appears to have continued for a while after his death. Winifred Coombe-Tennant wrote to Gerald Balfour in April 1930 describing her first sense of Arthur Balfour's post-mortem existence: 'I have been feeling very exhausted since my return from Eton—W.O.'s affairs to see to by day, & apparently—A.J.B's by night!... apparently the process of "finding his feet" over there involves this drain on my vitality.' She was told by the Dark Young Man that Arthur Balfour needed temporarily to stay in touch with her world, through her, till the confusion of transition settled. However, by August that had gone and in sleep she had contact with him: 'I found myself face to face with A.J.B. — he clear-eyed, vigorous, full of radiant life... his whole frame the embodiment of strength & energy, as of a man in the full zenith of his powers.' But, again, these psychic impressions contained nothing that could be assessed and verified (Balfour 1938).

There is also some uncertainty about the third broad aim, both the timing, and the specific role of Henry Coombe-Tennant. It is quite possible, of course, for a variety of reasons outside the communicators' control that the script interpretation could be generally correct but the predictions too complex, idealistic, and problematic to fulfil in an earthly environment. Indeed, one consistent theme in the scripts was that the communicators did not claim infallibility or complete command of the situation, either in the accuracy and clarity of their messages or their ability to shape and influence individuals and events. There is no doubt that the emphasis on Henry Coombe-Tennant as a world leader and initiator of peace (remarkable man though he was) was a failure, and the documents in the Kremer collection at Cambridge and the Coombe-Tennant archive at Harvard suggest some possible reasons for this. There were perhaps certain features in his character — a lack of drive, a certain detachment from the everyday world, not unlike his father? He had brains and courage and when faced with challenges rose well to them, but he was not a self-starter and perhaps found obvious political rhetoric and solutions too simplistic. Yet, huge expectations were placed on him by Gerald Balfour and Piddington, without his having, for many years, any direct sense of this or the challenge he had to rise to, and, thankfully for him, that failure on his part might discredit the intense interpretive efforts of more than thirty years. For, as Gerald Balfour put it, on one level the whole business appeared 'in the highest degree fantastic and improbable' and 'if the promises do not come to fruition who will wade through these scripts?'

But it is possible to rescue the above aims and intentions from total failure. As Brookes-Smith (1964) has stated, provided one interpreted the Plan in a more general sense without the focus on one charismatic and gifted individual, there are arguments (from a UK-centric perspective) in favour of the theme of progressive world improvements interspersed with considerable periods of conflict: the creation of the Welfare State, the move for international control of nuclear weapons, the United Nations, all seemed to be suggesting a move in the right direction. On the other hand, it is easy at almost any time in history to select pointers making for peace and indicators suggesting the trend was in the opposite direction. Moreover, in terms of acceptance by the general educated public, the two main claims in the scripts can work against each other. It is quite possible for someone to take very seriously the evidence in the scripts for a sophisticated approach towards proving survival, but that evidence is in great danger of being contaminated by the inherent and ridiculously implausible claim made for the status and future role of Augustus Henry Coombe-Tennant.

Moreover, the concentration on this topic and the inevitable climate of secrecy surrounding the cross-correspondences, with the frequent hints that, though remarkable evidence had been provided, there was still much that was too private and intimate to be revealed, could well have damaged the SPR. Dingwall (1930-1), a tenacious critic of what he saw as the 'Old Guard' of the SPR, lamented that the SPR, to the detriment of a broader, more objective approach, concentrated on 'the investigation of manifestations produced by private persons in their own immediate entourage'. If one adds this sense of almost Masonic-like secrecy to the already academic, rarified, and exclusive ambience of the core leadership, one can see why, after the First World War, so many members were restive. A number of people, particularly those of the Spiritualist persuasion, became frustrated by what they saw as a lack of vigour and leadership in investigating (or dismissing without adequate enquiry) the remarkable physical and mental mediumship and spontaneous phenomena that was reported to them (Hamilton 2013b).

In addition, as has been seen, the Messianic element can cast doubt on the whole body of the scripts and reduce them, in many eyes, to the status of sub-theosophical mumbo jumbo, and millenarian dottiness, of which there was much in the years 1900-1930. Gerald Balfour's consistent emphasis in *Notes and Excursuses* on the seven separate influences of the communicators blending to form the octave, the Messianic Child, smacks a little of this: the seven rays, and the seven types of personality outlined in in the books of Alice Bailey, an erstwhile disciple of Blavatsky (Balfour 1927; Hastings 1991: 91-4).

Therefore, it is perfectly reasonable to ask to what extent the scripts, their production and interpretation, are indicative of a cult like the Panacea Society (which was also based on automatic writing initially and, in that case, in the return of the actual Christ: see Shaw 2011) or many of the organisations surveyed in Barrett's *The New Believers* (2001). Or the case of Marion Keech mentioned above. Superficially, the comparison is invalid. The academic enquiry of the SPR investigators was conducted in a balanced and critical way quite alien to the above cases and none of them made drastic personal lifestyle changes and commitments or sealed themselves off from conventional society, in ways reminiscent of cultish behaviour. But it could be argued that there were some similarities in that their initial premises and conclusions were irrational and delusional, that together, as a small core of elite and secretive individuals within the SPR, they mutually reinforced these beliefs, and that, as mentioned before, they suffered a certain cognitive dissonance as time went on, which made

Piddington, particularly, burrow deeper and deeper and more ingeniously into the scripts for further confirmation.

This point, again, is only partially accurate. The first period of the scripts, up to 1912, bore witness to the investigators, without any doubt, examining and testing the material with great rigour and not from a prior commitment to survival, except in the case of Lodge. It took much solid documentary evidence for them to shift, gradually, towards a survivalist position. They were, of course, on much more dubious ground, with regard to the Messianic element. Yet, even here, though Gerald Balfour's final statement on all this was unambiguous with regard to interpretation, it was much more nuanced with regard to expectation (1938: 2-4): 'Do we still believe that the facts of the case are best explained on the hypothesis that the Communicators are really what they claim to be, and that, they have been genuinely engaged in an effort to bring about the birth of a child of Messianic order? To this our answer is emphatically in the affirmative. No more now, than then, do we accept the evidence for this belief as amounting to conclusive proof. But we are, and have long been, sufficiently convinced of its truth to act as if it were true.' Moreover, unlike Krishnamurti, no cultic behaviour (except the embarrassing name 'Wise One') ever developed around Henry.

As to Henry's role, or knowledge of the destiny intended for him, Gerald Balfour wrote: 'The central figure round whom the Scripts turn is now a young man of twenty-five; but signs and wonders are still to seek. Here again we can but wait and see.' Henry Coombe-Tennant had outstanding intellectual gifts and so for a while it seemed not such a totally implausible prediction, particularly if the scripts were interpreted as the development of a body of remarkable young people rather than the emphasis on one charismatic and inspirational leader (and if the specific embarrassing comparisons with Christ were dropped), but, however interpreted, the plain fact was that Henry, though a remarkable individual, did not have the impact that the scripts suggested.

Finally, how well have the cross-correspondences stood up against the arguments of critics past and present? There has not been a huge amount of published criticism of them and what there is varies in quality. There are thoughtful criticisms by Carrington, Pigou, Maxwell, Hude, and others published by the SPR itself, and there are broader more knockabout criticisms that are not so well informed and show no real engagement with the material. One problem, as Wilson (2013a) has pointed out, is that the whole tranche of movements that developed from the 1880s—Occult Societies, Magical Orders, Theosophy, the Spiritualist Movement, etc.— were not using these activities purely for social reasons or creative ones and, as Yeats put it, 'metaphors for poetry'. Many of them actually believed in the reality of the phenomena, as eventually, after a long intellectual struggle, did those involved in the cross-correspondences. To the modern reader, therefore, any involvement in this field must feel like a step back into a pre-Enlightenment world, with all the terrors, superstitions, and stupidities that that might bring. The issue then is how to overcome one's inevitable initial prejudice against the very idea of the cross-correspondences, their genesis and their purposes, in order to engage in depth with them and assess them fairly.

Maxwell (1912-13), a highly educated French investigator with an excellent command of English, produced the longest and most detailed early 'outsider' criticism of the cross-correspondences. Much of his analysis mentioned 'the usual suspects': accidental coincidence; subconscious impersonation; arbitrary selection from scripts; automatists too closely involved in the assessment of scripts; cryptomnesia; the banality of many of the correspondences; and a too easy and unthinking acceptance of the spiritist hypothesis. Mrs Sidgwick (1912-13) was able to counter a number of these points. She stressed (as has been seen *passim* through this current book) the efforts taken to trace every statement back to its potential source in the automatist's normal experience; that the best cross-correspondences were not simple banalities or accidental coincidences and demonstrated purposive intention and creativity beyond the automatists' own powers; and that rather than coming from 'spirits' most of the material came to a large extent from 'a dissociated phase or portion of the automatist's own personality': through which, of course, sometimes came substantial veridical material. However, her response to Maxwell's point that there were issues with regard to the good faith of the automatists themselves and the blurring of the automatist/investigator role was only partially convincing: 'I should like to know how M. Maxwell would propose to investigate automatic script, produced otherwise than in a trance, without letting the automatists share in the responsibility. Would he keep them in solitary confinement?' Because of the nature of the material and its production, and the nature of the relationships between automatists and investigators, tensions between objectivity and control and understanding, support, and motivation were inevitable, and on one level Maxwell was right, particularly as the interpretations became more extreme and the emotional investment in them more intense.

A more sympathetic and subtle commentator on the cross-correspondences was the Swiss psychologist Flournoy (1911: 174-87). Like Pigou, he argued that 'the caprice shown by the phenomena of the association of ideas' could, accepting that telepathic impressions existed, give the illusion of external design. But he went further and agreed with the investigators 'that we are in the presence of a new and original method, deliberately adopted by some superior intelligence in order to prove its existence independent of the medium which it employs'. But though the creator of this method might claim to be Myers and show elements of his intellectual and personal qualities across the automatists, nevertheless both personality and puzzles could be a group subliminal creation steered and led by Margaret Verrall, who perhaps felt his loss the most keenly. But, sensibly and modestly, he stated 'that it would be ridiculous to decide so early upon a question so complex'. It is surprising another European, the great polymath Richet (1923: 173-6), a pioneer of psychical research and an intimate of Myers (Hamilton 2009), did not study the cross-correspondences in the depth that Maxwell and Flournoy did. He acknowledged the role of cryptesthesia (clairvoyance) and telepathy in their production; he sided with Carrington that much of the material was the product of 'simple subconscious memory associations'; and with Maxwell and Flournoy that the subconscious was very good at producing dramatic personifications of individuals. He realised that they had to be studied in depth in order to make a proper judgement: 'Any analysis of them, however, would be lengthy and if not minute would be unenlightening.'[1]

Amy Tanner (1910) in her *Studies in Spiritism* also criticised the cross-correspondences. But her book was riddled with errors, as both Hyslop (1911) and Mrs Sidgwick (1911) pointed out, and she failed to comprehend the essentially nuanced and literary nature of the material. Eric Dingwall (1985), from within the SPR, as has been seen, launched possibly the most personal attack, accusing the original investigators of obstruction, evasion, and the destruction of documents. And he returned to this theme in later years, using as evidence of this the later automatic writing of Geraldine Cummins in *Swan on a Black Sea*, which he summarised in a misleadingly truncated and inaccurate form.

More broadly, and more significantly, it is argued, the existence of the cross-correspondences despite all their ingenuity and their later symbolic glory do not conclusively prove the survival hypothesis. As Podmore (1975) has lucidly pointed out: 'We cannot assign limits to the power of telepathy.' And Braude (2003) and Sudduth (2016) have perceptively expanded this basic point, stressing uncertainty as to the nature and range of such powers and that, regardless of the methodology devised to generate evidence for it, there are unproven and unexamined assumptions that lie behind statements that individual human personalities survive bodily death.

Jean Balfour (1958-9: 171), herself, stated in regard to the enormous Palm Sunday cross-correspondence, and despite her intimate familial involvement with the subject, 'We do not yet know the full extent of

---

[1] A good example of this is Gray's (2011) treatment of the cross-correspondences. He elegantly restates the general criticisms but fails to engage with them in any way that helps inform detailed study.

subliminal activity, and so it must be admitted that there is nothing in this case that was not known to somebody somewhere and therefore could not be explained by telepathy from persons still alive who knew, or had once known, the facts.' One should stress that Myers himself (and his colleagues knew this) was well aware of the complexities in stating what might or might not survive and in what form and how this related to other cosmic variables. This can be clearly seen in his articles on the subliminal self in relation to both retrocognition and precognition and his diagrammatic representations of the issues (Myers 1895b: 334-407; Myers 1895c: 408-593).

Louisa Rhine (1967: 234-5) was incorrect in asserting that the early leaders of the SPR did not realise the implications of unconscious mental action both in the narrower sense of subliminal interactions between people in close contact and the wider Myersian sense quoted above. She also criticised the apparent lack of method by which the cross-correspondences' allusive references were judged and does not seem to have read or to have followed Alice Johnson's complex argument. But, from her perspective on the latter point, she was correct. It was a definite clash of methodologies and approaches.

Behind these arguments lie unresolved and possibily unresolvable questions about the nature of personal identity both before and after death: in other words, what does it mean to say that one has survived death? The philosopher Parfitt, using the model of Star Trek/teleportation, has argued that mental continuity and psychological identity are one model for survival (Dainton 2014: 129-8, 133). If all the information about a person, their dispositions, talents, life history, memories, knowledge, capacities, and skills, is transferred to another location and rehoused in another material unit, is one entitled to talk of the survival of that person? It certainly highlights the two main components of personal identity—the physiological and the psychological (Braude 2013). What is missing from that definition is the lived experiential consciousness of the individual going through the change from life to death and communicating post-mortem. Unless one can find some way to share, access, and validate that (as the best mediums appear to be able to do), there will always be concerns about impersonation and deception. In some ways this is less an issue for the cross-correspondences since traditional survival evidence (though there is plenty *en passant* in the scripts) was not, as Alice Johnson pointed out, the prime aim of the communicators. One is always, however, left with the uneasy feeling that on this issue one can never outflank or rule out deception from another source: a non-human intelligence with a desire to play games, a psychic husk that just contains static memories, or the creative imagination of a living mind.

Carter (2012) has argued robustly against a number of the above objections. He asserts that the script personalities displayed, in convincing detail, the persistent and dynamic purpose, the point of view, and the skills associated with them in life. Their tenacity was remarkable. As Jean Balfour stated at the end of her Palm Sunday study: 'There can be no doubt about one thing, that there was *purpose* behind it all.' But whose purpose, one might ask?

Earlier sections have clearly demonstrated that evidence broadly characteristic of Myers particularly could be found in the scripts and that the construction of the cross-correspondences suggested an external intelligence that was trying to circumvent the argument from living agent telepathy or psi. But was there more specific evidence than this? Piddington wrote a thoughtful letter on the subject published in the *Journal* for 1910 which introduced a useful distinction. As he stated: 'though the *form* of the cross-correspondences may be evidence of an active intelligence, it affords no evidence, positive or negative, of the identity of that intelligence. This kind of evidence may, however, be afforded by the content of cross-correspondences…' In other words, the selection of the content was highly characteristic of Myers' interests and preoccupations in life and was, on occasions, demonstrably beyond the capacity of any of the living individuals, like Margaret or Helen Verrall, from whom it might otherwise have been derived. Both Margaret Verrall and Piddington exhaustively explored and evidenced this point. A number of such examples are quoted in this text.

It is important not to be too Anglo-Saxon centred in this context. Certain features of the cross-correspondences are very impressive but are they the best that the psychical research/parapsychological community is aware of? For example, Moreira-Almeida (2012: 204–6) has pointed out that an analysis of a number of poems by deceased Brazilian and Portuguese poets in the automatic writing of Chico Xavier go well beyond 'simple literary imitation'. Moreover, there is an 'intricate and sophisticated intertextuality' in them and references to writings 'that were not in the public domain when the mediumistic texts were produced'. The more cross-cultural evidence of this sort that can be obtained, the less likely that the cross-corresppondences will be seen as some kind of literary sport or freak.

What light did the scripts themselves shed on the deeper issues addressed by Braude, Sudduth (2016), Griffin (1997), *et al*? The answer is very little. There was a detailed account by Winifred Coombe-Tennant on the process of communication which was ably summarised by Gerald Balfour and has been discussed above, and also some philosophical/mystical material on the relationship of individual consciousness to group consciousness; there was a recognition of the uniqueness of each individual medium and a reluctance to generalise; there was the clear distinction made in Trix Fleming scripts between the nature and appearance of the discarnate entity and the projection or eidolon used in an apparitional sense for recognition. This seems to the current writer a position quite consonant with what one knows of the academic backgrounds of the three men. Just as they avoided the convential Spiritualist approach in the content of their communications, so too they largely steered clear of the fundamental questions—what survives, what is the survival vehicle, how long does the what survive, and is that survival for all or just some, and does the what that survives reincarnate? They were academically cautious and focused on their specific task. In essence one will find very little in the scripts of, say, the detailed metaphysical or pseudo-metaphysical content of the *Seth* books or the other channelled material referred to in studies of channelling (Klimo, Hastings).

To what extent does other automatic writing or mediumistic communications support the cross-correspondence case either directly or indirectly? There is some impressive evidence from Mrs Leonard of a personal nature linked to some of the investigators—Lodge, Piddington, Edith Lyttelton, and Winifred Coombe-Tennant. There is the broader, cosmic writing of Geraldine Cummins which has certain Myersian flourishes and touches. Do the ideas expressed by Myers in her scripts fit in with other automatic writing on the nature of the afterlife, or with the very limited comments expressed in the scripts themselves? Certainly, her scripts address the difficult process of designing and communicating the cross-correspondences (see Carter 2012) and they also catch the urgent energy of Myers, though they partially contradict him on reincarnation (see *Beyond Human Personality*). Do the messages of Robert Hugh Benson (a son of Edward Benson, Archbishop of Canterbury), an alleged communicator after death through automatic writing (Borgia 1954), and whose brother Martin, it was hinted at in the scripts, was in the background helping with the preparatory work on the cross-correspondences, shed any insight on the problem? They do not appear to do so.

Though the context and the detail may vary, the persistence of the Myers communicator over the years has been very impressive. Do the latest manifestations of Myers and colleagues as described in *The Scole Report* (Keen et al. 1999) ring true with what is known about the earlier material? Myers (and Lodge) was also alleged to have taken part in the physical mediumship and literary puzzles developed by the mediums under the controlled conditions laid down by T.G. Hamilton in Canada (Hamilton ML 1969). Juliet S. Goodenow (1923) published *Letters to Juliet*, supposedly produced via telepathic contact with Myers. This might appear outrageously flakey and otherworldly but she was a practical campaigner for social reform and, at one stage, was the Chair of the Industrial Committee of Michigan State Federation of Women's Clubs in which capacity she agitated long and hard against the exploitation of child labour. Both Florence Upton (Lyttelton 1926) and Aelfrida Tillyard (Mann 2013) wrote material supposedly directed by him. All this content is variable in quality, some quite reminiscent in style and approach of Myers in life, but much of it shares the common characteristic (as in some of the channelled material alleged to have come from William James) of operating at a lower intellectual level than the named communicator in their actual life. It would be a huge task to map, compare, and analyse this material, and the questions raised above go beyond the limits and resources of this current enquiry. An additional weakness appears to be the lack of awareness of these 'Myers Personae' of each other.

But what about the communicators? Granted that they were who they claimed to be, what was the environment which they inhabited and were they any more likely to be free from the conditioning assumptions than their incarnate colleagues? Broad has commented quite tartly on this (in Cummins 1965: intro). Without either accepting or rejecting the ontological status of the content, the evidence from surveys of automatic writing generally, which purports to describe the afterlife and from the more celebrated individual examples, suggests that there is not necessarily an immediate expansion in knowledge and spirituality after death and that like-minded consciousnesses tend to cohere in environments that they have mentally created to meet their temperaments and beliefs. Could one argue that this narrowly academic and highly technical approach to demonstrating survival, and the hugely ambitious emphasis on supporting the development of gifted children who would work for world peace and a new world order, was the product of a sheltered and impractical idealism, but, on this occasion, from the other side of the grave? Certainly, the Glastonbury scripts of John Alleyne (Hopkinson-Ball, T. 2007) and the Cleophas scripts of Geraldine Cummins (1974) would suggest such a posthumous group think and clustering.

One last point: are the cross-correspondences as impressive as the best mediumship evidence from other sources past and present? Do they meet tight modern criteria — regardless of any literary flourish or decoration? The same basic demands, often phrased in slightly different language reflecting the predominant discourse of the intended audience, crop up again and again when attempting to assess the paranormal. *The first is the sealing off of all normal channels for acquiring the paranormal content.* An interesting modern example is the work by Main (2007: 14) in which he proposed four criteria that needed to be met if a coincidence were to qualify as an instance of synchronicity:

1. 'two or more events parallel one another through having identical, similar or comparable content;

2. there is no discernible or plausible way in which this paralleling could be the result of normal causes;
3. the paralleling must be sufficiently unlikely and detailed as to be notable;
4. the experience must be meaningful beyond being notable.'

These criteria though referring to synchronicity relate closely to the assessment statements outlined in this study — they emphasise 'identical, similar or comparable content'; they stress the lack of a normal cause for the paralleling of content or communication; they emphasise the notable and meaningful nature of the paralleling of communication. One expects to apply all these criteria and see all of them satisfied if the scripts' claims are to stand up, and in many cases they do.

However, there is one extra factor that characterises the cross-correspondence scripts which goes well beyond the identification of synchronicity. In the case of synchronicity one has no sense of the cause. Is it a random conincidence or purposive agency? The script communicators positively and unambiguously claim purpose and design in the construction of cross-correspondences and the demonstration of paranormal cognition. And, for this reason, Salter called the 'the production and interpretation of the automatic writings of the S.P.R. group' the most important work they had done. But how does the assessment of the scripts stand up to the best practice developed by parapsychologists over the ensuing years after the founding of the Society for Psychical Research?

The second demand that seems to crop up again and again when assessing paranormal research is the objective assessment of the paranormal content. The fundamental issue was and is how to objectively demonstrate the paranormality of the cross-correspondences. This is a little (but not completely) like the identifying of coherent messages and recognisable images in remote viewing and the Ganzfeld experiments. A considerable body of expertise has developed with regard to these activities (Tart 2009; Sheldrake 2003) which was not available at the time the cross-correspondences were produced. Nowadays one would expect blind judging and the training of disinterested assessor panels. This point must be taken seriously since there is little doubt that the original investigators (though they did their best to guard against this) were deeply involved on a personal level with the scripts and their contents, and Margaret Verrall, particularly, had a difficult dual role as both automatist and investigator. However, though these points do compromise the material to a certain extent, they do not fatally compromise it.

Unfortunately, by dismissing the kind of simple outcomes-based tests that they had, to some extent, used in the telepathic hypnosis experiments of 1889–1891 (see *Proceedings* 1889, 1892) as irrelevant to the phenomena they were assessing, the investigators were inevitably going to encounter, from critics then and now, the problems raised above. In addition, they also ignored the expertise of the best elements of the Spiritualist community. Their view of the Spiritualist tradition was coloured by the disappointing and depressing investigations of earlier years. But this meant that they did not have access to the long experience Spiritualists had through training and development (Payne 1992; Boddington 1995) of the ways in which mediums could deceive themselves.

Was Winifred Coombe-Tennant someone with great natural gifts who eventually, to some extent, fell prey to this? Had Gerald Balfour not been her lover and the father of her coming child during the crucial period, had Margaret Verrall been a little younger and fitter and lived longer, and had Alice Johnson, too, not been ill for some of this time, there might have been less Messianic colouring in Coombe-Tennant's scripts. One could argue that the SPR leadership, while clearly seeing the dangers of traditional Spiritualism and the desire for immediate, direct, straightforward evidence of survival, failed to fully appreciate the issues of need, emotion, and bias that were masked by their own more dry-as-dust approach.

Broad (1925) laid down criteria which, he argued, would, if satisfied, tilt the argument more in favour of the survival hypothesis by strengthening the argument from design. 'It seems to me that we should have grounds for postulating the *survival* of a *mind*, and not the mere persistence of a psychic factor, if and only if the communications showed traces of an intention which persisted between the experiments and deliberately modified and controlled each in the light of those which had preceded it.' He asserted that if the cross-correspondence material came up to the specifications for an ideal cross-correspondence (reminiscent of the Latin Message), 'I think we should have to admit that it looks as if a single intelligent being were deliberately trying in an extremely ingenious way to produce evidence of its continuous existence'. His specifications were: three automatic writers in three different places with no communications between them; scripts to be produced over a number of years and sent to an impartial authority; the scripts of A, B, and C to be separately unintelligible; injunctions in A to refer to past, present, and future scripts of B and C, and these injunctions to also be found in B and C scripts. The independent assessor then works through the criteria, compares the scripts, and 'finds that these separately unintelligible sentences combine to to convey something which is highly characteristic of a certain deceased person who is alleged to be communicating'.

His conclusions were tentative. He did not believe that 'most of the alleged Cross-Correspondences accurately exemplify this ideal type'. He was suspicious of the enormous effort and ingenuity required to extract meaning from the scripts. 'Would not the same amount of patience, learning and ingenuity discover almost as good Cross-Correspondences between almost any set of manuscripts?' He wanted lots of negative evidence, no matter how laborious the process, 'before I was able to stake so much on this argument for human survival'.

There can be little doubt, based on the evidence in this book, that some of the cross-correspondences went some way towards meeting Broad's criteria, and he was writing without access to the *Notes and Excursuses* of Balfour and Piddington. But the bar was set very high by Broad and when one studies the ecologies of psychical phenomena they are rarely if ever amenable to such complex and stringent demands. Broad also ignored the fact that the cross-correspondences' production might require particular gifts and conditions that only occurred irregularly in time, and that they also require great emotional resonance (Palmer 2014) between the living and the discarnate. Such conditions, like astronomical conjunctions, may only take place a few times in a century.

Broad (1925) also asserted that, even if the above hurdle was jumped, the race to prove discarnate survival still had not beem won. Suppose it was 'rendered practically certain that some other mind was involved' — might it not be Margaret Verrall's? He gave three reasons: intense interest in a problem often involves unconscious processes; telepathy may take place 'between the unconscious parts of living minds'; the unconscious is often extremely obliging in providing the conscious mind with what it wants. Points one ignores at one's peril. And, of course, although Margaret Verrall died in 1916, her gifted daughter Helen lived long beyond the termination of the cross-correspondence phenomena.

So, a hundred years or more on from the inception of the phenomena how do the cross-correspondences stand up to the formidable challenges posed by Broad and other critics (many of them sympathetic to the aims and objectives of psychical research)? It is not possible to distinguish between the living agent psi hypothesis and the survival hypothesis in this or any other case. The hypothesis that there was subconscious collaboration between automatists and investigators in order to produce scripts that were shaped and selected to fit a range of hidden desires and purposes, including proof of survival after death, is certainly worth examining. The fact that such a task would be fiendishly complex is not fundamentally destructive of it as a hypothesis (*pace* Gauld 1983; Carter 2012). One just does not know. But one must always be cautious since explaining away the spiritist hypothesis by other contested hypotheses like telepathy, clairvoyance, or some kind of cosmic reservoir may mean substituting one species of ignorance for another.

It may be more sensible to avoid such speculation and to continue to refine methods for exploring the more manageable hypothesis of Broad that there must always be the suspicion that equally plausible meanings could be derived from the same mass of complex data. So, why should one privilege the Piddington/Balfour interpretation—apart from the self-evident intelligence, expertise, and effort they put into it? It is a fair point but no one has risen to the challenge of providing an alternative holistic explanation, though Carrington provided a superficially plausible one for the Statius case (see above). Nor have attempts to generate cross-correspondences of the same intellectual quality and persuasiveness from the random selection of passages in literary texts been successful.

There are two fundamental generic weaknesses (apart from the above) that stand out with regard to the phenomena as proof of survival, and both reflect the historical context in which the scripts developed. They are too elitist and they are not cost effective. The researchers adhered vigorously to the canons of evidence laid down by the founders of the SPR in their books and articles, but while they were fully alive to the prejudices, passions, and delusions of the uneducated, were they fully alive to their own? The cross-correspondences are permeated with an unchallenged elitism and the privileging of one set of associations, one way of knowing, over others. Were alternative meanings and interpretations really rigorously pursued? Were the links they finally established strong enough to bear the weight put on them? To fully explore these questions across all three thousand six hundred plus scripts and associated commentary would be many years' work for a team of researchers now, and the team and the funding are most unlikely to be available. This current book has just scratched the surface. And, in terms of a cost–benefit analysis, would it be worthwhile? For most people the, unfortunately rare, opportunity of sitting with a highly gifted medium under sensibly controlled conditions would probably provide (allowing for all the obvious caveats) much greater personal and intimate evidence for survival.

Information technology has helped in making the physical process of comparing scripts and identifying clusters of symbols much easier than for Piddington with his stack of books, concordances, articles, and encyclopaedias piled high on tables in his eyrie at the top of Fishers Hill (Roy 2008), but there is still a literary and psychological judgement to be made (and the same would apply in the application of any style recognition or author attribution software that might be devised for the cross-correspondences). Moreover, in that field, though results could well be extremely interesting and suggestive of further lines of enquiry, they would not be based on secure foundations (a problem acknowledged throughout this study) since the automatic writing will have been heavily coloured by the individual personality of the medium involved; and even though enough material from Myers and Gurney has been digitised (*Phantasms of the Living*/*Human Personality*) for matching purposes, the main automatists were familiar with some if not all of that literature.

But, on the other hand, to ignore the best examples of cross-correspondence and paranormal cognition outlined in this book and in more detail in the *Proceedings*, the original volumes of scripts, and the commentaries on them, is pure intellectual dishonesty. There is design, there is purpose (consistent over a number of years), there is insight and self-reflection, there is a sense of a continuing consciousness post-mortem. And this is clearly there even allowing for all the very valid cautions about the misinterpretation of evidence. But it does not quite meet the standards Broad set for it, or the more recent criteria Braude (2013: 31–2) has laid down that really persuasive mediumistic communications would have to meet. These are (slightly adapted): the evidence is not contaminated by psychological disorders; the evidence should not serve the psychological needs of the living; the evidence should make best sense if attributed to the agendas and interests of the deceased; the evidence should begin and be documented before the recipient has identified and researched the life of the deceased; verifiable intimate details of that life should be provided; these details should be recognised by several individuals on separate occasions; idiosyncratic skills or traits should be displayed; they should be as foreign or alien to the medium as possible, ideally from a different culture; skills associated with the deceased should be of a high level, require practice, and of a kind not usually associated with savants or prodigies; evidence should come from multiple remote physical and cultural sources.

As indicated in the text, the best of the cross-correspondences stand up well against some of these criteria (the character of the automatists, their physical separation from each other, the confirmation of content from multiple sources, the demonstration of knowledge and skills beyond their known abilities), but less so against intellectual and emotional separation from the alleged communicators.

As an exercise in interpretation, the *Notes and Excursuses* and the printed volumes of scripts with their notes are absolute triumphs of intellectual energy, organisation, and persistence. This should be fully recognised, and the best of the cross-correspondences of the earlier period stand the test of detailed assessment even though, complex and moving as they are, they do not circumvent the fundamental problem discussed above. Nor should one assume that the investigators deprived of their God by nineteenth-century science rushed to re-enchant the universe by swallowing the cross-correspondences at once and whole. Mrs Sidgwick's Presidential Addresses of 1908 and 1932 should be read as a record of her long path to conviction. Parts of the cross-correspondences are highly persuasive of paranormal knowledge, both of facts, events, and of individual personality traits, but there is no absolutely certain demonstration of such. They cannot, however, be dismissed. They deserve study, respect, and attention and they have certainly tilted the balance a little more in the direction of the possibility of survival. Apart from this central point, there is much unexplored material in them for the cultural historian on the nature of evidence, reception studies in the classics, the Bible, Victorian literature generally, the Edwardian class structure and its mores, the nature of psychological automatisms, and particularly the important role of highly gifted women in this huge interpretive enterprise (see, for example, Wilson 2013b; Kontou 2009, Galvan n.d.).

However, the cultural historian of psychical research sometimes needs to treat this work with a little care, particularly if the material is being framed in the context of another discipline or subject-specific thesis. For example, Wilson (2007: 19) writes of the 'potentially transgressive appropriations of cultural and literary mastery' in giving the female automatic writer power in the way the female medium in the séance had but suggesting that the male authority reasserted itself in the interpretive role. The power relations in the cross-correspondences were much more nuanced than that. The interpreters in the early years of the cross-correspondences were Margaret Verrall, Alice Johnson, and J.G. Piddington, with support from Eleanor Sidgwick who also wrote a massive study on Leonora Piper's mediumship. And Lodge, who was also part of the team, relied heavily on Margaret Verrall's expertise in his reports. Hardly a male dominated environment.

As the above example illustrates, one can say with some degree of confidence that the conclusions any investigator comes to concerning the cross-correspondences will depend on the cultural procedures and traditions of their professional discipline and their own preferred cognitive style (see Hudson 1972, Becher 2001, Gardner 1985, for some of the classic British and American exploratory work in this field.) The fuzzy, descriptive approaches of the arts and the humanities which seem to be what assessment of the cross-correspondences demands (with its constant cross-referencing of a range of quotations) may well irritate and unsettle those for whom objective analysis in terms of clear outcomes calculated against chance is crucial. Many, whether from a humanities or science background, would also point to the possible role of vanity and emotional investment in the construction of the Messianic Child element of the scripts; they would, rightly, point out the lack of external assessment by impartial observers; and would begrudge the investment of time and energy in painstakingly applying detailed assessment criteria to a mass of complex data, over a century old, and not produced under properly controlled conditions.

But in conclusion (though the position and role of Leonora Piper sits a little uneasily in all of this), if nothing else ultimately registers, it is hoped that this point is taken: Margaret Verrall and her daughter Helen, Winifred Coombe-Tennant, and Trix Fleming were different personalities facing different life situations and events but their gifts, dedication, stamina, and their courage (perhaps especially the fragile Trix Fleming in her particularly difficult family circumstances) still demand our attention and regard.

Afterword

A number of conclusions (some more firmly based than others) have emerged from this initial enquiry. They cannot be airbrushed out of the history of psychical research by those who a priori regard the whole field as preposterous and unworthy of study and who make no attempt to engage with the material in a significant way. (Nor must the silliness associated with the Messianic Child theme be allowed completely to discredit the scripts.) These points include:

- The remarkable prefiguring in Margaret Verrall's first three hundred scripts of the symbolism later linked to Laura Lyttelton, May Lyttelton, and Arthur Balfour. No other automatist ever read these scripts except Helen Verrall who worked on them from May to December 1912.
- The display by Leonora Piper and Winifred Coombe-Tennant of skills, knowledge, and semantic understanding beyond their normal, everyday capacities.
- Despite the close social and cultural connections between most of the automatists, the best cross-correspondences appear to have been independently generated, clearly signalled (though the origin of the signal must remain in dispute), to have occurred within a reasonable timeframe, and to have been broadly unambiguous.
- The impossibility (or perhaps even the irrelevance) of attempting to calculate the above chance appearance of cross-correspondences as opposed to their natural occurrence in an equally large body of random literary material. The small quantitative element in this study was purely provisional and partly intended to illustrate the pitfalls of that approach in this context.
- The impressive powers of paranormal cognition displayed particularly by Trix Fleming.
- The intellectual richness and colour of much of the automatic writing going well beyond that associated with low-level dissociation. See Balfour (1935) for example.
- The fact (difficult to present in the conventional format of a book) that there was often more than one example of cross-

correspondence or paranormal cognition in the scripts quoted leading to multiple links and associations between them.

This last issue is not easily illustrated or evidenced in detail in a written text with a prescribed wordage, and it highlights the fundamental questions that have always dogged and still dog the examination and presentation of this vast body of material. Any examples selected from the automatic writings will always be suspected as being the product of cherry-picking and wishful thinking. Only easy access to the full body of scripts will allow a proper assessment of those objections and the physical strains involved in a paper-based approach are intense. They need to be online with a good search facility. In addition, the cross-correspondences cry out for the detailed exploration of patterns and groupings that linguistic, authorship attribution, and stylometrics software (as reported on in the *Journal of Digital Scholarship in the Humanities*, for example) can provide (given the caveats mentioned earlier). It is hoped that this initial, limited, and tentative attempt to go back to the original documents and grapple with the nature of the wider patterns and meanings claimed for them might stimulate efforts to make the full body of scripts available online and the formation (given appropriate funding) of a more substantial team-based enquiry (encompassing a wide range of disciplinary expertise) into the complex, sometimes tedious, but ultimately fascinating riddle that is the cross-correspondence automatic writings.

Appendix 1

The flow of Scripts 1901–1936

	MV	HV	TF	WCT	Macs	Wilson
1901	3000–091					
1902	3092–071					
1903	3172–258	A–U	1–33			
1904	3259–307	V–Y	34–48			
1905	1–56		49–81			
1906	57–120	1–21	82–168			
1907	121–218	22–260	169–205			
1908	219–290	61–142	206–218	1–24	1–38	
1909	291–346	143–193	219–258	25–160	39–53	
1910	347–397	194–225	259–293	161–228	54–55	
1911	398–438	226–247		229–276	56–60	
1912	439–502	248–297		277–306		
1913	503–573	298–336		307–324		
1914	574–668	337–376		325–346		
1915	669–716	377–458		347–362		1–39
1916	717–739	459–493		363–382		39A–67
1917		494–517		383–384		68–87D
1918		518–529		385–386A		87E–87S
1919		530–535		387		87T–87W
1920		536–538		387A–388		88–96
1921		539–555		389–392		97–112
1922		556–585		393–401		113–121
1923		586–599		402–408		122–139
1924		600–612		409–410		140–156
1925		613–618		411–414		157–159
1926		619–620		415–418		160–172
1927		621–624				173
1928		625–625				174–183
1929				419–421		184–192
1930				422–427		193–197
1931						198
1932				427A–429		
1936				430		

Notes

1. There may be some minor numerical errors both in this chart and in the original numbering and counting of the scripts but at least it demonstrates the scale of the task the interpreters faced. The scale is increased when one remembers that Winifred Coombe-Tennant, at times, produced both scripts and Daylight Impressions and in the printed volumes the interpreters counted them as one item.

2. This study has been based on the printed scripts available but examples of the handwritten originals can still be found in the Salter papers at Trinity and in the voluminous Piper, Lyttelton, and Richmond papers in the SPR/CUL archive.

3. Note the very heavy load between 1908 and 1911 when up to five automatists were writing (in addition there were the Piper sittings with George Dorr and Winifred Coombe-Tennant's sittings with Leonora Piper).

4. Not all the scripts were of equal length. Many were short and fairly laconic but the Coombe-Tennant script was quite often voluminous.

5. To get a sense of the total task one should add the 141 Kenneth Richmond scripts, the 143 Zoë Richmond scripts, the 854 Mrs Lyttelton scripts (there may be more: these were just those spotted) quoted in the *Notes and Excursuses*. The total number of scripts is in excess of 3,600 without including the Piper material mentioned above or the scripts of Mrs Raikes.

6. In addition, one has to consider the sheer volume of commentary on these scripts: the thousands of pages in the *Notes and Excursuses*; the thousands of pages in the *Journal* and the *Proceedings*; and the secondary literature in book form.

Appendix 2
The Ave Roma Immortalis Complete Scripts

Ave Roma Immortalis is an example of one of the deceptively simpler cross-correspondences. The evidence comprising the Ave Roma Immortalis cross-correspondence is displayed below in chronological order. Laying out the matter in this way, one can see that a puzzle is posed in the three scripts of Margaret Verrall and the clue to solving it is provided by Alice Fleming's single script.

Margaret Verrall 2/3/1906:

> Dovedale and Derwentwater write to Lotta Leaf about Kitty's nurse she will understand [Drawing of bulrushes] bulrushes
> Not with such help will you find what you want. Not with such help, nor with those defenders of yours.
> Keep the two distinct — you do not hear — write regularly — give up other things.
> First among his peers, himself not unmindful of his name; with him a brother related in feeling, though not in blood. Both these will send a word to you through another woman. After some days you will easily understand what I say; till then farewell.

Margaret Verrall 4/3/1906:

> Pagan and Pope. The Stoic persecutor and the Christian. Gregory not Basil's friend ought to be a clue but you have it not quite right. Pagan and Pope and Reformer all enemies as you think.
> The cross has a meaning. The Cross-bearer who one day is born.
> The standard-bearer is the link.
> Now otherwise.
> Evidence is there for the seeker the papers should be carefully looked through there are things in them not for publication accept in faith confirm by search. To-morrow's news will help.
> (Last three lines in Richard Hodgson's writing.)

Margaret Verrall 5/3/1906 11.40:

> It was the old story nothing new. You have not heard clock beat with time and a bell what more unlikely and yet all true
> The club/key-bearer with the lion's skin already well described before this in the writings. Some things are to be corrected.

Ask your husband he knows it well
There stands the column where Calpe has been left. That is the end. no you have left something out. The columns [broken] by incessant reading.

Trix Fleming 7/3/1906:

The white winged bird is struggling to the shore
Not May—May would be much too late for those latitudes. Tell him to go the second week in April—A white beach with purple waves breaking on it—A group of palm trees—rising above a low flat house—The trading station is away to the left—A burial ground—with three named graves and one nameless lies beyond—Mariposa
The mixed blood gives a fatal fluency of speech—but remember the sense of <u>truth</u> is non-existent in this particular case—look at the <u>nails</u> they will tell the truth even if face and accent conceal it—Couldn't Alice F—undertake the book? Not the scribe but the Surrey Alice F. Bletchworth. It will need exactly the treatment she can best give it—P. hasn't quite got it the right way up—Miss J's way of looking at it is better but too analytical—It's a pity opinions can't be fused a little—
What are the printers thinking of? Those accents are scattered as if from a pepper pot—A.W. should slay them by return of post—Not enough bulbs—and—it's a pity the quince tree has suffered so.
Ave Roma immortalis. How could I make it clearer without giving her the clue? How cold it was that winter—Even snow in Rome—we might have stayed at home for that—
The sunshine has brought out the bees before the tulips are ready for them—Poor premature butterfly—
I can't admire your inkstand. More open air for both of you—especially A.W. The sunlight brings out the dust with startling brilliance—
Brittleworth—Brickdale—Britleton—No—not him and not James—Brit—Brick Brickleton—Hugo—H.M—Minster Berg. Hugo. Was he not aware? R. <u>Why</u> are they so brutally dense. H. I always had a quick temper.
(Script ceased at 11.10—leaving me feeling <u>annoyed</u>).

Mrs Verrall recognised that her very first sentence referred to a passage in the *Aeneid* describing the aged King Priam of Troy buckling on his armour to defend his city against the Greeks. However, the other statements puzzled her. Her husband said that he had an idea what they meant but did not tell her except to say that the phrase first among his peers (*primus inter pares* in Latin) was often applied to the Pope. On March the 11th she received extracts from Alice Johnson of Mrs Holland's script on March 7th. On reading it, her husband declared that it confirmed his original intuition. The statement of March 4th reminded him of Raphael's picture of Attila the Hun frightened by the vision of St Peter and St Paul who appeared as Pope Leo I rode out to stop Attila invading Rome in 452. The picture is in the Vatican. This was one of four paintings produced by Raphael between 1512 and 1514 for Julius II and then Leo X to symbolise divine help afforded to

Rome and its Popes against internal and external enemies. In the picture there is a cross-bearer to the Pope's left and to the right of Attila is a standard-bearer. St Peter and St Paul descend from the sky with swords and St Peter carries keys in his left hand. The background shows the city of Rome and the Coliseum.

Given the original guiding phrase (Ave Roma etc.) Alice Johnson, after substantial research, concluded that the cryptic words and sentences all indicated different aspects of Roman history; and that the overall theme was the triumphant rise of Rome—starting with Aeneas leaving Troy to found Rome in Italy. Key incidents in the history of Rome are alluded to: St Peter and St Paul, the guardians of Rome, and the Rock on which the Roman Church was founded; Pope Leo I repulsing the barbarian challenge and saving Rome; Pope Gregory I establishing his spiritual and military independence from the Emperors at Constantinople; Popes Julius II and Leo X who developed Rome artistically and intellectually; and Pope Sixtus V, who rebuilt Rome and laid out its modern streets and put St Peter and St Paul on the two great columns (replacing Trajan and Marcus Aurelius—the stoic persecutor of Christianity). In addition, the story of the growth of Rome was a symbol for the evolution of the human race and its developing civilisation and spirituality which Myers, when alive, deployed on several occasions in his writings. See his essay on *Virgil* and his *Human Personality and Its Survival of Bodily Death* (vol. 2).

Almost everything in Mrs Verrall's three scripts is used in the interpretation, and the statements, though terse, are obviously in the form of puzzles to be solved. They are not just a collection of random, semi-surrealistic offerings. Moreover, Mrs Fleming's single script is on a number of quite different topics, which have references to other cross-correspondences entirely, with, however, the statement re Ave Roma inserted apparently and solely to provide a specific clue to Mrs Verrall's material.

In addition, there are indicators in the scripts of conscious design and intention. The scripts are close in time and the intention is clearly signalled. For example:

- Gregory not Basil's friend ought to be a clue but you have it not quite right
- Pagan and Pope and Reformer all enemies as you think
- The cross has a meaning
- The standard-bearer is the link
- Some things are to be corrected
- Ask your husband he knows it well
- No you have left out something
- How could I make it any clearer without giving her the clue?

In addition, a cross-correspondence is clearly anticipated in the instruction to wait a few days and a woman will send a message and then you will understand. Equally clearly, the relevant clue is announced in Trix Fleming's script of a few days later. And the correspondence is not the repetition or near repetition of a word or part of a word which could easily be explained by mere chance or over-interpretation. It is a phrase, Ave Roma Immortalis, that throws a searchlight on Mrs Verrall's scripts and clearly links them all together in a coherent form. In addition, these very words were used as the title of a popular history of Rome, at the time of Myers' death, by F. Marion Crawford. Note, too, that all this took place within six days and not over months or years; and Ave Roma Immortalis only occurs twice again in the 3,600-plus published scripts between 1901 and 1936, and on each occasion in an appropriate context.

Re the Trix Fleming script of 7/3/1906:

The white bird references are fairly consistent symbols for Annie Marshall. Next come references to Feilding's travels in the Far East and then, by association, links to the grave of Robert Louis Stevenson; then references to deceptions in psychical research; references to a book, probably containing Greek (Margaret Verrall's 1906 report?); one untraceable name; slight differences in the approaches of Piddington and Alice Johnson to psychical research; and a return to Verrall's book; the bulb/bees and sunshine reference is a possible reference to Margaret Verrall's visit to the Botanic Gardens in Cambridge on 7/3/1906; the next three lines refer to the cross-correspondence and Myers' death though the source re the snow might be Trix Fleming who was in Rome around that time; there seems some clairvoyant perception of Margaret Verrall's inkstand (verified by her); then Trix Fleming's usual insertion of medical advice; then a possible shift to Hodgson as a communicator trying by alliteration to get to the name Münsterberg. Hodgson intensely disliked him and his approach to psychical research; a characteristic hint of Hodgson's quick temper which may or may not be veridical depending on what Trix Fleming knew at the time.

The point is that the vast majority of the script can be classified as dealing with paranormal cognition—only the white bird symbol for Annie Marshall and the Ave Roma cross-correspondence are obviously part of the wider structure and design of the scripts. One must not claim, and sometimes Piddington strayed dangerously near this cliff edge (though never quite toppled over), that virtually every element in the scripts was imbricated in the Story and the Plan.

But Piddington, as usual, eventually unearthed a symbolic cross-correspondence buried in the script based on Shelley's *The Sensitive Plant*, which was one of the symbols in scripts for Edith Lyttelton's child Antony. He stated (Piddington 1943b: 50-6) that this theme went back to Margaret

Verrall's script of 18/5/1902: 'Write for me in the woods it will be found the sweetest flower that blows—then you may know that I sent you this message all in a month of May.' The line from Shelley's poem was: 'The sweetest flower for scent that blows.' He further stated that this script was written of the first Whit Sunday after the death of Antony Lyttelton who had been born on Whit Sunday 1900 and that there was an obvious allusion to Pentecost in that script: 'Manifold are the words, but the interpretation is simple for those in whom speaks a mind conscious of God, not by flames or by tongues, but by the mind and the spirit which appertains to thought itself.'

The link to the Shelley poem in the Trix Fleming script is rather tortuous and comes via the references to Robert Louis Stevenson (the ship, the Mariposa, was a ship he had sailed on in the South Seas) and his grave on Samoa which was meant to point to the road built for him to his estate at Vailima, a road which after his death was covered by plants and vegetation like the neglect of the Sensitive Plant in winter: 'When Winter had gone and Spring came back/The Sensitive Plant was a leafless wreck.' He partially based his conclusion on two other Fleming scripts of the period which also linked, he argued, the overgrown road to the Sensitive Plant symbol.

Piddington's argument is difficult to follow and to summarise fairly. To the modern reader it seems strained and far-fetched. Can one (see earlier) claim the sweetest flower as both a reference to syringa (Phyllis) and the Sensitive Plant (Antony Lyttelton)? The stretching of symbolism by a) allowing a symbol to have multiple applications and b) allowing a variety of related symbols to apply to one individual can weaken the persuasiveness and coherence of the interpretation.

One curious section in the script has possibly more to do with certain subconscious personal fears of Trix Fleming than external design from the discarnates. Piddington argued that the section from 'the mixed blood gives a fatal fluency of speech… face and accent conceal it' in conjunction with 'Sensitive plant. Mellow moons and tropic skies' is a misquotation of 'mellow moons and happy skies' from Tennyson's *Locksley Hall* in which the writer imagines himself mating with a native woman and producing children of mixed race. Trix Fleming was certainly conscious of the fact that unpleasant and snobbish gossip sometimes suggested that she and Rudyard (who had a dark complexion) were partially Indian (Lee 2004).

Appendix 3
The Hope Star Browning Complete Scripts

This cross-correspondence involves, in essence, five scripts: Margaret Verrall 23/1/1907 and 28/1/1907; Helen Verrall 3/2/1907 and 17/2/1907; and Leonora Piper 11/2/1907. By 2/1/1907 a message had been dictated in Latin to the entranced Leonora Piper urging Myers to give apparently unrelated messages to two different mediums and then a communication to a third which would reveal the underlying links between all three. On 16/1/1907 Piddington suggested to Myers through Leonora Piper that Myers draw a circle with a triangle inside it to indicate such a cross-correspondence. The full Margaret and Helen Verrall scripts now follow with the relevant Piper extract.

Margaret Verrall 23/1/1907:

> JUSTICE HOLDS THE SCALES. That gives the words but an anagram would be better
> Tell him that—rats stars tars and so on. Try this. It has been tried before RTATS rearrange
> Those five letters or again tears stare seam same and so on. Skeat takes Kate's Keats stake
> Steak. But the letters you should give tonight are not so many—only three ast.

Margaret Verrall 28/1/1907:

> Star Wonder the world's wonder and all a wonder and a wild desire the very wings of her A WINGED DESIRE winged love—then there is Blake and mocked my loss of liberty. But it is all the same thing—the winged desire passion the hope that leaves the earth for the sky—Abt Vogler—for earth too hard that found itself or lost itself—in the sky. That is what I want—On the earth the broken sounds threads In the sky the perfect arc. The C major of this life But your recollection is at fault. [Drawing of of a semi-circle with a triangle in it. Drawing of a triangle inside a complete circle with ACB at top and D at bottom.] ADB is the part that unseen completes the arc.

Helen Verrall 3/2/1907:

> Vulliamy not to be confused with the other Williams more precious than rubies what was the name of the younger child Cecil at Mundellier

wherefore in Sicily he sets out a green jerkin and hose and doublet where the song birds pipe their tune in the early morning a healer from aliens. [Drawing of a monogram Drawing of a star Drawing of a crescent moon.] The crescent moon remember that and the star. Like a thunder riven oak the grim remains/stand on the level desolation of the plains/ a record for all ages of the span/which nature gives to the weak labour of a man. [Drawing of a bird.] bird.

Leonora Piper 11/2/1907:

> JGP. Do you remember what your exact reference to Browning was?
> Myers. I referred to Hope and Browning...I also said Star.
> (The next private sitter with Leonora Piper was then announced)
> JGP. Now, Myers, I must say goodbye as the friend is here.
> Myers. Do I U.D. that I am to go.
> JGP. Yes...
> Myers. Mean while look out for Hope, Star and Browning.

Helen Verrall 17/2/1907:

> Androsace Carthusian candelabrum [Drawing of an arrow] many together [Drawing of a star] that was the sign she will understand when she sees it diapason rhythm through all no arts avail the heavenly harmony as Plato said the mystic three (?) and a star above it all <u>rats</u> everywhere in Hamelin town now do you understand Henry (?)

Finally, Mrs Sidgwick took over the sittings with Leonora Piper from Piddington and asked Myers which poem particularly lay behind this cross-correspondence. After some difficulty, he got out Abt Vo and variations on the word Vogler which Mrs Sidgwick completed for him (but he had got the essentials). Leonora Piper's writing hand waved with excitement and then wrote—'Now dear Mrs Sidgwick in future have no doubt or fear of so called death as there is none.'

With regard to the cherry-picking or manipulating of data, the whole of Margaret Verrall's script of 23/1/1907 was quoted in the *Proceedings* and it virtually all referred to the Hope, Star, Browning case. The only line which did not was the first line—Justice holds the scale—which was part of a major theme developed later in other scripts. The whole of Margaret Verrall's script on 28/1/1907 was quoted and it was all relevant to the theme. Moreover, it included the triangle in the circle drawing which Myers promised Piddington through Leonora Piper that he would draw to signal a cross-correspondence.

One has to assume that Margaret Verrall was not told of this sign by Piddington. Margaret Verrall's two scripts which started the cross-correspondence were not seen by Helen Verrall or by Leonora Piper before their contributions to the cross-correspondence. Helen Verrall saw them on 23/2/1907 after she had written her two scripts on the 3rd and the 17th of February respectively. The whole of Helen Verrall's scripts were quoted.

The first and last parts of the 3rd and the first part of the 17th referred to important themes that are later developed in the scripts but were not recognised at this stage. Leonora Piper provided the essential clue on the 11th of February with her Browning, Hope, Star, so Margaret Verrall could not have been influenced by it in her earlier scripts or Helen Verrall in her script of the 3rd. The crucial question is, had Helen Verrall any access to the Piper script of 11/2/07 before she wrote rats everywhere in Hamelin town? Her mother told her on 15/2/07 about a correspondence but gave her no clue as to its focus or detail.

Piddington picked up the general references to Browning's poems, to *The Ring and the Book* (and all a wonder and a wild desire), to the *Pied Piper of Hamelin* (jerkin, hose doublet, a healer from aliens) and through the star theme (aster was star in Latin and teras in Greek and they were anagrams of each other), to *Abt Vogler* and to the one of only two places where star occurred in the poem: 'But here is the finger of God... such gift be allowed to man / That out of three sounds he frame, not a fourth sound but a star.'

Piddington argued the scripts fulfilled the demands of the Latin message. Script A was Margaret Verrall's script of the 23rd of January 1907: *Try also to give to A and B two different messages between which no connexion is discernible*. Script B was Helen Verrall's script of 3rd of February 1907, reinforced by her script on 17th of February 1903), and Script C was Leonora Piper's of the 11th of February 1907: *Then as soon as possible give to C a third message which will reveal the hidden connexion*. There was, of course, a fourth script, Helen Verrall's of the 17th of February. But this could be read as anxiety on the part of the communicators for the connection not to be overlooked.

In addition, a related meaning of *teras* was wonder or sign and the actual quotation Piddington discovered in *Abt Vogler* had been deployed in Liddell and Scott's *Greek Lexicon* to illustrate that very point. The anagrams used were of the sort Myers and Hodgson frequently constructed; the bird theme in the quotations and drawings, a symbol for soaring heaven-wards, was also a pointer to *Abt Vogler* since Vogler derived from the German for bird (vogel) and Vogler was a bird hunter or trapper. The mystic three were obviously the three automatists.

It should also be noted that the communicators signed or pointed up their actions: 'now do you understand Henry'; plus the drawing of the triangle in the circle as requested. They commented on failure—'but your recollection is at fault'—meaning that 'perfect arc' rather than 'perfect round' was quoted from *Abt Vogler*. They also (and this happens throughout the cross-correspondences) altered quotations to suit their particular purposes: for example, 'the hope that leaves the earth' rather than 'the passion' of the original. Note, too, the relatively short timescale of the scripts and the fact that Margaret and Helen Verrall did not see each other's scripts till after the cross-correspondence was over, apart from a brief mention by Margaret Verrall to her daughter on the 15th of February that something interesting appeared to be developing.

An extra layer of complication (mentioned above) was added a few years later when Piddington and Balfour saw many of the references, in this cross-correspondence and others, as referring to the underlying theme and purpose of the scripts which was the prediction, after many wars and troubles, of an era of peace, a new Pax Romana, established by a new Messiah and a race of spiritually developed children, the Children of Light. For example, Balfour connected the star with the Magi, with the advent of a Child of Destiny and a return of the 'Golden Age' citing 'Justice holds the scales' which was the first line of Margaret Verrall's script on 23rd of January. He saw this as a clear allusion to Virgil's *Messianic Eclogue IV*: '*Jam redit et Virgo redeunt Saturnia regna*' — Justice (Virgo) returns and the reign of Saturn returns (i.e. the Golden Age).

Note: there was very little irrelevant chaff: Vulliamy, Cecil at Mundellier, Androsace, Carthusian, candelabrum. But even this could be winnowed down by Balfour (1927) and Piddington (1943b): Androsace (a pink star-shaped Alpine flower); Cecil at Mundellier (a garbled script reference to Anthony Mundella, a Liberal politician who had links to Myers' work as an Inspector of Schools and who in scripts stood as a symbol for Antony Lyttelton); candelabrum (the seven candle sticks a symbol for Henry Coombe-Tennant); leaving only Vulliamy and Carthusian.

Appendix 4
List of Types of Symbols in the Scripts

In broad terms, four types of symbolism were deployed in the scripts: A. allusions to personal and family details; B. allusions from history and literature to situations that clearly matched aspects of the personal and family details of the individual concerned; C. highly indirect allusions from history and literature that matched aspects of the personal and family details of the individual concerned; D. general symbolism drawn from the natural world and general language that in a poetic and descriptive sense matched aspects of the personal and family details of the individual concerned. In C the links may be too tortuous, esoteric, and fine-spun to stand up. Conversely, in D, the symbolism may be so commonplace and general that it could immediately and vaguely apply to almost anyone.

It should be stressed that a commonplace symbol can become more convincing if it occurs in the context of other relevant material and that the symbols quoted are examples and by no means the totality of references to the individual named.

May Lyttelton

An enormous number of additional symbols, more than for any other of the communicators, were eventually identified as referring to May Lyttelton. The type A list is reasonably comprehensive but only illustrative examples are provided in the other categories.

Type A: play on her names—Mary, Mary, quite contrary, May blossom, Catherine/Kate/Cat; photograph of her as the lady with the candle, candle drawings, candle quotations and the indirect allusions in Macbeth (the sleep-walking scene), the Catherine Wheel and the bells of St Catherine of Alexandria; frequent references to the colour and abundance of her hair; her old-fashioned dress; her pearls; the emerald ring Balfour placed in her coffin and the silver box he had made for a lock of her hair; Lyttelton family references: references to her sister, Lavinia Talbot, and to Keble College, Oxford (she married the warden); the family crest which was of a Moor's head wreathed and three scallop/ cockle shells on the shield and the motto *Ung Dieu Ung Roy*; her love of music; the day of her death, Palm Sunday; the Palm Maiden; her family home, Hagley Hall.

Type B: Ariadne; Berenice, Beatrice; *The Blessed Damozel*; Persephone; Diana; Artemis; Shelley's *The Cloud*, 'the beat of her unseen feet'; Arethusa; Camilla; references to Tennyson's Maud (abandoned by her lover); the story of Hero and Leander and her lighting the beacon to guide Leander in his nightly swim across the Hellespont as 'the lonely hope of Sestos' daughter', etc.

Type C: the frequent use of lighthouses generally (particularly St Catherine's lighthouse); the White Ship that sank on St Catherine's Day (via quotations from Rossetti and Gray); sigma M, sigma C, sigma curl of hair, etc.; use of male symbols for Palm Maiden (Keats), etc.

Type D: phantom of delight, vision of hope, dew on parched earth, water in a thirsty land, nightingale, lark, lily, rose, water lily, stolen joy, still small voice, stars, deep calls to deep, responsive chord, etc.

Arthur Balfour

Type A: Arthur Balfour name or initials, family motto and coat of arms, Scottish and Irish references, Duke of Wellington his godfather, Excalibur, Perseus paintings in the Long Room, the silver/bronze casket.

Type B: Ariadne and Theseus, Hero and Leander, Dante and Beatrice, Orpheus and Eurydice, etc.

Type C: Oedipus, Hippolytus, Endymion, Faust, Integer Vitae, Aes triplex, Aeneas, Ulysses, Virgil, Shelley, etc.

Type D: London Pride, Shamrock, Thistle, Meditation, Pilgrim, Wanderer, etc.

Francis Maitland Balfour

Type A: his Christian name or initials—Frank, Francis, F.M.B.; reference to the brother or the three brothers; references to the lowlands of Scotland (East Lothian); references to Alpine mountaineering/ice axes and an accident (it was on the Aiguille Blanche de Peuteret that he died); his scientific work in Naples and his laboratory in Cambridge (he had the chair of Animal Morphology at Cambridge), etc.

Type B: references to great scholars and makers and magicians—Felix qui potuit, Opifex the great Artificer, Daedalus, Abt Vogler, Michael Scott and Melrose Abbey, the Magi; to the Franciscan order and St Francis; to a brother or brothers as in Catullus's *Frater Ave*, etc.

Type C: Bizarrely, Piddington and Gerald Balfour interpreted references to gifted men dying young as symbols for May Lyttelton. So there appear to be no examples in this category except occasional mentions of a 'broken column'.

Type D: Fish, coral, sea, ice and snow on mountain peaks, mountain references, broken column, brown monk, etc.

Laura Lyttelton

Type A: names of Laura and her husband Alfred, her Peacock Memorial in Mells Church, the bequeathing of her cradle to Lady Elcho, Easter Eve, etc.

Type B: Dido, Cleopatra, Rosamund, a Siren, a Mermaid, Circe, Dolores, Helen of Troy, a Will o' the Wisp, a Wizard of Delight, etc.

Type C: Panopticon Sphaerae, Volatile Ferrum, etc.

Type D: Peacock feather, Ophelia, general flower references, etc.

Henry Coombe-Tennant

Type A: It is interesting that there are none in this category which go across the automatists.

Type B: references in the *Aeneid* and Horace to Augustus and the Golden Age, Epiphany, the Magi, the Angels of the Annunciation, etc.

Type C: all references in scripts to psychological eugenics and the failed prototypes, Antony and Christopher Lyttelton, etc.

Type D: orb and sceptre, seven colours of the rainbow, seven notes of the scale and the octave, seven stars, seven pillars of wisdom, promised land, etc.

There is not space to explain all the allusions in this book. With modern reference books and internet access it is a fairly painless exercise to see why the early assessors of the scripts thought the symbols relevant and persuasive. Take Artemis, for example. She was concerned with virginity and the transition of women to married life. She was linked to the Greek moon goddess Selene and the Roman moon goddess Diana (Howatson 2011: 76). This clearly chimes with much of the May Lyttelton symbolism.

Archives

Society for Psychical Research archive. Cambridge University Library, Cambridge: SPR 1/1, 2/1, etc. This archive includes: Kremer papers (not fully catalogued at time of consulting), Osborne Leonard papers, Oliver Lodge papers.

American Society for Psychical Research archive. New York.

Tennant and Coombe-Tennant family papers. West Glamorgan Archives, Swansea.

Winifred Coombe-Tennant Papers. Houghton Library Harvard University (uncatalogued at time of consulting).

Balfour family papers. The Scottish National Archives, Edinburgh. Online access.

Wren Library, Trinity College, Cambridge: papers include those of F.W.H. Myers, W.H. Salter, and C.D. Broad.

Kipling Archive. University of Sussex.

Royal Museum for Central Africa (Stanley/Tennant papers).

Trix Fleming/Maud Diver letters. Professor R. Crane, University of Tasmania.

The printed books of original scripts and commentaries on them by the SPR Group (Gerald Balfour, Alice Johnson, J.G. Piddington, and Margaret Verrall: there are thirty one volumes) are included in chronological order in the bibliography. Roy (2008: 569–70) lists a number of locations where complete sets are held. The most accessible sets are those in the Cambridge University Library and the Wren Library at Trinity College. Detailed extracts from the original scripts and commentaries thereon require membership of the Society for Psychical Research in order to study them. See Important Note on the Selection, Presentation and Assessment of Material.

Select Bibliography and References

Note: when two dates are given, the earlier is the first edition and the later is the one cited. The automatic writing scripts (with the exception of Geraldine Cummins') have been listed under the editor's name, given the sheer amount of editing, commentary, and notation added to them by Gerald Balfour and J.G. Piddington.

Adams, R.J.Q. (2007) *Balfour: The Last Grandee*, London: John Murray.
Aldcroft, C.C. (1985-86) Is the Hope, Star and Browning cross-correspondence a prophecy of Auschwitz?, *Journal of the Society for Psychical Research*, 53, pp. 31-37.
Allen, C. (2007) *Kipling Sahib: India and the Making of Rudyard Kipling*, London: Little, Brown.
Almeder, R. (1992) *Death and Personal Survival: The Evidence for Life after Death*, Maryland: Littlefield Adams.
Almeder, R. (1996) Recent responses to survival research, *Journal of Scientific Exploration*, 10, pp. 495-517.
Alvarado, C.S. (1989a) Nineteenth century medical explanations of psychic phenomena, *Parapsychology Review*, 20, pp. 4-7.
Alvarado, C.S. (1989b) Dissociation and state-specific psychophysiology during the nineteenth century, *Dissocation*, 2, pp. 160-168.
Alvarado, C.S. (2009) Discussions of telepathy and nonphysicality by early members of the Society for Psychical Research, *Psypioneer*, pp. 373-378.
Alvarado, C.S. (2016) Introduction: Classic Text, No. 107. Joseph Maxwell on mediumistic personifications, *History of Psychiatry*, 27 (3), pp. 350-366.
Annan, N. (1955) The intellectual aristocracy, in Plumb, J.H. (ed.) *Studies in Social History: A Tribute to G.M. Trevelyan*, pp. 242-287, London: Longmans, Green.
Ankers, A.R. (1988) *The Pater: John Lockwood Kipling, His Life and Times 1837-1911*, Kent: Hawthorns Publications.
Anon (1865) *Routledge's Every Boys Annual*, London: Edmund Routledge.

Anon (1882) Objects of the Society, *Proceedings of the Society for Psychical Research*, 1, pp. 3-6.

Anon (1902) Private meeting for members and associates, *Journal of the Society for Psychical Research*, 10, pp. 291-295.

Anon (1905-1906) Opening of an envelope containing a posthumous note left by Mr. Myers, *Journal of the Society for Psychical Research*, 12, pp. 11-13.

Anon (1930) Sir Arthur Conan Doyle's resignation, *Journal of the Society for Psychical Research*, 26, pp. 45-52.

Anon (1950) Leonora Piper, *Journal of the Society for Psychical Research*, 35, pp. 341-344.

Anon (1959) Mrs W.H. Salter, *Journal of the Society for Psychical Research*, 40, pp. 98-99.

Appignanesi, L. (2008) *Mad,Bad and Sad: A History of Women and the Mind Doctors from 1800 to the Present*, London: Virago.

Asquith, M. (1920) *The Autobiography of Margot Asquith*, 2 Vols., Thornton Butterworth.

Asprem, E. (2014) *The Problem of Disenchantment: Scientific Naturalism and Esoteric Discourse 1900-1939*, Leiden: Brill.

Baggini, J. (2015/2016) *Freedom Regained: The Possibility of Free Will*, London: Granta Books.

Baird, A.T. (1949) *Richard Hodgson: The Story of a Psychical Researcher and His Times*, London: Psychic Press.

Balfour, A.J. (1881) Professor Watson on transcendentalism, *Mind*, 6 (22), pp. 260-266.

Balfour, A.J. (1884) Green's Metaphysics of Knowledge, *Mind*, 9 (33), pp. 73-92.

Balfour, A.J. (1894) Address by the President, *Proceedings of the Society for Psychical Research*, 10, pp. 2-13.

Balfour, F. (1930) *Ne Obliviscaris*, 2 Vols., London: Hodder and Stoughton.

Balfour, G.W. (1906) Presidential address, *Proceedings of the Society for Psychical Research*, 19, pp. 373-396.

Balfour, G.W. (1909) Psychical research and current doctrines of mind and body, *The Hibbert Journal*, pp. 543-561.

Balfour, G.W. (1911) Professor Pigou on cross-correspondences, *Proceedings of the Society for Psychical Research*, 25, pp. 38-56.

Balfour, G.W. (ed.) (1914) *Mrs Willett's Automatic Phenomena*, Vol. III, privately printed.

Balfour, G.W. (1914-15) [Statius] Some recent scripts affording evidence of personal survival, *Proceedings of the Society for Psychical Research*, 27, pp. 221-243.

Balfour, G.W. (1918a) The Ear of Dionysius: further scripts affording evidence of personal survival, *Proceedings of the Society for Psychical Research*, 29, pp. 197–243.

Balfour, G.W. (1918b) The Ear of Dionysius: a reply, *Proceedings of the Society for Psychical Research*, 29, pp. 270–286.

Balfour, G.W. (ed.) (1920) *Mrs. Willett's Automatic Phenomena*, Vol. IV, privately printed.

Balfour, G.W. (1927) *Notes and Excursuses: List of Passages in the Scripts of 1901–1924 with an introduction and commentary*, Vol. II, privately printed.

Balfour, G.W. (ed.) (1928) *Mrs. Willett's Automatic Phenomena*, Vol. V, privately printed.

Balfour, G.W. (1935) A study of the psychological aspects of Winifred Coombe-Tennant's mediumship and of the statements of the communicators concerning process, *Proceedings of the Society for Psychical Research*, 43, pp. 41–318.

Balfour, G.W. (ed.) (1938) *Mrs. Willett's Automatic Phenomena*, Vol. VI, privately printed.

Balfour, J. (1958–1960) The 'Palm Sunday' case: new light on an old love story, *Proceedings of the Society for Psychical Research*, 52, pp. 79–267.

Barczewski, S.L. (2000) *Myth and National Identity in Nineteenth-Century Britain: The legends of King Arthur and Robin Hood*, New York: Oxford University Press.

Barrett, D.V. (2001) *The New Believers: Sects, 'Cults' and Alternative Religions*, London: Cassell.

Barrett, W.F. (1911/2006) *Psychical Research*, Montana: Kessinger.

Barrett, W.F. (1917) *On the Threshold of the Unseen: An Examination of the Phenomena of Spiritualism and of the Evidence for Survival After Death*, London: Kegan Paul, Trench and Trubner.

Barrett, W.F. (1924) Some reminiscences of fifty years' psychical research, *Proceedings of the Society for Psychical Research*, 34, pp. 275–297.

Barrington, M.R. (1965–1966) Swan on a black sea: how much could Miss Cummins have known?, *Journal of the Society for Psychical Research*, 43, pp. 289–300.

Bates, E.K. (1906) Leonora Piper and her controls, *Occult Review: A Monthly Magazine Devoted to the Investigation of Supernormal Phenomena and the Study of Psychological Problems*, 3 (3), pp. 136–143.

Bayfield, M.A. (1914–15) [Statius] Some recent scripts affording evidence of personal survival, *Proceedings of the Society for Psychical Research*, 27, pp. 244–249.

Becker, C.B. (1993) *Paranormal Experience and Survival of Death*, New York: State University of New York Press.

Beard, M. (2000) *The Invention of Jane Harrison*, Cambridge: Harvard University Press.

Beard, M. (2015) *SPQR: A History of Ancient Rome*, London: Profile Books.
Beard, P. (ed.) (1987) *The Barbanell Report Transmitted to Marie Cherrie*, Norwich: Pilgrim Books.
Becher, T. and Trowler, P.R. (1989/2001) *Academic Tribes and Territories*, Buckingham: Society for Research into Higher Education and Open University Press.
Beer, J. (1998) *Providence and Love: Studies in Wordsworth, Channing, Myers, George Eliot, and Ruskin*, Oxford: Oxford University Press.
Beer, J. (2003) *Post-Romantic Consciousness: Dickens to Plath*, Basingstoke: Palgrave Macmillan.
Beischel, J. and Rock, A. (2009) Addressing the survival versus psi debate through process-focused mediumship research, *Journal of Parapsychology*, 73, pp. 71-90.
Beischel, J. (2010) The reincarnation of mediumship research, *Edgescience*, 3, pp. 10-12.
Beloff, J. (1993) *Parapsychology: A Concise History*, London: Athlone Press.
Benson, A.C. (1911) *The Leaves of the Tree: Studies in Biography*, London: Smith, Elder.
Benson, E.F. (1930) *As We Were: A Victorian Peep-Show*, London: Longmans, Green.
Bentley, M. (2001) *Lord Salisbury's World: Conservative Environments in Late-Victorian Britain*, Cambridge: Cambridge University Press.
Berger, A.S. (1987) *Aristocracy of the Dead: New Findings in Postmortem Survival*, North Carolina: McFarland.
Berger, A.S. (1988) *Lives and Letters in American Parapsychology: A Biographical History, 1850-1987*, North Carolina: McFarland.
Birkenhead, Lord. (1978) *Rudyard Kipling*, London: Weidenfeld and Nicolson.
Blackmore, S. (2003) *Consciousness: An Introduction*, London: Hodder & Stoughton.
Bobbit, M. (1960) *With Dearest Love to All: The Life and Letters of Lady Jebb*, London: Faber and Faber.
Boddington, H. (1947/1995) *The University of Spiritualism*, Stansted: Psychic Press.
Bolt, R. (2011/2012) *The Impossible Life of Mary Benson: The Extraordinary Story of a Victorian Wife*, London: Atlantic Books.
Borgia, A. (1954) Foreword, Anderson, J., *Life in the World Unseen*, London: Odhams Press.
Bradley, A. (1901/1910) *A Commentary on Tennyson's In Memoriam*, London: Macmillan.
Braude, S.E. (1978) Telepathy, *Nous*, 12, pp. 267-301.
Braude, S.E. (1986) *The Limits of Influence: Psychokinesis and the Philosophy of Science*, London: Routledge and Kegan Paul.

Braude, S.E. (1995) *First Person Plural: Multiple Personality and the Philosophy of Mind*, Maryland: Rowman and Littlefield.
Braude, S.E. (2003) *Immortal Remains: The Evidence for Life after Death*, Maryland: Rowman and Littlefield.
Braude, S.E. (2013) The possibility of mediumship: philosophical considerations, in Rock, A.J. (ed.), foreword, Storm, L., *The Survival Hypothesis: Essays on Mediumship*, pp. 21–39, Jefferson: McFarland.
Broad, C.D. (1925) *The Mind and its Place in Nature*, London: Kegan Paul.
Broad, C.D. (1962) *Lectures on Psychical Research*, London: Routledge and Kegan Paul.
Broad, C.D. (1953/2010) *Religion, Philosophy and Psychical Research: Selected Essays*, Abingdon: Routledge.
Broad, C.D. (1959) Mrs W.H. Salter, *Journal of the Society for Psychical Research*, 40, pp. 129–130.
Broad, C.D., et al. (1970) W.H. Salter, *Journal of the Society for Psychical Research*, 45, pp. 203–211.
Brookes-Smith, C. (1964) A humanist reaction to S.P.R. literature, *Journal of the Society for Psychical Research*, pp. 45–56.
Brown, A.W. (1948/1973) *The Metaphysical Society: Victorian Minds in Crisis 1869–1880*, New York: Octagon Books.
Browning, O. (1910) *Memories of Sixty Years at Eton, Cambridge & Elsewhere*, London: Bodley Head.
Burd, A. van (1982) *Ruskin, Lady Mount-Temple and the Spiritualists*, London: Brentham Press.
Burrow, J.W. (2000) *The Crisis of Reason: European Thought 1848–1914*, Newhaven and London: Yale University Press.
Burt, C. (1975) Gregory, A. (ed.) *ESP and Psychology*, London: Weidenfeld and Nicoloson.
Bush, J. (2000) *Edwardian Ladies and Imperial Power*, Leicester: Leicester University Press.
Cannadine, D. (1990/2005) *The Decline and Fall of the British Aristocracy*, London: Penguin Books.
Cardena, E. and Winkelman, M. (eds.) (2011) *Altering Consciousness: Multidisciplinary Perspectives*, 2 Vols., Santa Barbara: Praeger.
Cardena, E., Lynn, S.J. and Krippner, S. (eds.) (2014) *Varieties of Anomalous Experience: Examining the Scientific Evidence, (2nd Ed.)*, Washington: American Psychological Association.
Cardena, E., Palmer, J. and Marcusson-Clavertz, D. (eds.) (2015) *Parapsychology: A Handbook for the 21st Century*, North Carolina: McFarland.
Carey, J. (1992) *The Intellectual and the Masses: Pride and Prejudice among the Literary Intelligentsia, 1880–1939*, London: Faber and Faber.
Carpenter, J.C. (2012) *First Sight: ESP and Parapsychology in Everyday Life*, Lanham: Rowman & Littlefield.

Carrington, H., et al. (1914–15) [Statius] A discussion of the Willett scripts, *Proceedings of the Society for Psychical Research*, 27, pp. 458–491.

Carter, C. (2012) *Science and the Afterlife Experience: Evidence for the Immortality of Consciousness*, Vermont: Inner Traditions.

Cerullo, J.J. (1982) *The Secularisation of the Soul: Psychical Research in Modern Britain*, Philadelphia: Institute for the Study of Human Issues.

Chevalier, J. and Gheerbant, A. (1969/1996) Buchanan-Brown, J. (trans.), *The Penguin Dictionary of Symbols*, London: Penguin.

Childs, D.J. (2001) *Modernism and Eugenics: Woolf, Eliot, Yeats, and the Culture of Degeneration*, Cambridge: Cambridge University Press.

Clennell, W.H. (1966) *Index to Cross-Correspondence Scripts*, Vol. 1: Wren Library, Salter C/1/1.

Clennell, W.H. (1967) *Index to Cross-Correspondence Scripts*, Vol. 2: Wren Library, Salter C/1/2.

Coleman, M.H. (1997–8) [cross-correspondences et al.] *Journal of the Society for Psychical Research*, 62, pp. 372–375.

Coleman, M.H. (1998) [Letter on Leonora Piper] *Journal of the Society for Psychical Research*, 63, pp. 62–63.

Collini, S. (1991) *Public Moralists: Political Thought and Intellectual Life in Britain 1850–1930*, Oxford: Clarendon Press.

Crabtree, A. (1993) *From Mesmer to Freud: Magnetic Sleep and the Roots of Psychological Healing*, Newhaven: Yale University Press.

Crabtree, A. (2014) *Memoir of a Trance Therapist*, Victoria: Friesin Press.

Crawford, E. (1999) *The Women's Suffrage Movement: A Reference Guide 1866–1928*, London: UCL Press.

Crookall, R. (1961) *The Supreme Adventure: Analyses of Psychic Communications*, London: James Clarke.

Cuddin, J. (1977/1999) Revised, Preston, C., *The Penguin Dictionary of Literary Terms and Literary Theory*, London: Penguin.

Cummins, G. (1928/1974) *The Scripts of Cleophas: A Reconstruction of Primitive Christian Documents*, London: Psychic Press.

Cummins, G. (1932/1967) *The Road to Immortality*, London: Psychic Press.

Cummins, G. (1935/1952) *Beyond Human Personality*, London: Psychic Press.

Cummins, G. (1965) Tostvig, S. (ed.), Broad, C., Introduction, *Swan on a Black Sea: A Study in Automatic Writing. The Cummins-Willett Scripts*, London: Routledge and Kegan Paul.

Cunningham, P.F. (2012) The content-source problem in modern mediumship research, *Journal of Parapsychology*, 76 (2), pp. 295–319.

Dainton, M. (2014) *Self: Philosophy in Transit*, London: Penguin 2002.

Dakers, C. (1993) *Clouds: The Biography of a Country House*, New Haven: Yale University Press.

Dallas, H.A. (1910) Introduction, Barrett, W.F., *Mors Janua Vitae? A discussion of certain communications purporting to come from Frederic W.H. Myers*, London: William Rider & Son.

Dallas, H.A. (1929) *Comrades on the Homeward Way*, London: Collins.

Darwall-Smith, R. 4/6/2014. Personal communication on J.G. Piddington.

Davis, P. (2002) *The Victorians: The Oxford English Literary History, Volume 8*, Oxford: Oxford University Press.

Deacon, R. (1985) *The Cambridge Apostles: A History of Cambridge University's Elite Intellectual Secret Society*, London: Robert Royce.

De Courcy, A. (2001/2009) *The Viceroy's Daughters: The Lives of the Curzon Sisters*, London: Phoenix.

Demarest, M. 14/6/2013. Personal communication on J.G. Piddington.

Demarest, M. November 2014. Personal communication on Rosalie Thompson.

Dingwall, E.J. (1930-31) Recent developments in psychical research, *Psyche*, XI, pp. 56-64.

Dingwall, E.J. (1985) The need for responsibility in parapsychology: my sixty years in psychical research, in Kurtz, P. (ed.) *A Handbook of Parapsychology*, pp. 161-174, Buffalo: Prometheus Books.

Dixon, J. (2001) *Divine Feminine: Theosophy and Feminism in England*, Baltimore: Johns Hopkins University Press.

Dodds, E.R. (1934) Why I do not believe in survival, *Proceedings of the Society for Psychical Research*, 35, pp. 147-172.

Dodds, E.R. (1977) *Missing Persons: An Autobiography*, Oxford: Clarendon Press.

Downie, A. (2015) *Stalin's Englishman: The Lives of Guy Burgess*, London: Hodder & Stoughton.

Doyle, A.C. (1926/2001) *The History of Spiritualism*, 2 Vols., Surrey: Spiritual Truth Press.

Ducasse, C.J. (1961) *A Critical Examination of the Belief in a Life After Death*, Michigan: University of Michigan.

Ducasse, C.J. (1962) What would constitute conclusive evidence of survival after death?, *Journal of the Society for Psychical Research*, 41, pp. 401-406.

Eagleman, D. (2015) *The Brain: The Story of You*, Edinburgh: Canongate.

Egremont, M. (1977) *The Cousins: The Friendship, Opinions and Activities of Wilfred Scawen Blunt and George Wyndham*, London: Collins.

Egremont, M. (1980) *Balfour: A Life of Arthur James Balfour*, London: Collins.

Eisenbeiss, W. and Hassler, D. (2006) An assessment of ostensible communications with a deceased grandmaster as evidence for survival, *Journal of the Society for Psychical Research*, 70, pp. 65-97.

Ellenberger, H.F. (1970/1994) *The Discovery of the Unconscious*, London: Fontana.

Ellenberger, N.W. (1982) The Souls and London "Society" at the end of the nineteenth century, *Victorian Studies*, 25 (2), pp. 133–160.

Ellenberger, N.W. (2015) *Balfour's World: Aristocracy and Political Culture at the Fin de Siècle*, Woodbridge: The Boydell Press.

Ellis, A. (1949) *"Vitesse": The Story of 'Continental Express' 1849–1949*, London: Burrup, Mathieson.

Epperson, G. (1997) *The Mind of Edmund Gurney*, New Jersey: Associated University Press.

Feilding, E. (1963) Introduction, Dingwall, E.J., *Sittings with Eusapia Palladino and Other Studies*, New York: University Books.

Fernyhough, C. (2012/2013) *Pieces of Light: The New Science of Memory*, London: Profile Books.

Festinger, L., Riecken, H. & Schacter, S. (1956) *When Prophecy Fails: A Social and Psychological Study of a Modern Group that Predicted the Destruction of the World*, Minnesota: University of Minnesota Press.

Fisher, B. (2014a) *Trix – The Other Kipling: The Kipling Journal*, 88 (357), pp. 44–57.

Fisher, B. (2014b) *Personal communication*, [Draft chapter on Trix Kipling and the SPR].

Flanders, J. (2001/2002) *A Circle of Sisters: Alice Kipling, Georgiana Burne-Jones, Agnes Poynter and Louise Baldwin*, London: Penguin Books.

Fletcher, C. (2016) *The Black Prince of Florence: The Spectacular Life and Treacherous World of Alessandro de' Medici*, London: The Bodley Head.

Fletcher, S. (1997) *Victorian Girls: Lord Lyttelton's Daughters*, London: Hambledon Press.

Flew, A. (1953) *A New Approach to Psychical Research*, London: Watts.

Flournoy, T. (1911) Carrington, H. (trans.) *Spiritism and Psychology*, New York: Harper.

Flournoy, T. (1900/1963) Introduction, Chakiri, C., Vermilye, D. (trans.) *From India to the Planet Mars*, New York: University Books.

Fodor, N. (1934/1969) *Encyclopedia of Psychic Science*, New York: University Books.

Fontana, D. (2005) *Is there an Afterlife? A Comprehensive Overview of the Evidence*, Hampshire: O Books.

Foster, R. (1997) *W.B.Yeats: A Life. 1. The Apprentice Mage 1865–1914*, Oxford: Oxford University Press.

Foster, R. (2003) *W.B.Yeats: A Life. II. The Arch-Poet 1915–1939*, Oxford: Oxford University Press.

Freud, S. (1912) A note on the unconscious in psychoanalysis, *Proceedings of the Society for Psychical Research*, 26, pp. 312–318.

Galvan, J. (n.d.) *Tennyson's Ghosts: The Psychical Research Case of the Cross-Correspondences, 1901–c.1936*, [Online], www.branchcollective.org.

Galvan, J. (2010) *The Sympathetic Medium: Feminine Channeling, the Occult, and Communication Technologies 1859-1919*, Ithaca: Cornell University Press.

Gardner, H. (1984/1985) *Frames of Mind: The Theory of Multiple Intelligences*, London: Paladin.

Gauld, A. (1964) Frederic Myers and 'Phyllis', *Journal of the Society for Psychical Research* 42, pp. 316-323.

Gauld, A. (1968) *The Founders of Psychical Research*, London: Routledge and Kegan Paul.

Gauld, A., et al. (1971) In Memoriam Professor C.D. Broad 1887-1971, *Journal of the Society for Psychical Research*, 46, pp. 103-113.

Gauld, A. (1982/1983) *Mediumship and Survival: A Century of Investigations*, London: Paladin.

Gauld, A. (1992/1995) *A History of Hypnotism*, Cambridge: Cambridge University Press.

Gauld, A. (2014) Two cases from the lost years of Leonora Piper, *Journal of the Society for Psychical Research*, 78 (2), pp. 65-84.

Gauld, A. (2015) Essay review of the survival hypothesis, *Journal of Scientific Exploration*, 29 (2), pp. 305-330.

Gaythorpe, E. (ed.) (1950) *Unpublished F.W.H.Myers' Scripts (selected from the Richmond material). C.P.S. Paper 4*, London: College of Psychic Studies.

Gladstone, M. (1930) Masterman, L. (ed.) *Mary Gladstone (Mrs Drew): Her Diaries and Letters*, London: Methuen.

Goldhill, S. (2011) *Victorian Culture and Classical Antiquity. Art, Opera, Fiction, and the Proclamation of Modernity*, Princeton: Princeton University Press.

Goldney, K. (14/1/1966) [*Letter to W.H. Salter re Geraldine Cummins*] Salter D1/10/1-3.

Goodenow, J. (1923/2012) Introduction, Ellis-Behnke, J., Afterword, Boylan, G.D., *Letters to Juliet: Is there Life after Death? Letters delivered by telepathic communication by the late English author Frederic W.H. Myers*, Minus the Ink. Digital Publishing Group.

Goodrick-Clarke, N. (2008) *The Western Esoteric Traditions: A Historical Introduction*, Oxford: Oxford University Press.

Gray, J. (2011) *The Immortalization Commission: Science and the Strange Quest to Cheat Death*, London: Allen Lane.

Graves, R. (1955/2000) Introduction, McLeish, K., *The Greek Myths*, 2 Vols., London: Folio Society.

Griffin, D.R. (1997) *Parapsychology, Philosophy and Spirituality: A Postmodern Exploration*, New York: State University of New York Press.

Gurney, E., Myers, F.W.H. and Podmore, F. (1886) *Phantasms of the Living*, 2 Vols., London: Trubner.

Gurney, E. (1887a) Peculiarities of certain post-hypnotic states, *Proceedings of the Society for Psychical Research*, 4, pp. 268–323.

Gurney, E. (1887b) Stages of hypnotic memory, *Proceedings of the Society for Psychical Research*, 4, pp. 515–531.

Gutierrez, C. (ed.) (2015) *Handbook of Spiritualism and Channeling*, Leiden: Brill.

Hackett, J.T. (1919/1920) *My Commonplace Book*, London: Fisher Unwin.

Hacking, I. (1995) *Rewriting the Soul: Multiple Personality and the Sciences of Memory*, Princeton: Princeton University Press.

Hall, E. (2008/2012) *The Return of Ulysses: A Cultural History of Homer's Odyssey*, London: I.B.Tauris.

Hall, E. (2015) *Introducing the Ancient Greeks*, London: The Bodley Head.

Hall, M.P. (2003) *The Secret Teachings of All Ages*, New York: Tarcher.

Halliday, R. and Murdie, A. (2010) *Cambridge Ghosts*, Suffolk: Arima Publishing.

Hamer, M. (2012) *Kipling and Trix*, Twickenham: Aurora Metro Books.

Hamilton, M.L. (1969) *Is Survival a Fact? Studies of deep-trance automatic scripts and the bearing of intentional actions by the trance personalities on the question of human survival*, London: Psychic Press.

Hamilton, T. (2009) *Immortal Longings: F.W.H. Myers and the Victorian Search for Life after Death*, Exeter: Imprint Academic.

Hamilton, T. (2011) F.W.H. Myers and the synthetic society. Christianity and psychical research: a historical case study, in *Papers presented at the Annual Conference of The Churches' Fellowship for Psychical and Spiritual Studies*, pp. 46–54.

Hamilton, T. (2012) *Tell My Mother I'm Not Dead: A Case Study in Mediumship Research*, Exeter: Imprint Academic.

Hamilton, T. (2013a) F.W.H. Myers, William James and Spiritualism, in Moreman, C.M. (ed.) *The Spiritualist Movement: Speaking with the Dead in America and around the World*, Vol. 1., pp. 97–127, Santa Barbara: Praeger.

Hamilton, T. (2013b) The cross-correspondence automatic writings and the Spiritualists, in Moreman, C.M. (ed.) *The Spiritualist Movement: Speaking with the Dead in America and around the World*, Vol. 2, pp. 265–282, Santa Barbara: Praeger.

Hamilton, T. (2016) F.W.H. Myers, *Online Encyclopedia of the Society for Psychical Research*.

Hamilton, T. (in press) The cross-correspondence automatic writings, *Online Encyclopedia of the Society for Psychical Research*.

Hardie, P. (2014) *The Last Trojan Hero: A Cultural History of Virgil's Aeneid*, London: I.B. Tauris.

Harrington, A. (1987) *Medicine, Mind and the Double Brain: A Study in Nineteenth-Century Thought*, Princeton: Princeton University Press.

Harris, P. (1989) *Life in a Scottish Country House: The Story of A.J. Balfour and Whittingehame House*, Whittingehame House: Whittingehame House Publishing.

Harris, J. (1993) *Private Lives, Public Spirit: A Social History of Britain 1870-1914*, Oxford: Oxford University Press.

Harrison, J. (1917) In Memoriam—Mrs A.W. Verrall, *Proceedings of the Society for Psychical Research*, 29, pp. 376-385.

Harrison, J. (1925) *Reminiscences of a Student's Life*, London: The Hogarth Press.

Harrison, S. (n.d.) *Horace and the Construction of the English Victorian Gentleman*, conference paper, accessed 9/1/2017.

Hart, H. (1959) *The Engima of Survival: The Case For and Against an After Life*, London: Rider.

Hassin, R.R., Uleman, J.S. & Bargh, J. (eds.) (2005) *The New Unconscious*, Oxford: Oxford University Press.

Hastings, A. (1991) *With the Tongues of Men and Angels: A Study of Channeling*, Fort Worth: Holt, Rhinehart etc.

Haynes, R. (1982) *The Society for Psychical Research 1882-1982: A History*, London: Macdonald.

Hazelgrove, J. (2000) *Spiritualism and British Society between the Wars*, Manchester: Manchester University Press.

Heath, D. (1998) *Roden Noel 1834-1894: A Wide Angle*, London: DB Books.

Hearnshaw, L.S. (1964) *A Short History of British Psychology 1840-1940*, London: Methuen.

Heitland, W.E. (1926) *After Many Years*, Cambridge: Cambridge University Press.

Hellman, J. (2002) *Communitarian Third Way: Alexandre Marc and Ordre Nouveau, 1930-2000*, Toronto/Montreal: McGill-Queen's Press.

Heywood, R. (1959) *The Sixth Sense: An Inquiry into Extra-Sensory Perception*, London: Chatto & Windus.

Heywood, R. (1959-60) The Palm Sunday case: a tangle for unravelling, *Journal of the Society for Psychical Research*, 40, pp. 285-291.

Highet, G. (1949) *The Classical Tradition: Greek and Roman Influences on Western Literature*, Oxford: Clarendon Press.

Hilton, T. (2002) *John Ruskin*, Newhaven and London: Yale University Press.

Hinshelwood, R.D. (1991) Psychodynamic psychiatry before World War 1, in Berios, G. and Freeman, H. (eds.) *150 Years of British Psychiatry*, pp. 197-205, London: Royal College of Psychiatrists.

Hinshelwood, R.D. (1995) Psychoanalysis in Britain: points of cultural access 1893-1918, *International Journal of Psychoanalysis*, 76, pp. 136-151.

Hoare, P. (2005) *England's Lost Eden: Adventures in a Victorian Utopia*, London: Fourth Estate.

Holt, H. (1914) *On the Cosmic Relations*, 2 Vols., Boston and New York: Houghton Mifflin.

Hopkinson-Ball, T. (2007) Foreword, Gilbert, R.A., *The Rediscovery of Glastonbury: Frederick Bligh Bond Architect of the New Age*, Stroud: Sutton Publishing.

Horace (2004/2012) Rudd, N. (ed. and trans.) *Odes and Epodes*, Cambridge: Harvard University Press.

Howard, J.N. (1964) Eleanor Mildred Sidgwick and the Rayleighs, *Applied Optics*, 3 (10), pp. 1120-1122.

Howarth, T.E.B. (1978) *Cambridge Between Two Wars*, London: William Collins.

Howatson, H.C. (1937/2011) *The Oxford Companion to Classical Literature*, Oxford: Oxford University Press.

Hude, A. (1912-13) The Latin Message Experiment, *Proceedings of the Society for Psychical Research*, 26, pp. 147-173.

Hude, A. (1913) *The Evidence for Communication with the Dead*, London: Fisher Unwin.

Hudson, D.R.C. (2003) *The Ireland That We Made*, Akron: Akron University Press.

Hudson, L. (1966/1972) *Contrary Imaginations: A Psychological Study of the English Schoolboy*, Harmondsworth: Penguin.

Hutton, R. (1996) *The Stations of the Sun: A History of the Ritual Year in Britain*, Oxford: Oxford University Press.

Hynes, S. (1968) *The Edwardian Turn of Mind*, Princeton: Princeton University Press.

Hyslop, J.H. (1905) *Science and a Future Life*, Boston: Herbert B. Turner.

Hyslop, J.H. (1911) President G. Stanley Hall's and Dr Amy E. Tanner's *Studies in Spiritism*, *Journal of the American Society for Psychical Research*, V (1), pp. 1-99.

Hyslop, J.H. (1911) A review of recent English Proceedings, *Journal of the American Society for Psychical Research*, V (3), pp. 142-216.

Hyslop. J.H. (1919) *Contact With the Other World: The Latest Evidence as to Communication with the Dead*, New York: Century.

Inglis, B. (1984) *Science and Parascience: A History of the Paranormal, 1914-1939*, London: Hodder and Stoughton.

Irwin, H.J. and Watt, C. (2007) *An Introduction to Parapsychology*, Jefferson: McFarland.

Irwin, H.J. (2009) Foreword, Watt, C. and Wiseman, R., *The Psychology of Paranormal Belief: A Researcher's Handbook*, Hatfield: University of Hertfordshire.

Irwin, H.J. (2015) Thinking style and the making of a paranormal disbelief, *Journal of the Society for Psychical Research*, 79 (3), pp. 129-139.

Iverson, J. (1992) *In Search of the Dead*, London: BBC Books.

Jacoff, R. (1993/2000) *The Cambridge Companion to Dante*, Cambridge: Cambridge University Press.

Jalland, P. (1986) *Women, Marriage and Politics 1860–1914*, Oxford: Clarendon Press.

Jalland, P. (1996) *Death in the Victorian Family*, Oxford: Oxford University Press.

James, W. (1960) Murphy, G. and Ballou, R.O. (eds.) *William James on Psychical Research*, New York: Viking Press.

James, W. (1986) Burkhard, F.W., Bowers, F. and Skrupskelis, I.K. (eds.) *Essays in Psychical Research*, Harvard: Harvard University Press.

Jenson, O. and Munt, S.R. (eds.) (2013) *The Ashgate Research Companion to Paranormal Cultures*, Farnham: Ashgate.

Joad, C.E.M. (1949) *Shaw*, London: Victor Gollancz.

Johnson, A. (1907-09) On the automatic writing of Mrs. Holland, *Proceedings of the Society for Psychical Research*, 21, pp. 166–391.

Johnson, A. (1910a) Second report on Mrs. Holland's script, *Proceedings of the Society for Psychical Research*, 24, pp. 201–263.

Johnson, A. (1910b) Third report on Mrs. Holland's script, *Proceedings of the Society for Psychical Research*, 25, pp. 218–303.

Johnson, A. (1914–15) A reconstruction of some 'concordant automatisms', *Proceedings of the Society for Psychical Research*, 27, pp. 1–156.

Johnson, A. (ed.) (1916a) *Mrs. Holland's Script*, Vol. I, privately printed.

Johnson, A. (ed.) (1916b) *Mrs. Holland's Script*, Vol II, privately printed.

Johnson, A. (1927) *George William Johnson: Civil Servant and Social Worker*, Cambridge: privately printed.

Johnson, A. (1934a) "Mrs Holland" (Trix Fleming, née Kipling), Salter A6/4/10/1-16.

Johnson, A. (1934b) *The Gurney "Control" in Holland Script*, Salter A6/4/3/1-12.

Johnson, A. (1934c) [*Gurney's message in Piper Script to Winifred Coombe-Tennant*], Salter A6/4/4/1-12.

Johnson, A. (1935) [*A Letter re Gurney's Message in Piper Script to Winifred Coombe-Tennant*], Salter A6/4/1-3.

Johnson, A. (1936) Mrs Henry Sidgwick's work in psychical research, *Proceedings of the Society for Psychical Research*, 44, pp. 53–93.

Johnson, G.M. (2006) *Dynamic Psychology in Modernist British Fiction*, Basingstoke: Palgrave Macmillan.

Johnson, G.M. (2015) *Mourning and Mysticism in First World War Literature and Beyond: Grappling with Ghosts*, Basingstoke: PalgraveMacmillan.

Johnson, R.C. (1964) *The Light and the Gate*, London: Hodder and Stoughton.

Jolly, W.P. (1975) *Sir Oliver Lodge: Psychical Researcher and Scientist*, New Jersey: Associated University Presses.

Jones, L.J. (1928) Presidential address, *Proceedings of the Society for Psychical Research*, 38, pp. 17–48.

Katz, S.L. (2003) *Dearest of Geniuses: A Life of Theodate Pope Riddle*, East Hartford: Tide-Mark Press.

Keen, M. (1997-8) [cross-correspondences et al.], *Journal of the Society for Psychical Research*, 62, pp. 473–475.

Keen, M., Ellison, A. and Fontana, D. (1999) The Scole Report, *Proceedings of the Society for Psychical Research*, 58, pp. 150–392.

Keen, M. and Roy, A.E. (2004) Chance coincidence in the cross-correspondences, *Journal of the Society for Psychical Research*, 68, pp. 57–59.

Kelly, E.W. (1910) Some directions for mediumship research, *Journal of Scientific Exploration*, 24, pp. 247–282.

Kelly, E.F., Kelly, E.W., Crabtree, A., Gauld, A., Grosso, M. and Greyson, B. (2007) *Irreducible Mind: Towards a Psychology for the 21st Century*, Maryland: Rowman and Littlefield.

Kelly, E.F., Crabtree, A. and Marshall, P. (eds.) (2015) *Beyond Physicalism: Towards Reconciliation of Science and Spirituality*, Lanham: Rowman & Litlefield.

Keynes, G. (ed.) (1968) *The Letters of Rupert Brooke*, London: Faber and Faber.

Keynes, M.E. (1976) *A House by the River: Newnham Grange to Darwin College*, Cambridge: Heffers.

Kingsford, S.M. (1920) *Psychical Research for the Plain Man*, London: Kegan Paul.

Klimo, J. (1998) *Channeling.Investigations on Receiving Information from Paranormal Sources*, Berkeley: North Atlantic Books.

Knight, G.W. (1975) *Jackson Knight: A Biography by G. Wilson Knight*, Oxford: The Alden Press.

Kontou, T. (2009) *Spiritualism and Women's Writing: From the Fin de Siècle to the Neo-Victorian*, Basingstoke: Palgrave Macmillan.

Kontou, T. and Willburn, S. (eds.) (2012) *The Ashgate Research Companion to Nineteenth-Century Spiritualism and the Occult*, Farnham: Ashgate.

Kripal, J.J. (2010/2011) *Authors of the Impossible: The Paranormal and the Sacred*, Chicago: University of Chicago Press.

Krippner, S. and Friedmann, H.L. (eds.) (2010) *Mysterious Minds: The Neurobiology of Psychics, Mediums, and Other Extraordinary People*, Santa Barbara: Praeger.

Krippner, S. and Friedmann, H.L. (eds.) (2010) Foreword, Richards, R., *Debating Psychic Experience: Human Potential or Human Illusion?*, Santa Barbara: Praeger.

Lambert, A. (1984) *Unquiet Souls: The Indian Summer of the British Aristocracy*, London: Macmillan.

Lambert, G.W. (1928) The psychology of Plotinus and its interest to the student of psychical research, *Proceedings of the Society for Psychical Research*, 36, pp. 393–413.

Lambert, G.W. (1959) Frank Podmore, *Journal of the Society for Psychical Research*, 40.

Lambert, G.W. (1965) The Blue Vase, *Proceedings of the Society for Psychical Research*, 54, pp. 233–248.

Lambert, G.W. (1971) Studies in the automatic writing of Margaret Verrall: X. Concluding Reflections, *Journal of the Society for Psychical Research*, 46, pp. 217–221.

Lamont, P. (2004) Spiritualism and a mid-Victorian crisis of evidence, *Historical Journal*, 47, pp. 897–920.

Lamont, P. (2013) *Extraordinary Beliefs: A Historical Approach to a Psychological Problem*, Cambridge: Cambridge University Press.

Larsen, T. (2012) *A People of One Book: The Bible and the Victorians*, Oxford: Oxford University Press.

Lazlo, E. (2004/2007) *Science and the Akashic Field: An Integral Theory of Everything*, Vermont: Inner Traditions.

Leaf, C.M. (1932) *Walter Leaf: Some Chapters of Autobiography with a Memoir*, London: John Murray.

Ledger, S. and Luckhurst, R. (eds.) (2000) *The Fin de Siècle: A Reader in Cultural History c. 1880–1900*, Oxford: Oxford University Press.

Lee, L. (2003/2004) *Trix Kipling's Forgotten Sister*, Peterborough: Forward Press.

Lemprière, J. (1984/1990) *Lempriere's Classical Dictionary: Proper Names Cited by the Ancient Authors*, London: Bracken Books.

Leslie, A. (1973) *Edwardians in Love*, London: Hutchinson.

Lewis, G. (2005) *Edith Somerville: A Biography*, Dublin: Four Courts Press.

Lilienfeld, S.O. and Lynn, S.J. (eds.) (2015) Foreword by Tavris, C., *Science and Paeudoscience in Clinical Psychology*, London: The Guilford Press.

Lodge, O. (1901) In memory of F.W.H. Myers, *Proceedings of the Society for Psychical Research*, 17, pp. 1–12.

Lodge, O. et al. (Myers, Wilson, Hodgson, Johnson, Verrall) (1901–02) Reports of sittings with Mrs Thompson, *Proceedings of the Society for Psychical Research*, 17, pp. 61–244.

Lodge, O. (1905) Opening of an envelope containing a posthumous note left by Mr. Myers, *Journal of the Society for Psychical Research*, pp. 11–13.

Lodge, O. (1909a) Report on some trance communications received chiefly through Leonora Piper, *Proceedings of the Society for Psychical Research*, 23, pp. 127–285.

Lodge, O. (1909b) *The Survival of Man: A Study in Unrecognised Human Faculty*, London: Methuen.

Lodge, O. (1909c) A reply to Professor Pigou's criticism of cross-correspondences, *Journal of the Society for Psychical Research*, pp. 134–136.
Lodge/Pigou (1909d) Letters on Prof. Pigou's criticism of cross-correspondences, *Journal of the Society for Psychical Research*, pp. 161–162.
Lodge, O. (1911) Evidence of classical scholarship and of cross-correspondence in some new automatic writings, *Proceedings of the Society for Psychical Research*, 25, pp. 113–175.
Lodge, O. (1916) *Raymond or Life after Death*, London: Methuen.
Lodge, O. (1918) *Christopher: A Study in Human Personality*, London: Cassell.
Lodge, O. (1922) *Raymond Revised*, London: Methuen.
Lodge, O. (1930) *Conviction of Survival: Two Discourses in Memory of F.W.H. Myers*, London: Methuen.
Lodge, O. (1931) *Past Years: An Autobiography*, London: Hodder & Stoughton.
Lord, P. (2007) *Winifred Coombe-Tennant: A Life through Art*, Aberystwyth: National Library of Wales.
Lord, P. (ed.) (2011) *Between Two Worlds: The Diary of Winifred Coombe-Tennant 1909–1924*, Aberystwyth: National Library of Wales.
Lorimer, D. (1984) *Survival? Body, Mind and Death in the Light of Psychic Experience*, London: Routledge.
Lubenow, W.C. (1998) *The Cambridge Apostles: Liberalism, Imagination and Friendship in British Intellectual and Professional Life*, Cambridge: Cambridge University Press.
Lubenow, W.C. (2005) Intimacy, imagination and the inner dialectics of knowledge communities: The Synthetic Society 1896–1908, in Daunton, M. (ed.) *The Organisation of Knowledge in Victorian Britain*, pp. 357–371, Oxford: Oxford University Press.
Luckhurst, R. (2002) *The Invention of Telepathy 1870–1901*, Oxford: Oxford University Press.
Luckhurst, R. (2008) *The Trauma Question*, London: Routledge.
Lurie, A. (2001) *Familiar Spirits: A Memoir of James Merrill and David Jackson*, London: Viking.
Lycett, A. (2007) *Conan Doyle: The Man Who Created Sherlock Holmes*, London: Weidenfeld and Nicolson.
Lyttelton, E. (1917) *Alfred Lyttelton: An Account of His Life*, London: Longmans, Green and Co.
Lyttelton, E. (1926) *Florence Upton: Painter*, London: Longmans, Green and Co.
Lytton, C. (1925) *Letters of Constance Lytton: Selected and Arranged by Betty Balfour*, London: Heinemann.
MacCarthy, F. (2011) *The Last Pre-Raphaelite: Edward Burne-Jones and the Victorian Imagination*, London: Faber and Faber.
MacInnes, C. (1961) *England, Half English*, London: Macgibbon & Kee.

Mackay, R.F. (1985) *Balfour Intellectual Statesman*, Oxford: Oxford University Press.
Mackenzie, A. (1968) Introduction, Broad, C.D., *Frontiers of the Unknown: The Insights of Psychical Research*, London: Arthur Barker.
Mackenzie, A. (1982) *Hauntings and Apparitions*, London: Heinemann.
Mackenzie, A. (1987) Mrs Zoë Richmond, *Journal of the Society for Psychical Research*, pp. 166–167.
Mackenzie, J. (1986) *The Children of the Souls: A Tragedy of the First World War*, London: Chatto and Windus.
Mackenzie, N. and Mackenzie, J. (1973/1974) *The Time Traveller: The Life of H.G. Wells*, London: Weidenfeld and Nicoloson.
Main, R. (2007) *Revelations of Chance: Synchronicity as Spiritual Experience*, Albany: The State University of New York Press.
Mann, S. (2013) *Aelfrida Tillyard Hints of a Perfect Splendour: A Novel Biography*, Hitchin: Wayment Print and Publishing.
Maraldi, E. (2014) Medium or author? A preliminary model relating dissociation, paranormal belief systems and self-esteem, *Journal of the Society for Psychical Research*, 78 (1), pp. 1–24.
Marsh, E. (1939) *A Number of People: A Book of Reminiscences*, New York: Harper.
Marsh, J. (2008/2010) *The Penguin Book of Classical Myths*, London: Penguin Books.
Martin, M. and Augustine, K. (eds.) (2015) *The Myth of an Afterlife: The Case Against Life after Death*, Lanham: Rowman & Littlefield.
Mauskopf, S.H. and McVaugh, M.R. (1980) Afterword, J.B. and L.E. Rhine, *The Elusive Science: Origins of Experimental Psychical Research*, Baltimore and London: Johns Hopkins.
Maxwell, J. (1912–13) Les correspondances croisées et la méthode expérimentale, *Proceedings of the Society for Psychical Research*, 26, pp. 57–144.
Mayor, J.B., Fowler, W.W. and Conway, R.S. (1907) *Virgil's Messianic Eclogue: Its Meaning, Occasion, & Sources*, London: John Murray.
Mcluhan, R. (2010) *Randi's Prize: What Skeptics Say about the Paranormal, Why They Are Wrong, and Why It Matters*, Leicester: Matador.
[Merrifield, F.] (1903) A sitting with D.D. Home, *Journal of the Society for Psychical Research*, 11, pp. 76–80.
Milbank, A. (1998/2009) *Dante and the Victorians*, Manchester: Manchester University Press.
Mlodinow, L. (2012) *Subliminal: How Your Unconscious Mind Rules Your Behaviour*, New York: Random House.
Mollon, P. (1996/2001) *Multiple Selves, Multiple Voices: Working with Trauma, Violation and Dissociation*, Chichester: Wiley.
Monroe, J. Warne (2008) *Laboratories of Faith: Mesmerism, Spiritism, and Occultism in Modern France*, Ithaca: Cornell University Press.

Moorehead, C. (2000) *Iris Origo: Marchesa of Val d'Orcia*, London: John Murray.

Moreman, C.M. (2003) A re-examination of the possibility of chance coincidence as an alternative explanation for mediumistic communication in the cross-correspondences, *Journal of the Society for Psychical Research*, 67, pp. 225-242.

Moreman, C.M. (2004) [A letter re the cross-correspondences], *Journal of the Society for Psychical Research*, 68, pp. 60-61.

Moreman, C.M. (2010) *Beyond the Threshold: Afterlife Beliefs and Experiences in World Religions*, Lanham: Rowman & Littlefield.

Moreman, C.M. (ed.) (2013) *The Spiritualist Movement: Speaking with the Dead in America and Around the World*, 3 Vols., Santa Barbara: Praeger.

Moreira-Almeida, A. (2012) *Research on Mediumship and the Mind–Brain Relationship*, in Moreira-Almeida, A. and Santos, F.S. (eds.) *Exploring Frontiers of the Mind–Brain Relationship*, pp. 191-213, New York: Springer.

Morgan, S.de. (1863) *From Matter to Spirit: Ten Years' Experience in Spirit Manifestation, Intended as a Guide to Enquirers*, London: Longman.

Moses, W.S. (1883/1912) *Spirit Teachings*, London: London Spiritualist Alliance.

Moyle, F. (2011) *Constance: The Tragic and Scandalous Life of Mrs Oscar Wilde*, London: John Murray.

Muhl, A. (1930) *Automatic Writing: An Approach to the Unconscious*, Dresden: Steinkopff.

Munves, J. (1997) Richard Hodgson, Leonora Piper and 'George Pelham': a centennial reassessment, *Journal of the Society for Psychical Research*, 62, pp. 138-154.

Murphy, G., with Dale, L.A. (1970) *Challenge of Psychical Research: A Primer of Parapsychology*, New York: Harper & Row.

Murphy, M. (1992) *The Future of the Body: Explorations into the Further Evolution of Human Nature*, Los Angeles: Tarcher.

Murray, G. (1902/1904) *Euripides translated into English Rhyming Verse*, London: Longmans.

Myers, A.T. (1888) Recent experiments by M. Charles Richet on telepathic hypnotism, *Journal of the Society for Psychical Research*, 3, pp. 222-226.

Myers, A.T. and Myers, F.W.H. (1893) Mind-cure, faith-cure, and the miracles at Lourdes, *Proceedings of the Society for Psychical Research*, 9, pp. 160-209.

Myers, F.W.H. Papers: Trinity College Library, Cambridge: Myers 1/1, 2/1 etc.

Myers, F.W.H. (1867) *St. Paul*, London: C.J. Clay.

Myers, F.W.H. (1870) *Poems*, Macmillan: London.

Myers, F.W.H. (1879a) Victor Hugo, *Nineteenth Century*, 5, pp. 773-787, 970-995.
Myers, F.W.H. (1879b) Virgil, *Fortnightly Review*, 31, pp. 163-196.
Myers, F.W.H. (1880/1929) *Wordsworth*, London: Macmillan.
Myers, F.W.H. (1881a) Ernest Renan, *Nineteenth Century*, 9, pp. 949-968.
Myers, F.W.H. (1881b) Renan and miracles, *Nineteenth Century*, 10, pp. 90-106.
Myers, F.W.H. (1882a) *Marcus Aurelius Antoninus*, 37, pp. 564-586.
Myers, F.W.H. (1882b) *The Renewal of Youth and Other Poems*, London: Macmillan.
Myers, F.W.H. (1883a) *Essays Classical*, London: Macmillan.
Myers, F.W.H. (1883b/1897) *Essays Modern*, London: Macmillan.
Myers, F.W.H. (1883c) Rossetti, *Cornhill*, 47, pp. 213-224.
Myers, F.W.H. (1884) On a telepathic explanation of some so-called spiritualistic phenomena, *Proceedings of the Society for Psychical Research*, 2, pp. 217-237.
Myers, F.W.H. (1885a) Automatic writing or the rationale of the planchette, *Contemporary Review*, 47, pp. 233-249.
Myers, F.W.H. (1885b) Human personality in the light of hypnotic suggestion, *Proceedings of the Society for Psychical Research*, 4, pp. 1-24.
Myers, F.W.H. (1885c) Automatic writing—II, *Proceedings of the Society for Psychical Research*, pp. 1-63.
Myers, F.W.H. (1886a) On telepathic hypnotism, and its relation to other forms of hypnotic suggestion, *Proceedings of the Society for Psychical Research*, 4, pp. 127-188.
Myers, F.W.H. (1886b) Planchette writing, *Journal of the Society for Psychical Research*, 2, pp. 192-194.
Myers, F.W.H. (1886c) [Automatic writing and moral duality], *Journal of the Society for Psychical Research*, 2, pp. 224-229.
Myers, F.W.H. (1886d) Multiplex personality, *Journal of the Society for Psychical Research*, 2, pp. 443-453.
Myers, F.W.H. (1887a) Automatic writing—3, *Proceedings of the Society for Psychical Research*, 4, pp. 209-261.
Myers, F.W.H. (1887b) Multiplex personality, *Proceedings of the Society for Psychical Research*, 4, pp. 496-514.
Myers, F.W.H. (1888a) Matthew Arnold, *Fortnightly Review*, 49, pp. 719-728.
Myers, F.W.H. (1888b) The work of Edmund Gurney in experimental psychology, *Proceedings of the Society for Psychical Research*, 5, pp. 359-373.
Myers, F.W.H. (1888c) French experiments on the strata of personality, *Proceedings of the Society for Psychical Research*, 5, pp. 374-397.
Myers, F.W.H. (1888d) Remarkable instances of automatic messages, *Journal of the Society for Psychical Research*, 3, pp. 214-221.

Myers, F.W.H. (1889a) Automatic writing—IV: The daemon of Socrates, *Proceedings of the Society for Psychical Research*, 5, pp. 522-547.

Myers, F.W.H. (1889b) Tennyson as prophet, *Nineteenth Century*, 25, pp. 381-396.

Myers, F.W.H. (1889c) [Review of *Automatisme Psychologique* by Pierre Janet], *Proceedings of the Society for Psychical Research*, 6, pp. 186-199.

Myers, F.W.H. (1889d) Binet on the consciousness of hysterical subjects, *Proceedings of the Society for Psychical Research*, 6, pp. 200-206.

Myers, F.W.H. (1889e) Duplex versus multiplex personality [a letter], *Journal of the Society for Psychical Research*, 4, pp. 60-63.

Myers, F.W.H., et al. (Lodge, Leaf, James) (1890) A record of observations of certain phenomena of trance, *Proceedings of the Society for Psychical Research*, 6, pp. 436-659.

Myers, F.W.H. (1891a) [Review of *The Principles of Psychology* by William James], *Proceedings of the Society for Psychical Research*, 7, pp. 111-131.

Myers, F.W.H. (1891b) Science and a future life, *Nineteenth Century*, 29, pp. 628-647.

Myers, F.W.H. (1891c) Two new cases of spontaneous change of personality, *Journal of the Society for Psychical Research*, 5, pp. 93-96.

Myers, F.W.H. (1891d) The case of "Edina", *Journal of the Society for Psychical Research*, 5, pp. 100-105.

Myers, F.W.H. (1892a) The subliminal consciousness. Chapter 1: General characteristics and subliminal messages, *Proceedings of the Society for Psychical Research*, 7, pp. 298-327.

Myers, F.W.H. (1892b) The subliminal consciousness. Chapter 2: The mechanism of suggestion, *Proceedings of the Society for Psychical Research*, 7, pp. 327-355.

Myers, F.W.H. (1892c) The subliminal consciousness. Chapter 3: The mechanism of genius, *Proceedings of the Society for Psychical Research*, 8, pp. 333-361.

Myers, F.W.H. (1892d) The subliminal consciousness. Chapter 4: Hypermnesic dreams, *Proceedings of the Society for Psychical Research*, 8, pp. 362-404.

Myers, F.W.H. (1892e) The subliminal consciousness. Chapter 5: Sensory automatisms and induced hallucinations, *Proceedings of the Society for Psychical Research*, 8, pp. 436-535.

Myers, F.W.H. (1893/1961) *Fragments of Inner Life*, privately printed then S.P.R. published.

Myers, F.W.H. (1893a) The subliminal consciousness. Chapter 6: The mechanism of hysteria, *Proceedings of the Society for Psychical Research*, 9, pp. 3-25.

Myers, F.W.H. (1893b) The subliminal consciousness. Chapter 7: Motor automatism, *Proceedings of the Society for Psychical Research*, 9, pp. 26–128.

Myers, F.W.H. (1893c) Modern poets and the meaning of life, *Nineteenth Century*, 33, pp. 93–111.

Myers, F.W.H. (1893d) *Science and a Future Life with Other Essays*, London: Macmillan.

Myers, F.W.H. (1894–95) The experiences of W. Stainton-Moses, *Proceedings of the Society for Psychical Research*, 9, pp. 245–352; 11, pp. 24–113.

Myers, F.W.H. (1895a) Resolute credulity, *Proceedings of the Society for Psychical Research*, 9, pp. 213–234.

Myers, F.W.H. (1895b) The subliminal self. Chapter 8: The relation of supernormal phenomena to time — Retrocognition, *Proceedings of the Society for Psychical Research*, 11, pp. 334–407.

Myers, F.W.H. (1895c) The subliminal self. Chapter 9: The relation of supernormal phenomena to time — Precognition, *Proceedings of the Society for Psychical Research*, 11, pp. 408–593.

Myers, F.W.H. (1895d) The need for experiments in automatism, *Journal of the Society for Psychical Research*, 8, pp. 30–31.

Myers, F.W.H. (1896a) Glossary of terms used in psychical research, *Proceedings of the Society for Psychical Research*, 12, pp. 166–174.

Myers, F.W.H. (1896b) [A. Le Baron's automatism], *Proceedings of the Society for Psychical Research*, 12, pp. 295–297.

Myers, F.W.H. (1897) Recent experiments in normal motor automatism, *Proceedings of the Society for Psychical Research*, 12, pp. 316–318.

Myers, F.W.H. (1898a) On the possibility of a scientific approach to problems generally classed as religious, in Balfour, A.J. (ed.) *Papers read before the Synthetic Society 1896–1908: and written comments thereon circulated among members of the Society*, pp. 187–197, London: Spottiswoode.

Myers, F.W.H. (1898b) One door will open, in Balfour, A.J. (ed.) *Papers read before the Synthetic Society 1896–1908: and written comments thereon circulated among members of the Society*, pp. 212–216, see above.

Myers, F.W.H. (1898c) The psychology of hypnotism, *Proceedings of the Society for Psychical Research*, 14, pp. 100–108.

Myers, F.W.H. (1899) Provisional sketch of a religious synthesis, in Balfour, A.J. (ed.) *Papers read before the Synthetic Society 1896–1908: and written comments thereon circulated among members of the Society*, pp. 264–274, see above.

Myers, F.W.H. (1900) Presidential address, *Proceedings of the Society for Psychical Research*, 15, pp. 110–127.

Myers, F.W.H. (1901a) Pseudo-possession, *Proceedings of the Society for Psychical Research*, 15, pp. 384–415.

Myers, F.W.H. (1901b) In memory of Henry Sidgwick, *Proceedings of the Society for Psychical Research*, 15, pp. 452-462.

Myers, F.W.H. (1903/1904a) *Human Personality and Its Survival of Bodily Death*, 2 Vols., London and New York: Longmans.

Myers, F.W.H. (1904b) [Lines on] G.F. Watts, R.A., *Journal of the Society for Psychical Research*, 11, pp. 268-269.

Myers, F.W.H. (1904c) *Fragments of Prose and Poetry Edited By His Wife Eveleen Myers*, London: Longmans.

Myers, F.W.H. (1919) Eds., Abridgment, Introduction S.B. and L.H.M., *Human Personality and Its Survival of Bodily Death*, London: Longmans, Green and Co.

Myers, F.W.H. (1921) *Collected Poems with Autobiographical and Critical Fragments Edited By His Wife Eveleen Myers*, London: Macmillan.

Myers, F.W.H. (1960/2001) Smith, S. (ed.), Foreword, Huxley, A., Introduction, Mishlove, J., *Human Personality and Its Survival of Bodily Death*, Virginia: Hampton Road.

Newsome, D. (1980) *On the Edge of Paradise. A.C. Benson: The Diarist*, London: John Murray.

Nicol, F. (1972) The founders of the SPR, *Proceedings of the Society for Psychical Research*, 55, pp. 341-367.

Noakes, R. (2008) The historiography of psychical research: lessons from histories of the sciences, *Journal of the Society for Psychical Research*, 72, pp. 65-85.

Noel, R. (1902) *The Collected Poems of Roden Noel*, London: Kegan Paul.

Oberhausen, J. (2009) Sisters in spirit: Alice Kipling Fleming, Evelyn Pickering de Morgan and 19th-century spiritualism, *British Art Journal*, 9 (3), pp. 38-42.

Oppenheim, J. (1985) *The Other World: Spiritualism and Psychical Research in England 1850-1914*, Cambridge: Cambridge University Press.

Oppenheim, J. (1991) *"Shattered Nerves": Doctors, Patients and Depression in Victorian England*, Oxford: Oxford University Press.

Oppemheim, J. (1995) A mother's role, a daughter's duty: Lady Blanche Balfour, Eleanor Sidgwick, and feminist perspectives, *Journal of British Studies*, 34 (2), pp. 196-232.

Ormerod, R. (1984) *Una Troubridge: The Friend of Radclyffe Hall*, London: Jonathan Cape.

Ovid (Publius Ovidius Naso) (1916/1984) Miller, F.J. (trans.), revised Goold, G.P., *Metamorphoses*, Books IX-XV, Cambridge: Harvard University Press.

Owen, A. (1989) *The Darkened Room: Women, Power and Spiritualism in Late Victorian England*, London: Virago Press.

Owen, A. (2001) Occultism and the 'Modern' self in fin-de-siècle Britain, in Daunton, M and Rieger, B. (eds.) *Meanings of Modernity: Britain from the Late Victorian Era to World War II*, pp. 71–96, Oxford: Berg.

Owen, A. (2004) *The Place of Enchantment: British Occultism and the Culture of the Modern*, Chicago: University of Chicago Press.

Paget, W. (1924) *In My Tower*, 2 Vols., London: Hutchinson.

Palfreman, J. (1979) Between skepticism and credulity: a study of Victorian scientific attitudes to modern spiritualism, in Wallis, R. (ed.) *On the Margins of Science: The Social Construction of Rejected Knowledge*, pp. 201–236, Staffordshire: University of Keele Press.

Palmer, J. (2001) Motor automatism as a vehicle for ESP expression, *Proceedings of Presented Papers: The Parapsychological Association 44th Annual Convention*, pp. 205–217.

Palmer, J. (2017) Anomalous cognition, dissociation, and motor automatisms, *Journal of Parapsychology*, 81 (1), pp. 46–62.

Palmer, T. (2014) *The Science of Spirit Possession*, Newcastle upon Tyne: Cambridge Scholars Publishing.

Parker, A. (2004) Psi and altered states, in Storm, A. and Thalbourne, M. (eds.) *Parapsychology in the 21st Century*, pp. 65–89, Jefferson: McFarland.

Payne, P. (1938/1992) *Mankind's Latent Powers*, Cambridge: Pelegrin Trust.

Pettigrew, T.J. (1849) *Memoirs of the Life of Vice-Admiral Lord Viscount Nelson*, London: T and W Boone.

Pick, D. (1989/1996) *Faces of Degeneration: A European Disorder c.1848–c.1918*, Cambridge: Cambridge University Press.

Piddington, J.G. (1903–04a) The trance phenomena of Mrs Thompson, *Journal of the Society for Psychical Research*, 11, pp. 74–76.

Piddington, J.G. (1903–04b) On the types of phenomena displayed in Mrs Thompson's trance, *Proceedings of the Society for Psychical Research*, 18, pp. 104–307.

Piddington, J.G. (1907–08) On the relation between Myers and Rector, *Journal of the Society for Psychical Research*, 13, pp. 330–333.

Piddington, J.G. (1908) A series of concordant automatisms, *Proceedings of the Society for Psychical Research*, 22, pp. 19–416.

Piddington, J.G. (1916) Correspondences of a Gallic type, *Proceedings of the Society for Psychical Research*, pp. 1–45.

Piddington, J.G. and Lodge, O. (1920) Fresh light on the 'one-horse dawn' experiment, *Proceedings of the Society for Psychical Research*, 30, pp. 175–305.

Piddington, J.G. (ed.) (1913) *Miss Helen de G. Verrall's Script*, Vol. I, privately printed.

Piddington, J.G. (ed.) (1913) *Miss Helen de G. Verrall's Script*, Vol. II, privately printed.

Piddington, J.G. (ed.) (1914) *Mrs. Verrall Script*, Vol. II, privately printed.

Piddington, J.G. (ed.) (1919) *Mrs. Verrall's Script*, Vol. III, privately printed.

Piddington, J.G. (ed.) (1919) *Mrs. Verrall's Script*, Vol. IV, privately printed.

Piddington, J.G. (1921) *Notes and Excursuses with Ariadne, Berenice and the Lock of Hair and List of Scripts in Chronological Order by G.W. Balfour and Mrs Henry Sidgwick respectively*, Vol. I.

Piddington, J.G. (1923) Forecasts in scripts concerning the war, *Proceedings of the Society for Psychical Research*, 33, pp. 439–605.

Piddington, J.G. (1924) Presidential address, *Proceedings of the Society for Psychical Research*, 34, pp. 131–152.

Piddington, J.G. (1928) One crowded hour of glorious life, *Proceedings of the Society for Psychical Research*, 36, pp. 345–375.

Piddington, J.G. (1928) The Master Builder, *Proceedings of the Society for Psychical Research*, 36, pp. 477–505.

Piddington, J.G. (ed.) (1929) *Helen Verrall's Scripts*, Vol. IV, privately printed.

Piddington, J.G. (ed.) (1930) *Helen Verrall's Scripts*, Vol. III, privately printed.

Piddington, J.G. (1934) *Notes and Excursuses*, Vol. III, privately printed.

Piddington, J.G. (1935a) *Notes and Excursuses*, Vol. IV, privately printed.

Piddington, J.G. (1935b) *Notes and Excursuses*, Vol. V, privately printed.

Piddington, J.G. (ed.) (1938a) *Mrs. Wilson's Scripts*, Vol. I, privately printed.

Piddington, J.G. (ed.) (1938b) *Mrs. Wilson's Scripts*, Vol. II, privately printed.

Piddington, J.G. (1943a) *Notes and Excursuses*, Vol. VI, privately printed.

Piddington. J.G. (1943b) *Notes and Excursuses*, Vol. VII, privately printed.

Piddington, J.G. (1943c) *Notes and Excursuses*, Vol. VIII, privately printed.

Piddington, J.G. (1943d) *Notes and Excursuses: Index to Vols. VI., VII., VIII*, Vol. IX, privately printed.

Piddington, J.G. (1947) *[Note on Augustan References in Scripts]*, Salter A/6/6/2/1-45.

Pigou, A.C. (1909) Psychical research and survival after bodily death, *Proceedings of the Society for Psychical Research*, pp. 286–303.

Piper, A.L. (1929) *The Life and Works of Leonora Piper*, London: Kegan Paul, Trench, and Trubner.

Platt, C.B. (2015) *In Their Right Minds: The Lives and Shared Practices of Poetic Geniuses*, Exeter: Imprint Academic.

Podmore, F. (1910/1975) *The Newer Spiritualism*, New York: Arno Press.

Podmore, F., et al. (1909) [Discussion of cross-correspondences], *Journal of the Society for Psychical Research*, 14, pp. 3–30.

Porter, K.H. (1958) *Through a Glass Darkly: Spiritualism in the Browning Circle*, Kansas: University of Kansas Press.

Poynton, J. (2015) *Science, Mysticism and Psychical Research: The Revolutionary Synthesis of Michael Whiteman*, Newcastle: Cambridge Scholars.

Prince, W.F. (1917) The 'St. Paul' cross-correspondence reviewed, *Journal of the American Society for Psychical Research*, 11 (9), pp. 502–533.

Radclyffe Hall, Miss and Una, Lady Troubridge (1918-19) On a series of sittings with Mrs Osborne Leonard, *Proceedings of the Society for Psychical Research*, 30, pp. 339–554.

Raia, C.G. (2005) *The Substance of Things Hoped For: Faith, Science and Psychical Research in the Victorian Fin de Siècle*, PhD dissertation, University of California.

Raia, C.G. (2007) From ether theory to ether theology: Oliver Lodge and the physics of immortality, *Journal of the History of the Behavioural Sciences*, 431, pp. 19–43.

Raverat, G. (1953) *Period Piece: A Cambridge Childhood*, London: Faber and Faber.

Rayleigh, Lord (1919) Presidential address, *Proceedings of the Society for Psychical Research*, 30, pp. 275–290.

Renton, C. (2014) *Those Wild Wyndhams: Three Sisters at the Heart of Power*, London: William Collins.

Rhine, J.B. (1937) *New Frontiers of the Mind: The Story of the Duke Experiments*, New York: Farrar & Rhinehart.

Rhine, L.E. (1967) Parapsychology, then and now, *Journal of Parapsychology*, 31 (3), pp. 231–248.

Richet, C. (1923) de Brath, S. (trans.) *Thirty Years of Psychical Research*, New York: Macmillan.

Richmond, M. (1997) A lab of one' own: The Balfour Biological Lab for Women at Cambridge University 1884-1914, *Isis*, 88, pp. 422–455.

Ridley, J. and Percy, C. (eds.) (1992) *The Letters of Arthur Balfour & Lady Elcho*, London: Hamish Hamilton.

Rimmer, W.G. (1960) *Marshalls of Leeds: Flax Spinners 1788-1886*, Cambridge: Cambridge University Press.

Rock, A.J. (ed.) (2013) Foreword, Storm, L., *The Survival Hypothesis: Essays on Mediumship*, Jefferson: McFarland.

Root, J.D. (1978) The philosophical and religious thought of Arthur James Balfour, *Journal of British Studies*, 19 (2), pp. 120–141.

Rose, N. (ed.) (1973) *Buffy: The Diaries of Blanche Dugdale 1936-1947*, London: Vallentine.

Rothblatt, S. (1968) *The Revolution of the Dons: Cambridge and Society in Victorian England*, London: Faber and Faber.

Rose, J. (1986) *The Edwardian Temperament 1895-1919*, Ohio: Ohio University Press.

Roy, A.E. (1996) *The Archives of the Mind*, Essex: SNU Publications.

Roy, A.E. (2008) *The Eager Dead: A Study in Haunting*, Brighton: The Book Guild.

Ryan, A. (2012) *On Politics: A History of Political Thought from Herodotus to the Present*, London: Penquin Books.

Salter, H. (1928) A report on some recent sittings with Mrs. Leonard, *Proceedings of the Society for Psychical Research*, 36, pp. 187–332.

Salter, H. (1931–32) The history of George Valiantine, *Proceedings of the Society for Psychical Research*, 40, pp. 389–410.

Salter, H. (1931–32) [Review of Dennis Bradley's *And After*], *Journal of the Society for Psychical Research*, 27, p. 170.

Salter, H. and Newton, I. (1940) Alice Johnson, *Proceedings of the Society for Psychical Research*, 46, pp. 16–22.

Salter, H. (1950a) Impressions of some early workers in the SPR, *Journal of Parapsychology*, 14, pp. 29–41.

Salter, H. (1950b) Mrs Leonora Piper, *Journal of the Society for Psychical Research*, 35, pp. 341–344.

Salter, W.H., Papers, Trinity College Library, Cambridge: A/1, B/1, etc.

Salter, W.H. (1928) An experiment in pseudo-scripts, *Proceedings of the Society for Psychical Research*, 36, pp. 525–554.

Salter, W.H. (1947) Augustan references in the scripts, Salter A6/6/1–5.

Salter, W.H. (1948) *An Introduction to the Study of Scripts*, privately printed.

Salter, W.H. (1949) The Hon. Mrs Alfred Lyttelton, G.B.E. (with reminiscences by Mrs Richmond), *Proceedings of the Society for Psychical Research*, 48, pp. 333–335.

Salter, WH. (1950) *Trance Mediumship: An Introductory Study of Leonora Piper and Mrs Leonard*, Glasgow: Society for Psychical Research.

Salter, W.H. (1952) J.G. Piddington and his work on the cross-correspondences, *Journal of the Society for Psychical Research*, 36, pp. 708–716.

Salter, W.H. (1955a) *Memoirs*, unpublished, Trinity College Library, Cambridge.

Salter,W.H. (1955b) The S.P.R. and the Myers' 'Sealed Packet', *Journal of the Society for Psychical Research*, 38, pp. 18–20.

Salter,W.H. (1958a) F.W.H. Myers' posthumous message, *Proceedings of the Society for Psychical Research*, 52, pp. 1–32.

Salter, W.H. (1958b) Frederic W.H. Myers, *Journal of the Society for Psychical Research*, 39, pp. 261–266.

Salter, W.H. (1959–60) The Palm Sunday case: A note on interpreting automatic writings, *Journal of the Society for Psychical Research*, 40, pp. 275–285.

Salter, W.H. (1960) Our pioneers: Richard Hodgson, *Journal of the Society for Psychical Research*, 40, pp. 329–334.

Salter, W.H. (1961) *Zoar: The Evidence of Psychical Research Concerning Survival*, London: Sidgwick and Jackson.

Salter, W.H. (1963) The Rose of Sharon, *Proceedings of the Society for Psychical Research*, 54, pp. 1–22.

Salter, W.H. and Piddington, J.G. (1924) Elucidation of two points in the 'one-horse-dawn' scripts, *Proceedings of the Society for Psychical Research*, 34, pp. 153–165.

Saltmarsh, H.F. (1938/1975) *Evidence of Personal Survival from Cross Correspondences*, New York: Arno Press.

Schneer, J. (1999) *London 1900: The Imperial Metropolis*, New Haven and London: Yale University Press.

Schueller, H.M. and Peters, R.L. (1967–69) *The Letters of John Addington Symonds*, 3 Vols., Detroit: Wayne University Press.

Schultz, B. (2004) *Henry Sidgwick: Eye of the Universe. An Intellectual Biography*, Cambridge: Cambridge University Press.

Searle, G.R. (2004) *A New England: Peace and War 1886–1918*, Oxford: Clarendon Press.

Shamdasani, S. (1993) Automatic writing and the discovery of the unconscious, *Spring: A Journal of Archetype and Culture*, 54, pp. 100–131.

Shamdasani, S. (2003/2004) *Jung and the Making of Modern Psychology: The Dream of a Science*, Cambridge: Cambridge University Press.

Shaw, J. (2011) *Octavia Daughter of God: The Story of a Female Messiah and her Followers*, New Haven: Yale University Press.

Sheldrake, R. (2003) *The Sense of Being Stared At and Other Aspects of the Extended Mind*, London: Hutchinson.

Sherry, N. (1989) *The Life of Graham Greene: Volume One 1904–1939*, London: Jonathan Cape.

Shils, E. and Blacker, C. (eds.) (1996) *Cambridge Women: Twelve Portraits*, Cambridge: Cambridge University Press.

A.S. and E.M.S. (Arthur and Eleanor Sidgwick) (1906) *Henry Sidgwick: A Memoir*, London: Macmillan.

Sidgwick, E. (Mrs. H.) (1886) Results of a personal investigation into the physical phenomena of spiritualism, with some critical remarks on the evidence for the genuineness of such phenomena, *Proceedings of the Society for Psychical Research*, 4, pp. 45–74.

Sidgwick, E. (Mrs. H.) (1900–01) Discussion of the trance phenomena of Leonora Piper, *Proceedings of the Society for Psychical Research*, 15, pp. 16–38.

Sidgwick, E., et al. (1907) Richard Hodgson: In memoriam, *Proceedings of the Society for Psychical Research*, 19, pp. 356–72.

Sidgwick, Mrs. H. (1908) Presidential address, *Proceedings of the Society for Psychical Research*, 10, pp. 1–18.

Sidgwick, Mrs. H., Verrall, Mrs A.W. and Piddington, J.G. (1910) Further experiments with Leonora Piper in 1908, *Proceedings of the Society for Psychical Research*, 24, pp. 31–200.

Sidgwick, E., et al. (Verrall, Johnson, Piddington) (1912–13) A reply to Joseph Maxwell's paper on cross-correspondences and the experimental method, *Proceedings of the Society for Psychical Research*, 26, pp. 375–418.

Sidgwick, E. (1911) Review [Studies in Spiritism, by Amy E. Tanner], *Proceedings of the Society for Psychical Research*, 11, pp. 102–108.

Sidgwick, E. (1915) A contribution to the study of the psychology of Leonora Piper's trance phenomena, *Proceedings of the Society for Psychical Research*, 28, pp. 1–652.

Sidgwick, E. (1916) Mrs A.W. Verrall, *Proceedings of the Society for Psychical Research*, 29, pp. 170–176.

Sidgwick, E. (1923) On hindrances and complications in telepathic communication, *Proceedings of the Society for Psychical Research*, 34, pp. 28–69.

Sidgwick, E. (1929) [Reply to E.J. Dingwall's attack on the cross-correspondences], *Journal of the Society for Psychical Research*, 25, pp. 69–72.

Sidgwick, E. (1932) The SPR: A short account of its history and work on the occasion of the Society's jubilee in 1932, *Proceedings of the Society for Psychical Research*, 41, pp. 1–26.

Sidgwick, Ethel. (1938) *Mrs Henry Sidgwick: A Memoir*, London: Sidgwick and Jackson.

Sidgwick, H. Papers, Trinity College Library, Cambridge: Add.Ms.c.100, etc.

Sidgwick, H. (1882) Address by president at the first general meeting, *Proceedings of the Society for Psychical Research*, 1, pp. 7–12.

Skidelsky, R. (2003) *John Maynard Keynes 1883–1946: Economist, Philosopher, Statesman*, London: Macmillan.

Skrupskelis, I.K. and Berkeley, E.M., et al. (eds.) (1992–2004) *The Correspondence of William James*, 12 Vols, Charlottesville: University Press of Virginia.

Smith, H.W. (1900) *Greek Melic Poets*, Glasgow: Robert Maclehose.

Smith, J.C. (2010) *Pseudoscience and Extraordinary Claims of the Paranormal: A Critical Thinker's Toolkit*, Chichester: Wiley-Blackwell.

Solomon, G. & Solomon, J. (1999) *The Scole Experiment: Scientific Evidence for Life after Death*, London: Piatkus.

Souhami, D. (1998) *The Trials of Radclyffe Hall*, London: Weidenfeld & Nicolson.

Stanley, H.M., Papers, Royal Museum for Central Africa, Brussels: RMCA correspondence section 2.6., 432 onwards.

Stawell, F.M. (1918) The Ear of Dionysius: a discussion of the evidence, *Proceedings of the Society for Psychical Research*, 29, pp. 260–269.

Stein, R.D. (1968) *The Impact of the Psychical Research Movement on the Literary Criticism of Frederic W.H. Myers*, PhD, Northwestern University.

Stevenson, I. (1978) Some comments on automatic writing, *Journal of the American Society for Psychical Research*, 72, pp. 315–332.

Stevenson, I. (1983-84) Cryptomnesia and parapsychology, *Journal of the Society for Psychical Research*, 52, pp. 1-30.

Stevenson, I. (1990) Thoughts on the decline of major paranormal phenomena, *Proceedings of the Society for Psychical Research*, 57, pp. 149-162.

Stevenson, I. (1998) [Letter on Munves and Leonora Piper], *Journal of the Society for Psychical Research*, 62, pp. 282-283.

Stevenson, I. (2013) Kelly, E.W. (ed.) *Science, the Self, and Survival After Death: Selected Writings of Ian Stevenson*, Lanham: Rowman & Littlefield.

Stewart, J. (1959) *Jane Ellen Harrison: A Portrait from Letters*, London: The Merlin Press.

Stone, D. (2002) *Breeding Superman: Nietzsche, Race and Eugenics in Edwardian and Interwar Britain*, Liverpool: Liverpool University Press.

Storm, L. & Thalbourne, M. (eds.) (2003) *Parapsychology in the 21st Century*, Jefferson: McFarland.

Stray, C. (1998) *Classics Transformed: Schools, Universities and Society in England, 1830-1960*, Oxford: Oxford University Press.

Sudduth, M. (2013) Is postmortem survival the best explanation of the data of mediumship?, in Rock, A.J. (ed.), Foreword, Storm, L., *The Survival Hypothesis: Essays on Mediumship*, Jefferson: McFarland.

Sudduth, M. (2016) *A Philosophical Critique of Empirical Arguments for Postmortem Survival*, Basingstoke: Palgrave Macmillan.

Sutherland, G. (2006) *Faith, Duty and the Power of Mind: The Cloughs and their Circle*, Cambridge: Cambridge University Press.

Sword, H. (2002) *Ghostwriting Modernism*, Ithaca: Cornell University Press.

Tabori, P. (1972) *Pioneers of the Unseen*, London: Souvenir Press.

Tanner, A.E. (1910) *Studies in Spiritism*, New York: Appleton & Co.

Targ, R. (2004) Foreword, Huston, J., *Limitless Mind: A Guide to Remote Viewing and Transformation of Consciousness*, California: New World Library.

Tart, C. (2009) *The End of Materialism: How Evidence of the Paranormal is Bringing Science and Spirit Together*, Oakland: Noetic Books & New Harbinger Publications.

Taylor, A. (1992) *Annie Besant: A Biography*, Oxford: Oxford University Press.

Taylor, E. (1996) *William James on Consciousness beyond the Margin*, Princeton: Princeton University Press.

Taylor, G. (n.d.) How Martin Gardner bamboozled the skeptics, [Online], www.dailygrail.com [accessed 14/01/2015].

Taylor, I. (1987) *Victorian Sisters: The Remarkable Macdonalds and the Four Great Men They Inspired*, London: Weidenfield and Nicolson.

Taylor, J.B. & Shuttleworth, S. (eds.) (1998/2003) *Embodied Selves: An Anthology of Psychological Texts 1830-1890*, Oxford: Clarendon Press.

Taylor, J.B. (2007) Psychology at the fin de siècle, in Marshall, G. (ed.) *The Cambridge Companion to the Fin de Siècle*, pp. 13-30, Cambridge: Cambridge University Press.

Tennant family papers, West Glamorgan Archive Service, Swansea, D/DT.Vol 3: 2532 onwards.

Thalbourne, M.A. (2003) Preface, Beloff, J., *A Glossary of Terms Used in Parapsychology*, Charlottesville: Puente.

Thornton, A. (2015) *Reading Room Notes: History Meets Archaeology*, [Online], www.readingroomnotes.com [accessed 22/3/2016].

Thorpe, D.P. (2003) *Eden: The Life and Times of Anthony Eden, First Earl of Avon, 1897-1977*, London: Chatto and Windus.

Thouless, R.H. (1963) *Experimental Psychical Research*, Middlesex: Penguin Books.

Thouless, R.H. (1972) *From Anecdote to Experiment in Psychical Research*, London: Routledge.

Thurschwell, P. (2001) *Literature, Technology and Magical Thinking 1880-1920*, Cambridge: Cambridge University Press.

Tillyard, E.M. (1958) *The Muse in Chains*, London: Bowes and Bowes.

Tomes, J. (1997/2002) *Balfour and Foreign Policy: The International Thought of a Conservative Statesman*, Cambridge: Cambridge University Press.

Tresidder, J. (1997/2008) *The Watkins Dictionary of Symbols*, London: Watkins Publishing.

Treffert, D.A. (1989) *Extraordinary People*, London: Bantam Press.

Treitel, C. (2004) *A Science for the Soul: Occultism and the Genesis of the German Modern*, Baltimore: Johns Hopkins University Press.

Tromp, M. (2006) *Altered States: Sex, Nation, Drugs, and Self-Transformation in Victorian Spiritualism*, Albany: State University of New York Press.

Tuchman, B.W. (1966/1997) *The Proud Tower: A Portrait of the World before the War, 1890-1914*, London: Hamish Hamilton/Folio Society.

Tucker, K. (1994) *Chronicle of Cadoxton*, Neath: Historical Projects.

Tullberg, R. (1975/1998) Introduction, Sutherland, G., *Women at Cambridge*, Cambridge: Cambridge University Press.

Turnbull, M.P. (1902/1905) *A Short Day's Work: Original Verses. Translations from Heine and Prose Essays*, London: John Murray.

Turner, F.M. (1974) *Between Science and Religion: The Reaction to Scientific Naturalism in Late Victorian England*, Newhaven and London: Yale University Press.

Turner, F.M. (1981) *The Greek Heritage in Victorian Britain*, New Haven and London: Yale University Press.

Turner, F.M. (1993) *Contesting Cultural Authority: Essays in Victorian Intellectual Life*, Cambridge: Cambridge University Press.

Tymn, M. (2008) *The Articulate Dead: They Brought the Spirit World Alive*, Minnesota: Galde Press.

Tymn, M. (2013) *Resurrecting Leonora Piper: How Science Discovered the Afterlife*, Guildford: White Crow Books.
Tyrrell, G.N.M. (1946) *The Personality of Man*, London: Penguin Books.
Tyrrell, G.N.M. (1953/1961) *Science and Psychical Phenomena & Apparitions in one volume*, New York: University Books.
Tyrell, G.N.M. (1954) Foreword, Price, H.H., *The Nature of Human Personality*, London: Allen and Unwin.
Verrall, A.W. (1884) *Studies Literary and Historical in the Odes of Horace*, London: Macmillan.
Verrall, A.W. (1913) Bayfield, M.A. and Duff, J.D. (eds.) *Collected Literary Essays Classical and Modern with a Memoir*, Cambridge: Cambridge University Press.
Verrall, Mrs. A.W. (1902) Some recent experiments in automatic writing, *Journal of the Society for Psychical Research*, 10, pp. 291–295.
Verrall, Mrs. A.W. (1903) A further account of experiments in automatic writing, *Journal of the Society for Psychical Research*, 11, pp. 71–74.
Verrall, Mrs. A.W. (1906) On a series of automatic writings, *Proceedings of the Society for Psychical Research*, 20, pp. 1–432.
Verrall, Mrs. A.W. (c.1910a) *The 'Delta' Case*, privately printed.
Verrall, Mrs. A.W. (c.1910b) *Mrs Willett's Automatic Phenomena*, Vol. 1, privately printed.
Verrall, Mrs. A.W. (c.1910c) *Mrs Willett's Automatic Phenomena*, Vol. 2, privately printed.
Verrall, Mrs. A.W. (1910d) A new group of experimenters, *Proceedings of the Society for Psychical Research*, 24, pp. 264–318.
Verrall, Mrs. A.W. (1910e) Classical and literary allusions in Leonora Piper's trance, *Proceedings of the Society for Psychical Research*, 24, pp. 39–85.
Verrall, Mrs. A.W. (1911) Notes on Mrs Willett's scripts of February 1910, *Proceedings of the Society for Psychical Research*, 25, pp. 176–217.
Verrall, Mrs. A.W. (1911–12) Cross-correspondences as a vehicle for literary criticism, *Journal of the Society for Psychical Research*, 15, pp. 98–100.
Verrall, Mrs. A.W. (ed.) (1913) *Mac Script*, privately printed.
Verrall, M. de G. (ed.) (1914) *Mrs Willett's Automatic Phenomena*, Vol. I, privately printed.
Verrall, M. de G. (ed.) (1915) *Mrs. Willett's Automatic Phenomena*, Vol. II, privately printed.
Verrall, Mrs. A.W. and Verrall, H. (eds.) (1914) *Verrall Script*, Vol. I, privately printed.
Verrall, H. (1911) The element of chance in cross-correspondences, *Journal of the Society for Psychical Research*, 15, pp. 153–173.

Virgil (Publius Vergilius Maro) (1919/2002) Fairclough, H.R. (trans.), revised Goold, G.P., *Aeneid VII–XII*, Cambridge: Harvard University Press.

Virgil (Publius Vergilius Maro) (1916/2004) Fairclough, H.R. (trans.), revised Goold, G.P., *Eclogues, Georgics, Aeneid I–VI*, Cambridge: Harvard University Press.

Waller, D. (2009) *The Magnificent Mrs Tennant*, Newhaven and London: Yale University Press.

Warcollier, R. (1959-60) Charles Richet, *Journal of the Society for Psychical Research*, 40, pp. 157–162.

Warner, M. (2006) *Phantasmagoria: Spirit Visions, Metaphors, and Media into the Twenty-first Century*, Oxford: Oxford University Press.

Warwood, L. November 2014. Personal communication on J.G. Piddington.

Wegner, D.M. (2002) *The Illusion of Conscious Will*, Cambridge, MA: MIT Press.

West, D.J. (1954/1962) *Psychical Research Today*, Middlesex: Penguin.

West, W.J. (1987) *Truth Betrayed*, London: Duckworth.

West, W.J. (1998) *The Quest for Graham Greene*, London: Phoenix.

Whiteman, M. (1986) *Old and New Evidence on the Meaning of Life: The Mystical World-View Journal of the Society for Psychical Research and Inner Contest. Volume 1 An introduction to scientific mysticism*, Gerards Cross: Colin Smythe.

Wiener, M. (1981) *English Culture and the Decline of the Industrial Spirit, 1850–1980*, Cambridge: Cambridge University Press.

Williams, J.P. (1984) *The Making of Victorian Psychical Research: An Intellectual Elite's Approach to the Spiritual World*, PhD thesis, University of Cambridge.

Williams, J.P. (1985) Psychical research and psychiatry in late Victorian Britain: trance as ecstasy or trance as insanity, in Bynum, W.F., Porter, R. and Shepherd, M. (eds.) *The Anatomy of Madness: Essays in the History of Psychiatry. Vol 1 People and ideas*, pp. 233–254, London and New York: Tavistock Publications.

Wilson, A.N. (1999) *God's Funeral*, London: John Murray.

Wilson, L. (2013a) *Modernism and Magic: Experiments with Spiritualism, Theosophy and the Occult*, Edinburgh: Edinburgh University Press.

Wilson, L. (2013b) *The Cross-Correspondences, the Nature of Evidence and the Matter of Writing*, in Kontou, T. and Willburn, S. (eds.) *The Ashgate Research Companion to Nineteenth-Century Spiritualism and the Occult*, pp. 98–119, Farnham: Ashgate.

Wilson, L. (2007) Dead letters: Gender, literary history and the cross-correspondences, *Critical Survey*, 19 (1), pp. 17–28.

Wilson, T.D. (2002) *Strangers to Ourselves: Discovering the Adaptive Unconscious*, Cambridge: The Belknap Press.

Wingfield, K. (1923/1948) Preface, Radnor, H., Introduction, Marshall Hall, E., *Guidance from Beyond*, London: Psychic Book Club.
Wise, S. (1912) *Inconvenient People: Lunacy, Liberty and the Mad-Doctors in Victorian England*, London: The Bodley Head.
Wiseman, R. (2011) *Paranormality: Why we see what isn't there*, Basingstoke: Macmillan.
Wolman, B.B. (ed.) (1977) *Handbook of Parapsychology*, New York. Van Nostrand.
Wyles, R. and Hall, E. (eds.) (2016) *Women Classical Scholars: Unsealing the Fountain from the Renaissance to Jacqueline de Romilly*, Oxford: Oxford University Press.
Young, K. (1963) *Arthur James Balfour*, London: G. Bell.
Zimmerman, J. (2015) *Hermeneutics: A Very Short Introduction*, Oxford: Oxford University Press.

Index

Albemarle Club 229
Apostles 230
Ariadne's Crown 108, 215
Arnold, Matthew 51, 237
  To Marguerite: Continued 237
Asquith, H. 4, 106, 111, 246
Asquith, Margot 4, 111, 179
Automatic writing
  Nature of 6-7, 196-98
  See entry under each automatist
  Number of scripts 281
  Location of scripts 294

Bailey, Alice 263
Balfour, Blanche 11, 134, 142, 185
Balfour, James 11
Balfour, Arthur
  Plate
  Family 11
  Personality 11, 41, 110
  Career 107, 137
  Attitude to psychical research 110-11
  Attitude to the Story and the Plan 109, 141
  May Lyttelton and her family 105
  The silver bronze box and the ring 105, 108, 214, 230-32
  Sittings with Winifred Coombe-Tennant 136, 139-40, 141-43
  And Eugenics 246
  Symbols for in the scripts. See Appendix 4 and separate references to Knight 120, 130, 151; Theseus 120,169; Excalibur 174-75
  And the Souls 111, 151, 155, 178, 184, 229-30, 240-41
  At 4 Carlton Gardens 105-07, 136, 173, 175, 231
  At Fishers Hill 105, 139, 141-42, 252
  At Whittingehame 12, 105, 138, 140, 143, 230, 255
  General: 1,4, 96, 101, 104-07, 110-11, 118, 120, 130, 136-42, 150-51, 154, 165, 167-68, 170, 172-73, 175, 178, 185-85, 188, 214, 216, 227-32, 236-37, 242, 246, 248, 253, 255, 260-61, 278, 292
Balfour, Eleanor (see Sidgwick) 4, 11
Balfour, Evelyn 4, 11, 71
Balfour, Francis Maitland (FMB, Frank)
  Plate
  Background and scientific career 4, 44, 11,173
  Symbols for in the scripts 173, 174, 245, 292
  Leading role in scripts/spiritual eugenics 104, 111, 139, 242
  Closeness to Winifred Coombe-Tennant 136-38, 144
  Script interchanges with Gerald Balfour 101
  Dark Young Man symbol and photograph 104, 111, 138, 139. See appendix 4
Balfour, Gerald 4, 11
  Plate
  Background and career 4, 11, 99
  Character 99
  Marriage to Betty Lytton 99
  Love affair with Winifred Coombe-Tennant 5, 98-99, 100-01
  End of love affair 133-35
  On the Story and the Plan 160-61
  On Henry Coombe-Tennant, the Messianic Child 5, 100-01, 121, 139, 144-45, 165, 174, 248
  On Winifred Coombe-Tennant's

mediumship 190-92
Script discussions with Gurney
  102-03
On methods of interpreting scripts
  161, 167, 182, 206, 208, 209, 227, 255
On interpretive disagreements with
  Pigou 206-08, Carrington 118, 246,
  249, Margaret Verrall 122, Miss
  Stawell 119
Influences shaping his interpreta-
  tion 246-47, 257
Friendship with Piddington 122,
  123, 210
General: 34, 41, 59, 60, 91, 98, 99,
  100, 105, 106, 107, 108, 110, 111, 113,
  122, 123, 135, 140, 145, 165, 166, 191,
  203, 210, 215, 220, 229, 230, 241, 246,
  249, 252, 258, 261, 272
Balfour, Eustace 11, 111
Balfour, Cecil 11, 111
Balfour, Alice 11, 107, 111
Balfour, Betty (see Lytton)
  Early life, marriage, acceptance of
  Gerald Balfour's affair 99-100
  Friendship with Piddington 123
  Birth of her daughter Kathleen
  resented by Winifred Coombe-
  Tennant 133
  Acceptance of Henry Coombe-
  Tennant 145
  Friendship with the Richmonds
  149
  Knowledge of May's hair in the
  silver bronze box 232
Balfour, Jean (see Traprain)
  On Palm Maiden 109
  On Arthur Balfour 110
  On Henry Coombe-Tennant 145
  On Winifred Coombe-Tennant 146,
  203
  On meaning of Dido in the scripts
  241
  On telepathy in the scripts 266-67
  On purpose in the scripts 268
Bates, Katherine 42
  On Mrs Piper's trance states 65
Bayfield, M.A. 118
Benson, Arthur 111-12
Benson, Edward 90
Benson, Martin 269

Benson, Robert Hugh 269
Besant, Annie 111
Bible, The, and texts from 75, 245,
  276, 45-46, 50, 105
Blavatsky, Madame 239, 263
Boer War, The (Wagon Hill) 19, 38
Braude, S. 5, 7, 206, 266, 275
Broad, C.D. 129, 145, 190-91, 255,
  270, 272-73, 275
Broadlands 15, 185, 231
Brooke, Rupert 128
Browning, Elizabeth
  The Romance of the Swan 120
  A Musical Instrument 181
  A Child's Grave at Florence 216
Browning, Robert
  Abt Vogler 67, 107, 297
  La Saisiaz 97
  Aristophanes' Apology 162
  The Ring and the Book 289
  The Pied Piper of Hamelin 289
Burne-Jones, Edward
  Plate: Peacock Memorial 177
  Perseus Panels 106, 136, 175
  The Depths of the Sea 177
  The Morning of the Resurrection 177,
  179
  General: 37, 39, 106, 112, 178, 185-
  86, 229
Butcher, S.H. (Henry) 21, 101, 115-16,
  118, 168, 230

Cadoxton 59, 60-61, 83, 85, 89-90, 98,
  107, 130, 167, 187-89, 240
Cambridge
  Intellectual atmosphere 13
  Ladies Dining Club 14
  Attitude to higher education for
  women 14
Candle symbol across scripts for May
  Lytelton 170-73
Carrington, Hereward 118, 264, 266,
  274
Carlton Gardens (see Arthur Balfour
  entry)
Castanette 220
Clandeboye 38
Classics, status of 243
Clairvoyance 3, 37, 109, 131, 191, 206,
  222, 226, 260, 266, 273

Coma Berenices 108, 215
Communications, difficulties of 65–66, 88, 168, 200, 201, 204, 211
  Need for 'stupid' sensitives 199
  Need for calm and stillness to receive clearly 92
  Need to still fears of deception 92
Coombe-Tennant, Alexander 88, 97–98, 133, 146, 248
Coombe-Tennant, Charles 83–84, 89, 91, 99, 135
Coombe-Tennant, Christopher 88, 133–35, 146, 198, 203, 248
Coombe-Tennant, Daphne
  Death 84–85
  Memoir of 87
  Role in the Story and Plan 86, 87, 88, 92, 199, 216, 255
  Symbols for 167, 216
  In Helen Verrall scripts 89, 130, 257
  General: 61, 91, 106, 113, 134, 147, 194, 203, 241, 242
Coombe-Tennant, Henry (Augustus: Wise One)
  Plate
  Messianic child and the Plan 113, 141, 143, 144–46, 165, 179–83
  One Messiah/Child of Light or many? 255
  Career 145–46
  And Palm Maiden 242
  See appendix 4
  General: 2, 5, 83, 88, 98, 100, 132, 240
Coombe-Tennant, Winifred (Mrs Willett)
  Plate
  Nature of automatic writing 33, 85–86, 91, 92, 95, 96, 97–98, 101–03, 107, 109, 139, 140, 199, 203, 215, 242, 268
  Background, family and marriage 3, 83–84, 203
  Affair with Gerald Balfour 98–99, 133–35
  Sittings with Arthur Balfour. See his entry
  Her public life 136
  See list of cross-correspondences
  See paranormal cognition
  Knowledge of the Story and the Plan 192, 233
  As investigator and automatist 234
Cognitive dissonance 257
Cross-Correspondences
  Assessment of 7–8, and Part 2
  Types of 159–61: Latin message 66
  List of: Fawcett 15, Sevens 28, 164, Selwyn Text 45, St Paul 69, Arrow 70, Thanatos 70, Light in West 74, Blue Flower 161, Violet 162, Yellow 162, Euripides 162, Prometheus 163, The Cloud 166, Theseus 168, Candle 170, Naples 173, Excalibur 174, Dorr 94, Lethe 80, 92, Electra 207, Eheu Fugaces 207, Angel 209, Diana 213, Medici Tombs 217, Medusa's Head 223, Procession 223, Savonarola 244, Hope Star Browning (app), Ave Roma (app), Statius 117, Ear of Dionysius 118 (also examples of paranormal cognition)
  Critics of (see separate entries)
    Braude, Broad, Carrington, Dingwall, Doyle, Flournoy, Hude, Hyslop, Moreman, Podmore, Richet, Louisa Rhine, Sudduth, Tanner
  Theory and purposes of 46–47
Cryptesthesia (see clairvoyance, telaesthesia) 26
Cryptomnesia (see Source Amnesia) 53, 62, 233, 235, 265
Crystal bars 216

Dallas, H. 198
Dante 75, 94, 96, 117, 154, 257, 292
  Purgatorio 165
Dark Young Man (see Francis Maitland Balfour)
Darwin, Charles 88, 104, 195, 242
Diamond Island (see Muirhead) 53
Desborough 138
Dingwall, E. 58, 263, 266
Diotima 25, 28
Diver, Maud 40–41
Dissociation 65, 151, 278
Douglas, Alfred 186
Doyle, Conan 5, 26

Index

Driesch, Hans
Plate

Elcho 112, 138, 178, 179, 184, 293
Elitism 243, 246, 258, 274
Eugenics, terrestrial 246–47
Eugenics, spiritual 22, 88, 100, 111, 113, 246, 248, 253, 257, 293
Excalibur symbol across scripts for Arthur Balfour 174–75

Fawcetts 14, 15, 185, 186, 229, 253, 254
Feilding, Everard 42, 58–59, 62, 253–54, 285
Fishers Hill 98, 99, 100, 121, 123, 145, 167, 210, 261, 274
Fleming (Kipling) Trix (see Mrs Holland)
Plate
  Background and life 3, 36–43, 70, 110, 179, 184–85, 203–04, 230
  Personality 37, 38, 42, 43
  Marriage and the Fleming family 38–43
  Nature of automatic writing 40–42, 48–49, 52, 55, 62, 90, 127, 178, 187, 192, 200, 254
  Knowledge of the Story and the Plan 231
  See list of cross-correspondences
  See paranormal cognition
  General: 8, 13, 15, 16, 29, 31, 38, 50, 51, 53, 61
Fleming, Jack 38–43
Flournoy, Theodore 118, 203, 265–66
Fox-Pitt 132, 252
Freud, S. 44, 128, 191 203

Graham, Francis (see Horner) 177
Gray, John 266
Gray, Thomas 117
  The Progress of Poetry 117
  Elegy written in a Country Churchyard 237
Greene, Graham 149–50
Gurney, Edmund
Plate
  Life and career 3, 51–52
  Personality in life and in scripts 19, 25, 51–52, 120, 128
  Role in Winifred Coombe-Tennant

scripts 87, 89, 92, 97, 98, 102–03, 111, 187, 190–91, 203, 216, 248
See cross-correspondences
See paranormal cognition

Hair in Temple 214
Hall, Radclyffe 132, 252
Hallam, Arthur 74, 75
Hallsteads 24, 26, 27, 51, 189, 190
Harrison, Jane 13, 16, 229
Hill, Annie (see Marshall, Annie; Phyllis)
Hodgson, Richard 26, 28, 29, 30, 44, 46, 47, 57–58, 63–66, 69, 76, 77, 79, 81, 129, 162, 187–90, 194, 198, 282, 285, 289
Holland, Mrs (see Trix Fleming)
Home, D.D. 14
Homer 50, 192
Horace 70, 71–73 (C.1.28 *Archytas*), 141, 172–73, 181, 207, 237, 250, 293
Horner, Francis (Graham) 177
Hude, Anna
  Career 66
  On Latin Message 67
  Criticises cross-correspondences 55, 207–08, 264
Hunt, Holman
  Light of the World 106
Hyslop, James 5, 64, 82, 194, 198, 266

Irving, Henry 129, 172

James, William 24, 29, 47, 50, 63, 76, 101, 111, 172, 188, 254, 270
Jebb, Caroline 14, 99
Jebb, Richard 230, 253
Johnson, Alice
  Plate
  Work for the SPR 4, 44
  Her family 18, 44–45
  Theory of cross-correspondences 2, 3, 46–47
  Relations with Winifred Coombe-Tennant 242
  Relations with Trix Fleming 44
Jones, Lawrence
  Plate
Jung 44, 150, 203

Keble College, Oxford 106, 108, 229, 232, 291

Kipling, Alice 37, 38, 39, 104–05
Kipling, Lockwood 37, 38, 39, 104–05
Kipling, Rudyard 3, 36, 37, 38, 39, 42, 114, 186
Kipling, Trix (see Fleming; see Mrs Holland)
Krishnamurti 145, 240

Leaf, Walter 101, 230
Leonard, Gladys Osborne 26, 129, 132, 135, 198, 209, 211, 251, 252
Leckhampton House
Plate
18, 27, 125
Liddell, A.G. and Laura Tennant 112
Living agent psi (see clairvoyance, telepathy etc.) 273
Llangattock (see Cadoxton) 88–89, 188
Lodge, Oliver
Plate
Career 26
President of the SPR 26
Investigator 23, 26
And Winifred Coombe-Tennant 91–94, 96, 97, 134, 135, 161, 249
In scripts 52–53
And Mrs Piper 64, 232
And Arthur Balfour 184, 261
On Myers 195
On cross-correspondences 208
And Synthetic Society 229
The Survival of Man 34
Man and the Universe 86
General: 28, 33–34, 41, 42, 44, 46, 79, 81, 87, 95, 189, 264, 269, 276
London Clubs for women (see Albemarle; Sesame)
Long Room (see Music room) 22, 106–07, 136, 173–74, 292
Lutyens 99
Lyttelton, Alfred 34, 48, 109, 111, 112, 134, 140, 151, 152, 178, 233, 242, 293
Lyttelton, Arthur 231, 236
Lyttelton, Antony 4, 113, 151, 236, 255, 286, 287, 290, 293
Lyttelton, Christopher 4, 112, 113, 168, 241, 255, 293
Lyttelton, Edward 112

Lyttelton, Edith
Life and personality 3, 151–52, 231
Nature of automatic writing 151
Predictions in scripts 152–54
Knowledge of Palm Maiden story 154
Networks 229, 241, 249
Lyttelton, May
Plate
Life and death 103–105
Personality 105
And Arthur Balfour 105, 108
Symbols for in the scripts. See appendix 4
Lyttelton, Lavinia (Talbot) 105, 106, 108, 229, 232, 291
Lyttelton, Laura (Tennant)
Plate
Life and death 111–12
Personality 111–12
Symbols for in the scripts. See appendix 4
Lyttelton, Spencer 105, 110
Lytton, Betty (see Balfour)
Lytton, Emily (Lutyens) 99–100, 145
Lytton, Constance 99–100

Macs, The 3, 86, 95, 147, 218
Scripts 94, 218, 280
Magdalen College, Oxford x, 122
Maitland, F. 101
Maria Angélique de Gaudrion (see Verrall, Margaret)
Marshall, Annie (Hill)
Early life and death 4, 27
Marriage 24, 27
Symbols for in the scripts 20, 30, 32, 51
Marshall, Reverend G. 24
Marshall, Walter 27
Mells Church (see Peacock Memorial; Burne-Jones) 112, 176, 177, 239, 293
Merrifield, Frederic (see Verrall, Margaret) 14, 15, 129, 253
Messianic Child (see Coombe-Tennant, Henry)
Moreman, C. 5, 225
Moses, S.M. 65, 185, 196, 253, 254
Mount-Temples 167, 185, 186, 231, 253

Muirhead, Alexander (see Diamond Island) 53, 219
Multiple Personality 44, 198, 199
Music Room (see Long Room) 106, 175
Münsterberg, Hugo 58, 285
Murray, Gilbert 169
Myers, Arthur 197
Myers, Eveleen
Plate
And F.W.H. Myers' autobiography 24, 27
Attitude to automatic writing and mediumship 12, 20, 24, 28, 30, 86
Visit to Mrs Piper in America 32
Relations with family 86
Myers, F.W.H.
Plate
Life and career 1, 4, 45–46, 49, 50, 79, 84, 89, 128–29, 185, 229, 232, 237, 253
Annie Marshal, the Valley, the Sealed Envelope 23–32
On automatic writing 6, 7, 21, 200–01
On telepathy, On the subliminal. See separate entries
On evolution 72–73, 181, 194, 195, 201, 240
On his autobiography. See under Myers, Eveleen
And Mrs Thompson 12, 20, 26, 28
In Winifred Coombe-Tennant scripts 87–97
See also separate entries for paranormal cognition and cross-correspondences
Human Personality 1, 25, 28, 40–41, 44, 52, 56, 71, 146, 181, 192–94, 240, 274, 284
Fragments of Prose and Poetry 52, 79, 185
Immortality 73, *On Teneriffe* 30, *Ode to Nature* 73, *Love and Death* 30
Myers, Harold 133, 162, 163
Myers, Leopold 32, 84, 163
Myers, Silvia 84, 128, 134, 163, 203

Neptune 216
Newnham, Reverend P.H. 21

Newnham College, Cambridge 3–5, 12–14, 16, 18, 21, 24, 44–45, 119, 125, 128, 229, 230
Naples, symbol across scripts for Francis Balfour 173–74
Noel, Roden
Life 53–54
See list of cross-correspondences
See paranormal cognition

Old Church 24, 27
Ovid
Metamorphoses 80–81, *Fasti* 193

Paget, W. 40
Palmer, Robert (see Selborne) 249–51
Palm Maiden 104
Incorrect date of death in scripts 131
Paranormal Cognition (see living agent psi; telepathy; clairvoyance; cryptesthesia; telaesthesia; telergy):
Fir-tree 19, One-horse dawn 21, America visit 32, cross and wreath 33
Myers/Lodge/Feilding/Hodgson/Verralls/Gurney/Noel in Fleming script 47–59, Coombe-Tennant properties in Fleming script 59–61, window seat and autobiography 24, Robert Palmer 250, Daphne's memoir 86, *Aeneid* 77–79, eidolon 192, Inns of Court bird 33, pars casiam 193, questions to Myers 71–74
Peacock Lady, symbol for Laura Lyttelton 112–13
Peacock Memorial (see Mells Church)
Pharaoh's daughter 216
Phyllis (see Hill: see Marshall, Annie)
Pickering de Morgan, Evelyn 39
Piddington, J.G.
Plate
Life and character 4, 122–23
And Mrs Verrall 121–22, 124–25
Ingenious interpretations 74, 75, 109, 130–31, 160–61, 237–39, 252–55, 259
On Palm Maiden 94, 130
Arthur Balfour and the Empire as indicated in scripts 4, 137–38

On Laura Lyttelton 176–79
On Spiritual Eugenics and sacrifice 113
Influences on his interpretations 239–47, 257
Friendship with Gerald Balfour 122, 123, 210
Piper, Leonora
Plate
Life and personality 63, 228, 232–33
Nature of automatic writing 64–82, 91, 97, 163, 187, 198, 199, 200, 215
Controls: Rector 20, 65, 67, 72, 74, 237, Prudens 237, Imperator 65, Gurney's Child 248
See cross-correspondences
See paranormal cognition
Plan, The 4, 5, 114, 137, 148, 161, 179–80, 206, 248, 253, 262
Podmore, Frank 89
On Latin Message 67
On telepathic explanation for cross-correspondences 266
Plotinus 74

Raikes, Diana 3, 18, 19, 20, 25, 52, 127
Rhine, L. 267
Richet, Charles 266
Richmonds, The 3, 149–51, 227, 249, 261, 281
Riviere, Joan 128
Rossetti, Dante Gabriel
Beata Beatrix 186
Blessed Damozel 108, 137, 139
General: 28, 104, 229, 243, 292
Ruskin, John 84
Sesame and Lilies 82, *Fors Clavigera* 120

Salter, Helen (see Verrall, Helen)
Plate
Early life and education 128
Marriage to W.H. Salter 129
Nature of automatic writing 127, 130–31, 204–05, 215
Sitting with Arthur Balfour 261
Community involvement 130
SPR work 129, 131–32
Experiments with pseudo scripts 224
Knowledge of the Story and the Plan 231
See paranormal cognition, cross-correspondences
Salter, W.H. 13, 28, 123,148
Plate
Marriage to Helen Verrall 129
On experiments with pseudo scripts 224
On automatists' prior knowledge of script content 231
On importance of scripts 271
Salter archive 247, 281
Sealed Envelope 23–28, 50–51
Sesame Club 229
Selborne, William Waldegrave 249–51
Scott, Michael (see Wizard of Melrose) 111
Scott, Walter 111
The Lay of the Last Minstrel 111
Shakespeare, William 43, 242
Hamlet 244
Macbeth 150, 170
The Merchant of Venice 150, 170
Twelfth Night 70
Shelley
The Cloud 116, 165–67, *Prometheus Unbound* 163–64, *The Sensitive Plant* 285–86
Sidgwick, Arthur 71
Sidgwick, Eleanor (see Balfour)
Plate
And Myers' unexpurgated autobiography 24
Questioning Myers on proposed Sidgwick life 71–72
On Selwyn Text issue 45–46
Admiration for Arthur Balfour 255
At Fishers Hill 123, 210
Study of Leonora Piper 161, 198, 217
On the subliminal 208, 222
Critical of Maxwell 265
Critical of Tanner 266
Presidential Addresses of 275
Her record of when automatists first saw each other's scripts 234
General: 4, 11, 14, 23, 24, 26, 28, 44–45, 71, 72, 74, 82, 85, 91, 110, 125,

163, 166, 213, 216, 221, 230, 232, 233, 276, 288
Sidgwick, Henry
And Myers' autobiography 29
His meditation texts 45
And Roden Noel 55
His memoir 55-56, 86
In Mac script 147
Cambridge names linked to him in scripts 227
See cross-correspondences
See paranormal cognition
Smith, J.G. (see Piddington, J.G.)
Society for Psychical Research
20 Hanover Square 23, 30, 41, 46, 81, 129, 205
Opening of Myers' sealed envelope 23-28
Piper records transferred from United States 63-64
Conduit for early psychoanalytic ideas 128
Close links between investigators 228
And Spiritualists 5, 29, 272
Dingwall's attacks on 263, 266
Louisa Rhine's criticism of 267
Souls, The 4, 109, 111, 138, 151, 178, 184, 210, 229-30, 240-41
Source Amnesia (see cryptomnesia)
Stawell, Miss (see Newnham College) 119
Stevenson, I.
On automatic writing 196
On cryptomnesia 235
Stevenson, R.L.
As symbol in scripts 285-86
Spiritualism 14, 39, 123, 127, 198, 272
Story, The 4, 5, 130, 137, 161, 206, 255
Subliminal 6, 7, 52, 56, 59, 61, 80, 102, 103, 109, 119, 124, 158, 172, 191, 201-02, 205, 208-10, 221-22, 237, 247, 248, 266-67
Supraliminal 102, 109, 201, 205, 222
Sudduth, M. 266, 268
Syringa 27, 30, 51, 96, 126, 128, 189, 190, 215, 235, 286

Talbot, Warden 106, 108, 229
Tanner, A. 82, 266

Telepathy 3, 13, 21, 22, 32, 34, 41, 47, 55, 72, 73, 109, 110, 131, 147, 159, 190, 191, 200, 201, 206-08, 221-22, 226, 245, 253, 260, 266-68, 273
Telergy 190
Telaesthesia 190
Tennant, Charles 4, 111
Tennant, Dorothy 84, 133
Tennant, Edward 179
Tennant, Laura (see Lyttelton)
Tennant, Margot (see Asquith)
Tennyson, Alfred
Maud 51, 75, 182 292, *In Memoriam* 74, 75, 182, 210, *The Sea-Fairies* 176, *Locksley Hall* 286
Theosophy (see Bailey, Alice; Besant Annie; Blavatsky, Madame) 240, 264
Thompson, Rosalie 2, 11, 12, 13, 16, 18, 20, 26, 28, 29, 46, 123
Tolstoy
Resurrection 100
Traprain (see Balfour, Jean)
Troubridge, Una 132, 252

Unconscious 201-02

Vermala 125
Verrall, A.W.
Plate
3, 16, 17, 21
Marriage 12,18
One-horse dawn 21, Statius 117, Ear of Dionysius 118
Verrall, Margaret
Plate
Background, personality and career 1, 3, 13, 15, 16, 18
Family: Merrifield, de Gaudrion, Fawcett 14, 15, 129, 253
Nature of automatic writing 13, 14, 17, 205
Marriage 12, 18
Disagreements with J.G. Piddington and Gerald Balfour 121-22, 124-25, 238
See cross-correspondences
See paranormal cognition
Knowledge of the Story and the Plan 231
As investigator and automatist 35

Virgil
   Eclogues 30, 290, *Georgics* 174
   Aeneid 70, 77, 78, 93, 94, 121, 150, 176, 177, 179, 180, 283, 293

Whittingehame (see Arthur Balfour)
Wilde, Constance 186
Wilde, Cyril 186
Wilde, Oscar 186
Willett, Mrs (see Coombe-Tennant, Winifred)

Wilson, Mrs Stuart
   Nature and content of automatic writing 147–49
Wingfield, K. 11, 12
Wise One (see Coombe-Tennant, Henry)
Wordsworth, William 75
   Laodamia 50–51